disagreement w/ townsend p 7

174 crackdown on theatre - include

82 - his books + his ways

292

The Duke of Newcastle

Engraved by W. Holl.

THOMAS PELHAM, DUKE OF NEWCASTLE.

OB. 1768.

FROM THE ORIGINAL OF HOARE, IN THE COLLECTION OF

HIS GRACE THE DUKE OF NEWCASTLE.

London, Published May 1, 1835, by Harding & Lepard, Pall Mall East.

THE DUKE OF
NEWCASTLE

Reed Browning

New Haven and London, Yale University Press

1975

Designed by John O.C. McCrillis
and set in Baskerville type.
Printed in the United States of America by
The Murray Printing Co., Forge Village, Massachusetts.

Published in Great Britain, Europe, and Africa by
Yale University Press, Ltd., London.
Distributed in Latin America by Kaiman & Polon,
Inc., New York City; in Australasia and Southeast
Asia by John Wiley & Sons Australasia Pty. Ltd.,
Sydney; in India by UBS Publishers' Distributors Pvt.,
Ltd., Delhi; in Japan by John Weatherhill, Inc., Tokyo.

To the memory of my father

Contents

Preface

The study of eighteenth-century English political history is finally taking on renewed vigor. Over four decades ago Sir Lewis Namier began constructing a model of mid-eighteenth-century politics. His heirs in more recent years have elaborated upon it. This model placed mere factions where political parties had once stood; it portrayed political behavior as rooted in obedience to self-interest rather than commitment to principle; it rejected that peculiar distorting lens of Victorian standards previously invoked to judge a pre-Victorian era.[1] This great Namierian model has proved at once compelling and ennervating. It is compelling insofar as it appears to restore realism to our view of the age: the energetic, self-seeking politicians who now people the eighteenth-century world strike us today as more credible than the rhetorical giants and bold visionaries who competed with indolent peers and aspiring agents of absolutism in the picture that was dominant before Namier. This is its achievement. But the model is ennervating, and this has increasingly been its drawback, insofar as it has exercised something close to a paralyzing impact upon those among the professional students of the period who did not share Namier's assumptions and programs. Powerful among these assumptions was the tendency, in light of the evanescence of parties, to view cynically all eighteenth-century appeals to principle. Powerful among the programs was the prescription that reduced the story of ongoing politics to quarrels among self-seeking atomized individuals, both simple and confined in their political thinking. The potent Namierian demolition leveled much that deserved to crumble: our facile generalizations about Whigs and Tories, our confident denunciations of spectral politicians like Bute and ambitious monarchs like George III, our ready recourse to implicit theories of progress. But the perspective bequeathed us by the Namierians, with these assumptions and programs, was not without its difficulties. It is by addressing themselves to these difficulties, by accepting but then building upon the Namierian landscape, that historians are at last quickening the study of the age of Walpole and Pitt, Pope and Hume, Hogarth and Wilkes.

One of the major difficulties with Sir Lewis's legacy is its peculiar pessimism about the force and importance of ideas. Indeed, it is the effective public surmounting of this very tendency in 1967–68 that permits us to date with some precision the emergence of the new vigor in the study of eighteenth-century politics. During those two years three works appeared which collectively demonstrated that the legacy had been absorbed and that new questions were finally being posed and new answers generated.[2] Geoffrey Holmes argued that Tories and Whigs were political realities during Anne's reign and that they were ideologically divided from one another. Isaac Kramnick analyzed the thought of the Tories, concluding that their ideas were patterned, coherent, and determinative of action. J. H. Plumb, concurring in these views, went on to identify the techniques employed by Sir Robert Walpole to quash the Tories and thereby to initiate the factional world of mid-century Whiggery that Namier surveyed. These three works reintroduced to the historiography of the eighteenth century the notion of party as a controlling element in politics, and they demonstrated the utility of undertaking analyses of political thought in trying to account for party. In brief, they took ideas seriously, an achievement that must be accounted a great gain since it should allow historians of England to begin to view the eighteenth century with the same awareness of the capacity of ideology to control perception that historians of America have recently acquired.

But another difficulty emerging from the Namierian model of politics needs now also to be addressed. It is, put simply, the incapacity of that static model to make important chronological distinctions and hence its basic irrelevance to efforts to relate and explain the course (in contrast to the structure) of politics. The Namierians made us aware of the fragmentation of party; they drew our attention to that permanent parliamentary body of ministerial supporters for whom the holding of appointive office meant a commitment to whoever exercised power; they discovered the primal inclination of the country gentry, save in time of patent national confusion and mismanagement, to support a monarch. But lost in this new structuralization of politics was any real sense of movement through time. And yet changes actually did occur.

During the 1720's Sir Robert Walpole, as skillful a politician as was ever entrusted with authority in Britain, acted systematically to consolidate his power. He won two monarchs over through his sheer usefulness; he mastered the House of Commons with his shrewd insight into the fears and hopes of the gentry and his willingness to remain among them; he imposed docility upon his ministry by expelling rebels. Within a few short years he had Crown, Commons, and cabinet under his control. Henry Pelham succeeded Walpole and, finding so much talent outside the ministry that he felt threatened, he abandoned Sir Robert's policy of excluding able opponents. Pelham thereby secured skilled colleagues, but he lost the heavy-handed prime-ministerial control of the government that had characterized Sir Robert's era. Pelham's successor, the duke of Newcastle, feared the rising influence of the Commons and, trying to find techniques whereby to control the house from afar, inadvertently squandered much of another portion of the Walpolean legacy, influence in the popular chamber. He thereupon lost confidence in his own capacity to guide the Parliament. Thus within a generation Sir Robert's patrimony was dissipated, and numerous politicians mindful of pre-Hanoverian days began once again to look to the king as the chief and final source of their security in office. It was a barren hope, however, for even as the foundations of prime-ministerial power had been allowed to rot, the strength and self-confidence of the House of Commons had grown. Hanoverian monarchs, deprived of the prerogative weapons of their Stuart predecessors, lacked the might to keep popularly distrusted ministers in office for very long.

This stretch of time, from the days of Sir Robert Walpole's struggle for respectability and then power to the days of public tumult over the government's treatment of Wilkes, was the arena in which Thomas Pelham-Holles, Duke of Newcastle, lived out his influential career. For almost half a century he held high office. He was dominant secretary of state during one war and first lord of the treasury during another. He was the most celebrated political boss of his day. He loved being busy and became a byword for frenetic activity. Ultimately he was a failure. His leadership was weak and subject to irrational promptings. His chief political and diplomatic plans foundered. He never discovered the formula for converting a passion for politics into a capacity for command. But a variety of fellow politicians found him a useful, even indispensable colleague. He was perceptive, diligent, and rich; he was a fervent partisan; he took politics seriously. He is one of the most important political figures of the eighteenth century.

Not surprisingly therefore the duke figures prominently in most accounts of eighteenth-century English politics. But the way in which he figures is generally misunderstood. It seems to be widely believed that he has, with only a few exceptions, been depicted as a buffoon or fool. The historiographical truth is, however, more complex. In almost every generation the duke has had his talented defenders. In his own day Lord Waldegrave, both wise and well-informed, saw him as a diligent and competent civil servant; early in the nineteenth century William Coxe adjudged as sound his comprehension of Britain's foreign policy requirements; in the present century Evan Charteris praised his broad strategic vision and Bernhard Knollenberg his shrewd imperial understanding. Stebelton Nulle, in a short biographical study of the opening phase of the duke's life, portrayed a man capable of growth, insight, and hard work.[3] After a cautious reckoning I have concluded—by impression rather than by count—that the duke has had as many defenders as detractors.

What has blocked our perception of this ambivalence among historians is the unmistakable truth that some of the most prominent craftsmen in the discipline have sketched portraits of the duke which in unforgettable ways celebrate his eccentricities, underline his errors, and indict his follies. His lettered contemporaries, Lord Hervey and Horace Walpole, ridiculed his foibles and denounced what they saw as his wickedness. The great Thomas Babington Macaulay taught the age of Victoria to scorn the duke's successes as the achievements of a man who employed deceit and a kind of animal cunning to rise past far abler rivals. The generation prior to our own fed on Sir Lewis Namier's characterization of the duke as a psychological invalid. Basil Williams authored a brief biography of the duke, but his compact treatment testified chiefly to the author's massive contempt for his subject.[4]

I do not dispute that much of this contempt, whether from Walpole or Macaulay or Williams, was merited. There was a great deal in Newcastle's career to contemn. His pusillanimous sacrifice of Admiral Byng was inexcusable by any standard, and his treatment of Lords Harrington and Chesterfield was petty. He was often unable to conceive broad plans and tended to use much of his power ineffectually, almost aimlessly. He sought responsibility and, having acquired it, too often fled it. His tenure as Walpole's and Pelham's successor was a disaster. By no possible accounting can Newcastle be envisioned heroically. But I quarrel with the duke's critics, especially Williams, insofar as they implicitly suggest that heroic standards are the only appropriate ones.

They are not, and in two ways. First, one must sometimes be simply less demanding in judging careers: instead of heroics we should look for competence, instead of bold triumphs, for patterns of small successes. Newcastle, I shall argue, handled both foreign and financial affairs in a fashion we can call professional. He was a good subordinate minister. Second, one must not forget that the assessment of the career is not the assessment of the man. Newcastle undoubtedly behaved vilely at times, but he was not a vile person. Rather, he was generous and softhearted, a man whose chief notion of manipulating people was simply to be agreeable to them. He worked hard, enjoyed life in his own anxious fashion, and never forgot his family. Contempt for such a man should be generously alloyed with pity and tinctured with a trace of respect. Our own experience with humankind tells us that human beings are exceedingly complicated and contradictory creatures. We ought not to expect less complexity from our forebears, nor should we, for the sake of simplicity, filter out the complexities we find.

Ulrich B. Philips wrote in the preface to *Life and Labor in the Old South*:[5]

> Every line which a qualified student writes is written with a consciousness that his impressions are imperfect and his conclusions open to challenge. If he put upon paper all that is in his mind, every third or fourth sentence would contain a saving clause—"it seems to me", "the weight of evidence tends to show", or "as others have said and I accept." If the pages do not bristle with such phrases it is not a mark of duplicity or cocksureness. In history, science and philosophy the tentative is implicit.

I concur in this judgment. In doing so I do not seek to evade the customary prefatory acceptance of responsibility for error: like any author, I must bear full culpability for the mistakes that undoubtedly still mark this work. But Philips's point is nevertheless valid, as anyone knows who has tried to put a coherent story together from no more than shreds of evidence. At least faint clouds of doubt hang about almost every key interpretive point. There are, moreover, certain types of uncertainty which evidence cannot resolve, and I have generally dealt with them by reliance on the particular biases or tendencies of thought which collectively constitute the apparatus wherewith I explain to myself the social world man inhabits. The following prejudices (using that word in its Burkean richness) are the ones that I feel to have been most influential: I am a Christian rather than an agnostic or atheist, a conservative rather than a liberal or radical, a formalist rather than a romantic, a humanist rather than a social scientist. Furthermore, I believe that the historian should pay the closest heed to the explanations and interpretations of events advanced by those who lived through them. It is usually an act of unjustified arrogance to presume, without powerful reasons, to correct the judgments of individuals who were contemporary with the occurrences being described. Forewarned of these controlling views, the reader should make such allowances as he deems appropriate.

It is always a pleasure to acknowledge the kindnesses and help of others. Professor Lewis P. Curtis first aroused my interest in the Duke of Newcastle; he remains a mentor whose animated prose style exemplifies what in places I have, without complete success, tried to emulate. Mr. Wilmarth S. Lewis permitted me access to the microfilmed Newcastle Papers kept at the Sterling Memorial Library at Yale University. The late Mr. George Lam guided me in the use of the papers and became in addition the personification of scrupulous and almost anonymous scholarship. Portions of the manuscript were read by Professor Curtis, by Professors H. Landon Warner and Robert L. Baker of Kenyon College, and by the late D. B. Horn of Edinburgh. The opportunities to engage in the research behind this biography were made available by a Fulbright Fellowship and grants from the National Endowment for the Humanities, the American Philosophical Society, and Kenyon College. Without this necessary help this book would not exist. No less indispensable for the production of a monograph in history is the isolation with which an author must cloak himself when he writes. I thank my parents, Mr. and Mrs. Arthur M. Browning, and my parents-in-law, Mr. and Mrs. W. L. Lampley, for the consideration they showed to an aspiring and idiosyncratically demanding author. Most of this work was drafted in their homes. The Lampleys also donated valuable typing time and skills.

Finally, I wish to express publicly my deep thanks to my wife Susan. I used to think it amusing that so many prefatory statements closed in this manner. I now understand the reasons.

1

Young Whig

I

The Pelham family had ancient roots in the Sussex earth.[1] Long before the Tudors ascended the throne of England Pelhams had been men of merit in the county, and the attentive husbanding of resources and a series of lucrative marriages had made them men of means as well. In the final decade of the seventeenth century the leadership of the family lay with Thomas Pelham, a Whig by self-designation, a man of the "Centre" in his actions, and a useful though undistinguished politician during the political complexities of William III's reign. Like his forebears Thomas Pelham loved Sussex, and he revealed both his compassion and his sectional loyalty by providing for the poor of the county in his will. He was largely unaffected by the steady economic transformation that saw the once flourishing iron industry of Sussex reduced to stagnation and a consequent turn—fortunately one that prospered—to the soil. He was touched rather by the carefree, easy temper of the isolated county—a temper which condoned a variety of illegal activities and was neatly captured in the old Sussex toast: "May the smuggler's heart be free from the pirate's spirit."[2] But as part of his service to his county Thomas Pelham represented Lewes in Parliament; public affairs often drew him and his family away from the county. Thus, it was in London, not Sussex, that on 21 July 1693 his eldest son was born.[3] The infant was named after the father: Thomas Pelham.

Young "Tommy" grew to manhood almost tracelessly.[4] He was doubtless not lonely, for in addition to two half-sisters, offspring of his father's first marriage, he had one younger brother, Henry, and six sisters: Grace, Frances, Mary, Gertrude, Lucy, and Margaret.[5] But little can confidently be said of Tommy's youth. His attitude toward his mother, the former Lady Grace Holles, is unknown. She died in

1

1700, and he scarcely ever referred to her in his correspondence. Toward his brother and sisters he clearly felt real affection. He attended Westminster School in the days of the famous Knipe, having perhaps already received some instruction from Richard Newton, an educational reformer of the day. At the school he was taught by the Tory poet Robert Freind. Whether he absorbed much learning at Westminster cannot be determined, but his later fondness for the school and his eagerness to assist its graduates into public employment suggest that his memories of it were not unpleasant. In 1710 Tommy matriculated at Clare Hall (later Clare College), Cambridge, and was tutored by the noted Newtonian Richard Laughton. He left the university before taking a degree,[6] but retained for this second alma mater a large measure of affection which she, decades later, would reciprocate. Tommy was, in fine, no scholar, but in light of his later facility with French and his ability to conform to the epistolary standards of the age by invoking relevant classical allusions, neither was he a dunce.

Tommy's father, meanwhile, received several marks of distinction during Queen Anne's reign. In 1703 he inherited the family baronetcy and three years later, in recognition of political moderation and services at the Treasury Board, he was raised to the peerage as Baron Pelham of Laughton. A few years after he received this dignity, however, his health began to fail, and early in February 1712 he died. To his younger son, Henry, Lord Pelham left some annuities and £5,000 in cash; for each of his daughters he provided generous portions. But his principal heir was Tommy, to whom the father left his title and the Pelham estates in Sussex with their annual rent–roll of £4,000 and timber resources later valued at £9,000.[7] Tommy was heir as well to his father's ties with the county; throughout his career he would operate by a principle later expressed openly to several Nottinghamshire electors who sought a Pelham as their parliamentary candidate: "I will never abandon Sussex."[8]

But by 1712, when Tommy acquired his father's title and estate, he was already a very wealthy young man, for in July of the previous year, at the death of his Holles uncle, John, duke of Newcastle, Tommy had been the principal heir to a vast estate. After leaving to his widow her jointure and to his daughter some lands in the North worth about £5,000 a year, Duke John bestowed upon Tommy a group of properties bringing in close to £35,000 annually in rents. In return, Tommy had only to adopt "Holles" as his name, an obligation he faithfully observed throughout the rest of his life. Duke John had no male children, but since he had a daughter and several nephews older than Tommy, it is unclear why he passed them over and chose the young Pelham, only fourteen years old when the will was drafted, as his heir. Perhaps the decision reflected Duke John's affection for his late sister Grace, Tommy's mother; perhaps it indicated that Duke John saw unusual promise in the boy; certainly it flowed at least in part from the close friendship and confidence which Duke John and his brother-in-law, Baron Pelham, shared and their common adherence to a centrist form of Whiggery. But whatever its origin, the decision—carefully hidden by Duke John from his duchess and daughter—brought consternation and then anger to those neglected ladies upon its disclosure.[9] The dowager duchess, in fact, vowed to fight the testament.

Challenging a will was not an easy task, but the dowager duchess believed she had grounds. She had been born Lady Margaret Cavendish, daughter of Henry Cavendish, an earlier duke of Newcastle, and after marrying John Holles she had inherited the bulk of her father's property. Thus, Duke John's great estate was actually a union of Holles and Cavendish wealth. The dowager duchess ruefully acknowledged her late husband's right to dispose of Holles property as he saw fit, but she believed that the Cavendish acres were not his to distribute so freely. She argued in fact that her father's will prohibited Duke John from alienating the Cavendish estate from descendants of Cavendish blood. Such a claim had, it soon appeared, no foundation, for the dowager duchess herself had agreed in 1693 that the debt-ridden Cavendish estate would be limited to Duke John's heirs. Thus, every judicial decision bearing on the dispute, whether handed down in Chancery or the House of Lords itself, found against the dowager duchess. But for two reasons, despite the feebleness of her case, the educated of the kingdom followed the litigation with considerable attention. First, to a landed class deeply involved with entails and testaments, an issue of principle rode on the fate of Duke John's will. An unidentified attorney stated the situation bluntly: "All the wills in England are concerned in this case."[10] Second, to a politically divided nation it was a matter of much interest that the dowager duchess enlisted her strongest support from none other than the Harley family, and above all from the lord treasurer himself, the earl of Oxford.

The dispute over Duke John's will was not ultimately resolved until 1719. It was marked by an intense struggle between the dowager duchess and young Lord Pelham for the rent-paying loyalty of tenants, by Lord Pelham's unsuccessful effort to mollify her with a proposal to marry her daughter Henrietta, by the duchess's flagrant obstructiveness in preventing the Prerogative Court of Canterbury from proving the will, and by chancery orders for the sequestration of the duchess's property. By 1713 Pelham declared a readiness to compromise—to accept less than his lawful due if amicable terms with the dowager duchess could be reached. The Harleys, tiring of the costs of their champion's antics, soon accepted the offer; and in July 1714, aided by Lord Paget and Lord Cowper, the Harleys and Lord Pelham came to terms which can only be called generous to the outraged duchess. Lord Harley, now himself married to Henrietta, was to receive over half of the old Cavendish estate. Pelham was to have the rest—chiefly Nottingham Castle—and the entire Holles estate. Pelham's chief concession was his renunciation of Welbeck Abbey. Convivial and costly celebrations in late July and August, marking also Lord Pelham's coming of age and Lord Oxford's efforts to ingratiate himself with the Whigs as the queen's day passed, seemed to seal the agreement, but the dowager duchess remained dissatisfied, pouring forth demands for justice and cursing her tepid allies. Only after her death in 1716 could steps be taken, ratified by Parliament three years later, to have the compromise legalized. Henrietta finally received lawful title to parts of the old Cavendish estate plus numerous lands purchased by her father after 1707.[11] Still, despite these difficulties, as early as 1714 Lord Pelham was safely enjoying most of the fruits of his vast ducal inheritance.

He was thus, at the outset of the Hanoverian age, clearly a rich man. But it would nevertheless seem that many accounts have exaggerated Lord Pelham's wealth at this time. An annual income figure of approximately £40,000 is often cited, and a few eighteenth-century sources raised that amount by another £10,000.[12] But in fact the annual revenues of his estate can scarcely have exceeded £32,000. Duke John's rent–rolls produced about £40,000 per year at his death; but by the terms of the compromise agreement, lands providing £11,500 of this total passed to Duke John's daughter, and others worth £700 were left to his wife. Apparently, therefore, at a maximum Lord Pelham received lands bringing in less than £28,000 per annum from Duke John. His inheritance from his father was much smaller, comprising by his own testimony lands with an annual revenue of about £4,000. Since he had no other sources of regular income, his estate thus could not have produced more than £32,000 annually.[13] This figure placed him somewhat below the rank of the wealthiest landlords in the kingdom.

It was a scattered estate. Lord Pelham inherited lands in London and eleven counties: Sussex, Nottinghamshire, Yorkshire, Lincolnshire, Middlesex, Dorset, Wiltshire, Hertfordshire, Derby, Kent, and Suffolk. The chief residences which he acquired by inheritance were in Nottinghamshire, London, and Sussex. Nottingham Castle, which had been rebuilt during the Restoration, was initially the object of much Pelhamite horiticultural attention, but after 1720 it passed into desuetude. A skeleton staff maintained the stately building over the following decades, but its distance from London made it politically inconvenient and hence an obvious target in any of the many campaigns to find painless economies.[14] Clumber Park, another part of the Nottinghamshire inheritance, was allowed to decay into a black heath. In London Lord Pelham inherited a house at the northwest corner of Lincoln's Inn Field. Built in James II's reign, it was later bought by Duke John and became known in his lifetime as Newcastle House. Lord Pelham hired his political friend, the already illustrious John Vanbrugh, to remodel the three-storey mansion. One contemporary called it a "noble palace,"[15] and it became for over half a century its owner's chief London headquarters for politicking and entertaining. In later years the splendor of its furnishings, especially its wealth of gold and silver plate, impressed even continental visitors accustomed to the magnificence of princes. Nearby lay squalid Clare Market, another legacy from Duke John, which brought in £5,000 per annum and earned for its owner in later years the designation "King of Clare Market."

In Sussex Lord Pelham inherited three residences. Laughton Place was the oldest, the traditional family seat. But the young peer scarcely used it, finding its meager proportions too confining for his expanding needs. Within a few years it was mortgaged. Bishopstone, close by Seaford and the Channel, was also small, but it became a useful hunting lodge. After its owner reached the years of more sedentary recreations, however, it too passed into disuse. The third residence, Halland, located in the parish of East Hoathly, was Lord Pelham's favorite Sussex domicile. Dating from Tudor days, the mansion was a veritable museum, filled with suits of armor and tapestries. The park grounds, marked by many impressive chestnut trees, provided protection for a herd of deer and was a setting lovely to behold. But for reasons both political and commodious—the house was, it seems, filthy—a country residence closer to London was needed.[16] Hence it was in Surrey, near Esher, that the young peer bought a portion of land from John Vanbrugh and established his largest and most luxurious seat. This was Claremont.

From insignificant origins Claremont rose to be one of the great country homes of England. Vanbrugh had acquired the land in Anne's reign and had built a small brick domicile for himself upon a hill, but in late 1714 or 1715 he sold the estate to his noble friend, recently elevated in the peerage to Earl of Clare (a title with Holles associations). Vanbrugh then stayed on for several years to direct the construction of numerous additions to the core house on the hill, "Claremont," as it was soon called. Improvements never ceased; throughout his life the elder Pelham brother devoted burdensome amounts of his income to the development and beautification of Claremont. Steadily as the years passed he bought adjacent properties and enclosed the surrounding heath. To Vanbrugh's imposing structure, famed for its great reception room within, its turrets and battlements without, and conveying even in its massiveness that sense of proportion so characteristic of England's leading baroque architect, a splendid garden was added in later years by the master of landscapes, William Kent. The famous Kent tricks—a pond and a winding bank—created a striking visual composition when conjoined with the great house and the belvedere on the hill. Antelope roamed the woods, salmon glided through the streams, and the renowned fruit gardens delighted noble and royal palates throughout Europe with apricots, strawberries, raspberries, cherries, peaches, nectarines, pineapples, and melons. Ideally located for a politician—a messenger from Whitehall could arrive in two hours—Claremont became alternately a showroom for entertaining the illustrious and a refuge from the hurly-burly of the capital. Above all other residences, "dear Claremont" quickly became the young peer's preferred seat, "the only place where I am really easy."[17]

II

Like his father and his uncle, Lord Pelham was a Whig. But the ferocity of his partisanship contrasted keenly with their rather amiable political behavior. Although Lord Pelham's father had served on the

Treasury Board in periods of Whig ascendancy during William's and Anne's reign, his vote against the Fenwick attainder stamped him as a centrist, unwilling to follow the Junto into virulent Whiggery. And if the older Lord Pelham's politics were moderate, Duke John's were downright ambiguous. He viewed officeholding chiefly as a way to amplify his local influence. Hence he had been the only important Whig to remain in office in 1710 when the Tories swept into power. From such men the young Lord Pelham clearly did not learn his pugnacious Whiggery. Perhaps he acquired it in the vigorously Whiggish atmosphere of Clare Hall. Certainly Lord Townshend, husband of his half-sister Elizabeth until her premature death in 1711, was a central figure in the young man's political socialization. Indeed, though the evidence is sparse, it seems probable that between 1712 and late 1716 the young peer saw himself primarily as a political follower of his brother-in-law.

Lord Pelham first revealed his commitment to the Whig cause, somewhat beleaguered as it was in the final years of Anne's reign, by joining the party's chief clubs. The famous Kit-Cat club provided Pelham with the opportunity—if he had not had it before—to meet the artistically creative men who associated with the Whigs: John Vanbrugh, who would build his homes; Samuel Garth, who would celebrate the most palatial of them; Sir Godfrey Kneller, who would paint his portrait; and Richard Steele, who would (for a while) sing his praises. But more exciting, if less prestigious, was the Hanover Club, a political action group pledged to defend the coming Hanoverian succession and to harry Tories and Jacobites. Through this club Pelham and other young bulls of the party—Paul Methuen, William Pulteney, Horace Walpole, Joseph Addison, and Richard Steele among others—organized large parades and encouraged demonstrators to chant Protestant and Hanoverian slogans and burn effigies of the pope.

A somewhat different indication of Pelham's readiness to strike a blow for Whiggery appeared in 1713 with his effort to place Whigs in Parliament from Aldborough and Boroughbridge. Influence in these two Yorkshire boroughs had been part of Pelham's inheritance from Duke John. But unlike his uncle in 1710, Pelham was willing to use his power in these boroughs to replace wavering with loyal Whigs. He reckoned on being able to return two members from Aldborough and one from Boroughbridge, but his plans in this earliest of his electioneering efforts went awry. Control over the Aldborough seats, or more precisely,

over the ownership of the manor, was being contested by the dowager
duchess, and the two candidates put forward by the indomitable old
lady won on election day. Lord Pelham's nominees then petitioned the
Commons to be seated, but the effort came to naught. It is not unlikely
that Lord Pelham's decision to seek a compromise with his bitter aunt
reflected in part at least a recognition of the damage she could do to his
political influence if she remained unreconciled.

The young peer's devotion to the Hanoverian cause received dramatic recognition after George I acceded peacefully to the throne in
August of 1714. Lord Pelham had just come of age and had taken his
seat in the House of Lords. He was scarcely a familiar figure in the
politics of the capital. Still, the young peer was promptly permitted to
kiss the new royal hand, and in October he was raised in the peerage
with the titles of Viscount Houghton and earl of Clare, both previously
borne by Duke John. Other honors quickly followed. He became lord
lieutenant and custos rotulorum of Middlesex and Nottinghamshire; he
was appointed lord warden of Sherwood forest; he was made vice
admiral of the coast of Sussex. Such an effusion of royal largesse seems,
in light of the recipient's accomplishments and potential, rather extravagant; and again, though positive evidence is lacking, it is likely that
Lord Townshend, the dominant ministerial figure in the opening years
of the reign, was in fact practicing the respectable nepotism of the day
by procuring favors for his brother-in-law. The young man was, after
all, if not a leading Whig, at least a rich one—and wealth, as all knew,
was a crucial component of a political party's success.

Lord Clare proved a useful Whig retainer. In the general election
held early in 1715 he exercised his considerable electoral influence in
energetic and costly behalf of the party. It was a bitter contest throughout the kingdom, with the incumbent Whigs raising the spectre of
popery and the office-seeking Tories conjuring up phantoms of Luther
and Calvin. Those Sussex constituencies from which Clare could expect
some measure of obedience performed superbly; nursed along by his
agents in the county, Captain James Pelham and Anthony Trumble,
an attorney from Hastings, they returned a coterie of devoted Whigs,
including Spencer Compton, soon to be speaker in the new Commons.
In Yorkshire, Aldborough was not on this occasion permitted to stray;
eviction punishments meted out to several who had defied Clare's
interests in 1713 served to secure the remaining voters. Even in Nottinghamshire, where the dowager duchess could still exercise a modest

Pelham

influence, Lord Clare won some seats for the Whigs. In all, he seems to have significantly assisted the election of fourteen members to the new House of Commons. An impressed monarch and a grateful ministry rewarded Clare in August with further promotions in the peerage. Once again old titles of Duke John's were revived: the earl of Clare became the marquess of Clare and the duke of Newcastle-on-Tyne.

The new duke was promptly called upon to serve the young dynasty again. The king's foreign origins and the German background of many of his advisers galled numerous Britons; his failure to reward Hanoverian Tories incensed a portion of the governing elite; and the partisan activities of the restored Whigs, especially in the election of 1715, suggested to the Tories that recourse to orthodox political action would be futile. Unrest, associated with Tory and Jacobite discontent, became widespread in the kingdom in 1715, and after midyear it often intensified into local riots. The Jacobites who invaded Scotland later in the year in support of the Pretender could give no material aid to the dissidents in England, but their presence in the North encouraged the restless and alarmed the authorities in the South. In his capacity as lord lieutenant of Middlesex and Nottinghamshire, Newcastle bore primary responsibility for maintaining peace in the two counties. From September on, this responsibility absorbed a major portion of his time. Since he could not be in both counties simultaneously, he chose to direct peace-keeping activities in Middlesex personally and to handle Nottinghamshire affairs through agents. It was an unsatisfactory arrangement, and preparations in Nottinghamshire remained confused until a group of local loyalists independently organized their own defense force. But Newcastle did not totally ignore the county, and even offered to pay the expenses of sending troops into Nottinghamshire in preference to compelling the towns to accept the financial burden.

Meanwhile, he worked conscientiously in Middlesex during the crisis. As early as April he had had himself represented as neglecting no means "to prevent and suppress the least tendency to commotion." Several months later he was quoted as publicly declaring his readiness to venture "all I have . . . for the service of the Royal Family, and of my Country."[18] By the early fall, when the Jacobite threat was unmistakable, he was complying with Privy Council instructions in directing the arrests of men suspected of disloyalty. To the task of interrogating those detained he devoted daily attention; over 800 men submitted to questions from the duke and his deputies. Still later he

decided to create for Middlesex a copy of the voluntary defense association that had sprung up in Nottinghamshire. At times his activities
against the Jacobites may have become considerably more risky: if a
tale dating from 1768 can be believed, Newcastle participated in a riot
during 1715 in which two men were shot dead and from which he
escaped only by fleeing across rooftops.[19] That such a story is not implausible is suggested by incontrovertible evidence of his leadership of
mob demonstrations the following year. Indeed, bands of pro-Hanoverians who took to the streets in defense of the new monarch sometimes
styled themselves "Newcastle mobs." Jacobites cursed his audacity in
organizing tumults, Whigs celebrated his zeal for the Protestant cause,
and many years later a reminiscing Newcastle declared: "I love a mob.
I headed a mob once myself. We owe the Hanoverian Succession to a
mob."[20]

In early 1716 the Jacobite cause received two insurmountable setbacks in the military defeat at Preston and the unbecoming flight of
the Pretender. Thereafter, the Jacobite problem became a matter for
parliamentary manipulation, and the young duke, already immensely
useful in electoral matters and marginally effective as a peace-keeper,
revealed that he could also serve the new dynasty in the legislature.
Along with Lord Townshend in the House of Lords and Townshend's
brother-in-law Robert Walpole in the Commons, he argued against
moderation and for the imposition of severe penalties on rebels. More
important, he endorsed the ministry's proposal to extend the maximum
lifetime of a parliament from three to seven years. A postponement of
the next general election from 1718 to 1722, he contended, would
destroy the Jacobites, whose power was declining each year, and
demonstrate to those foreign nations hesitant to accept the new dynasty
that the house of Hanover was determined to retain command of
Britain. These two arguments were commonplaces, but at the second
reading of the Septennial Bill Newcastle introduced an element of
novelty with a harangue based, as an opponent phrased it, on the
"pretty odd maxim, that, since the King had lost the affections of the
people, he must rule by the sword."[21] It may have been the first—but
was certainly not the last—occasion on which the champion of Whiggery exalted the royal prerogative. The Septennial Bill, meanwhile,
became law.

But even as Newcastle was exercising his somewhat exuberant
forensic talents in behalf of the Whigs in 1716, that party was itself

beginning to split. The causes of the division, which eventually pitted Townshend and Walpole against lords Sunderland and Cadogan and James Stanhope, were numerous. It was a quarrel over both issues and personalities. For a while Newcastle stood with Townshend and Walpole, the men who had served him so well already. During the king's fateful absence at Hanover, for example, while the Prince of Wales stood in for his suspicious father as regent and gave kisses of political death with many of the friendships bestowed, Newcastle provided lavish entertainments at Claremont for the heir to the throne. But for reasons not entirely clear— perhaps they provide the earliest intimation of the duke's extraordinary ability to foretell the victors in political struggles— his allegiance began to shift from his former brother-in-law Townshend to his second cousin, the Earl of Sunderland, whose close association with George I suggested where royal favor would fall in any struggle for power. Relegated to Ireland in the ministerial shuffling attendant on George's accession, Lord Sunderland, last survivor of the Junto of Anne's reign, had chosen the king's visit to Hanover in 1716 as the opportunity for reviving his political fortunes. Feigning an illness, he traveled to the continent and soon joined the king and Secretary Stanhope in the electorate. Not long thereafter Newcastle changed patrons; Townshend's future was clouded while Sunderland's seemed bright.

It would be inaccurate, however, to attribute Newcastle's shift of allies solely to a concern for future political advantage. Several considerations in 1716 were forcing the young duke to contemplate matrimony, and the girl to whom he directed his attentions was, fortuitously it would seem, a politically innocent member of the Sunderland–Cadogan network—in fact, the niece of Sunderland's second wife. Thus, as the prospects for the marriage improved, the duke found himself associating ever more frequently with friends of the earl. One motive for marriage was social: a young man of twenty-three, ostentatiously wealthy, was expected to have a wife. But Newcastle's requirements for a mate, if not high, were at least restrictive: his wife, in the words of a confidant, had to be "a useful and faithful friend, as well as an agreeable companion."[22] Moreover, she had to bring with her a sizeable portion, for if satisfying society's expectations was the duke's first motive for matrimony, satisfying his own creditors was the second. Construction and renovation on the vast scale then being supported by Newcastle in London, Surrey, Sussex, and Nottinghamshire cost a great deal of money. The political demonstrations he organized also drew greatly upon his wealth. Archdeacon Thomas Bowers, one of the duke's guardians until 1714, and for several years thereafter his financial adviser and conscience, had already written with chilling explicitness in 1715: "I am very sure your Ldp. cannot go on six months in ye way you are in without plunging yourself into such difficulties as will make you uneasy all your lifetime."[23] The prophecy was unheeded, but nevertheless sound.

The girl upon whom the duke's eye fell was Lady Harriet Godolphin, daughter of the second Lord Godolphin and granddaughter of both the illustrious lord treasurer and the still more illustrious duke of Marlborough. Indeed, it was Sarah, duchess of Marlborough, young Harriet's grandmother and a principal financier of the Sunderland faction, who stepped in for her infirm husband and impecunious son-in-law to negotiate the settlement for the Godolphin side. Who initiated the discussions, whether Newcastle or Sarah, is unclear, but their intermediary was Sir John Vanbrugh, whose work at Blenheim and Claremont made him known to both parties. Sir John found the commission taxing, for just as Newcastle's financial needs were inordinate, so too was Sarah's cupidity. "As in all her other traffick," Sir John advised the duke, "so in a husband for her Grand Daughter, she would fain have him good, and cheap."[24] This attitude proved a serious obstacle to success, for Newcastle wanted a portion of £30,000— Bowers regarded that amount as indispensable—and the Marlboroughs were hoping to pay no more than £10,000.[25]

Thus, despite the blessings of Godolphin and Townshend, the negotiations became stalled in late 1716, and Sarah turned to another matchmaker, Peter Walter, whose position as steward for the duke gave him confidential access to the prospective bridegroom. Vanbrugh resented Walter's intrusion, but he and Walter remained at the task, and the differences between Sarah and Newcastle were finally worked out. A compromise sum of £20,000 proved acceptable to both sides, and the fact that Newcastle was obliged to provide a jointure of only £1,400 suggests that Sarah was pleased to get her dull and unattractive granddaughter married off so well. Newcastle in any event was clearly enchanted at the thought "of having a posterity descend from the Duke of Marlborough."[26] On 2 April 1717 the couple was married. A reception followed at Marlborough House. Though there is no indication that the match was one of love at the beginning, over the years the two cultivated an affection for each other that makes their marriage stand out as one of the happiest among the great of the eighteenth century.

The split in the Whig party, meanwhile, became unbridgeable during the winter of 1716–17, and Newcastle moved firmly into the Sunderland–Stanhope–Cadogan camp. Perhaps he received a promise of office from Lord Sunderland; certainly his name was bandied about in late 1716 when the mastership of the horse fell open. In any event, even as his marriage approached, the duke busied himself in the Lords with defending the foreign policy of Stanhope against Townshend's criticisms. It was a public declaration of independence from his former brother-in-law, and although the two men had many more years of ministerial cooperation ahead of them, the old personal warmth was a permanent casualty of Newcastle's shift to new allies at this time. Ultimately Townshend, Walpole, and their followers left office, unable to endure the frustrations of giving unheeded advice and suffering royal contempt. Their departures opened up a series of places in the administration which Sunderland, Stanhope, and the king moved quickly to fill with friends. It was the duke's great opportunity. Already a frequent debater in the House of Lords—he had recently been chosen to move the address of thanks—he possessed all that the leading ministers might hope for in a subordinate: wealth and a willingness to use it, loyalty reinforced by a marital tie, diligence energized by partisan enthusiasm. The position of lord chamberlain had been vacant for several months. On 13 April 1717, less than two weeks after his marriage, the duke took the oath for the office. Thus began a public career that would not end for half a century. p. 18

2

Rising Politician

Newcastle was only twenty-three when he assumed the post of lord chamberlain, the most important and powerful of the court offices. As director of the household "above stairs," he commanded the largest of the household departments and had fully two-thirds of all household servants under his coordinating authority. The chief concerns of the post were technically ceremonial, but through his wide patronage powers the lord chamberlain could exercise impressive political influence. He exercised his authority with relish and with an eye to service to self and friends. In 1717, for example, he bestowed a chaplaincy-in-ordinary upon his old counsellor Dr. Bowers, and five years later he saw Bowers elevated to the see of Chichester. In 1718, on the death of Nicholas Rowe, the duke bypassed John Oldmixon to reward Laurence Eusden, a drunkard who had brought attention to himself by celebrating Newcastle's marriage in verse, with the honor of poet laureate. He appointed his relative James Pelham to the post of secretary to the lord chamberlain. Power of this sort made the duke a formidable figure, and all whose hopes for advancement lay along the road of official favor found it wise to flatter the new lord chamberlain.[1]

Another responsibility that devolved upon the lord chamberlain was supervision over the physical condition of the buildings which housed the government. Shortly after assuming his office the duke was confronted with a series of conflicting reports, the more extreme of which suggested that the leaky palace of Westminster, in which both houses of Parliament convened, was in imminent danger of collapsing. Newcastle directed the officers of the works to undertake immediate repairs, but he also joined a committee of peers which investigated the various reports and determined the more sensational of them to have been "false and groundless." He thereupon discharged from his office the surveyor general, William Benson, whose signature had lent much credibility to the baseless scare stories.[2] Meanwhile, he busied himself with authorizing alterations in or furnishings for such diverse facilities as the king's chapel at Kensington, Lady Kielsmanegge's rooms in St. James's, the record room of Parliament, the kitchen at Hampton Court, and the royal barge. Since he acted in effect as chief procuring agent for the king, it was often necessary for him to be in attendance upon George I, and as a consequence of these frequent royal exposures to the duke's convivial nature, a mutual friendship between monarch and subject emerged. "The King," Newcastle later remarked of George I, "was always good to those who had got into his service."[3] But to Newcastle he was uncommonly gracious. In March 1718 the duke received that most signal mark of royal approbation, the blue ribbon of the Order of the Garter. Of the three kings Newcastle served in his lifetime, only George I employed him as a courtier, and only George I truly liked him.

Newcastle enjoyed power. Though not yet at the heart of governmental activities, he had at least penetrated to the heart of court activities. He handled himself in these years so as to expand, through almost sycophantic attention, his influence among the real wielders of power, Lords Sunderland and Stanhope, while simultaneously defending with all vigor his prerogatives as lord chamberlain. It was this latter concern that lay behind his celebrated run-in with the playwright Sir Richard Steele. The two men had once been friends and Whig allies. Steele had even sat for Boroughbridge, and he had clearly not been backward in heaping encomia upon the man he called his "patron": the duke had been, in a ringing and representative phrase, *"the Terror of Ill, and the Refuge of Good Men."*[4] But Steele was also a manager of Drury Lane theatre, while Newcastle, become lord chamberlain, bore responsibility for overseeing London's theatrical life. As a manager Steele was both independent and careless of regulations; Newcastle, as noted, was sensitive to any decay of his official prerogatives. It was a further complication that in the years before the Regulating Act of 1737 there existed no consensus about precisely what those prerogatives were. Herein, therefore, lay the stuff of conflict, and the dispute that ensued should be viewed primarily as a struggle between two proud men over the locus of ultimate authority in theatrical matters, although it is patently true that the intensity of the quarrel was heightened by Steele's prior decision to support Walpole's and Townshend's Whig opposition rather than Sunderland's and Stanhope's Whig government.[5]

Steele based his claims to independence from governmental supervision on the theatrical patent that he, Colley Cibber, Robert Wilks,
and Barton Booth had received in early 1715. Such patents were rare
but not unprecedented and had already given rise to several jurisdic-
tional disputes between lords chamberlain and patentees. In fact, it
was Newcastle's predecessor, the duke of Bolton, who had first grown
alarmed at Steele's disregard of the lord chamberlain's authority and
who had initiated an investigation of the rights of the court office and
its options should Steele continue refusing to accede to its direction.
Newcastle, in short, far from picking a quarrel with Steele, inherited it.
But he prosecuted it with gusto. Almost immediately upon becoming
lord chamberlain he asked Steele to exchange his patent for a license,
and when Steele rejected a request that he rightly recognized could
only circumscribe his authority, Newcastle began to raise the fundamental issue of accountability. For a while he was restrained by the
realization that the king, a frequent patron of Drury Lane, enjoyed
Steele's theatrical work. But by 1719 the monarch was growing disenchanted with a theatrical manager whose antigovernmental polemics
had become effective ammunition for disaffected Whigs. In those
changed circumstances the duke could safely resume his campaign to
assert his official authority. Armed with legal advice from high quarters,
Newcastle sought in late 1719 to intervene directly in the activities of
the Drury Lane company. But he failed in his effort to intimidate
Steele's colleague, Colley Cibber, into giving a part to an actor of his
own designation; and he apparently failed as well to get Steele to provide an account of playhouse finances. Cibber meanwhile retaliated
against the lord chamberlain's assaults with a denunciation of the
duke in the dedication to *Ximena*. Cibber in turn was attacked by a
foe of Drury Lane, the playwright John Dennis, who called on the duke
to exercise his prerogatives firmly in defense of "the cause of dramatic
poetry, the cause of the British Muses and of all those whom they vouch-
safe to inspire. 'Tis your grace who is to determine whether these shall
flourish for the future and do honor to Great Britain."[6]

The verbal affray lent color to the dispute, but it was under the
auspices of the law that settlement in fact came, and with the lord
chamberlain triumphant. Newcastle struck at Cibber first, requiring
Steele to suspend him from the company. But the step was apparently
taken simply to humiliate Steele, for Sir Richard, not Colley Cibber,
remained Newcastle's chief target; and just as a far harsher penalty

lay in store for Sir Richard, so too did the duke's final solution involve the restoration, even the enhancement, of Cibber's authority. In January 1720 the duke took an unexpected step; rather than recall Steele's patent, he revoked Drury Lane's license. This action punished Steele and his three colleagues equally, but within a week, having first released a warrant regulating London theatres, the duke issued a license for a new company to Steele's three former partners. Only Steele himself remained under suspension, and despite appeals from this self-styled "oppress'd innocent" for reconsideration of his case, he was prohibited from participating in theatrical affairs for sixteen months. In fact, not until 1721, almost a year after the Whig schism had closed, were Steele's privileges restored, and by then the theatrical entrepreneur had learned what Newcastle deemed the appropriate lesson in humility. The duke had vindicated his authority. And while it seems evident that during the altercation he had been moved largely by personal concerns, a majority of those involved in theatrical affairs thought that the reassertion of the lord chamberlain's authority, by ending Drury Lane's exclusivism, benefitted the growing body of London playwrights. The "British Muses" had, it would seem, not been entirely neglected.

The young lord chamberlain was in fact serving several muses. Even as he waged war on an independent Drury Lane in 1719 he saw himself invested with full veto authority over a new theatrical organization, the Royal Academy of Music. The academy's aim was to produce operas, and while it is true that the nobility who supported the enterprise hoped to turn a profit through their participation, the company was more than a simple commercial venture, for, as the statement of proposal averred, opera was "the most harmless of all publick diversions," and efforts to channel popular enthusiasm into nondisruptive activities were considered commendable.[7] Newcastle's office in the academy was governor, a post that apparently fell to him by virtue of his court position, and he subscribed £1,000 to the company, matching the sums advanced by three notable patrons of the arts, the duke of Chandos, Lord Burlington, and the king. The new cultural entrepreneurs immediately showed good judgment in seeking the services of George Frederick Handel, the German born Baroque master who had preceded George I to England. But even if their taste was good—and they sought such able singers as Senezino, Durastante, and Orsini—they can scarcely claim to have been promoters of native British art.[8]

The duke had been made lord chamberlain because the leaders of the Whigs felt he could be politically useful to them. Thus, whatever his success as supervisor of theatrical activities or of repair work on governmental edifices, he would be appraised by those to whom he had to look for advancement largely on the basis of his political contributions. These were not inconsiderable during these years, for the duke continued as a vigorous if rough defender of the government in the House of Lords, and emerged as both a recruiter of needed talent for the ranks of the ministerial Whigs and an adviser of insight.

The recruitment activities bore special significance. By 1720 Newcastle had introduced into politics the two talented friends whose careers would be most closely linked with his own in the years ahead and who would, with the duke, rise to become a ruling triumvirate a quarter of a century later. The first, Henry Pelham, was Newcastle's younger brother. More reserved than the duke, Pelham lived his life within a narrower emotional range. His abilities, as they emerged, would prove to be considerable, both as a leader of the Commons and as a shepherd of national finances, but they were neither obtrusive nor quickblooming. Moreover, unlike most men who have the capacity to command others, Pelham was a follower as well. His rise therefore was silent and shadowy. Long before the nation at large would know of his power he would be the intimate adviser of the mightiest subject in the kingdom. Pelham was, in short, cast in a different mold from the engaging Newcastle. The two brothers could love each other; less easily could they reach mutual understanding. But blood made them allies. In 1717 Newcastle brought Pelham into Parliament at Seaford, and two years later Pelham succeeded to the lucrative post of treasurer of the chamber. In 1721 Sunderland placed him on the Treasury Board. His politics, of course, were Newcastle's. The second political intimate was Philip Yorke, a lawyer from Kent, three years the duke's senior. He first met the duke about 1718 and the two men founded what would become the most powerful friendship of eighteenth-century politics. Almost half a century later Newcastle would refer to Yorke— by then the famous Lord Hardwicke—as "my sheet-anchor."[9] Yorke's legal talents were enormous; yoked to his firm Whig convictions and his commonsensical wisdom, these talents quickly made him a formidable political figure. Newcastle introduced him into Parliament for Lewes in 1719 and had him returned for Seaford in 1722. Meanwhile, in 1720 he became solicitor general. For this assistance—and for unfailing comradeship—Yorke remained grateful to Newcastle as long as he lived.

The duke's ability to formulate sound advice unfolded itself against the background of the Whig split. In 1717 Walpole, Townshend, and several of their friends, having left office, embarked deliberately upon a course of opposition designed to make them so troublesome to the administration that it would be compelled to accept them back into power on generous terms. Newcastle, who had ridden into office as a supporter of Sunderland during the months of the widening breach, remained faithful to the ministers. As so often in his career, self-interest and principle can be discerned directing the duke to the same course; for if it was clearly to his advantage to achieve high office, it remains true that his foreign policy thinking in the early decades of his career found Stanhope's imaginative boldness far more attractive than Townshend's sterile and perhaps incautious inflexibility.

Complicating the political picture was the Whig opposition's effective use of divisions within the royal family, for Walpole and his friends grouped around the Prince of Wales, the scorned son of a father he in turn reviled. Late in 1717 the duke became the central, if somewhat passive, figure in a sensational public demonstration of the tensions that wracked the royal family.[10] The Princess of Wales had given birth to a son, and the king, following custom, had designated his lord chamberlain as second godfather to the infant. To the prince this action seemed a calculated affront, for he would have preferred his uncle, the duke of York, to be godfather, and he had little use anyway for a young lord chamberlain who behaved like a royal lackey. Newcastle served as messenger in the negotiations about this matter and, according to one report, was unnecessarily rude to the heir to the throne.[11] On 28 November, immediately after the christening, the unhappy prince finally lost control of his temper and, drawing on a German idiom that made little sense in his awkward English, declared to Newcastle "I will find you." The duke believed he had heard the Prince say "I will fight you." He reported this apparent challenge to Stanhope, Sunderland, and the king's Hanoverian adviser, Baron Bernstorff, and after a cabinet meeting, convened hastily the very next morning, an investigation was set in motion. To a group of official inquirers the prince acknowledged that he had insulted the lord chamberlain, but he denied that he had challenged him, and he refused to believe that Newcastle had not deliberately sought the role of godfather. Meanwhile, George I raged against his contumacious son, had him briefly confined to his apartment, and then commanded him to leave St. James's. He later proposed a rapprochement, but on terms so harsh that the prince could only reject them. For weeks the political gossips of the kingdom could talk of little else, and a set of conflicting accounts of the postchristening encounter made the rounds. Early in 1718 the king struck again at his son—through the medium of his lord chamberlain—by forbidding peers who hoped to be received at court from visiting the prince, and then by prohibiting the prince admittance to Drury Lane. Tension had finally led to open rupture in the royal family.

Interestingly, the long-term consequences of this clash turned out to be far less momentous than some contemporaries predicted: within three years the breaches in the Whigs and in the royal family would be mended, albeit uneasily, and within ten years the humiliated prince would succeed to the throne of England and yet take into his confidence the very same duke who he believed had insulted him in 1717. What was important about the duke's run-in with the Prince of Wales was its immediate impact. It further polarized the two Whig factions, it gave Newcastle a notoriety in the politics of the kingdom, and it turned the attention of the ministerial Whigs to the problem of how to insure their continued maintenance of power in the coming reign of the son. In the deliberations on this last point the duke played a major—and perhaps a decisive—advisory role, although Sunderland was the prime mover in the new ministerial strategy. The keystone of the strategy, revealed early in 1719, was a proposed peerage bill that would sharply confine the Crown's power to create new peers. The ministry was seeking to save itself in the coming reign by denying the Crown its most formidable weapon for insuring its own independence. The other two components of the Whig strategy were a bill to repeal the Septennial Act and there-by give immortality to the existing Commons, and a bill to gag the Tory-minded faculties of Oxford and Cambridge. Although it is clear that the peerage bill was the key measure, all three together would constitute a comprehensive legislative assault on the chief enemies of the Whig ministry, the Jacobites, the high churchmen, and the dis-affected Whigs, and on the institutions which actually or potentially served as their staging areas.

Newcastle approved of all three bills; they were, as Lord Stanhope told him, "measures you and your friends wish."[12] And the duke vigorously defended the peerage bill in the House of Lords, first early in 1719, when with characteristic unguardedness he blurted out the ministry's desire to tie the hands of the future king, and then late in the year, when it was taken up again at a new session. But the measure encountered unexpectedly strong opposition, skillfully led by Walpole, and by the fall of the year the duke began to have second thoughts about Sunderland's strategy.

On the wisdom of the peerage bill he still had no doubts. At the very core of his Whiggery lay the conviction that the well-being and liberty of the kingdom depended upon a strong and independent aristocracy beholden to nothing but its own good judgment and invulnerable to royal intimidation. The Tory sensibilities of the late Queen Anne had unhappily induced her to launch the most massive attack on an independent peerage in English history, and the duke believed that it was imperative to eliminate the possibility of future royal assaults. He thus supported the peerage bill not only for its immediate political advantages but also because it was directed at constitutional rectification. But of the other two measures he was less certain. The university bill, of less moment than the peerage bill, was stirring up discontent in the Commons; by abandoning it the government might well avoid offending some whose votes would be needed on the more vital issue. And the repeal of the Septennial Act, although perhaps designed in part as a sop to M.P.'s short of funds for reelection campaigns, seemed similarly unwise to the duke. He questioned the ministerial assumption that such bribery would ease the passage of the peerage bill, and he shrewdly speculated that the ministry, far from trying to preserve a Parliament that had not always been responsive, ought to be looking forward eagerly to the advent of the new Parliament, which it could reasonably expect to be more, not less, tractable. Those views he addressed to Lord Stanhope in a letter in October, and this communication is the earliest piece of extant evidence clearly demonstrating the duke's insight into the operations of politics.

In accordance with Newcastle's views, though not demonstrably as a direct consequence of them, both the university bill and the repeal bill were abandoned by late 1719. The ministry then devoted its undivided energies to securing passage of the peerage measure. The duke's views on the bill were plain: "I must own I can never think our Constitution settled or ye King entirely safe till it be passed." Walpole was depicted as the enemy, the malign force trying to dupe the Com-

mons into abandoning the path of reason. He and his allies, including
Sir Richard Steele, were, Newcastle wrote, "the most virulent kind of
men, the most abandon'd to all pretence of principle." The proper way
to handle them, Newcastle argued, was to drive them to rash extremes
and force them to make common cause with the Jacobites; after that,
the duke concluded, "we shall have but little difficulty in dealing with
them."[13] Like many others, the duke underestimated his opponent from
Norfolk. Walpole read the mind of the Commons as no one before him
had, and he combined with this uncanny understanding a capacity to
strike just the right tone in his addresses to the house. By appealing to
the M.P.s' hopes to see their families rewarded with ennoblment in
the years ahead Walpole mustered a majority against the peerage bill.
On 8 December 1719 the ministers witnessed the humiliating defeat of
the centerpiece of their scheme for self-preservation.

Stanhope and Sunderland were realists: Walpole was too dangerous
to be left in the wilderness, especially since he was rumored to be
consulting with the recently discredited Hanoverians Bernstoff and
Bothmer about a mutual effort to storm the closet and drive the current
ministry out. Acting to forestall any such alliance, Stanhope and
Sunderland, through the mediation of the younger Craggs, came to
terms with the dissident Whigs, and in the spring of 1720 both the party
schism and the division in the royal family were formally pronounced
healed. Newcastle was privy to the secret negotiations that led to the
settlement, but there is no evidence that he actively assisted in effecting
it. Indeed—though again speculation must suffice where evidence is
absent—it is likely that he was uneasy about the reunion, not only
because he had spoken uncommonly harshly of Walpole but also
because he was an obviously dispensable figure if a cabinet of non-
offensive ministers was the goal of the negotiations. But, as it turned
out, he retained office, silently endured insulting neglect by the Prince
of Wales at their first postreunion encounter, and by July he was the
drinking partner of the very men he had dubbed as "virulent" less than
a year earlier. Nor, despite ministerial forebodings, did the reunion
work seriously to the disadvantage of officeholding Whigs. For if
Walpole and Townshend could brandish the threat of an alliance with
Bernstorff to make the ministry more amenable to compromise, they
were themselves financially straitened by their three years out of office
and now, for compelling personal reasons, needed a resumption of
salaries and perquisites. Thus the ministry retained the upper hand,

and in the redistribution of places Townshend emerged with the honorific but nonvital office of lord president of the council, while Walpole could command no more than the lucrative paymastership and the duties, though not the title, of chancellor of the exchequer. Since the Hanoverians got nothing at all, the end of the schism may legitimately be regarded as a ministerial victory.

Financial exigency aside, there was one other reason why the dissident Whigs demanded and got so little. The kingdom by early 1720 was entering the frenzy of the South Sea Bubble, and the ministry was a major beneficiary of the mood of euphoria that infected the political nation. Against a ministry that presided over such prosperity, Walpole reckoned, opposition would be folly. Thus, for this reason too, the rapprochement was effected largely on ministerial terms, and just in time. The crude manipulations by which greedy men rigged the market and duped the unsuspecting were losing their efficacy. In August, as foreigners began withdrawing from the market and Englishmen as well turned to new Dutch projects, the disastrous decline in the price of shares in the South Sea Company began; by the end of the year numerous fortunes both paper and real had been wiped out, and bitter vindictiveness had replaced optimistic insouciance as the mood in the Parliament, now reconvening. Making the already awkward situation worse for the ministry were the various rumors—soon corroborated—of profit-making collusion between officials of the company and highly placed politicians.

Like most ministers, Newcastle had joined the subscriptions, but his hands appear to have been clean of any finagling. There is no evidence that he borrowed on his stock,[14] and his name was not among those bandied about in accusations of ministerial complicity. He participated for the first time in the second money subscription, in April of 1720, subscribing £2,000. In June he entered the third subscription, again investing £2,000. On this latter occasion the duchess subscribed a separate and identical sum. All this money was eventually counted as loss. Other Pelhams, including Henry, took drubbings too. Newcastle also enlisted acquaintances for the transactions and expressed disappointment when in August he was unable to pry open the closed fourth subscription to admit some of his friends.[15] For a while he had hopes that the magical money-making powers of the South Sea Company would so enrich him that he could purge himself of his debts: "I really believe," he confided to Lord Stanhope, "I shall by this get

quite clear." But when the day of reckoning came he had, in fact, not
so thoroughly committed his fate to the market that the losses were
personal catastrophes; he felt, in truth, that he had come out of the
debacle less scathed than most.[16] For once, the duke's disinclination to
pursue wealth through business enterprises worked to his comparative
advantage.

But the resultant ministerial shake-up did not. It was Walpole to
whom the Whigs looked for protection against public wrath, not
because he had forewarned them about imminent financial catastrophe
—he had in fact lost money himself—but because his reputation
emerged unsullied from the sordid affair. Thus, he alone among major
politicians appeared to combine both integrity and financial ability.
Luck moreover was with him: death and disgrace conspired to eliminate
several other notables and thereby clear the path forward to his political
dominance. Early in the new year both of the Craggses died, one by
suicide and the other of smallpox. Lord Stanhope, his brilliant reputation somewhat tarnished by the South Sea troubles, collapsed in the
House of Lords and passed away the next day. Since he had just attended one of Newcastle's famous parties—a thirteen-hour "debauch"
one contemporary called it[17]—baseless rumors circulated that the secretary had fallen victim to overindulgence. Even Sunderland, though
apparently in good health, had to make way for Walpole at the
Treasury and retreat to the less conspicuous post of lord steward,
where he nonetheless continued to exercise wide-ranging influence.
Thus, within a year of Walpole's return from opposition, he had swept
past several significant rivals to assume the lead in the political derby.
It was a change not to the duke's liking. He continued to regard Sunderland as the key minister and remained distrustful of Walpole. During
the summer of 1721 he bluntly informed the new lord steward of his
opinion of the new first lord of the Treasury and his friends: "You know
I neither like their persons nor credit their interest." And Sunderland
in turn, abetted by his young and able lieutenant, the new southern
secretary Lord Carteret, intimated to the duke that a plot to unseat
Walpole was imminent.[18]

But death had not claimed its final prize when Newcastle wrote and
heard those words: in April 1722 Sunderland himself lay suddenly
stricken, and Walpole stood unrivalled and unassailable. The duke's
political options were thus foreclosed. If he hoped to remain in politics
he had to come to amicable terms with the nation's preeminent politi-

cian. It remains unclear precisely how the duke accomplished this *volte-face*, or, to put the issue more tellingly, why Walpole—unquestionably no fool—chose to forget Newcastle's recent antipathy and admit the duke into the very heart of the government. That he found the duke's wealth, Whiggery, electoral influence, and diligence attractive are doubtless relevant considerations; but judging from Walpole's entire career, it would seem as well that his desire to surround himself with men who fell short of first-rate talents also played a significant role. Walpole liked to keep capable potential rivals out of office. He was inclined therefore to turn to men like Newcastle for his colleagues— ambitious men, it is true, but inclined to see the key to political success lying in service to, not contention with, the most powerful men in the kingdom. Newcastle, Walpole reckoned, was made to be a flunkey; if Sunderland was no longer around to command him, the duke could only turn to Walpole. It was an imperfect reading of the duke's character, but it bore enough resemblance to reality to permit policy based on it to succeed for a while.

Even before Sunderland's death Walpole had been maneuvering to detach the duke and other Sunderland followers from their patron, and Henry Pelham, although installed at the Treasury Board by Sunderland, had been quick to recognize the merits and sheer power of Walpole and had shifted allegiances. The lord chamberlain and the new first lord drew together somewhat more slowly. But by June 1723 the duke had emerged as the third most powerful man in the administration, though a wide gap separated him from the two above him, Walpole and Townshend. Domestic affairs fell to Walpole, foreign affairs to the new northern secretary, Townshend. Newcastle served both. His total acceptance of Walpole's thesis that Jacobitism remained a grave threat made him useful to the prime minister. His willingness to accept the novel Whig policy of friendship with France that Lord Stanhope had inaugurated, coupled with his reluctance to follow Townshend into the anti-Austrian implications of that policy, made him helpful in struggles against Carteret and others who advocated a proimperialist line. By the summer of 1723 the man who two years earlier had been reviling Walpole and Townshend was occasionally—in the temporary absence of both leaders—directing affairs in the capital. More frequently he attended the brothers-in-law at their famous "Norfolk Congresses," repairing with Walpole, Townshend, and sometimes Henry Pelham to the Houghton library for private discussions of affairs of state. New-

castle loved his new importance, and his mood stands revealed in a
postscript he penned in those days: "My love to Harry, and tell him a
Secretary of State (though only deputed) never writes to his brothers
except they are foreign ministers, plenipos, &c."[19] Meanwhile, a remarkable degree of intimacy developed among Walpole, Townshend,
and Newcastle. "I beg," wrote Townshend in a typical conclusion to
Walpole, "that these particulars may not be mentioned to any body
but the duke of Newcastle."[20]

Beyond the show of intimacy, moreover, Walpole and Townshend
were also quite ready to seek the duke's advice on political affairs; and
while this gesture is in part explicable as an effort to humor their
sensitive new colleague, it was also a recognition that in some fields—
particularly, in these years, ecclesiastical politics—the duke had knowledge and well-founded views. Walpole in 1723 was creating a new
political order, and his scheme included gaining control of the national
church. As his chief adviser for ecclesiastical politics Walpole chose
Edmund Gibson, translated in 1723 to the see of London. In light of
the political unreliability of both archbishops, it was Gibson, not they,
who became the recipient of such political authority as quickly served
to make him the most powerful churchman in the kingdom—"Walpole's pope," as the catchword had it. Newcastle assisted Walpole in
these activities. He enjoyed church politics. He had already begun
cultivating friends on the episcopal bench—it would be a lifetime
habit—and he had shrewd insight into the reliability of these awkwardly positioned clerics, would-be stewards of an Erastian church. The
duke helped persuade Walpole of the value of close cooperation with
Gibson: "Our man must be the Bishop of London. He has more sense,
and I really think more party zeal than any of them."[21] The duke also
helped persuade Gibson of the utility of a close liaison with the Whigs.
Meanwhile, insofar as he could, he denied the lord chamberlain's
patronage to those clerics whose loyalty was suspect. Newcastle was on
his way to becoming Walpole's great disciple in church–state relations.

More important for his immediate future, however, was the duke's
readiness to follow Townshend into the unexplored reaches of a foreign
policy based on friendship with France. Against the harassment of men
like Carteret and Cadogan, spokesmen for cooperation with Vienna,
Townshend stood firm in the commitment made by Stanhope to
cooperate with Versailles in maintaining tranquillity in Europe. Alert
to the fiscal and commercial benefits of peace, Walpole thoroughly

endorsed Townshend's decision. So did the duke, though the reasons
for his support were more motley. To war itself in these years he had
no deep aversion, and so his advocacy of Anglo-French cooperation was
not rooted in the same sort of considerations that impelled Walpole.
Rather it was his admiration for Stanhope,[22] reinforced by the pru-
dential judgment that the gifted Carteret posed a political threat, that
induced him to support Townshend. In doing so he broke with traditional Whig foreign policy and with the legacy of the great Marlborough, and later, after France resumed its customary role as Britain's
adversary, he lamented the shortsightedness of the French connection.
But of doubts expressed in the mid-1720's no evidence exists. There is
no reason to think that any were harbored.

The duke's interest in foreign policy was almost as old as his official
career. In 1717 he had entertained the Abbé Dubois at Claremont and
had hosted important diplomatic meetings. By 1723 he could describe
himself to Walpole as "a great dabbler in foreign politicks."[23] As
Carteret continued to prove obstructive Newcastle began to emerge as
one of several potential replacements for the single-minded southern
secretary. The duke also had a private reason for aspiring to Carteret's
post. He had drawn very heavily on his wealth to insure maximum
success in the general election of 1722, and the emoluments of the
secretarial office looked increasingly attractive as a possible means of
restoring health to his personal financial situation. While a lord
chamberlain could realize only about £1,300 annually from his office,
a secretary of state could expect about £6,000. The differential explains
the duke's jubilation in 1723 at "some prospects I have had of ex-
changing my place for one infinitely more profitable."[24]

The prospects were not immediately fulfilled, however, for the king
liked Carteret, the only minister with whom he could speak German.
But when George finally realized that his secretary was pushing a
marriage scheme at Versailles that annoyed Louis XV and the duc de
Bourbon, the king withdrew his protection from his secretary. Carteret
was soon required to hand over the seals. Robert Walpole's former
friend William Pulteney hoped to be nominated in Carteret's stead,
but Pulteney, a comrade from Walpole's days in the wilderness, was too
bright for the prime minister's taste and had already begun quarreling
with him as well. So in April 1724, in a series of shifts that also saw
Henry Pelham become secretary of war and the duke of Grafton become
lord chamberlain, the post of southern secretary was conferred on

Newcastle. Despite his lack of experience in foreign courts—despite too
his tender years—the duke had acceded to one of the greatest offices of
state. Submissiveness toward superiors and a capacity for earnest
application to any assigned task had been his chief recommendations.
Many commentators were surprised at the selection; to exchange a
seasoned diplomat with achievements to his credit for a somewhat
muddleheaded bon vivant who had never left the kingdom scarcely
seemed the height of political or diplomatic wisdom. But shrewder
heads saw that Walpole and Townshend wanted a follower, not a
leader. "Il leur suffit," wrote the French envoy, "qu'il ait la docilite
pour agir et parler comme ils [Walpole and Townshend] lui dic-
teront."[25] For several more years the duke would be able to fulfil that
expectation.

II

One field of Newcastle's activity that seemed likely to be especially
useful to Walpole was electioneering. Like his Holles uncle, Newcastle
possessed both the territorial foundation and the personal inclination to
be a manager of wide influence. In three counties—Yorkshire, Nottinghamshire, and Sussex—he could in effect choose some of the members of Parliament. As early as 1719 Lord Stanhope had noted that in
electoral affairs Newcastle "can judge as well as anybody."[26] Thus it
was wealth, a far-flung estate, and sound judgment—brought together
in one man—that made the duke a formidable political figure. If Walpole had needed convincing that the duke could be a useful ally, the
evidence was provided in the general election of 1722. The contest
created an even larger majority for the Whigs than the happy election
of 1715. After petitions were resolved 389 Whigs confronted only 169
Tories. And Newcastle, working on behalf of Lord Sunderland, threw
his energy and money into a personal campaign that secured seats for
over a dozen Whigs. Such influence could not be scorned, and if the
duke's docility was one recommendation in Walpole's eyes, his borough-
mongering was another. Votes in Parliament were the chief currency
of politics.
Eighteenth-century electioneering has been closely scrutinized in the
past half century. A variety of studies has exposed a lively political
world marked by parochialism, factionalism, and venality. Organizing
a victory in a constituency involved much effort and, often, much
money. Even if all the expenditures were, to use an ambiguous term,

legitimate—even if, that is to say, the money was expended only on such items as transportation for voters, entertainment for the towns-folk, and meetings of the party faithful—costs could mount. When, as was often the case, the boundary of deviousness was overstepped and bribes were passed or hostile voters impeded, the costs could prove still more exorbitant. Even the most "closed" of boroughs could occasionally be obstreperous; no borough could be taken absolutely for granted. The duke knew this truth. He troubled himself with his constituencies not just in election years but at all times. He helped in solving local problems; he used his national influence to win favors for his local friends; and he kept open the lines of communication between himself and constituency leaders. Electoral influence was as much the reward of assiduity as it was the consequence of wealth.

In Yorkshire the duke exercised extensive influence in two neighboring boroughs, Aldborough and Boroughbridge.[27] Duke John had been lord of the manor at Aldborough and thereby director of its parliamentary fate. After the embarrassing exception of 1713, Aldborough became, above all others, preeminently Newcastle's borough; no other constituency in the kingdom lay so thoroughly under his thumb. With Boroughbridge the situation was initially different, for when Newcastle came into his inheritance the bulk of the burgages in the borough were owned by either of two families, the Wilkinsons and the Stapyltons. The duke began buying burgages himself, but since he had no hope of purchasing a clear majority of them, he allied himself with the Wilkinson family. By the time of the general election of 1715 an agreement between the duke and Charles Wilkinson, head of the family, had been effected whereby the two boroughs were to be treated as a unit in which the Wilkinsons would nominate one member to Parliament and Newcastle would nominate three. The Stapyltons made their final effort at defeating this coalition in Boroughbridge in 1718 and thereafter withdrew from the political wars.

In 1715 the duke gave one Aldborough seat to his chief legal adviser, William Jessopp, formerly an aide to Duke John and the man who had persuaded Charles Wilkinson to support Lord Clare rather than the dowager duchess. The second seat he gave to James Stanhope. When Stanhope chose to accept election from another constituency, Newcastle presented the seat to William Monson, one of his guardians by his father's will. The duke conferred the Boroughbridge seat at his disposal on Sir Richard Steele. In 1722, while renominating Jessopp,

Newcastle turned out both Steele and Monson. The famous row over
the theatre patent undoubtedly accounted for the first dismissal, and
it is possible, though evidence on the point is insufficient, that Monson
was being punished for voting with the opposition on such crucial
issues as the charges of fraud against Cadogan. In any event, the duke
replaced Monson with Charles Stanhope and Steele with Conyers
Darcy. The selection of Stanhope, cousin of the recently deceased Lord
Stanhope, was necessitated by the government's unwillingness to have
a man who had been only narrowly acquitted of malfeasance in the
South Sea scandal expose his political fate to a constituency that was
less than absolutely dependable. Darcy was a scion of the chief Whig
family in the North Riding and a man who had supported Walpole's
Whig opposition. In choosing him Newcastle demonstrated, aside
perhaps from a desire to please Walpole, his recognition of the need for
managers of even closed boroughs to court the gentry of the neighborhood. Darcy chose to sit for the county instead, however, and Newcastle
replaced him, at Lord Sunderland's behest, with Joseph Danvers. In
none of the elections was any formal opposition to a ducal candidate
offered.

The situation in Nottinghamshire was not so placid.[28] Newcastle's
holdings in the borough of Nottingham and in the vicinity of East
Retford and his role as lord of the manor of Newark gave him electoral
influence in all three boroughs and, by extension, in the county elections
as well. But nowhere in the county did his influence match the power he
could wield in his Yorkshire pocket boroughs. In the borough of
Nottingham he shared the Whig interest with the corporation and the
numerous body of dissenters; and the Tories, led by Lord Middleton,
posed a formidable opposition to any Whigs. Thus Newcastle was in no
position to dictate the choice of candidates, and in 1715 he lent his
support, both personal and financial, to George Gregory and John
Plumptre, members of established Whig families in the county. The
notably expensive Whig victory in that year ended Tory control of the
borough, but Newcastle was advised that the Tories would regroup for
later contests, and he made several visits to the town and his castle in
the next few years in an effort to consolidate his Whig influence.
Cajolery, flattery, and an open purse won him friends, and by 1720 he
could report to a ministerial colleague that "we have here a most
delightful place, & a country as well disposed as possible." An open
house every Tuesday and Friday allowed the citizens to sample ducal
largesse: "I have scarce," the duke added, "been sober since I came,

& did not go to bed 'till six this morning."[29] Such political carousing paid off. In 1722, despite a strenuous Tory effort concentrated on behalf of a single candidate, the sitting members narrowly won reelection.

At Newark the duke's interest was similarly contested. He led the Whigs, but the Sutton and Willoughby families directed a powerful Tory bloc. The contested election of 1715 saw victories for one Whig, Conyers Darcy, and one Tory, Richard Sutton. The election of seven years later saw a similar standoff, with Sutton, who for several years had been showing Whiggish inclinations, again winning one seat and James Pelham, second cousin to Newcastle and secretary to the duke in his capacity as lord chamberlain, replacing Darcy in the other. At East Retford, where the duke had succeeded his uncle as high steward, Newcastle shared the Whig interest with the White and Thornhagh families and faced powerful opposition from a Tory faction led by William Levinz and John Digby. During his 1720 visit to the county Newcastle met some of these Tories and, as Levinz exulted, "the Mob were ungrateful enough to shout him out of the Town."[30] Electoral results similar to those in Newark were obtained. In 1715 Thomas White, whom Newcastle called his "first friend" in the county, won one seat while John Digby gained the other. In 1722 White won reelection—he or his son would hold the seat until 1768—while William Levinz's son-in-law replaced Digby as the Tory member.

The struggle between Whigs and Tories that enlivened these borough elections was no less evident in the county polls for Nottinghamshire. Newcastle had powerful Whig allies in the county, but the gentry-based Tory strength was in general equal to Whig devices. In 1715 the Tories, in the persons of William Levinz and Francis Willoughby, carried the county, and it was primarily to have this electoral decision for knights of the shire reversed that Newcastle made his trips between 1717 and 1720 to the comparatively uncongenial and provincial atmosphere of the midlands. The election of 1722, long prepared for, was the political turning point for Nottinghamshire. In a very close, hard fought, and dear election, the Whigs in the persons of Lord Howe and Sir Robert Sutton ousted the Tories. The victory was painfully expensive. But precisely because it drained Tory coffers as well as Whig, it convinced Tory leaders that future elections would be prohibitively costly and disposed them to regard sympathetically various postelection suggestions for a moratorium on contested polls. It was in fact the last contested county race for over a century.

After 1720 Newcastle participated in various Nottinghamshire elections only by proxy, that is, through agents, friends, and allies. It was otherwise with Sussex.[31] Throughout his life he entered directly and personally into its elections. The county closest to his heart was naturally the county most deserving of his time. And the voters of Sussex, moved by regard and self-interest, returned Newcastle's respect. This attitude was strikingly displayed in a Sussex toast:[32]

> Then fill your glass. Full let it be.
> *Newcastle* drink while you can see.
> With heart and voice, all voters sing
> Long live great *Holles—Sussex King.*

Although Newcastle's neighbors in the county included such eminent peers as the duke of Dorset, the duke of Somerset, the duke of Norfolk, and the duke of Richmond, and although he could significantly influence electoral affairs only in the eastern half of the county, the remarkable appellation that concludes the toast accurately reflects the feeling of most politically conscious Englishmen in the years between 1720 and 1760. Sussex was Newcastle's arena. Sussex was the heart of his power.

Most Sussex boroughs were under the control of a small group of peers, local gentlemen, and, in some cases, governmental officials. The usual methods of nursing constituencies prevailed in Sussex, although the coastal location of the county had led to the cultivation of some idiosyncratic local customs. It was useful, for example, to be able to promise port work to the voters of certain coastal towns; and a handy way for those with governmental authority to curry favor was to pledge noninterference with illicit trade and to promise the release of some locally popular smuggler temporarily confined behind bars. Newcastle's favors for the county were legendary. Aside from such conventional practices as conferring the custom of his seats at Halland and Bishopstone upon the shopkeepers and artisans of the region or giving preference whenever possible in filling vacant places to men of Sussex background, the duke indulged in some unusual demonstrations of beneficence as well: for example, he offered protection from the press gangs to the inhabitants of the coast, and on an appointed day each December he invited the poor to one of his homes to give them money —4d. to each adult, 2d. to each child, and a meal of bread and beer.

The chief borough in the eastern half of the county was Lewes. It had a heritage of deference to the Pelham family, and reinforcing this tradition were the duke's holdings, including not only lands in the vicinity of the town but also houses within it. Still, Lewes was not quite a borough to be taken for granted. A sizable contingent of non-conformists gave ecclesiastical issues an uncommon importance in local politics, and a heterogeneous group of discontented men—often those who had been denied ducal favors—stood ready at most elections to mount at least a temporary opposition. In 1715 Newcastle nominated, and Lewes chose, Thomas Pelham, a resident of the borough and one of the duke's cousins, and John Morley Trevor, the husband of another cousin. Trevor's death four years later provided Newcastle with a seat with which to inaugurate the parliamentary career of Philip Yorke. In 1722, against an insignificant opposition, the duke's two candidates—Thomas Pelham again and yet another cousin, Henry Pelham of Stanmer—won easily. It is clear that the duke saw Lewes as a convenient constituency through which to meet his family obligations. But the proximity of the Stanmer estate to the town meant that the political interests of that branch of the Pelham family could not go unconsulted in the disposition of Lewes' spoils.

Hastings and Seaford, though technically two of the Cinque Ports, were treated by the duke as Sussex boroughs which he might influence. His interest in Hastings was initially founded upon his position as owner of the castle, lordship, and rape of Hastings. Early in 1715, in a colorful pageant, he also became a member of the corporation. To these varieties of interest he added a governmental one when he became, after 1717, the distributor of treasury patronage in a town peculiarly beholden to the Treasury for economic security. The borough invited the duke to name a candidate in 1715, and he chose Henry Pelham of Stanmer, the cousin who later sat for Lewes. Pelham's colleague was the independent Whig, Archibald Hutcheson, who broke with the government in 1716. Newcastle tried to unseat Hutcheson in 1722, nominating Sir William Ashburnham, one of the county's most eminent gentlemen, and John Pulteney, brother of William Pulteney. But when a disappointed office seeker, John Collier, turned against the duke and lent his assistance to Hutcheson, the embattled incumbent was enabled narrowly to outpoll Pulteney. Afterwards Newcastle commented sadly that "the disposition of the town is such that I could publicly recommend but one."[33] Seaford was more obliging. The estate at Bishopstone gave the duke his interest, and while he consulted with the Gage family, seated at nearby Firle, in making his decisions, the nominations

were largely his. In 1715 he chose George Naylor, his brother-in-law,
and Sir William Ashburnham. Two years later Ashburnham withdrew
to permit the duke to bring in his brother, Henry Pelham. In 1722,
annoyed at Naylor's opposition to the peerage bill, the duke abandoned
him for Sir William Gage, now one of his key advisers on Sussex
politics. And since Pelham was moving on to the more prestigious
constituency of Sussex, his seat was conferred upon Sir Philip Yorke.
Only Aldborough surpassed Seaford in giving the duke his way.

For the county elections in Sussex Newcastle spared no expense. His
territorial possessions and his governmental patronage assured him of
wide influence in Sussex; his readiness to lavish wealth upon an eager
electorate assured him of preeminence. His election trips through the
county were magnificent processions. A letter from 1722, penned to
the duchess, is as revelatory of electioneering as it is of its author: "I
can assure my dear I have thoroughly kept my word with you, for I
have been perfectly sober ever since I left you. We scarce ever drink a
drop & indeed I have quite left it off."[34] Everywhere he traveled his
largesse won him friends. The election of 1715 provided the first test for
such methods, and in a year which was, admittedly, favorable for the
Whigs, the two Whig candidates in Sussex—Spencer Compton, relative
of the Duke of Dorset, and James Butler, member of an old Sussex
family—handsomely defeated a Tory opposition. For 1722 the Whigs
ran Compton again, but Butler had earned their enmity by dabbling in
opposition and handling his sexual adventures indiscreetly, and Newcastle replaced him with his own brother, Henry Pelham. Since the
Tories thought it pointless to waste money on a hopeless contest, the
Whigs carried the day unopposed.

It was once believed that Newcastle could return as many as seventy
members in the government's interest. Such a view is no longer ten-
able.[35] The number of members who largely or entirely owed their
seats to Newcastle amounted to fourteen in 1715 and sixteen in 1722,
the latter figure agreeing exactly with the duke's own computation of
his influence in 1719.[36] This total was comprised of two members each
from Aldborough, Nottingham, Sussex, Lewes, Seaford and (in 1722
only) Nottinghamshire, and one each from Boroughbridge, Newark,
East Retford, and Hastings. And even these more modest sums are
subject to possible criticism, since they lump together such men as
George Naylor, entirely dependent on the duke for his seat, and John
Plumptre, whose independent parliamentary career antedated New-

castle's support by almost a decade. In truth, all such figures convey a false sense of precision. The nature and extent of the influence a manager could exercise varied from constituency to constituency and from year to year. Under such conditions the criteria for distinguishing significant influence from insignificant influence are inevitably arbitrary. For this reason, efforts to measure Newcastle's electoral power in quantitative terms must be cautious. It suffices for perspective to say that if earlier views erred in assessing the magnitude of the duke's influence, they were yet correct in adjudging Newcastle the most powerful electoral patron in the kingdom.

III

Throughout his life the duke was a family man. Ties of kinship and matrimony meant a great deal to him, as they did to most members of the eighteenth-century landed class, and as early as the opening years of his political career his familial affection was unmistakably manifest. It did not matter for his marital happiness that Harriet was homely, her features disfigured by a heavy and embarrassing growth of facial hair. Their marriage basked in the warmth of a mutual love that grew and matured over the years. Harriet was "my dearest dearest girl," the duke's confidant and helpmeet. She was ever there in the background, seeing her role as that of a subordinate, an aide, and a comforter. The correspondence surviving from Newcastle to his duchess, necessitated by her trips to spas and his to more distant territorial holdings, is at once trivial and yet revelatory. To the degree that it deals with the ephemeral and silly it is like most personal correspondence. But still it breathes an air of uncommon tenderness and concern. Absence clearly made the ducal heart grow fonder, and more anxious. Separation was invariably unhappy. Wherever he was, the duke sought out harmless gossip—"tittle tattle" they both called it—for the delectation of his duchess. And when the pressure of time prevented him from writing his usual full letter, he still tried to get off a "dabb," just to let Harriet know she was in his thoughts. This marriage eventually became a by-word for mutual devotion, and there is not the slightest reason to doubt what both the surviving epistolary evidence and the views of contemporaries testify to: that the match was uncommonly and genuinely happy.

This fortunate relationship did not rest on a total congruence of interests. The duke's official activities as lord chamberlain and then as secretary of state seem simply to have bored Harriet, who contented herself with exercising her modest talents for painting, music, and sewing. There was thus one side of the duke's life for which she had little appetite. But the duke's love of electioneering was a passion that Harriet shared. His latest electoral ploy he would quickly pass on to her. His hopes, triumphs, fears, and disappointments he poured out to her. Together they computed probabilities and gains and losses; together they fretted over ungrateful or stubborn boroughs. And besides the mad game of electioneering the two shared another keen interest, the improvement of Claremont. It was only at their Surrey home that they could be assured of "happy and quiet days,"[37] briefly isolated from the cacophony of London. Claremont came to symbolize escape for both duke and duchess. They were not, of course, unwilling to open the estate to the festive activities that ornamented high politics. The vast entertainments that Newcastle hosted at Claremont became famous. But while Claremont could be a showcase, it served more valuably as a retreat. Here duke and duchess could exercise their taste for landscaping and building. Here they could receive nonpolitical friends and relatives. Here lay the chance for solitude.

A side of the duke that neither his contemporaries nor posterity knew much about emerged in the ease of domestic privacy. Thus sheltered, Newcastle could cultivate a variety of hobbies, of which only the patronage of music acquired a public aspect. Upon the beautification of Claremont, for example, he poured out his fortune. Vanbrugh had direction of much of the early work on the estate, but the architect's hand was not free. The duke advised, suggested, and queried. Immensely proud of his seat, he demanded that it be kept neat, that its fruit gardens be diversified, and that it be provided with adequate supplies of water. Successive members of the Greening family were charged with the responsibility of maintaining Claremont's appearance, and it was doubtless through the duke's influence that John Greening later became gardener at Hampton Court. Among the duke's favorite guests was his friend from the days of the Kit-Cat Club, Jacob Tonson; and Tonson celebrated the expansion and improvement of Claremont in a bit of jovial doggerel:[38]

> When I belonged to Earl of Clare
> To call me Claremont was but fair.
> But since my master is raised higher,

> All things about him should aspire.
> The world must own my fashions new
> And that I'm like a castle too.
> To second thoughts let first then bow,
> And call me pray New Castle now.

Privacy also allowed the duke the opportunity to dabble in the composition of poetry, and while no samples of his efforts appear to have survived, there is a letter from his old tutor, Robert Freind, dutifully praising in well-chosen and studiedly noncommital words some Latin verses the duke had penned in Freind's honor.[39] Meanwhile the duke was building up impressive libraries at both Newcastle House and Claremont. An inventory of the London volumes included works of history (Clarendon, Rapin, Burnett, Josephus, Thucydides, Suetonius, Tacitus, Bede, Dugdale, Xenophon), of literature (Shakespeare, Jonson, Dryden, Chaucer, Congreve, Milton, Swift, Pope, Gay, Racine, Montaigne, Fontenelle, Virgil, Terence), and of philosophy and theology (Seneca, Tillotson, Halifax, Epictetus, Cato, Sherlock). Significantly, the library contained fourteen bound volumes of *The Craftsman* and Pope's translations of the *Iliad* and the *Odyssey*, possessions which hint that the duke did not allow politics to govern his reading taste.[40] There is even some evidence that the duke in these years nursed an interest in antique art.[41] None of these enthusiasms was remarkable, especially for the eighteenth century; still, in sum they suggest that the range of ducal interests was initially considerably wider than his later single-minded devotion to politics indicated.

Only two disappointments clouded the marriage. The first was the precarious nature of the duchess's health. An exceedingly nervous and fearful person, Harriet may have loved solitude chiefly because she needed it. Tension and excitement customarily brought on a not uncommon set of symptoms: headaches, indigestion, and giddiness. But in addition to these manifestations of what Newcastle was later to call her "hysterick fits," the duchess seems to have been unusually vulnerable to whatever contagious disorders were passing around. This vulnerability appeared early in the marriage, and by the mid-1720's the duchess had taken to visiting Bath in an effort to alleviate her ailments. Meanwhile, the parade of physicians that was to accompany her throughout life had begun. One medical man advised antimony treatments and a heavy consumption of alcoholic beverages. Another, persuaded that the headaches were merely a manifestation of an intestinal disorder, counseled moderation in eating and drinking, restricting Harriet's imbibing to small portions of watered-down red wine. Still another recommended the mineral waters that lay happily close at hand at Claremont.[42] There is no evidence that any of these treatments worked, and although Harriet would survive her husband by almost eight years, longevity may not have been counted an un-mixed blessing by a woman who seems to have known scarcely a day without pain in her entire adult life.

The second disappointment, probably related to the duchess's poor health, was the barrenness of the marriage. Newcastle's dreams of having a posterity descended from the great Duke of Marlborough were unfulfilled. It is true that Harriet became pregnant right after the marriage in 1717, but in the fall of that year she underwent a lengthy and serious illness that ended in a miscarriage.[43] Never again did she conceive. It seems likely that either the disorder of that autumn or the treatment for it made her sterile. As time passed the duke slowly came to understand that she would probably not have children. It was a sad realization, and two decades after his marriage he confessed to Lord Hardwicke that, unlikely as it might seem, he still hoped for a son. Perhaps, in the evening of his career, the duke would find resignation from office so difficult precisely because he, unlike Hardwicke, had no children through whom he could vicariously remain in political life.[44]

A less speculative consequence of the childless marriage, however, was the duke's deep interest in the welfare of his relatives. Denied offspring to lavish his affection upon, he found among the Pelhams and their in-laws fit objects for his concern. The more distant members of the clan he could assist through political patronage. Sir Francis Poole, husband of Newcastle's cousin Frances, was allowed to represent Lewes for twenty years. Sir Francis's son, Henry Poole, became deputy paymaster of Minorca and later commissioner of the excise. Colonel James Pelham, Newcastle's second cousin, served successively as secre-tary to the Prince of Wales and as deputy cofferer, meanwhile holding a seat in Parliament for almost forty years. Thomas Pelham, a first cousin, was appointed to the Board of Trade. He was later succeeded by his own son Thomas. John Shelley, a nephew, was provided with a seat at East Retford for seventeen undistinguished years.

The marriages of his sisters gave Newcastle further opportunities for bestowing favors. Of the six girls who were full sisters to the duke only

Mary failed to survive to adulthood. Gertrude married David Polhill, a great grandson of Oliver Cromwell and a fervent Whig at the opening of the century. Gertrude soon died, but Polhill kept her brother informed on Kentish affairs for many years and in return received a post in the Tower. Margaret wed Sir John Shelley, scion of an old Sussex family. Sir John exercised wide influence in the borough of Arundel and sat for it himself until 1741. Sir John's family, moreover, had been acquaintances of the Pelhams for a number of years, and in 1721, six years before Margaret's marriage, the duke had borrowed heavily from another of the Shelleys. In later years Margaret's son, also a Sir John, was the ultimately ungrateful recipient of much ducal largesse. Frances married less happily, choosing the notorious Christopher Wandesford, Lord Castlecomer, who within several years of the wedding was dead. Castlecomer's politics had doubtless been a recommendation, for he was a staunch Whig and a colleague of Newcastle's in the Hanover Club. Still, his reputation as a rake was thoroughly unsavory. In later years Newcastle and Lady Frances may have drifted apart; in any event, the duke was not among the Pelhams attending her funeral in 1756. The duke's eldest full sister, Grace, married George Naylor, member for Seaford, a distant cousin of Robert Walpole's, and one of Newcastle's key legal advisers in the opening years of his career. Naylor had served as one of the duke's guardians after his father's death and had aided in preparing the compromise whereby the young Lord Pelham and the Harley family had come to terms in 1714 over the disputed inheritance.

It was Lucy, however, who was the duke's favorite sister, and she wed Henry Clinton, Lord Lincoln, thereby initiating a tie between the Pelhams and the Clintons that would eventually permit the transfer of some of the duke's titles and the residue of his wealth to Clinton heirs. Like Newcastle, Clinton was a spirited Whig, still another of the duke's Hanover Club acquaintances. His official career had begun before the duke's, in the household of the Prince of Denmark in 1708, but it was largely through Newcastle's influence that Lincoln later received the prestigious garter. Kneller's portrait of the two Whig cronies, partners in a bottle, captures the spirit of their friendship, and Lincoln's marriage to Lucy clearly had the duke's blessing since he added £7,000 to the £5,000 dowry that the late Lord Pelham had already provided. Lord Lincoln died in 1728, so deeply in debt that his wealth could not cover his obligations. Newcastle thereupon acted to aid Lucy's family, and her

sickly son Henry, who would eventually prove as faithless a friend to the
duke as Margaret Shelley's son, became the beneficiary of much ducal
kindness over the course of several decades.

The most important family marriage was Henry Pelham's. Younger
than Newcastle, "Harry" was long forced to live in the shadow of his
brother. He entered Parliament in 1717 for Seaford, and three years
later became treasurer of the chamber. Soon thereafter Robert Walpole
fixed on him for his unusual combination of ability, loyalty, and self-
effacing diligence, and the younger Pelham rose smoothly as the prime
minister's most capable disciple. As head of the family, the duke dealt
generously with his brother, providing an annuity of £1,000 for Henry
immediately after their father's death and adding Sussex lands worth
£1,500 per annum when Henry came of age. For a number of years
thereafter Henry remained single while Newcastle considered the
possibility of marrying his brother to a rich heiress. Lady Katherine
Manners, daughter of the duke of Rutland, a suitable prospect, finally
caught Henry's fancy, and the two were wed in 1726. At this time
Newcastle made further provision for his brother, giving him Sussex
lands from both the Pelham and the Newcastle estates worth £800
a year and selling him still other Sussex lands that realized £500 per
annum. These transfers gave Henry more extensive holdings in the
county than the duke himself.[45] But the assertion found in some sources
that Newcastle also transferred part or all of the lucrative Lincolnshire
estate to his brother in the context of the marriage settlement is erroneous. The young couple produced a daughter in as brief a time as
decency permitted, and within a few years they bought Esher Place in
Surrey and settled there within view of the belvedere at Claremont.
This daughter, named after her mother, captured a large portion of
Newcastle's unrequited paternal affection—he believed in fact that the
infant resembled him—and she later married her first cousin, Henry
Feinnes Clinton, the second Lord Lincoln, son of Lucy. For Newcastle
the marriage betokened the union of his favorite niece and his favorite
nephew. And thus, with characteristic eighteenth-century complexity, a web of marriages reinforced a web of blood. It was because the
younger Lord Lincoln's tie with the duke was in this sense double that
Newcastle, decades later, felt his nephew's defection so keenly.

As the two Pelham brothers settled down in the 1720's as neighbors
in Surrey, they had years of effective political cooperation ahead of
them. But even though they were on the way to becoming the most

successful set of fraternal politicians in English history, they were already experiencing the tensions that would plague their relationship virtually unabated until Henry Pelham's death in 1754. The source of much of the friction lay in the awkward truth that while the duke's age and wealth made him the head of the broad Pelham family, he was far inferior to Henry as an administrator of the patrimony. Indeed, he was thoroughly inept. Early in the 1720's Newcastle began not only borrowing from Henry but even asking his brother to try to unravel the tangled skein of ducal finances.[46] What was needed, however, was far more than untangling. Nothing less than a reordering of ducal life coupled with broad reforms in land management would be necessary to restore the profitability of the estate. But Newcastle had not heeded Thomas Bowers on this point and was now similarly deaf to his brother's pleas. It is possible—though the assertion is entirely speculative—that the duke was encouraged in his commitment to extravagance by the self-interested advice of his matchmaking steward, Peter Walter. Apparently part of Newcastle's inheritance from Duke John, Peter Walter was, according to Pope, "a rogue of truly ministerial kind." His legal training and financial shrewdness, harnessed to a capacity for making friends among the great, allowed Walter to amass a fortune in his lifetime. An aura of the sharpster hung about him, and it is thoroughly conceivable that he might have offered subtle opposition to any proposals for a ducal austerity that could threaten his own lucrative position. Whatever the source of the duke's inability to live within his income, however, it was a trait that Pelham could only grieve over. Before his eyes, and despite his warnings, Henry Pelham watched his elder brother slowly destroy the foundation of family wealth.

The tale of Newcastle's feckless direction of his estate has never been recounted. But the broad outlines of the story—testimony to the duke's prodigality and infirmity of will—can be retrieved. The duke's annual estate income averaged about £32,000 when he came of age in 1714. Of that sum £28,000 came from the so-called Newcastle estate, i.e., the estate inherited from Duke John, while £4,000 came from the so-called Sussex estate, i.e., the estate inherited from his father. Although an ample income by any reasonable standard, this sum proved too confining for the ambitious and eager young Whig peer. There is little evidence to suggest exactly how his money was spent, but contemporary stories of ducal electoral campaigns, of entertainments, and of an ostentatiously framed style of life all suggest that much of it was conspicuously consumed. Scattered bits of direct evidence tell the same story. The duke's household expenses in 1717 amounted to no less than £5,574. His stables cost him another £2,000 a year. Additionally, he felt obliged to make appropriately magnificent contributions to charities: to the poor of several Halland parishes, toward the cost of dealing with smallpox visitations at Hastings, for the school at Seaford.[47] And these entries in account books apparently just hint at the scope of Newcastle's incautious spending, for if direct evidence of the purpose of most expenditures is lacking, clear proof that such expenditures exceeded the duke's income is easier to come by.

Newcastle proceeded with reckless haste to mire himself in ultimately unconquerable debt. As early as 1715 he mortgaged various lands to obtain £10,000 from William Guidott. He then turned to John Morice for £6,000 and Mary Turgis for £4,000. In 1721 Henry Shelley provided £2,746, in 1723 Henry Rogers supplied £2,100, and in 1729 the duke's father-in-law, Lord Godolphin, lent him £5,000. These sums are useful only as representative figures; of much of the duke's borrowing and mortgaging there seems to be no trace left, and no statistical argument can be derived from this set of randomly extant figures. Unquestionably some of these debts were repaid; the disposition of others is uncertain.[48] It appears that the duke was not at this time borrowing from Hoare's, the Fleet Street bank that served him and several generations of Pelhams. But it is clear beyond cavil from Thomas Bowers's mounting alarm at the young duke's insensitivity to financial concerns that the estate was being exhausted with terrifying speed. And others must have thought so too, for in 1721 Newcastle submitted to a humiliating arrangement. A trust was created—the first of many in his financially wayward lifetime—designed to pay off ducal debts and restrain ducal extravagance.

This trust was drawn up by one of the duke's lawyers, William Jessopp. It applied only to the old Newcastle estate, already somewhat reduced in size by virtue of land sales, but still realizing between £24,300 and £27,500 a year.[49] Most of this sum was now set aside for the repayment of debts and the redemption of lands, and Newcastle's allowance was to be only £6,500 per annum. This latter figure was to be supplemented by the Sussex revenues of £2,500 and the annual income of the lord chamberlain's office, totalling perhaps £1,300. His annual expendable income therefore still exceeded £10,000. But even this sum was too confining, and since the trust was not ironclad, Newcastle simply began diverting money from debt redemption to personal expenditures. In the ensuing years of the decade his debts were not at all wiped out; they were, if anything, still more sweepingly incurred. And simultaneously, as mortgaging and land sales deprived the duke of revenue from rents, the income from his holdings declined. To be sure, with the various proceeds of his new secretarial office totalling about £6,000 a year after 1724, the duke's personal income mounted to close to £14,000 annually.[50] But the ominous estate conditions that had once provoked Bowers now vexed Henry Pelham: debt mounted while revenue declined, and only through a program of prolonged austerity could the duke hope to undo the damage. Newcastle had many virtues, but a capacity to live abstemiously was not among them.

IV

The political adjustments of 1724 had eliminated the last rivals challenging Walpole for dominance. Now fixed in power, he acted with insight, imagination, and considerable courage to assure himself a long tenure in the seat of authority. Unlike Newcastle, who was also a beneficiary of the visitation of mortality and dishonor that swept the ranks of English politicians in 1721 and 1722, Walpole chose to command events rather than obey them. All his actions in the middle years of the decade can be understood as parts of a systematic effort to anesthetize or emasculate those elements in the kingdom that posed potential threats to his maintenance of power. In foreign policy his prime desideratum was peace. Only if war could be avoided would Britain's increasing prosperity touch enough people to insure his own retention of power. In particular he sought to please two groups through his calculated pacifism: the landed gentry, who would be spared a wartime land tax, and the merchants, to whom the channels of world commerce would remain open. In domestic policy Walpole moved to remodel the British government, or, more precisely, to amplify its unsuspected authoritarian potentialities, and in so doing to widen and deepen his own power to deal with dissidence and division. He found the emerging institution of the cabinet a nuisance, and he sought to subvert or circumvent it, entrusting power and influence only to a small circle of his most trusted subordinates.[51] For each of the other political institutions of state—the Crown, the Commons, the Lords, and the inchoate civil service—he developed a strategy of conquest. The Crown could be ruled by cultivating the friendship of women who stood close to the monarch. The Commons responded to the twin devices of visible leadership—Walpole rejected a peerage so that he might remain in the popular chamber—and well-organized election-eering. The House of Lords was controlled by the ecclesiastical machine, which created and maintained a bloc of progovernment bishops whose attendance at crucial moments could be relied upon. Meanwhile, from among the ranks of treasury officials throughout the kingdom Walpole purged men of dubious loyalty and replaced them with those he deemed trustworthy, thereby fostering what would later become the Pelhams' most powerful weapon, the Treasury Party. Newcastle revealed the swift success of Walpole's program when he awkwardly but accurately remarked to Horace Walpole in 1724 that "either before, or since His Maj^ty's happy accession, there never was a greater unanimity and zeal in both Houses of Parliament for His Maj^ty's service, or so universal a satisfaction and tranquillity throughout the whole nation, as there is at present."[52]

Newcastle had several responsibilities within this system. He was among the small inner circle in whom Walpole confided. At first only Townshend stood closer to the prime minister, but within several years the duke overtook even him. It is true that Newcastle was not very useful in ministerial plans to manipulate the king, especially in the early years of George II's reign, nor was he significant in Walpole's efforts to weed out infidelity in the Treasury. But in the prime minister's strategy for subduing parliamentary defiance the duke played a key role. In the Lords, though generally taking his cues from Townshend, he remained a forceful and willing advocate of governmental decisions and actions, and in a period in which few peers shone as speakers, the duke's doggedness sufficed for this purpose. For the Commons Newcastle was, of course, an influential patron. Walpole prized those sixteen seats and valued besides the duke's extensive knowledge of local politics. On top of all other considerations, the duke was entrusted with the office of secretary of state. It was a post of extensive power, for in addition to exercising wide patronage influence, the two secretaries conducted foreign affairs and also bore responsibility for maintaining order at home. To the latter task—whether the rioters were Jacobites or tin miners—the duke brought few scruples about using force.[53]

In the direction of foreign policy secretaries of state conventionally divided the world into two spheres: the northern department, which dealt with the Netherlands, the German empire, Russia, and the

Scandinavian states; and the southern department, which handled
diplomacy with France, Spain, Portugal, the Italian states, and the
colonies. But since this division was simply one of convenience, not law,
either secretary was in fact competent to correspond with and send
commands to any British diplomat in any court. The unhappy possibility thus existed for meddling in a colleague's department. But since,
as Newcastle put it, "the affairs of the North and South are so inter-
woven together, that any stand or rub that happens in either place must
in consequence affect the other,"[54] it was also useful that one secretary
could—if secretarial cooperation should break down—guide all
aspects of foreign policy. In his first years as secretary Newcastle was
little more than Townshend's shadow. Later on, with Walpole's approval, he became Townshend's rival. In each role, however, he served
Walpole's purposes. Rumors spoke frequently in the mid-1720's of the
duke's imminent exit from office, but in view of Newcastle's numerous
virtues in Walpole's eyes, these were baseless, and testify only to a
widespread contemporary failure to understand just what the prime
minister was up to.

Newcastle brought to his new secretarial office both the capacity for
exhaustive industry and the desire to expand the sphere of official competence that had characterized his days as lord chamberlain. He
throve on work. At most cabinet meetings he was the minister who took
minutes, both for private and royal use. After consultations with his
colleagues among the "Select Lords"—a group of ten to a dozen politicians who advised on foreign affairs—he drafted lengthy letters to the
diplomats in his department. Initially ignorant of colonial matters, he
diligently attended those Privy Council meetings at which colonial
subjects were discussed. He preferred not to work at the cockpit at
Whitehall, the usual office of secretaries, choosing instead an office
in Kensington; but he was often on the move, away from the capital,
keeping odd hours, and thereby driving his aides to distraction. Charles
Delafaye, the duke's undersecretary, wrote that "His Grace of Newcastle may be at midnight forty miles off at Tyrrel's near Oxford and
the next morning at seven at Kensington." Such bustle, Delafaye added,
"does *deranger* my poor noodle sometimes, as the uncertainty of the
time of dining does my stomach."[55]

Just as in 1720 the duke had been the willing instrument for the
elimination of elements of autonomy in theatrical affairs, so he became
five years later the instrument for the elimination of a similar autonomy

in Scottish affairs. In each instance it was his own office that incorporated what had formerly been functions exercised elsewhere. But there was a difference too: in 1720 the duke had acted on his own initiative, while in 1725,—since nothing was done without Walpole's consent,—he acted on the prime minister's. The Scottish problem was, for Walpole, political. His great fear was that the Scots, whose loyalty to the Hanoverians still remained in doubt, would organize a faction of their own and use its might as a weapon for extorting favors from the Crown. Walpole was determined to create loyalism in the northern kingdom and to make its politicians conform to standards of political behavior acceptable to the Whigs. His chief obstacle was the duke of Roxburgh, secretary of state for Scotland since 1717. Not only did Roxburgh hold an office the very existence of which bespoke Scottish separation from England, he also had been an ally of Sunderland and Cadogan, and hence an enemy of Walpole. Walpole's opportunity to remove the obstacle came in June 1725. Malt riots broke out in Glasgow, and although General Wade complained from Scotland that both Newcastle and Townshend had been dilatory in providing him with enough justices of the peace, the chief onus for the calamity fell on Roxburgh. Further darkening the Scottish secretary's image in ministerial eyes were reports that he was actually encouraging the rioters. At Walpole's request George I sent word from Hanover that Roxburgh was to resign the seals, and on 25 August Newcastle, by virtue of his secretarial post, added the control of Scottish affairs to his responsibilities.

In some respects the choice was puzzling. Of the two secretaries it was Townshend who knew more about Scotland; indeed, the duke promptly acknowledged his virtual ignorance of the northern kingdom's "laws and methods of proceeding."[56] Perhaps the selection is an early sign of Walpole's coming distrust of his brother-in-law. It is likelier, however, that Townshend, in Hanover at the moment of the switch and far more interested in the grand chess game of continental politics anyway, simply had no use for such new responsibilities. The duke's role, as Townshend may have foreseen, rarely rose above that of a clerk. Duncan Forbes, the new lord advocate, ran day-to-day affairs in Scotland, and the Campbell brothers—the duke of Argyll and the earl of Islay—advised on most patronage decisions. Newcastle insisted, and Walpole behind him probably also insisted, that all Scottish business pass through the southern secretary's office. But this requirement

merely made the duke a conduit, not a pump. The duke investigated
Scottish affairs, gained a nodding acquaintance with Scottish law, and
of course harried Jacobites in what still remained for them a comparative haven. Lord Islay and Duncan Forbes even penned appropriately
humble protestations of their faithfulness to Newcastle's authority. But
in truth, in Scottish affairs as in most other matters, power lay with the
prime minister.[57]

The one exception to this rule in 1724, the one area Walpole did not
directly control, was foreign affairs. He abstained, it is true, only
because he agreed with the general outlines of Townshend's policies
and fully trusted Townshend's judgment. Thus confident that the northern secretary was sound on the French alliance, Walpole could defer
to his wider experience and knowledge. But in effect this made Townshend foreign secretary. And for Townshend, as for Stanhope and
Bolingbroke before him, France was the prime foreign concern. Upon
good relations with Versailles depended not only the security of the
Hanoverian dynasty—a hostile France could become a sanctuary for
Jacobitism—but even the very peace of Europe. From the French point
of view the alliance was similarly useful. By nurturing Britain's friendship in Stanhope's day, the duc d'Orléans, the first regent for the
young and sickly Louis XV and himself legal heir to the throne, had
expected to earn London's support should the child king die and the
Spanish Bourbon, Philip V, reassert his claim. Orléans' successor in
1723, the duc de Bourbon, was also committed to retaining Britain's
friendship as long as the French king stood without direct heirs. It is
important to note, however, that France's reason for maintaining the
alliance was by its very nature transitory. Within a decade of 1724
Britain could expect Louis XV either to die or to marry and have
children; and whichever event transpired, the grounds for the alliance,
as seen by Versailles, would then dissolve. For this reason the British
worked arduously to persuade France that the broader purpose of
European tranquility also argued for the alliance.

Yet if France was the lodestone for British diplomacy in the 1720's,
it was Spain that demanded the greatest diplomatic attention. Madrid
had several reasons for being displeased with London. Britain was loath
to honor an earlier careless pledge to yield Gibraltar to Spain and disinclined to provide satisfactory guarantees to Spain that the Spanish
prince Don Carlos should succeed to several Italian principalities promised him by the Quadruple Alliance. In 1725 Bourbon Spain startled

Europe by breaking from Bourbon France and concluding a treaty of alliance with Habsburg Austria. It mattered little that the immediate provocation for the action had been a blunder by France, not by Britain. The effect was the same: Spain now had powerful Austria as an ally in its efforts to extract concessions from Britain. Nor was that all. Precisely because the public terms of the Treaty of Vienna seemed so preferential to Austria, Townshend could only conclude that a secret treaty also existed which contained Austria's compensatory pledges to Spain—pledges which perhaps offered assistance in Spain's efforts to drive the British from Gibraltar. Townshend thus responded to the new alliance by promoting a counteralliance. Within two years he recruited to his camp such allies as the Swedes, the Danes, and the Hessians. And at the core of his alliance was the Treaty of Hanover—Britain's response to the Treaty of Vienna—wherein the Dutch and the British pledged their joint opposition to belligerence by Spain or Austria.

As Townshend masterminded this riposte, Newcastle began his diplomatic career by serving as his willing clerk. The duke approached his new responsibilities in 1724 with fitting humility. To Horace Walpole he wrote that "nothing but my dependence upon the friendship and great ability of my Lord Townshend at home and the information and advice that I shall receive from you abroad could have induced me to undertake an office which at present must be so difficult to me." On the method he proposed to adopt he was quite explicit: "I shall in everything act in concert with my Ld. Townshend and according to the advice & instructions that I shall have the pleasure of receiving from him."[58] The duke dutifully accepted Townshend's orders. He formulated a scheme of alliance that, by mobilizing Britain's friends, would leave Spain and Austria isolated. He repeatedly admonished France to exercise its influence in Scandinavian courts to persuade them to join the alliance. When the Treaty of Hanover was dispatched to London in September 1725 for consideration by the lords of regency, he defended it vigorously, arguing its needfulness on the grounds that Vienna's behavior was patently unfair and Madrid's no less than a bit mad. When the House of Lords turned its attention to the treaty early in 1726 he led the ministry's forces in the chamber, countering opposition assertions that Spain was benign and the whole treaty a farce with a report that Spain's chief minister had recently confessed to the existence of secret pledges securing Austrian support for Spanish irredentism.[59] All the while Newcastle stood by uncomplainingly as Townshend, in his desire to unify all British foreign policy, wrote to British diplomats in France and the Iberian kingdoms. He was poaching in Newcastle's southern territory, but it was fitting that he do so: by virtue of his experience and talents he merited being boss in the cockpit.

Still, if it is legitimate to see in this British response to the Treaty of Vienna a demonstration of Townshend's dominance in foreign affairs, it is also true that this response laid the basis for the fundamental differences of opinion between the two secretaries that within four years, despite Newcastle's initial pledges, would shatter their cooperation. The treaty clearly gave Britain two enemies. But which of them, Austria or Spain, should be regarded as the prime foe? Townshend had no doubts: Austria, by virtue of geography and its new interest in the East Indies, had made itself the chief threat. But Newcastle, even while taking his cues from Townshend in drafting dispatches, was soon puzzling over some awkward facts. Recent military history had shown the value of treating Austria as a friend; geography and history had conspired to make Spain Britain's major rival on and off the coasts of America; and of the two states Spain was far more bellicose in its public declarations. These considerations raised doubts in Newcastle's mind about the wisdom of Townshend's command. At first these doubts drew attention to themselves solely in the duke's inability to say anything really severe about Austria. He distrusted Vienna and thought it potentially belligerent, but only rarely could he bring himself to condemn the Habsburg state with harshness. Spain elicited a different response. He described Queen Elizabeth Farnese, the real ruler of the Iberian kingdom, as "an ambitious, passionate woman, excited on the one hand by the excessive thirst of Revenge against France and on the other led away by the flattering prospect of the high pitch of power to which her family might possibly be raised by the match of Don Carlos with the eldest Archduchess." The Spanish were "notoriously and egregiously the aggressors," and by late 1726 he was urging Admiral Hosier, dispatched to prowl on the Spanish silver fleet, to "omit nothing that can possibly be done to prevent the bringing home of this treasure."[60]

Events soon seemed to confirm Newcastle's view. Spain undertook what was in effect war against Britain, interning the South Sea Company ship *Prince Frederick* at Vera Cruz and initiating a siege against Gibraltar. The duke chose this occasion to commit his beliefs to paper. In April 1727 he gave expression to the opinion he had been moving toward for two years: although Austria was behaving outrageously,

Spain posed the graver threat and was the only enemy meriting military action. The duke was not unaware that France shared Townshend's views rather than his own and preferred, if war there must be, a conflict with Vienna to one with Madrid; he thus expressed a readiness, if the French were adamant, to declare war on the Habsburg state. But he urged that Spain be isolated as the enemy in the present conflict and—so long as the imperial court did not aid His Most Catholic Majesty—that Austria be left untouched.[61] With this declaration he made public his disagreement with Townshend. Clearly the duke had in the course of three years become a man confident of his own ability and judgment.

The grounds for such confidence were several. He had learned something about the refined customs and habits of conducting foreign policy; what had once been strange and even exotic was becoming second nature. During Townshend's absences or illnesses he had handled northern affairs in addition to those of his own department. He had discovered that even commanders at sea obeyed his orders. He had developed, moreover, certain firm beliefs about the conduct of foreign policy—about, for example, the need to be "steady and resolute" in confronting enemies bent upon realizing "wild projects," or about the wisdom of handling foreign affairs in such a manner as to maintain at least the appearance of rectitude. Military strength, he deeply believed, was the key to making one's way in the world.[62] Above all, however, Newcastle's growth in self-confidence must be attributed to the encouragement given him by the prime minister; late in 1725, for example, Sir Robert Walpole, recently inducted into the Order of Bath, lauded some dispatches the duke had left for his perusal and added the remark that as Newcastle's writing became terser it also became better. The duke throve on such praise, and Sir Robert, a superb reader of human nature, had the measure of the southern secretary. But he was not flattering the duke merely out of disinterested motives. The cost of the subsidies that Townshend's new diplomacy would require alarmed him, and the northern secretary's blithe courting of war concerned him still more. Newcastle may not have been as pacifically inclined as Sir Robert would have wished, but his moderation toward the imperial court seemed sounder than Townshend's rage, and he was also far likelier, should Walpole choose to assume personal direction of foreign policy, to accept the status of a functionary. Newcastle was to be the lever wherewith Walpole would remove Townshend from power.

But the incipient division among the three politicians was abruptly healed in mid-June 1727 when word arrived from Hanover that George I, vacationing in his preferred haunts, had just died. It was a blow of fearful implications for the ministry, for it brought to the throne a man who had reason to dislike each of them. Even the omens were initially inauspicious: as Walpole and Newcastle departed the ceremony that had proclaimed George II king, their carriage broke down.[63] The duke—and most other observers as well—believed that the new monarch would entrust his affairs to Sir Spencer Compton, speaker of the House of Commons and one of his favorites when he had been Prince of Wales. For his own career the duke could only be deeply apprehensive. Though ten years had elapsed since the memorable christening fracas, the new king was known to be still contemptuous of and unforgiving toward the southern secretary. He had called the duke an "impertinent fool," and Townshend, still abroad, was a "choleric blockhead."[64] Newcastle was being unwontedly reserved when he wrote simply of "the concern and distraction we are all in here for the loss of our dear master."[65]

But Sir Robert, after an initial bout with despair, soon realized that the ministry's prospects were not entirely bleak. George II asked him to keep temporarily at his job, Compton himself made the same request, and while they thought perhaps to make some short-run profits from Sir Robert's experience, it was Walpole who perceived what might really be made of the unanticipated opportunity. In attendance on the new king every morning while Compton presided at the House of Commons, Sir Robert won over the monarch by his competence and congeniality. Queen Caroline proved a useful ally, artfully reminding her husband of Walpole's capacity for service. Walpole demonstrated this capacity by securing for George II an enlarged Civil List of £800,000 per annum. And as Sir Robert's future brightened, so did Newcastle's. Rumors that the duke would be shifted to Ireland quickly disappeared, and within a week of the proclamation of the new reign Newcastle could report that, though a final judgment remained yet uncertain, George II was behaving with unexpected civility to his inherited ministers. Compton soon thereafter began to read the signs aright, and in the peculiarly gutless manner that characterized so much of his public life he simply acknowledged Walpole's triumph. In return for that service he was made Baron Wilmington. Late in July the two secretaries of state kissed the royal hand as a symbol of their retention of office. And by November, the crisis over, it was clear that the

ministry was again in full command: "Things at home go extremely
well," Newcastle wrote to the earl of Carlisle, "the King is in mighty
good humour, very gracious to us all and I hope and believe perfectly
well satisfied with the management of his affairs."[66] Walpole's skill and
tact had played upon George II's chronic docility to procure for the
duke a new lease on political life.

Credit should not, however, go solely to the prime minister. The
general election that was attendant upon a change of monarchs in the
eighteenth century gave Newcastle an unparallelled opportunity to
show precisely how valuable he could be to the Crown.[67] As in 1722, he
delivered sixteen members to the Commons, a gain of power in Sussex
offsetting a loss in Nottinghamshire. The Sussex elections were virtually
free of difficulty. The duke spent the polling days in the county, politicking and partying and writing to his duchess of one ball "where I
danced like an arrow out of a bow."[68] The county returned Henry
Pelham and the humbled Sir Spencer Compton. Lewes returned two
Thomas Pelhams, both of them cousins of the duke. Hastings, with Sir
Archibald Hutcheson now dead, allowed Newcastle to propose two
candidates and then approved Sir William Ashburnham and still
another relative of the duke, Thomas Townshend. Seaford sent its
sitting members, Sir William Gage and Sir Philip Yorke, back for
second terms. For none of these contests did an opposition emerge.
Further northwards, however, in Nottinghamshire, the duke's electoral
affairs were less happily resolved. The duke was working assiduously—
though at a distance—to keep his friends happy. He accepted the office
of recorder of Nottingham; he secured red ribbons for seven county
neighbors after the revival of the Order of the Bath; he even dispatched
his brother Henry to reconnoiter the area in 1725. But the costly
struggle between Whigs and Tories of 1722 had disposed leaders on both
sides to compromise. The terms of the agreement by which the election
of 1727 was fought gave both county seats to the Whigs—Lord Howe
and Sir Robert Sutton again—but required that the Whigs let the
Tories retain one seat each at Newark, East Retford, and the borough
of Nottingham. In truth, since the Sutton family cannot now be easily
classified as Whig or Tory, and since the Tory leader of East Retford
picked a tepid Whig as his nominee, the compromise is perhaps best
understood in personal rather than party terms. Newcastle was able to
resecure the Newark seat for James Pelham, to see Thomas White
retain his East Retford seat, and to confer on John Stanhope, Lord

Chesterfield's brother, a seat at Nottingham. But the loss of any influence over the disposition of the other seat at Nottingham constituted a diminution of his interest in county electoral affairs. As for the Yorkshire boroughs, Aldborough reelected Charles Stanhope and William Jessopp, while Boroughbridge provided a haven for Newcastle's Nottinghamshire friend, George Gregory, who otherwise would have been a victim of the compromise in his own county.

Throughout the kingdom the Whigs fared well in the election. The duke had predicted that the new Parliament "no doubt, will be at least as good as the present."[69] Eager to impress his new master, he did not confine his activities to electoral affairs in his own three counties, but entered the frays, at least indirectly, in Kent, Lincolnshire, and Middlesex. His capacity to take pains, serving as a reinforcement for the powerful political machine that Walpole had constructed, helped propel that machine toward a crushing victory. Once the various petitions had been disposed of, the Whigs held an awesome majority of 430 to 128 in the Commons. It is true that a small number of these Whigs had mobilized behind the opposition banner unfurled by the disappointed William Pulteney. But such a defection, though a harbinger of later difficulties for the government, seemed no more than a quixotic gesture in the aftermath of the overwhelming ministerial triumph. Never again would Sir Robert Walpole see so tractable a Commons.

With a new king settled confortably on his throne and a new Parliament satisfactorily chosen, politics could resume its normal course by the end of 1727. The cooperation between Walpole and Newcastle that had been visible by late 1726 continued to grow; and the fissures dividing these two from Townshend continued to widen. The last personal tie among the three had dissolved in 1726 with the death of Dorothy, Townshend's second wife and Sir Robert's sister. A mutual love for Dolly had hitherto done much to soften disputes over policy; her passing allowed the divisive implications of these disputes to work their way unimpeded thereafter. Townshend continued to press for vigorous action against Austria. He condemned Charles VI's government as "despotick" and found it not a whit more satisfactory than Ferdinand II's oppresive reign. But Newcastle, Walpole, and, significantly, George II maintained that Britain's best interests would best be served by reaching an accommodation with Vienna. They shared Townshend's unhappiness over Austria's Ostend venture—no British politician dared to ignore London's vociferous commercial community on that point—but they believed that this disagreement could be adjusted by means short of war. If any bilateral peace were attainable, Newcastle declared, "it must be more advisable to make up singly with the Emperor than with Spain." Townshend, he added, disagreed "*toto caelo*."[70] By late 1728 it was customarily Newcastle, not Townshend, who transmitted notes to the king about foreign affairs, even if the problems discussed fell solely within the sphere of the northern secretary. Thus, just as he was proving himself useful to Walpole, so too was the duke winning over the new monarch.

Townshend knew full well that he was being isolated. A foreign policy success would have given him a boost, but the only consequences of the creation of the Hanoverian alliance had been subsidy payments and a two-year period of uneasy suspension somewhere between war and peace. Although Spain, its American revenue sharply reduced by Hosier's activities, had reluctantly accepted the preliminaries for peace in 1727, it continued to resist British efforts to regain lost commercial privileges and the detained ship. Young Benjamin Keene, Britain's minister to Spain, let himself be duped into accepting a convention that betrayed London's interests, and when his action was disavowed, Spain had all the more reason to maintain the ominous armament and defense program that the new minister, Don Jose Patiño, had determined upon. Irritated by Newcastle's carping, Townshend began in 1728 to bypass the duke by dispatching secret instructions to Horace Walpole at the French court. It was a technique Newcastle himself would later use with telling effect against fellow secretaries he distrusted. But in Townshend's hands it availed little. Though perhaps not privy to all that Townshend did, Newcastle soon learned that the northern secretary was undertaking activities he wished to keep undisclosed. The revelation only increased secretarial distrust, and by the middle of 1729 Townshend and Walpole had abandoned any efforts to conceal the differences that divided them. Walpole began withdrawing authority in foreign affairs from Townshend. Thus as Britain moved toward a showdown with the Vienna allies, it was Newcastle—and behind him, Walpole—who was calling the signals.

The Spanish situation, still confused, held center stage. Spanish policy continued to pursue two unrelated goals: the satisfaction of Elizabeth Farnese's family ambitions and the reassertion of Spanish commercial and maritime might. Elizabeth had entered into the Vienna alliance in 1725 to enable Don Carlos to get into the Italian principalities. By securing Austria's support she had ended long-standing Habsburg opposition to the admission of a Bourbon into the peninsula. But that very move had simultaneously aroused British and French suspicions, and since it was no more possible for Don Carlos to take his Italian possessions without British and French acquiescence than it would have been without Austrian acquiescence, the new alliance proved abortive. The Spanish blockade of Gibraltar in 1727, designed to pressure Britain into restoring the rock, and the ineffectual Anglo-Spanish sea war of the same year were manifestations of the second thrust of Spanish policy—the restoration of Spanish political influence in Europe. Where Townshend, his suspicions directed toward Austria, had steadily urged that Britain seek an accommodation with Spain, Newcastle had taken a firmer line. He believed that Britain was negotiating with Madrid from strength and that patience, backed by unmasked might, would suffice to let London prevail in the struggle. When Newcastle assumed command of foreign affairs, negotiators had recently gathered at Soissons, again trying to settle these persistent issues of the 1720's. But this time they held out considerable hope of success, since Vienna and Madrid had already accepted the preliminaries of peace. The duke's instructions to the British plenipotentiaries at the conference reflected his readiness to resort once more to force: "Unless they [Spain] will come to a speedy conclusion upon the foot of the provisional treaty which they have all along seemed disposed to, the Allys will be obliged to use the proper means for doing themselves justice."[71] Newcastle was becoming a resolute advocate of the efficacy of threats.

In May 1729 the Vienna alliance fell apart; the hardness that Newcastle had imbued London's Spanish policy with had borne its desired fruit. Renunciation of its Austrian tie compelled Spain to end its diplomatic and military harassment of Gibraltar and to seek a reasonable maritime settlement with Britain. The Spanish decision led Vienna's minister in London, Count Kinsky, to sound out Newcastle on Britain's willingness to drop France and resume friendship with the Habsburg state. The duke was jubilant at the double breakthrough. He doubted that Britain could come to terms with both enemies, for he feared that a settlement with one would destroy the hope of ties with the other. But even a partial conclusion of veiled hostilities—and Austria was, naturally, to be preferred to Spain—would mark an improvement for Britain: "Peace is best of all, and the present uncertain situation almost the worst."[72] Negotiating with the courts of Madrid and Vienna was notoriously slow, and as diplomacy made its tortuous way through the summer of 1729 there were several hints of abrupt changes in Britain's policy, especially when Newcastle and Walpole grew exasperated with Austrian dilatoriness. Still, the broad lines that the two men in their calmer moments imposed on British policy prevailed, and in November, after a lengthy airing of Spanish grievances against the illicit activities of the South Sea Company, Britain and Spain concluded the Treaty of Seville. By its terms the South Sea Company was to receive restitution, the *Prince Frederick* was to be released, the *Asiento* was to be observed, and, for the resolution of strictly commercial issues, a commission was to be created. Spain had, in effect, capitulated. To gain British support for the Spanish garrisoning of the principalities intended for Don Carlos—and Britain had long endorsed his claim—Madrid had abandoned a variety of maritime and commercial hopes.

This treaty was the first triumph for the new diplomatic course charted by Walpole and Newcastle.[73] It is true that by coming to terms with Madrid while remaining at odds with Vienna Newcastle seemed simply to be accomplishing what Townshend had sought, not breaking with his predecessor. But the appearance misleads. The treaty allowed the British government publicly to forecast a revival in trade. Moreover, it had been concluded, as Newcastle had believed it should be done, largely on Britain's terms, not Spain's; Madrid had yielded to London's power, and Britain had not been forced to make significant concessions to get a settlement. Nor did the incidental fact that Britain concluded first with Spain alter the truth that a treaty with Vienna now stood as Britain's chief foreign policy goal. Spain had simply been more tractable in 1729, less able to take care of itself. Moreover, if it was Austria's greater potential strength that allowed Vienna to remain for a longer time deaf to British offers of accommodation, it was precisely this potential strength that made Austria worth securing. Indeed, Austria represented more than merely the stronger of two possible allies; Vienna was as well the heart of the Empire, that Germanic entity that needed strengthening as a counterweight to French might. Walpole and Newcastle, by repudiating Townshend's anti-Habsburg policy, were preparing for the day when the artificial situation that induced Britain and France to be allies had dissolved. They were preparing their diplomatic defenses against a future sun king.

But this statement is perhaps too suggestive. With the advantage of hindsight the historian can see that Britain in 1729 was beginning to return to a conventional diplomacy that regarded the Bourbon kingdoms as a menace and Austria as potentially useful. But there is no evidence to read that motive into Sir Robert's actions. Cardinal Fleury had assumed command of French affairs after the duc de Bourbon's death in 1726, and Walpole, unprepared for the wiliness of the aged ecclesiastic, saw in Fleury a man after his own heart: a statesman who believed in the utility of peace and the value of Anglo-French cooperation. Newcastle harbored some doubts. Though initially enthusiastic about both the activity that the bishop of Frejus injected into French policy and the Anglophile spirit with which he led it, the duke by 1728 had noticed a strange gap between Fleury's words and performance: "He may not always act with that vigour and firmness with which he sometimes talks."[74] But the duke was too dependent on Walpole, both politically and psychologically, to press his suspicions very far, and he continued to muzzle whatever private concerns he had about Fleury's reliability.

Townshend's eclipse could only be construed as a humiliation for the proud Norfolk grandee. If he could no longer command foreign policy, it seemed but a matter of time until he either left or was asked to leave the government. By early 1730 he was talking of retirement, and by March Newcastle had received assurances that as soon as Parliament rose the northern secretary, with whom his relations were now frigid, would resign. It was joyous news. It meant not only the departure of a colleague with whom Newcastle could no longer get along; it meant as well the appointment of "the man in the world I wish,"[75] the earl of Harrington. Harrington, who until recently had been William Stanhope, kinsman of the great Lord Stanhope, had served for a number of years as Britain's ambassador to Spain. Newcastle had found him to be a kindred spirit—one who distrusted, albeit for different reasons, Townshend's conduct of foreign policy. The two men had corresponded frequently and a genuine friendship had emerged. In mid-1728, when Stanhope fought unsuccessfully for a peerage for himself and a preferment for his brother, a man whose reputation had suffered from apparent complicity in the machinations of the South Sea Company, Newcastle supported his cause. A year later, when Spain finally began to show signs of a new interest in conciliation, Newcastle recommended that Stanhope be chosen to represent Britain with full powers at the decisive negotiations. Thus, it was through Newcastle's —and Walpole's

—favor that Stanhope garnered the glory attendant upon negotiating a pact as important as the Treaty of Seville. He seemed a natural choice as Townshend's successor.

The actual departure of the northern secretary took place in May 1730, triggered by a quarrel between Townshend and Newcastle about policy toward Austria. Though both men seemed ready at that time to make war on a Vienna that stubbornly refused to recognize the Seville agreement, Newcastle favored giving the emperor one last chance to change his ways. When Townshend found king, queen, prime minister, and southern secretary arrayed against him, he chose to hand over the seals. Harrington—for Stanhope had received his peerage in January— was selected to replace him. Other changes followed. Carteret was driven from his Irish office into opposition; Wilmington was given an earldom; Chesterfield was made lord steward; and Henry Pelham was promoted to the paymastership. Newcastle was ecstatic in his gratitude: "God bless Sir Robert," he exulted to Harrington, "—'tis all his doing: and let us in return, resolve to make him happy as we can."[76] If the expression sounds somewhat puerile to twentieth-century ears, it cannot be denied that the duke had sufficient grounds for jubilation. He stood now virtually at the top. Loyalty to Sir Robert and a capacity for in- dustry had allowed him to overtake even the powerful Lord Towns- hend. He had survived a change of ministers in 1721–22 and a change of reigns in 1727. The replacement of Townshend with Harrington now promised to bring unity of purpose to British foreign policy and a thoroughgoing return to what Newcastle regarded as right principles.

3

Political Lieutenant

I

The departure of Townshend altered the political and diplomatic scene. Newcastle was now the senior secretary. Such deference as he had felt obliged to show his former colleague, a man whose distinguished career had had pre-Hanoverian roots, was not required toward the new northern secretary. In many eyes Harrington was merely Newcastle's protégé and creature. The duke handled him in ways that he had circumspectly avoided in his dealings with Townshend: he denied Harrington colonial appointive privileges that his predecessor had exercised, and he began covert correspondence with diplomats in Harrington's department. Meanwhile, an adjusted team of British diplomats was accredited to the key courts of Europe. Keene replaced Harrington in Madrid; Lord Waldegrave moved from Vienna to assume Horace Walpole's post at Versailles; and in September Thomas Robinson took over Waldegrave's duties at the imperial capital. The shifts did not necessarily signify disappointment at past performances. Harrington, after all, had been promoted, and Horace was returning to Britain chiefly because Sir Robert believed his considerable talents could be more usefully deployed in parliamentary endeavors. But the appointment of Robinson hinted at a British desire to purge Anglo-Austrian relations of recent unhappy memories associated with Waldegrave, and the departure of the prime minister's brother from France suggested a glimmering recognition of the truth that the special relationship with the court of Versailles was moving towards its inevitable dissolution. The repudiation of Townshend's diplomacy was to continue.

With Spain secured through the Treaty of Seville, Walpole and Newcastle pressed on in their efforts to reach an accommodation with

Austria. That in fact was Robinson's mission. But the path to accommodation, like all other diplomatic roads passing through Vienna, was rocky. The emperor, as Newcastle had feared, resented the Anglo-Spanish pact, especially its substitution of Spanish for neutral garrisons in Italy. He adamantly refused to accede to the introduction of Spanish troops into the duchies, and Newcastle responded with threats of punishment and preparations for an Anglo-French invasion of Sicily designed to intimidate Austria. Vienna, the duke reminded Waldegrave, had to be "convinced that we will not for ever be amusing ourselves and them with negotiations and without doing any thing essential."[1] Spain meanwhile grew impatient with Britain's inability to budge Vienna on the issue of garrisoning and finally declared its obligation under the Treaty of Seville null and void. But these developments were not omens. Robinson set to work in the fall to sweeten imperial tempers and plunged soon into secret negotiations with Viennese ministers. Newcastle felt uneasy about hiding this development from Britain's ally, France, but he feared still more the possible consequences of a premature public disclosure of such sensitive talks.[2] The secrecy paid off. In March 1731 Robinson and the imperial negotiators completed the Treaty of Vienna, ending six years of Anglo-Austrian animosity and restoring an alliance that Newcastle thought natural and Walpole thought politic. Britain gave Charles VI what he most wanted: a guarantee of the Pragmatic Sanction, the imperial document that specified the indivisibility of the Habsburg dominions on the emperor's death. In return Charles agreed to dissolve the Ostend Company and to accept the Spanish garrisons. Walpole's—and therefore Newcastle's—recasting of Britain's foreign policy was complete.

The Treaty of Vienna was the most important European settlement since Utrecht and Rastadt. Unlike various intervening agreements, it worked. George II, as Newcastle grandiloquently put it, had "given peace to all Europe."[3] And he had done so on British terms, for, as the duke explained to Robinson, the treaty had "at once answered, all that our friends could wish, or our enemies"—the duke could only mean France—"fear."[4] Elizabeth Farnese, at long last successful in her struggle to win the duchies for her son, agreed to have Spain reassent to the Treaty of Seville. Within a few months, despite a variety of petty disputes, Spanish troops had garrisoned the duchies and Don Carlos himself had finally entered Italy. Simultaneously, Spain reinstituted the British trading privileges specified in the Treaty of Seville, giving

Walpole the parliamentary ammunition he keenly wanted. Austria, meanwhile, had won the support of Europe's most potent state for a testamentary policy bearing on the very viability of the Habsburg confederation.

There was but one clear loser from the treaty, and that was France. Of this fact Newcastle was more aware than Sir Robert. The duke had already strikingly declared that "the cardinal is not dead, but dead to us."[5] Dubious of French intentions as early as 1728, he grew more so as time passed. He regarded the Anglo-French alliance as something unnatural and dimly perceived that, with the birth of a dauphin in 1729, and the consequent end of the basis for Franco-Spanish suspicions, Anglo-French conflicts of interest would reassume their traditional importance. The Treaty of Vienna promoted that very development. Aside from French pique at being kept in the dark by its ally—Newcastle dismissed this as "an omission of form"[6]—there were substantive grounds for French concern. Though Newcastle could argue, and truthfully, that the pact secured what Britain and France had long sought, namely, protection for Don Carlos's rights in the duchies, the duke also realized, as Walpole apparently did not, that Britain's acceptance of the Pragmatic Sanction, implying British support for the indivisibility of France's chief continental rival, could only be regarded by Versailles as a thoroughly unfriendly action. Had the continuation of Anglo-French cooperation been a real possibility, the treaty would thereby have been a mistake. But since all indications suggest that that cooperation was disappearing in any event, it was prudent that Britain once again proffer the hand of amity to the emperor. In the international affairs of Europe the highest wisdom is to avoid isolation by keeping friends.

These foreign policy successes of the early 1730's were matched by domestic triumphs as well. But in the elaboration and implementation of Sir Robert Walpole's domestic schemes Newcastle took little part; he was important chiefly as a defender, in the House of Lords, of policy devised by others. As long as Townshend had sat in the ministry it had been he who had served as the government's leading spokesman in the Lords. That responsibility now devolved upon Newcastle. It was not a light task, for in addition to demanding regular attendance and hours of preparation, it also required that the duke spar with abler public speakers. In all these activities Newcastle submitted to Walpole's instruction. When Sir Robert in 1731 adopted his customary expedient

of permitting an awkward pensions bill to pass the Commons, knowing
that the Lords' negative would spare him the necessity of revealing the
names of those favored with pensions, Newcastle obediently advanced
the remarkable argument that Parliament should not request such
revelations since, by its very request, it would suggest to the world that
unworthy men were among the recipients. When, a year later, Sir
Robert needed to restore revenue jobs for discontented followers and
decided to reintroduce the recently repealed salt duty, he prepared a
memorandum for Newcastle, outlining how the duke could most persuasively justify the government's embarrassing *volte-face*. Newcastle
performed effectively. When the duke called the bill "just" he was not
being heartless but rather appealing to a theory of taxation that equated
justness with universality of incidence; and when he called it "compassionate" he was simply being characteristically ingenuous about the
principles of eighteenth-century politics.[7] Lord Egmont relegated
Newcastle to the class of "declaymors" in the house, and it is true that
when the going became rough after 1733, the duke needed reinforcements. But until the great assaults on Sir Robert began in earnest,
Newcastle represented the government in the Lords. As with much
else that he did, his record was not distinguished, but neither was it
contemptible.

As a consequence of his heightened importance, the duke began
to play a larger role in the social life of the capital and court. Partying
had ever been one of his favorite pastimes, but early in the 1730's it
began regularly to embrace foreign dignitaries and members of the
royal family. Newcastle had a flare for giving sumptuous parties. Even
Lord Hervey, his most venomous detractor, had high praise for his
management of social affairs: "The entertainment last night was the
most magnificent, the easiest, the best understood, and the best ordered
thing, I ever saw in my life."[8] When in attendance at court entertainments the duke engaged avidly in cards and sometimes caroused too
much. He also began a flirtation with George II's homely daughter
Emily. It was by all accounts a harmless political dalliance rather than
an *affaire de coeur*, and there is no reason to believe that the duke was
unfaithful to his wife, especially since he was comically shy and awkward in his courting. But he and Emily became friends. And thus,
though never truly popular with the king in these years—George II
would never honor Walpole's request that the monarch select the duke
to accompany him on his visits to Germany—and frankly disliked by

the queen, Newcastle was able to assure himself of both intelligence about court affairs and some leverage in court decision making.

In August of 1732 Newcastle found a new and important comrade. While entertaining in Surrey, he was introduced to Andrew Stone, not yet thirty years old, and the two men immediately struck up a warm friendship. The duke wrote to his wife of the encounter: "I have had the charmingest man with us at Claremont I ever saw. . . . He has more learning, more parts, & as agreeable as any man I ever saw in my life."[9] Stone was the brother-in-law of William Barnard, Newcastle's chaplain at Claremont, and was an alumnus of Newcastle's Westminster. That he was ambitious cannot be doubted. But his ambition was of a peculiarly reticent variety. He cared less for acclaim than for influence and was prepared to forego the former in pursuit of the latter. If he could attach himself to a man of prominence he could rely on his own abilities to give himself a measure of power. The duke, meanwhile, though possessing wide authority by virtue of birth, wealth, and office, felt himself in need of an assistant to whom private matters, boring details, and the care of day-to-day correspondence could be safely entrusted. Within three weeks the two men with complementary needs had come to amicable terms: Stone would be Newcastle's secretary and receive £200 annually. Later, he would assume other tasks and become in a sense Newcastle's companion and factotum, and he would eventually receive sinecures bringing in £4,000 yearly as partial recompense. Self-interest—indeed, shrewdly perceptive self-interest—motivated both men. But serving oneself is not incompatible with bestowing affection. The new friendship was mutually genuine.

The opening years of the 1730's were thus remarkably placid and pleasant for the duke. He would not know such political tranquillity again for two decades. Sir Robert commanded affairs of state, and his regime effused order, prosperity, and satisfaction over the kingdom. There were, nevertheless, hidden weaknesses in the system. Sir Robert was not immune to complacency nor to the more serious character flaw of overconfidence. He forgot that a successful past could not prevent future misjudgments. Moreover, a policy of consistently excluding talent from high office, while providing short-run security, assured that in the long run an ambitious, skilled, and vengeful opposition would emerge. By the early 1730's such an opposition finally existed, composed of three branches.[10] First, there were the dissident Whigs, followers of William Pulteney, who asserted that Walpole had

abandoned true Whiggery for despotism. Then there were the Hanoverian Tories, combining an allegiance to the new dynasty with a
distaste for the emerging commercial ethos of Whiggery. Lord Bolingbroke, restored to his possessions but not his seat in the House of Lords
in 1725, led this faction. Finally, there were the Jacobites, looking to
"the king over the water" for leadership.

Clearly there were obstacles to any effective cooperation among three
such groups, each owing allegiance to a different notion of good governance. But the antipathy that all came to feel for Sir Robert proved a
sufficient binder. Pulteney and Bolingbroke made common cause in
promoting the opposition journal, *The Craftsman*, in the late 1720's,
and in 1730 the Pretender made the calculated decision to authorize
his followers to cooperate with other opponents of the ministry. These
opposition leaders had few scruples about passing awkward information
on to foreign diplomats, and their periodicals lashed the ministry with
splendid combinations of truths and fabrications, propelled, in their
highest moments, by vigorous and powerful prose. Newcastle tried to
move against the hostile press. He and his friend Philip Yorke, the
attorney general, deliberated frequently on how to defend the ministry
from slander. But because there was nothing illegal in reprinting old
journals, every opposition newspaper, even at times of governmental
crackdowns, was free to revive assaults against an earlier foreign born
king, William III. One thing alone truly protected Sir Robert from this
pack of baying hounds: his continued dominace in the House of Commons. Because he was secure in the house, his ministry was secure in the
kingdom. But in 1733 his burgeoning egotism pushed him to folly.

Sir Robert proposed in that year to extend the excise principle to
cover tobacco and wine. The new revenue to result from the taxes
would allow him to lower the land tax to the irreducible rate of one
shilling in the pound. All his key advisers—Yorke, Pelham, and
Newcastle—approved the proposal. They knew from the stir that the
reimposition of the salt duty had created that discontented voices
would exclaim against the excise scheme. But to a man they were confident. "Excise will be the grand affair," Newcastle predicted early in
the year, "but as it is right in every respect, it gains every day, and will
certainly be carried by a great majority in both houses."[11] The ministry
had, however, miscalculated. The opposition, united in its zeal to
embarrass Sir Robert, found in the proposal its great chance to galvanize the political nation and mobilize it behind a new banner, thereby

threatening to destroy the prime minister's strength in his very strong-hold, the House of Commons. A shrill, often hysterical campaign against the excise began. Critics pointed to the expenses that the presumed increase in the number of treasury officials would require; they assailed the right that such new officials would have to search private business establishments. Without excessive distortion it was possible to represent the proposal as a product of tyrannical cunning, designed to begin the task of undermining the precious freedoms of Englishmen. And through-out the kingdom, sympathetic to that appeal, the chorus of excise opponents swelled beyond measure.

For a long time Walpole did not yield. Convinced that he was right and his proposal sound, he kept on course, determined to weather the storm. But frailer men began to mutiny. Some felt pressure from their constituencies and deserted the prime minister to protect themselves in future elections. Others, though holding office, were privately jealous of Walpole's power and found in the excise ruckus a suitable excuse for abandoning their nominal leader. Among politically influential peers only Newcastle, Harrington, Grafton, and Devonshire stayed loyal to their chief. Ultimately Walpole bowed to what finally seemed to be the inevitable. It was not so much his steadily declining majority in the Commons that persuaded him to abandon his plan, but rather the likelihood of a defeat in the House of Lords. Bitter and humilated, Sir Robert moved in early April to postpone consideration of the motion until after the house had risen. He thereby killed his bill. But he was determined to avenge himself upon those of his opponents still subject to his authority, and he promptly instituted a purge of a scope unprecedented in Hanoverian Britain. The dukes of Bolton and Mont-rose and lords Chesterfield, Burlington, Clinton, Stair, Marchmont, and Cobham were deprived of various offices. This was a momentous decision. Those whom Walpole forced into opposition now supplied enough new talent to the dissident Whigs to let that group credibly offer an alternative Whig ministry. And those who stood by Sir Robert —Newcastle and Pelham, Yorke, Harrington, Devonshire, and Hervey —henceforth comprised the nucleus of what Newcastle would later call the "Old Corps." It would be the most authentic repository of Walpolean Whiggery for three decades to come.

The death of the excise measure did not, however, end the ministry's difficulties. An opposition that had won an important psychological victory hoped to gain a still more striking legislative one as well. The

opportunity came with reports that the confiscated estates of the South
Sea directors had been put to improper use. Opposition peers demanded
and, despite Newcastle's efforts, received authorization for a parliamentary inquiry into the matter. The ministry faced, at a minimum,
considerable embarrassment, especially when several minor divisions
showed its forces to be in the minority for the first time in many years.
So Walpole and Newcastle began whipping: friends of the ministry,
both lay and episcopal, were urged, sometimes with little subtlety,
to demonstrate their loyalty. The feverish maneuvering succeeded.
On 2 June, led in debate by Newcastle and Devonshire, the government
troops prevailed on the key vote, 75 to 70. With this division the will of
the opposition was finally spent. Promptly after the victory Newcastle
attended the court and later reported that "I never saw My Master &
Mistress in such Joy as they were last night, we are all in High Spirits,
I think our Affairs are retrieved."[12] In a sense, he was right. Political
tranquillity of a sort was now restored. But the events between February
and June 1733 were too violent to leave the foundations of politics
unchanged. Walpole had been proven vulnerable; the great man had
been compelled to retreat. Total retrieval of a former self-assuredness
was impossible. For Newcastle and the rest of Walpole's colleagues it
meant a reduction in the confidence they could repose in him; for
Walpole it meant a return to caution and conservatism in policy.

Walpole was thus in no mood to entrust his political fortunes to
hazardous enterprises when, in the summer of 1733, the Bourbon
powers and Austria approached war. Nominally this conflict—it would
be called the War of the Polish Succession—was fought on behalf of
competing candidates for Poland's elective crown. In reality, however,
France was choosing war in the hope of dismembering Maria Theresa's
eventual inheritance under the Pragmatic Sanction and—though it
long hid the fact—to secure itself territory on the Rhenish frontier.
Early in the year Newcastle, while arguing against a diminution in
troop strength, had obliquely warned Parliament that war was not out
of the question for Britain. As tensions mounted in July he tried to use
the kingdom's influence to preserve peace. The disputed royal election
in itself was inconsequential to London: "What relates singly to Poland
is a very remote consideration for His Majesty." But the likelihood that
armed conflict would alter the balance of power in Europe and thereby
threaten the "liberties of Europe"—a cant phrase of the era—was
deeply disturbing to London. Newcastle clearly saw what France's

indignation over the Polish election imported: Poland would be the convenient pretext, he told Waldegrave in June, but France really designed "to defeat the Emperor's settlement of his succession upon his daughters, and to divide the succession." In an effort to dissuade France from making war or Austria from stupidly legitimizing any French hostilities—for imperial troops were on the road toward the Polish frontier—Newcastle adopted the strategy of leaving Versailles and Vienna uncertain about Britain's response to belligerence. The French were informed that George II "will not fail to perform punctually and faithfully his engagement" to the emperor. But the Austrians were urged to recall their troops, since Britain could not promise military aid if hostilities commenced. "In these circumstances," Newcastle explained to Waldegrave, "His Majesty thinks the most prudent measure is to leave both parties in suspense, and when they both have reason to apprehend the consquences of what they may do, they may probably think twice before they venture upon it."[13]

When France declared war on the empire, however, the policy of fostering incertitude was proved bankrupt. Britain could no longer avoid the hard decision of how to respond to war on the continent. In the duke's mind there could be no question of not honoring the Treaty of Vienna. Britain's guarantee of the Pragmatic Sanction had come into play; an attack on the Habsburg dominions had triggered the *casus foederis*. More than national honor was at stake. To let the Habsburg state be dismembered by France would be imprudent, even reckless. With France slowly returning to its natural stance as Britain's foe, Britain dared not disoblige Austria, its anti-Bourbon ally, and dared still less to let this ally be weakened and its usefulness to London thereby impaired.[14] Newcastle was emboldened to espouse this conviction and become its most vigorous advocate by the knowledge that George II, for reasons pertaining to Hanoverian interests, shared it. So in fact did the queen, Lord Harrington, and the influential Hanoverian minister to the court of St. James, Hatorff. But it would be illegitimate to infer that Newcastle adopted his pro-Austrian view simply to curry political favor. If anything, his advocacy was politically disadvantageous. For although the king heartily wished to support Vienna, a still more powerful political figure did not. That in fact is why the debate occurred: Sir Robert Walpole opposed British entry into the war.

The prime minister had his reasons. He suspected it would be impossible to persuade the Dutch to follow Britain, and he disliked the idea that Dutch merchants should profit from wartime trade denied to Britain. He persuaded himself that Fleury wanted to preserve the balance of power in Europe and that, even if France were successful in arms, the cardinal would seek a quick and nonpunitive peace. He was annoyed that Vienna had been so clumsy in its handling of the Polish affair, virtually demanding French military intervention. He believed that peace promoted prosperity while war invited Jacobite scheming. But above all, he feared for the parliamentary consequences of a war. A general election was due within a year. Having already inflamed the nation with his excise blunder, he dared not saddle the administration with a foreign war as well. And so Sir Robert set himself against the beliefs and arguments of all his friends. And he prevailed. Lamely maintaining that the Treaty of Vienna involved a defensive obligation but not a guarantee of assistance, British spokesmen announced that George II would remain at peace with his cousins. It was a powerful proof of the personal authority the Norfolk squire exercised over his monarch and colleagues.

But while it is clear that Walpole's action demonstrated his sheer might, it has been less clear that it spoke well for his wisdom. The creation of hypothetical alternatives is always a speculative enterprise but nevertheless often instructive. It can be argued that Britain, by not coming to Vienna's aid, permitted its ally to be weakened, encouraged France and Spain to believe that London would not resort to arms save when in mortal danger, and resigned its rightful position as one of the powers whose views were to be consulted when European decisions were made. By this view British intervention, had it been launched, would probably have thwarted all Spanish designs in Italy and likely have checked France's Rhenish ambitions. The War of the Austrian Succession, a far more extensive and costly conflict than the one over Poland, might thereby have been averted by a manifestation of greater courage in 1733.[15]

Newcastle was certainly conscious of some of these general considerations—of the poor figure Britain would cut in the deliberative councils of Europe if it abstained from battle and of the dangers inherent in isolation. But this case against Walpole and for Newcastle is not ultimately sufficient, for it cannot be persuasively argued that Britain on balance was the loser by refraining from giving military aid to Austria in 1733. Britain's years of peace while Europe was bent beneath war must surely be reckoned an advantage. And if France profited from the conflict, as she did with the succession to Lorraine, it is hardly clear from the record of 1740–48 that British arms could have prevented the conquest. As for British isolation, it simply did not occur. It is true that when Britain went to war in 1739 it had no ally, but that struggle with Spain was essentially an American conflict for which Vienna in any case would not have been obliged to offer aid. And in 1740, when events in Europe led to a widened war, Britain and Austria resumed their earlier military cooperation. Whether Spain would have courted war so recklessly in 1739 had it been confronted by British might in 1733 is questionable. But then one must question too whether war in 1733, undertaken without popular demand, would have succeeded where war in 1739, backed by a strong mandate, failed. In short, with the benefits of peace so patent and its feared liabilities so intangible, it seems appropriate to conclude that Walpole's was the wiser advice even if Newcastle's was the more honorable.

Almost from the outset Britain hoped to provide a satisfactory plan of peace for the belligerents. But London regarded Dutch support for its peace-making activities as essential, and was delayed in undertaking them by Dutch slowness in approving the idea. Meanwhile, Don Carlos marched into Naples, a Habsburg territory, and Sardinia sided with France. Then Versailles and Madrid concluded the Bourbon *pacte de famille*. Newcastle had long feared that such a reunion might be in the offing. Keene quickly obtained a copy of the secret treaty and dispatched it to London, where its promise of French aid to help Spain regain Gibraltar confirmed Newcastle's fears about Britain's self-imposed impotence. "It is hardly possible," he lamented, "for a treaty to be more injurious to His Majesty than this in every respect."[16] But Walpole's chief concerns as 1734 opened were domestic—the need to protect his ministry against any renewed opposition assaults and to prepare for elections. To the former end he supplied Newcastle with formidable allies in the House of Lords where, spunky as he was, the duke could not cope with Carteret's forcefulness and Chesterfield's wit. Lord Hervey, effeminate in appearance and catty in manner but still an able debater, had been called to the Lords the previous summer. He was now joined by Baron Talbot, the new lord chancellor, and by Baron Hardwicke, formerly Philip Yorke, who took the dignity of lord chief justice. The arrival of Hardwicke was a special blessing to Newcastle. The duke detested Hervey, and while he respected Talbot, he could unburden himself only to his close friend Hardwicke; the baron's presence quickened the duke's spirit. And the parliamentary strategy succeeded. With Walpole and Pelham calmly guiding the Commons and Hardwicke, Hervey, Talbot, and Newcastle commanding the Lords, the government passed through a tranquil session.

But Newcastle's greater services to Walpole were revealed in the spring. The Septennial Act compelled the government to call a general election. With the opposition restless and the uproar over the excise proposals still echoing in the land, the times were scarcely propitious. The campaign of 1734, therefore, may be taken as constituting the first true test of Newcastle's electoral power.[17] The duke was most concerned about Sussex. Both he and important opposition Whigs thought a defeat for some of his candidates in the county eminently possible. William Hay, a hunchbacked dwarf married to a cousin of the duke, had gloomily reported in August of 1733 that many outraged inhabitants of the county believed the government had intended to impose the excise on such essentials as bread and meat. As a consequence, beginning in the fall of 1733, the duke spared no effort to mollify his neighbors. He made several personal trips to the county; he sent the county members, Henry Pelham and the frosty James Butler, on a tour of the region; he arranged for the release of the popular smuggler Thomas Newman from Horsham Jail; he established a coffee house and assembly rooms at Lewes for use by loyal Whigs; and he expended money as never before—£3,600 by a memorandum in his records and £10,000 by some accounts—in efforts to purchase the support of the county.[18]

The exhausting campaign paid off. When the votes were tallied, Seaford returned Sir William Gage and Sir Philip Yorke's recently elected replacement, the hardworking and loyal William Hay. In Hastings the duke had previously taken steps to strengthen his interest by appointing his former enemy John Collier to be his estate and electoral agent. Thus, he had no difficulty in securing the reelection of Sir William Ashburnham and his second cousin, Thomas Pelham Jr., son of Thomas Pelham of Lewes. But in that "ungrateful town of Lewes" a mighty struggle ensued. Both the incumbents were indifferent campaigners, prompting the duke to lament "there never were two such creatures as our candidates."[19] Thomas Pelham of Lewes was indolent; Thomas Pelham of Stanmer, nicknamed "Turk" because he had a background in commerce, was often drunk and then dangerously loquacious. Against these two stooges a powerful opposition, uniting both the Tory and the dissenting interests, emerged; and the opposition candidates campaigned vigorously and effectively. Ultimately, in a close contest, Newcastle's candidates won, largely because the duke's able agent Robert Burnett turned to wholesale treating of the town. Meanwhile, in the county election, the two ministerial Whigs, Henry Pelham and James Butler, won by a respectable margin over an energetic opposition. Sussex, though in peril, had remained loyal.

In Yorkshire the duke had his usual success, but in Nottinghamshire he once again, as in 1727, saw his influence diminished. Abandoning Charles Stanhope, who had personally disobliged George II, Newcastle asked Aldborough to choose William Jessopp and the duke's own brother Henry. For Pelham this pocket borough was clearly a safe and last resort, and when he resigned the seat promptly after the election to represent Sussex, the borough chose John Jewkes, one of Newcastle's Sussex agents. Boroughbridge reelected George Gregory, but only after a quarrel between Newcastle and the Wilkinsons had been amicably resolved. The three boroughs in Nottinghamshire continued to send up one Whig and one Tory each. James Pelham was again the Whig at Newark; John White, who had recently succeeded his late father, represented the party at East Retford; and John Plumptre, replacing the neglectful John Stanhope, carried the banner in Nottingham. But for the county the Whigs no longer monopolized representation. In 1732 both sitting members had left the house, Lord Howe because he had accepted an office and Sir Robert Sutton through embarrassing expulsion. They had been replaced by a Whig, Thomas Bennett, and a Tory, William Levinz, and in 1734 Bennett and Levinz won reelection. Thus, where in 1722 the duke had been instrumental in returning six Whigs from Nottinghamshire constituencies, by 1734 he could muster only four. He was paying the penalty of choosing to be an absentee landlord.

The duke was not pleased with the nationwide results of the election; in what some thought to be an unprecedentedly costly campaign, the ministerial Whigs had suffered a patent setback. After the petitions had been judged, 347 ministerial Whigs faced 87 opposition Whigs and 145 Tories in the House of Commons. It might have been worse—after all, the government still had a dominating majority—but Newcastle had expected a happier outcome. He was, in fact, a thoroughgoing realist about the new house at a time when Sir Robert remained excessively sanguine: "Our parliament is," the duke wrote to Horace Walpole shortly after the returns were known, "I think, a good one; but by no means such a one as the queen and your brother imagine. It will require great care, attention, and management to *sett out right*, and keep people in good humour."[20] In the narrower sphere of personal electoral power, even though he had in effect returned only fifteen members, the duke was far more cheered. An effort to expand his influence in Yorkshire to the county level had met little success. But otherwise all seemed well. The decline of influence in Nottinghamshire, unavoidable because of decisions made in 1732, did not really trouble him, and the triumphs in his own county, "notwithstanding the strongest & most violent opposition from ye Tories, y^t ever was known in Sussex," sent his spirits soaring.[21] Indeed, the duke could not refrain from a bit of gloating as he cast his eye over the "bad success of our friends in other counties, as Kent, Cheshire, Hampshire, Yorkshire, Gloucestershire, Essex, &c."[22] And that comparison was telling. Prior to 1734 Newcastle had been simply a peer with a taste for electoral machinations; in the general election of that year he first showed his masterful talents at organizing electoral victories. He had held a dike that had in many other places been breached. The lesson was not to be lost on Walpole— nor on Newcastle himself.

II

The course of the war in Europe continued to breed disagreements between Newcastle and Walpole. Its outbreak had been the occasion of the first serious difference of opinion to mar their years of concord. And because the war would not disappear new irritants were regularly provided to inflame a wound that really needed a balm. Britain's persevering efforts to find terms for a settlement acceptable to all belligerents or alternatively to impose a peace foundered on London's inability to get vigorous assistance from the Netherlands. Obedient to the prime minister's wish (which in time became the king's as well), Newcastle avoided any actions or promises that might threaten to suck London into the conflict. Though increasingly scornful of French professions of a will to peace, he faithfully requested Versailles to open talks with an emissary of George II concerning the purpose of the war and French ideas about its resolution. But Fleury and Chauvelin did not wish to commit themselves prematurely, and so they resorted to stalling tactics, putting British diplomats off with technicalities, pro- cedural questions, and all manner of contrived delay. Newcastle recognized the pattern of deceit behind the multitude of plausible excuses. But Walpole would not. The duke accused the French of double-talk, indicted Chauvelin's correspondence with the French ambassador Chavigny as "a heap of blustering nonsense," and declared Fleury's sworn word worthless.[23] Walpole merely continued to rely—perhaps desperately—on French discretion and Fleury's common sense. But while trusting the French minister, he apparently feared that Newcastle, deliberately or mistakenly, might let the ducal enthusiasm for combat commit Britain beyond his own wishes. In any event, by 1735 Walpole was cultivating private contacts with the French government, thereby bypassing and undercutting his secretary of state.

The outer limit to the possibility for French delaying was imposed by Versailles' fear that excessive stalling might drive London into the arms of Vienna. Thus, at appropriate moments, France made limited concessions to Britain. In May of 1734 Versailles finally accepted the proffered mediation of the maritime powers, but refused in the following months to give satisfactory answers to Anglo-Dutch questions about French engagements, independence, and intentions. Newcastle's patience was about exhausted when, in September, Fleury proposed secret talks between Horace Walpole, known to share his brother's myopia toward France, and an eminent Frenchman. Newcastle discerned in this suggestion a ploy to divide Britain from the United Provinces and to create new tensions between London and Vienna, and he counselled against accepting it; but Sir Robert again overrode the secretary and secret talks began. They moved quickly to a resolution of almost all ostensible issues, but in February of 1735 France repudiated the work of its negotiator on a flimsy pretext, and the whole mediation mission collapsed. Newcastle commended Horace Walpole and excoriated Fleury: "It is plain," he wrote the British diplomat, "you constantly drove him to the wall."[24] France's shoddy treatment of British hopes, while it did not purge Sir Robert of all his illusions, certainly confirmed Newcastle in his belief that he, not the prime minister, had a sounder grasp of foreign realities. In this instance the duke was right. Walpole may have been the wiser guide in keeping Britain out of the war; Newcastle was surely the more acute spectator of the character of the men directing it.

By the end of 1735 the terms for a settlement had been reached—and, as Newcastle had feared, without British participation. French and Imperial negotiators had come together in Vienna to work out an accord. That the conflict nominally continued for three more years while Spain obdurately refused to come to terms had little bearing on the fates of European states or Europeans. The compromise settlement had something for everyone. Austria placed its candidate on the Polish throne and acquired territory in northern Italy. France secured the reversion to Lorraine. A third Bourbon kingdom appeared in Europe as Naples passed from the Habsburgs to Don Carlos. Considering the drubbing that the imperial forces had taken in the war, the peace was regarded as a lenient one. Newcastle, though apprehensive about the method and uneasy about the disposition of Lorraine, was generally pleased with the terms;[25] and Bolingbroke commented grudgingly that "if the English ministers had any hand in it, they were wiser than he thought them, and, if they had not, they were much luckier than they deserved to be."[26]

Lord Hervey remarked in his *Memoirs* that foreign policy in 1735 was handled entirely by Walpole and the queen,[27] and while the evidence does not permit confirmation of Caroline's role, it is obvious that the judgment about Walpole is correct. Indeed, it would have been true of 1734 as well. Newcastle was reduced to such humiliating tasks as transmitting unopened letters back and forth between Waldegrave and Sir Robert. He learned too of the prime minister's secret negotiations with Chavigny. It was a novel and frustrating experience for him —clearly Walpole no longer trusted him—but he was still loyal enough and insufficiently weaned from political dependency to avoid undue recriminations: his lot was unhappy but, sometimes sullenly and often self-pityingly, he accepted it. This irritation is suggestive, for insofar as there was a similarity between the duke's earlier disagreement with Townshend and his present one with Walpole it points to one of the fixed stars in Newcastle's firmament of ideas. In each case he wanted to cultivate good relations with Austria. Townshend had viewed the Habsburg state as an enemy; Newcastle had believed it could be transformed into an ally. Walpole was ready to leave Austria to a harsh fate at the hands of its Bourbon foes; Newcastle was prepared to assist it on the grounds that an enemy of Britain's enemy was Britain's friend. The duke's foreign policy thinking, whether in the 1720's or the 1730's, cannot be understood without recognizing that just as he saw something natural in Anglo-French animosity, so he saw in Anglo-Austrian cooperation something almost equally in accord with the fundamental order of international relations.

Although the war receded from visibility after 1735, the relationship between the prime minister and the southern secretary remained rather prickly. In a sense, the confirmation of the soundness of his judgment that Newcastle had received from the war emboldened him to begin to take issue with Walpole on other matters as well. He did not undertake wholesale cavilling; both friendship for the man and regard for his own position prevented that error. But little by little he abandoned his former role of his master's echo. In May of 1735, when a position in the Treasury opened up, both Pelhams urged the claims of one candidate while Walpole wanted another (and better) man. Sir Robert dealt with the problem cautiously, choosing neither and disobliging no one severely. Late in 1736 Newcastle took far greater alarm than Walpole did at dubious evidence of Jacobite activities, moving Sir Robert to observe caustically that the duke's dispatches betrayed "too much fear." In 1737 the disagreements became still more public. First, Newcastle demanded harsh treatment for the murderers of Captain Porteous, victim of a vindictive act by Scots who regarded Porteous himself as a murderer. Newcastle had called the captain's death "cruel and barbarous" and an "outrage committed by the mob." But Walpole and Lord Islay thought moderation likelier to prevent future crimes, and they prevailed. Then, the duke persuaded George II to send a ducal nominee rather than Walpole's to acknowledge Don Carlos as King of Naples. Still later, both Pelhams spoke against some of Walpole's ideas concerning the very citadel of his ministerial power, the Treasury. Sir John Barnard had proposed a scheme in Parliament whereby the interest rate on the national debt would be reduced to 3 percent. Initially enthusiastic, Walpole later decided that the suggested rate would be dangerously low for economic safety. But Pelham and Newcastle approved the notion, puzzled over the prime minister's peculiar objections to a plan that to them seemed utterly benevolent, and were not backward in expressing their dismay.[28]

The most striking examples of divisions within the cabinet, however, were provided by the quarrels that surfaced in the royal family in 1737. Early in that year the advisers of the Prince of Wales induced him to present his need for a larger income to Parliament, with the hope that the legislature would address the Crown in his behalf. The demand had merit: though recently married, Frederick retained his earlier allowance of £50,000 a year, and this sum was charged not to a separate and independent establishment but to the royally directed Civil List. The issue, however, had political ramifications: as a supporter of the opposition the prince was expected to open his coffers to the enemies of the ministry. The king, who in good Hanoverian fashion disliked his son, would hear nothing of the proposed increase. Walpole too was opposed to the request. But Newcastle suggested to Caroline—an unsympathetic auditor—that an increase in the prince's allowance was the most appropriate solution to the problem. Ultimately, by a narrow vote, the Commons sustained Walpole's view.

This quarrel within the royal family, painful as it was, soon paled beside the spectacular altercation that the summer brought on. Enraged at his father, Frederick one evening swept out of Hampton Court with his wife Augusta, even though the princess was going into labor. After a hasty and jerky trip to St. James the princess gave birth to a daughter. The prince's absurd, almost malicious behavior pointed up his disjointed sense of perspective, but it revealed too how deeply the divisions in the royal family penetrated. George II and Caroline were incensed beyond measure at their son. They insisted that a total separation between their court and Frederick's be effected, that the prince be banished from their presence, and that those who showed favor to the son should be denied it by the parents. Walpole concurred in this extraordinary decision. Among his reasons was his resentment at Frederick's recent juncture with the opposition. But the Pelhams and Hardwicke, the only ministers whom Walpole consulted, demurred. Both for political reasons and out of regard for the dignity of the Crown, they sought to moderate the royal declaration of banishment from the court. Newcastle worked on Princess Emily to use her influence to soften the document. But it was all in vain. With only slight modifications Walpole and the royal couple had their way.[29]

If the foregoing catalogue demonstrates Newcastle's greater readiness to take issue with Walpole after 1734, it does not account for it. The explanation for the duke's liberation from Sir Robert must be sought in certain institutional and psychological developments of the middle years of the decade. For, on the one hand, Newcastle assumed in this period a variety of functions and hence powers which allowed him, as never before, to influence the business of the House of Lords and the distribution of offices within the colonial, ecclesiastical, and educational establishments. And, on the other hand, he found in Andrew Stone and still more in Lord Hardwicke persons in whom he could confide and on whom he could depend—persons who relieved him of the need he had hitherto felt to gain Sir Robert's approval. Thus, just as the acquisition of positions of power gave him independent leverage within the councils of government, so did the advice of his understanding friends encourage him to believe that an opinion at variance with the prime minister's was not necessarily erroneous. By 1737 Newcastle was, both politically and psychologically, a far stronger person than he had been in 1734.

It was natural that Newcastle should have risen to a sort of dominance in the House of Lords. As senior secretary of state after 1730 in a body in which most of the talent was arrayed with the opposition, Newcastle really had little competition for his claim. He himself later remarked how, though he had willingly been Townshend's subordinate, since Townshend's resignation he had refused to serve under anyone else and had come to be "the foremost in the scene of action there."[30] Though he often spoke in debate, no one regarded him as a great orator. His claim to power derived from his organizational contributions to the government's success. His lodgings were the site of the traditional preparliamentary meeting of ministerial peers at which the king's speech was informally read. He himself served as government whip whenever the troops were needed in the chamber of peers. He even kept track of how various peers voted on crucial divisions. In sum, it was his diligence and his characteristic absorption with detailed work that elevated him above other grandees; and one must understand therefore that when the duke called himself "foremost" he was not referring to oratorical talent—he recognized his own limitations in that field— but to leadership. For he became in the years after 1730—notwithstanding Devonshire's more eminent name, Hardwicke's greater incisiveness, and Hervey's more pointed humor—the leader of the government in the House of Lords.

Meanwhile, the duke was extending his influence in colonial affairs. The colonies fell within the southern department, but when Newcastle had become secretary of state in 1724 the Board of Trade was the chief governmental agency handling plantation affairs. From the beginning Newcastle diverted many sorts of business from the board to his own office. He assumed the correspondence with colonial governors, he issued them instructions independently of the board, and he granted licenses for colonial councilors desirous of temporarily leaving their colonies. On matters of patronage, however, he moved more circumspectly. Many appointees continued to owe their posts to the Board of Trade, and some even to Lord Townshend. Against these rival loci of

patronage power Newcastle waged a two-front war. The struggle against
his cosecretary was won in 1730; Harrington never exercised the
colonial patronage power that his predecessor had had. But the war
against the Board of Trade was more protracted. It was not unusual
in the early 1730's for even the plums among colonial offices to go to
nominees of the board rather than of Newcastle. But slowly this war too
was won. The personnel on the Board of Trade gradually changed;
more pliable men reached its table. In 1735 Lord Fitzwalter, a friend
of the duke's, became president, and in 1737 Sir John Monson, a
servile nonentity whose family was beholden to the duke, replaced
Fitzwalter. Monson's appointment signalled the total eclipse of the
board. From the mid-1730's, for better or for worse, colonial affairs
were Newcastle's affairs. And within the colonial office it was patronage matters that chiefly commanded his time and attention. A man
with control over so many offices was not a man to be scorned.

But control over still other offices was simultaneously falling to the
duke. The alliance established in 1723 between Walpole and Edmund
Gibson, bishop of London, had received Newcastle's hearty approval;
it had exonerated the Whigs from charges of hostility to the Church of
England and the episcopacy from charges of Jacobitism. Under Gibson's firm direction the episcopal bench had become a phalanx of
Whig clerics, orthodox in doctrine and reliable in politics. Their
twenty-six votes had often been crucial to Walpole's ministry. Throughout the vast ecclesiastical structure, moreover, Gibson's recommendations for office carried preeminent weight. He was, in effect, minister of
church affairs. But in the 1730's the alliance declined. Walpole felt
pressure to make good on some long-standing Whig promises to light-
en the burden still placed on dissent, but Gibson resisted any legal
change that might upset the existing balance of forces between Angli-
cans and Dissenters. Sir Robert was growing weary too of the bishop's
obstinacy—for Gibson could often discern principles where Walpole
preferred to see expedients—and came to believe that the alliance had
outlived its usefulness. Only the need for the episcopal votes in the
House of Lords induced Walpole to stay his hand, and the election of
1734 had sharply reduced that need. Bent on punishing those peers
who had broken with the ministry on the excise and South Sea bills,
Walpole and Lord Islay had cooperated to defeat every deserter in the
election of Scottish representative peers. Walpole and Newcastle thereafter redoubled their efforts to secure the attendance of peers who

supported the government.[31] The effect of these two changes was to diminish the importance of the episcopal votes, and hence of the alliance and Gibson.

The final rupture occurred in September 1736. Gibson had appeared to be trying to mobilize episcopal opposition to a ministerial bill designed to make payment of obligatory tithes less complicated for Quakers. Walpole lost his temper at the prelate, and Gibson resigned his unofficial post as ecclesiastical minister. The obvious candidate to replace him was Newcastle. No other politician had the duke's wide acquaintance with clergymen high and low, or his knowledge of the intricate ladder of preferment by which Gibson had rewarded the faithful and chastened the disobedient. The duke was himself a devout churchman who attended services twice daily when possible; he had earned a deserved reputation for charitable acts. The Christian faith, in short, was alive for Newcastle. But he was also remarkable because he stood well with both the established church and the dissenting sects. He had already demonstrated his opposition to Hoadly's controversial views on the nature of the visible church, and his recommendations for promotions in the (Anglican) Church of Ireland showed that he was not sympathetic to heterodox ideas within the established church. But his continuing friendships with dissenters, going back at least to 1715 when he introduced a delegation of dissenting clergymen to the king, and his sharp rebuke of bishops who opposed the government's tithe bill, pointed to the fact that, however firm an Anglican he might be, he stood well with the sectarians.[32] The duke had long been grooming himself to succeed Gibson. As early as 1723 he had called himself an "ecclesiastical politician" and in that same year he had given ecclesiastical advice with authority.[33] His assumption of the post of ecclesiastical minister in 1736 was thus thoroughly appropriate. But it gave him significantly widened influence in the government because it provided him with a vast new arena in which, by dispensing or withholding favors, he could foster political loyalties.

There remains but Cambridge to be mentioned. In May 1737 Lord Anglesey, high steward of the university, died. Newcastle had long nourished an affection for his university and had already gained a certain notoriety for preferring Cantabrigians above Oxonians in the distribution of places. But interest as well as devotion lent appeal to the vacant office: high stewards customarily succeeded to the post of chancellor of the university, and the present incumbent of that position, Newcastle's Sussex neighbor the duke of Somerset, was seventy-five. As chancellor—even as heir–presumptive to the doughty Somerset —Newcastle could add yet another field of patronage to his expanding collection. He allowed his name to be entered and, with only hints of opposition, was duly elected high steward.[34]

By securing significant control over colonial, ecclesiastical, and, to some degree, university patronage, Newcastle acquired the means to stand apart from Sir Robert Walpole. At least equally important, he was simultaneously nurturing the courage to do so. His political career had hitherto been an adjunct to Walpole's. During these years of close cooperation he had sometimes disagreed with his mentor but he had behaved as a loyal lieutenant. "I endeavoured," he characteristically wrote to Walpole in 1734, "to conform myself entirely to your way of thinking."[35] He was, to be sure, feeding an ambition; his rank and wealth, he believed, made him merit the mantle of leadership. But the duke was fundamentally an insecure man. He needed to rely on someone else. Walpole had fitted the role of dominator, not perfectly perhaps, but adequately. He was shrewd, sympathetic, capable of deceit but not its slave. Newcastle, grateful to Sir Robert anyway, acquired the habit of deferring to his judgment. Walpole thereby gained a useful aide while Newcastle gained a sense of security. Still there was an inner tension: if the duke derived satisfaction from obedience to Walpole, he felt anxiety that this obedience sometimes led him to deeds that he did not feel to be wise.

The blossoming comradeship with Lord Hardwicke offered a release from the tension. The law was Philip Yorke's chosen field, and he advanced quickly in it. First solicitor general, then attorney general, he became in 1734 lord chief justice and, on Talbot's death early in 1737, lord chancellor. He was a lawyer of sense and intelligence, a politician oddly lacking in the usual sort of ambition, an ally who shared Newcastle's view of the nature and limits of politics, and a man who liked Newcastle for what he was. Sometime in the middle of the decade of the 1730's the old friendship deepened; Hardwicke's willingness to advise linked up with Newcastle's need for direction. "Dear Hardwicke," the duke implored in one of his frequent entreaties to his friend to attend a cabinet session, "without you we are nothing."[36] And from it all Newcastle emerged, if not a stronger figure, then at least a politician prepared to strike out independently of the man who had hitherto nursed him. He was still psychologically dependent; he wrote to Hardwicke in 1738 of his "own personal happiness, in being so remarkably favoured with your private friendship, assistance, & of which I hope I shall ever retain the most grateful remembrance."[37] But with the relationship of dependence transferred to the lord chancellor there was this difference: the duke now received assurances of the rectitude of his own views. These assurances, applied one by one to his troubled spirit and reinforcing his own convictions, gave him the will to act on his beliefs. And this will in turn allowed him finally to reveal the ambitions that he had long kept secluded.

It is dubious, however, that even with his widening influence and his new self-assertiveness Newcastle could have gained effective equality of power with Walpole had it not been for Sir Robert's own failure of will. For if Newcastle can be seen as reaching for power, Walpole can be viewed as deliberately relinquishing it. The prime minister's confidence never completely rebounded from the shocks of 1733. Though aware of the informal league that the Pelhams and Hardwicke were creating and urged by Hervey to destroy them before they destroyed him, Walpole remained strangely impassive. A man who had shown no notable reluctance to punish deserters in the past now withheld any blow from what he called "the house of Pelham."[38] In part, advancing years were numbing his former taste for vengeance. But perhaps too he did not want to destroy the chief vehicle of Whiggery. It is known that Walpole saw Hardwicke as the ablest of his assistants and Pelham as his political heir. Yet these two were intimately bound up with Newcastle. By disabling one he would almost certainly have alienated the others. In short, the aging prime minister may have chosen not to punish the duke because to have done so would have been to dissolve the system that was intended to be his legacy to Britain. Whatever the reason, Sir Robert accepted affronts as never before, grumbled about but tolerated disobedience, and in so doing gave added encouragement to Newcastle in his hesitant exploration of a new course.

The final and strongest buttress of Walpole's capacity to keep Newcastle subordinated disappeared in November of 1737 with the death of Queen Caroline. This brave woman had been the chief source of the prime minister's success with the king. With her on his side Walpole could persuade George II to do almost anything. Caroline contemned Newcastle. Schooled by Hervey on the duke's foibles and informed by Walpole of the duke's new contrariety, the queen dismissed Newcastle as "such a mixture of fiddle-faddle and popularity that there was no

making anything of him." Her inclination supplied Walpole the power
to negative the duke. Her passing was unexpected and Walpole mourned her demise as sincerely as the king and with greater reason. Shortly
thereafter Newcastle wrote to Devonshire to assure him that, because
George's sentiments were identical to his late wife's, the death would
not alter governmental policy.[39] The statement about the king was
essentially true, though Caroline, of course, had helped make it so. But
a larger point was ignored. Policy is determined in part by the forcefulness of those espousing various views. With Walpole now disarmed
and Newcastle cocky, the balance of force within the ministry had
shifted still further against the former. From November 1737 until
Walpole's resignation early in 1742, Sir Robert had to share power
with Newcastle.

III

Newcastle's apprenticeship was now ending. At forty-three the duke
was in the prime of his life. His health remained sound, his appearance
distinguished. Taller than average for his century, the duke possessed
as well a slightly outsized head that lent him an air of magisterial dignity
befitting a peer of the realm. His nose was his most prominent facial
feature—large and somewhat hooked, but still not unduly obtrusive.
His forehead was high, sloping slightly backward. Despite years of
heavy eating and scarcely inhibited quaffing, his frame was well-
proportioned and his posture erect. He regularly used pince-nez
glasses, but in no other respect were his faculties impaired. By any
reckoning his body had come through the decades of self-indulgence in
excellent shape, and nothing testified better to his physical resilience
and remarkable stamina than the fact that his name had become a
byword for the frenetic expenditure of energy. More important for
Britain, however, was the shape his mind and spirit had taken on during
the years of training.

The duke was a pious man. Contemporaries recognized him as a
good Anglican, and in an age in which adherence to the Christian
faith did not always entail putting the church's moral directives into
practice, Newcastle led an uncommonly proper life. He was generous
with his wealth. He joined the Society for the Propagation of the Gospel
in Foreign Parts. If he committed sexual misdemeanors, they escaped
the notice of friends and critics alike; and the occasional and invariably
vague hints of amatory peccadillos which now and then found their

way into print sound more often like coarse slander than revelations of ducal misbehavior. Toward his family—the term embraced brother, sisters, cousins, nephews, nieces, and their spouses and children—the duke displayed deep love and interest. Childless himself, he lavished attention and affection on Henry Pelham's and Lord Lincoln's off-spring, and he spoke possessively of his brother's progeny as "our own daughters."[40] Even to mere acquaintances he was loyal, and the younger Horace Walpole's remark that Newcastle "never felt for a powerless friend" is base slander.[41] Many people, great and small, learned that the duke did not in general compute political advantage when responding to the entreaties of friends with personal needs. It is now impossible to determine the extent to which Newcastle's decency and humaneness were essentially rooted in his Christian faith, but whatever their origin, these traits appropriately complemented that faith and lent it a fuller dimension.

The duke was, by almost all accounts, an affable and gregarious individual and excessively eager to please his acquaintances. Some believed his friendliness an artifice, others found it genuine, but every-one thought it one of his most distinctive traits. He was a ready, though often a vacuous, conversationalist. His exuberant kisses of greeting gained a notoriety in an age far more tolerant of this custom than ours. He tended to grasp his conversational companions, often by the hand and sometimes by the cheek, in order to enhance intimacy. Whenever it was possible, he wanted to gratify others; and if it was impossible to comply with their wishes, he found it excruciating to refuse them with decent directness. Instead he tried to hide his inability to grant what had been asked behind a gushing torrent of protestations of devotion or, in more ticklish situations, behind lies. Though he already held consid-erable power and would, in the years to come, engross still more, the duke never learned the art of the simple negative.

Contemporary opinion also agreed that Newcastle was financially honest, and it is clear from an examination of his career that the duke in fact regarded it as a mark of his rank in society that he behave in a thoroughly disinterested fashion in any monetary dealings which should come before him. Early in his career he spoke of "the great backward-ness I have always had to ask or secure any sum of money of yᵉ king, how I detest it in others and consequently how unwilling I shall be to do yᵉ like myself".[42] Late in his career he would twice spurn offers of pensions. Like his brother—though subjected to greater personal temptation—he held it beneath the dignity of a royal servant to use public funds for private gain. Throughout his life the duke's management of his own wealth was disastrously inept, and debt dogged his career to its very end. Still, he refused while in office to engage in activities which, though unquestionably self-serving, were not even illegal and were in fact widely practiced. After Newcastle's death Lord Chesterfield would attribute the duke's poverty to this remarkable abstinence,[43] a judgment which, though exaggerated, errs only in magnitude. The primary cause of his difficulties was, of course, his profligate spending, but a contributory element was this refusal to compensate for personal expenditures in ways that most of his contemporaries who were fortunate enough to hold office availed themselves of without compunction.

The duke was quick to anger but also, with few exceptions, quick to forgive, and this second characteristic was more impressive to his contemporaries. The politics of revenge were not his. "My temper," he acutely wrote to Hardwicke, "is such that I am often uneasy and peevish and perhaps, what may be called, wrongheaded, to my best friends; but that always goes down with the sun and passes off as if nothing had happened."[44] These bursts of rage were often generously alloyed with jealousy. Newcastle was a suspicious man, easily hurt by unintended or even nonexistent slights, and he persistently feared that his place and power were threatened by the climbing of others. This suspicion and fear made him peculiarly vulnerable to two failings that could only impair his effective political leadership. First, fearful that others would believe him to be performing his duties poorly, he was a sucker for flattery, an easy mark for those whose honeyed words delighted him. Second, apprehensive of rivals, he was ill at ease when forced to serve with official colleagues who equalled him in competence, and so he generally sought to surround himself, in his ministerial capacity, with utter mediocrities.

He was a man of idiosyncracies, and these neurotic foibles attracted much attention from his contemporaries. Readers of Lord Hervey and Horace Walpole will be familiar with items on the list: a fear of travel by sea, an aversion to beds not previously slept in, an abhorrence of chills, a propensity to weep at the slightest provocation, a tongue that prattled on and on. Nor are the unsympathetic Hervey and Walpole the only witnesses. If Walpole regales us with the tale of Newcastle seeking relief from the cold pavement at George II's funeral by standing on the duke of Cumberland's robes, the same message is less strikingly conveyed by the entry among treasury records indicating that Newcastle, during his days at that office, had the treasury room made warmer.[45] If Hervey delights in depicting a duke "mightily out of breath though mightily in words," a far less biased clergyman also found the duke to be a ceaseless talker.[46] But too much can be made of these ducal peculiarities. Though the duke unquestionably believed that a bed was unhealthy unless aired beforehand by a sleeper, he was scarcely alone in this interesting conviction and need not be singled out—on these grounds, at least—as a man subject to oddly irrational beliefs. In fact, though the suggestion to the contrary is often made, the duke was not even notably hypochondriacal, at least for an age rather given to brooding about health. The multitude of doctors who swarmed through his household tended the duchess. Far from dwelling on illness, imagined or real, in his correspondence with his wife, he often withheld from her information about sicknesses he was passing through. To be sure, in those letters he dwelt on his defecatory irregularity to a degree that surprises the twentieth-century reader, but this writing habit seems to have been designed more to meet her needs than his. The true hypochondriac does not focus on constipation when bedridden with fever and weakness.

On matters of social taste Newcastle's preferences were unimaginatively subordinated to the shifting course of transient whims that passed through the upper levels of eighteenth-century English society. If his social judgment had any fixed star at all it was the conviction that French manners and fashion set the standards most worthy of emulation, and thus the man who was later to be accused of being German in his politics was decidedly French in his taste. When French food was the craze, the duke procured one of the most celebrated French chefs of the day, Cloué, to handle culinary affairs at Claremont. When the French dancing manikins called *pantins* became the rage, the duke acquired one and delighted friends with its antics. The duke's Sussex neighbor, Thomas Turner, was not the only Englishman who expressed disgust that the duke should employ "so many Frenchmen, there being ten of his servants, cooks, etc., which was down here of that nation."[47] But Francophilism did not make the duke any less English. In his fondness for hunting, for partying, and for games, in his dislike of Scots, and in his pleasure in landscaping and building on his Claremont estate, he was representative of the English landed class of his age.

Further, even among members of the English ruling elite—a group already markedly less concerned with social punctilio than their continental analogues—the duke was noted for his informality. In sum, he was thoroughly English, he enjoyed society, he was an able host, but he was—not surprisingly—a complete captive of the social conventions of his era.

As the years passed and experience gave Newcastle an education in the intricacies of human relations, the duke developed a series of techniques for handling the more conventional political situations that confronted him. He kept orderly memoranda of conversations held with suppliants, and while always ready to assume credit for himself whenever he coulid please a petitioner, he early developed the trick of attributing his frequent inability to satisfy a request to the obstinate refusal of the king—especially in George II's day—to entertain such a proposal. Newcastle found it convenient to divert the bitterness of disappointment from himself to the king. It was thoroughly credible that George II could be opposed to many of the requests for favors anyway, and while Newcastle and others close to the king knew that George could be bullied into acquiescing in decisions he did not like, they wisely realized that they ought to withhold the hand of intimidation except on matters of grave importance. Another technique that the duke used to refuse the requests made of him was to take the petitioner into his confidence, sketch in the complex situation in which several men were invariably vying for the same honor, reckon the various possible consequences of each promotion, and then ask the petitioner how he would handle the situation. Quite frequently the man would in effect withdraw his own request, or at least scale it down, and spare the duke the necessity of disappointing him. Newcastle was no fool in dealing with others: the ploys were scarcely ingenious, but the duke used them with effect.

For dealing with royalty Newcastle needed other devices. Although he was to serve each of the first three Georges, only during the last half of the reign of George II would he exercise powerful influence in the closet. For this monarch the duke developed a wide repertoire of manipulative techniques. A crushing power play, such as the resignations of 1746 or the calculated refusal to rejoin the government in 1757, was occasionally thought necessary. But in general the duke had to be far more discreet in his handling of the king: George's temper was ferocious and, while not insurmountable, was, when aroused, invariably a cause of delay. If George's papers had survived it might now be possible to estimate more accurately the extent to which he ruled the duke or was ruled by him. As it is, there exists only Newcastle's testimony, predictably confusing, and the divergent accounts of contemporaries upon which to base judgment. It is clear that the duke was never the king's commander. George had a mind of his own, a certain willfulness, and stronger internal resources of resistance than many have credited him with. But it is also clear that the duke was not the king's stooge. If he wanted to bend George to his own point of view he often found it useful to plant an idea in the king's mind, have it watered with casual reinforcing arguments from Hardwicke and Pelham, and let it bloom in royal soil with apparent spontaneity several months later. He treated all his royal masters with appropriate courtesy in the closet, and while he was unquestionably uncomfortable when the royal opinion diverged from his own, he was not as hesitant to push an unpopular point in the closet as some have suggested. He sensed, it would seem, that to be an effective minister he would have to be able both to serve and to nudge the king. Whether he caught the right balance between docility and forcefulness is a moot question. Still, it is clear that the duke's abundance of political difficulties did not in general take their origins in the closet.

Nor did they arise from his choice of close friends. For if Newcastle sought as official colleagues such inconsequential figures as Lord Harrington and, later, Lord Holderness, he chose as his confidential advisers men of superior talents. Lord Hardwicke would be the pre-eminent lord chancellor of the century; William Murray, later Lord Mansfield, would become the most able lord chief justice of the age; and Andrew Stone, if less distinguished than the others, was a man of consummate secretarial skill. These three comprised as resourceful and intelligent an advisory council as any politician in modern British history has had; and if it be remarked that the duke needed them as few other politicians did—a correct judgment—it can also be noted that it was the duke who chose them, not they who wormed their way into the duke's confidence. Some of the measure of any man can be taken by assaying his entourage of friends; by this criterion Newcastle gets high marks. And close friendship with the duke was no easy commitment. The duke bombarded these three, and others as well, with desperate pleas for advice whenever crucial issues arose. His correspondence gives the superficial impression that he was totally dependent on Hardwicke's judgment; contemporaries, seeing a different master, believed him a puppet dancing at Stone's behest. Only after the histories of the duke's connections with these men have been related will it be appropriate to examine and place in perspective the nature of the duke's various dependences, but it can at least be noted at this point that Newcastle was less suggestible than many have believed and that his close circle of confidants served more as a cheering section than as a steering committee. In 1737 he needed both.

IV

Difficulties with Spain were again looming large in the public consciousness. They were not, it is true, the difficulties of the 1720's, Gibraltar, Minorca, and Spanish support for Jacobitism. The Treaty of Seville and the solidity of the Walpolean regime had given these their quietus. The locus of the new disputes between the two crowns was shifting from the Old World to the New. In the emerging matrix of Anglo-Spanish conflict there were essentially three disputes about America. One concerned the young British colony of Georgia. A disagreement had arisen between the Georgia authorities and the governor of the Spanish colony of Florida about the location of the boundary separating the two plantations. The British settlers had built forts on the contested acreage; the Spanish authorities had fomented Indian raids on the British. It was a sticky situation rendered stickier still by the time it took queries and orders to traverse the Atlantic and by the fact that, although Spain's claim was better, Britain held possession. Newcastle, as the secretary of state charged with handling colonial affairs, had not been backward in trying to contain James Edward Oglethorpe's ambitions for Georgia's territorial expansion, but he was ready by the late 1730's to confess that "I fancy however the right may be, it will now be pretty difficult to give up Georgia."[48] The press agreed: "Our ministers," opined the *Daily Post,* "will as soon consent to part with their eyes as to part with Georgia."

A second conflict between the crowns arose from Britain's assertion of the right to cut logwood—a component of valuable dyes—at Spanish-claimed Campeachy Bay. Britons were in fact settled at the Bay and had been so for many years; they were therefore, the duke argued, entitled to cut wood "by right and custom." Not everyone in the British government concurred with the duke's understanding of law—the Board of Trade, for example, doubted the kingdom's title to undertake logging—but it was Newcastle who enunciated the government's position on the issue: "The right of his Majesty's subjects to cut logwood is what the king can never give up."[49]

Oddly, considering the course that events were to take, the duke was less truculent and adamant on the third and transcendent American issue, the Spanish depredations. British subjects claimed the right to sail freely in the West Indies and often used the right as a cover for smuggling goods into and out of Spanish settlements; Spanish authorities claimed the right to inspect suspicious ships and often used their right as a cover for stealing from innocent Britons so as to recompense themselves for losses to guilty Britons. The British government was notably less successful than Dutch and French authorities at curbing smuggling by its citizens, and the Spanish were inclined to see in this failure a sign of governmental complicity in the forbidden trade. The Spanish *guarda costas* were none too scrupulous in seeking out smugglers. Long accustomed to violence, and profiting only insofar as they could apprehend "smuggled" goods, they saw little reason to be punctilious about maritime law and custom, especially since Spain still laid claim, in theory at least, to almost all of America and its waters. Spain's prize courts were not in any systematic fashion unfair, so it was not infrequent that the Spanish government found itself trying to make restitution to a British merchant victimized by the *guarda costas*. But even with good will, the vast problems of ordering indemnification in Spain and effecting it in the Indies proved generally insuperable. British subjects turned to their government for relief.

In November of 1737, the very month in which Caroline died, Newcastle transmitted to Keene in Madrid a memorial outlining Britain's position on the issue of the depredations.[50] Though it would soon become notorious as an illogical, shoddily conceived document, the memorial was not a hasty composition. Newcastle had drafted it, Walpole had had opportunity to peruse it, and the cabinet had considered it. It had arisen as a response to a rising tide of petitions from West Indian merchants who claimed to have been victims of Spanish depredations. Newcastle heard that the parliamentary opposition, lying in wait for a new issue, would argue that Walpole's government, and especially the southern secretary, had failed to provide adequate protection for commerce. The unbending tone of the memorial may have taken its origin in the duke's fear of being singled out. Referring to the Anglo-Spanish treaty of 1667, Newcastle argued in the memorial that British merchants had "an indisputable right" to sail in American waters and that the searching of ships by the *guarda costas*, the confiscation of noncontraband cargo, and the imprisonment of crews were all illegal.

Keene was openly embarrassed by the memorial. He sympathized with its intention but found the duke's reasoning doubly flawed. First, Newcastle had confused contraband goods with smuggled goods. Second—an incredible blunder—Newcastle had invoked the wrong treaty. The pact of 1667, with respect to its commercial clauses, did not bear on America at all. The appropriate treaty, as Keene and then Horace Walpole gently pointed out,[51] was concluded in 1670. It was the one meant to provide some regulation for American trade. But the petitioning merchants had called the government's attention to the earlier of the two agreements because it specified, in a way the later one did not, that a search at sea had to be confined to an examination of a ship's papers—because, in short, it forbade any effective Spanish efforts to deter smuggling.

The Spanish minister La Quadra used the duke's error to delay responding to the question of the grievances themselves. Newcastle meanwhile was flustered at his mistake, and the British government, not eager to underline the egregious error of the secretary, shifted its ground to the more appropriate treaty behind a fog of words designed to suggest that the pact of 1670 confirmed the one of 1667. "We scramble out of it as well as we can," Horace Walpole confided to a friend.[52] Ultimately, because the treaty of 1670 left too much undefined, Newcastle came to rest his case on neither treaty but on the singularly ambiguous concept of the Law of Nations. This law was, the duke explained, "a rule for all countries, where particular treaties do not intervene."[53] Still, the government, though resorting to bluster, was not doing so in order to promote war—at least, not yet. To be sure, it thought war possible. For that reason parts of the Mediterranean fleet were secretly ordered from Gibraltar to Minorca. But in April Newcastle told Keene that Britain would accept Spain's right of search if it were exercised within a specified distance from Spanish islands.[54] And Sir Robert had already privately directed the ambassador to soften his representations to the Spanish government. Unhappily, the ministry undid whatever pacifying effect these steps might have had by offering letters of reprisal to any British merchants who wished them. Its European glove was velvet, but its American fist was iron.

The decision to authorize reprisals came early in March, and hence prior to the great uproar about Spanish villainies that reached and rocked Parliament later that month. It becomes therefore all the more blameworthy. The public rage itself, triggered by reports about the ill-treatment dealt out to British sailors held in Spanish captivity on dubious charges, produced an unprecedented number of memorials demanding governmental action. City after city sent up petitions, and as their attorney the merchants recruited the brilliant young Scot, William Murray. Then, as a capstone to the frenzy caused by the memorials, came the testimony before the Commons of the celebrated Captain Jenkins. Commander of the *Rebecca* when the *guarda costas* had assaulted it in 1731, Jenkins told of the barbarities to which the Spanish had subjected his English sailors. As dramatic proof of all his charges, he displayed his bottled ear, severed from his head, he said, by a Spanish blade on that infamous day. The story itself was not a surprise. When Newcastle had learned eight years earlier of the Spanish tortures aboard the *Rebecca* he had called them "violences . . . carried to a height of inhumanity unknown even in times of war."[55] But if the substance of the tale lacked drama, the manner of the telling did not. Jenkins presented himself as a British patriot, his honor as the national honor, and his vindication as the national objective. To the merchants, who still felt the government to be too hesitant, he was a godsend. "No Search!" became the fashionable cry. But merchants were not alone in seeing utility in Jenkins. The parliamentary opposition, as Newcastle had feared, saw capital to be made out of the Spanish issue. The emergence of the so-called "patriots" made the dispute doubly sensitive to the duke: already inflamed because his sense of national pride was offended by Spanish depredations, the duke now feared that his political career might be at stake as well.

The Spanish government was apprehensive about the fulminations in Britain. It did not want war because its ties with France had slackened of late, and it knew from past experience the folly of taking on Britain's maritime might without a naval ally of its own. But just as Spain began to sound concessive in May 1738, the arrival of Haddock and his squadron at Minorca was revealed and Britain dispatched a regiment to Georgia. Unwilling to appear intimidated, La Quadra thereupon resumed his harsh tone, and Newcastle in turn, fearing imminent war, advised British merchants to leave Spain and British ships to avoid Spanish ports.[56] The admiralty even sent out directions for impressment on a widened scale. Still, if Madrid feared seeming weak, it dreaded still more an open conflict. Thus in June Spanish officials again spoke of compromise, and this time the British government responded favorably. Fairly quickly the negotiating priorities were agreed on. In London the Spanish ambassador, Don Geraldino, would negotiate with British officials—he had actually been doing so for several months—to try to determine what sums of money might reciprocally be paid to indemnify each side for past losses. Then, in Madrid, Keene and Montijo, president of the council of the Indies, would try to resolve the more fundamental issue of reconciling Spain's right to protect itself against smuggling with Britain's right to have ships freely sail the seas. The first negotiations would treat past injuries; the second would then lay the basis for forestalling future injuries. Newcastle's hopes for a settlement ran so high that he dreamed of an Anglo-Spanish alliance emerging from the present fire: "Such an alliance," he rhapsodized, "would not only be for the mutual advantage of both kingdoms, but might also greatly tend to the security of the Balance of Power in Europe."[57]

The geographical separation between the negotiations broke down, but the talks themselves progressed well. In March 1738 a British commissioner had advanced a plan whereby Spain would pay £200,000 to the merchants to satisfy their claims. In July the British submitted this proposal to Spain with the sum scaled down to £140,000. Madrid thought the amount still too high, and so Keene, not afraid to assume personal responsibility, reduced it further to £95,000. Newcastle thought Keene's action a mistake, but Sir Robert, aching for peace and terribly world-weary after the recent death of his second wife, sought and received privy council approval for Keene's decision. Meanwhile, the counterclaim that the Spanish crown advanced against the South Sea Company for unpaid proceeds was fixed at £68,000. The company was in fact central to the proposed settlement: not only was it to pay Philip V the money it owed him but it was then to lend him a further £27,000 so that he in turn could pay the £95,000 he owed.

But in August, just when all seemed to be going smoothly, the company suddenly tried to use the leverage that its unusual position as financial middleman gave it: it revived claims against Spain for damages incurred in the wars of 1718–19 and 1727 and without much effort eventually found grounds for inflating these new demands to an astronomical £484,000. This claim—especially since the company lacked conclusive evidence to substantiate it—was totally unacceptable to Spain. And Madrid for its part began raising objections to the proposed modalities of payment. A period of hard bargaining ensued, in which Walpole assumed command for Britain and Newcastle stayed in the background. The duke was unhappy with the course the negotiations had taken, for, though no friend of the South Sea Company, like a good Whig he objected to governmental pressuring of private companies as a thing "very improper to do."[58] Ultimately, though the company remained unmoved, British pressures on the Spanish king did prevail, enough at least to let the provisional convention drafted in September be transformed in January 1739 with only minor alterations into the Convention of Pardo.

Pardo held out the hope of peace. The terms were those arrived at as early as the previous August: £95,000 for £68,000, with the difference owed to the Britons to be made up by a loan from the South Sea Company to Philip V. Each side had compromised, and if Britain's dismantling of the claims made by its own merchants was the more sensational compromise, Spain's implicit acknowledgement that there had indeed been depredations was the more fundamental. Andrew Stone had earlier reminded Newcastle of this point when the duke had been particularly dejected about British concessions. Pardo did not restrict itself to the issue of indemnification. Taking a broad and hopeful view, the negotiators had assigned other outstanding Anglo-Spanish difficulties, especially the Georgia boundary dispute, to commissioners. Men on both sides were pleased with what they had wrought, and both governments expected peace. Indeed, Spain began reducing its fleet, Haddock was recalled from the Mediterranean, and Newcastle, the most ardent warrior within the government, wrote again of the utility of an Anglo-Spanish alliance.[59]

Both ministries reckoned without the South Sea Company. Officials of the company took offense when, at the ceremonies concluding the convention, Philip V orally declared that he might suspend the *Asiento* —the company's contractual right to supply Spanish America with 4,800 slaves each year—if the company failed to make its payment to him. Newcastle had instructed Keene not to sign if the Spanish king employed such bluster,[60] but the circumstances of the occasion made obedience to that direction impossible. Eager to destroy the convention, company officials quickly alerted the parliamentary opposition to aspects of the pact they regarded as unsatisfactory. Among these aspects was the belief that by expressing a willingness to "regulate" British and Spanish rights Britain had already conceded its inability both to gain total freedom of navigation and to suppress Spanish searches completely. This objection was a peculiarly sensitive one for Newcastle, for although he had occasionally strutted about as the chief "patriot" in the cabinet, he had consistently—and as recently as November—expressed a private readiness to allow limited searches and to forbid British vessels from sailing in certain specified waters. The duke felt vulnerable, and whenever his political skin was at stake he was apt to take ill-considered actions. But far more remarkable was Sir Robert Walpole's response to the renewed public outcry about a pusillanimous ministry: he caved in and began sounding more ferocious even than the duke. Georgia would not be yielded, he declared, and Spain would not search British ships. He thereby won parliamentary endorsement for the convention, but only by a narrow margin and with young William Pitt's words still ringing: "The complaints of your despairing merchants—the voice of England—has condemned it." The leader had finally abdicated responsibility.

Within scarcely more than six weeks, therefore, the British government performed a *volte-face*. From prophets of peace they became advocates of arms. Public opinion was ugly, but that was not the sole explanation for the change. London learned late in the winter that Elizabeth Farnese's younger son, Don Philip, had married Louis XV's oldest daughter, and what had been desirable as concessions to an independent Spain thereupon became folly if they would serve chiefly to strengthen a united Bourbon front. Newcastle instructed Keene to insist on the restitution of several ships and—in a decisive action—sent counterorders to Haddock, directing him to return to the Mediterranean. Spain took understandable alarm at the latter development, clearly ominous at a time when Madrid was dismantling its fleet. Newcastle and Walpole told Don Geraldino that the counterorders were merely a sop to Parliament, but the ambassador dared not believe them.[61] Spain was similarly alarmed when Newcastle demanded that it abandon the right of search. Even Keene was losing hope: Spain, he wrote, summoning his best style, was governed by "three or four mean stubborn people of little minds and limited understandings . . . people who have vanity enough to think themselves reserved by Providence to rectify and reform the mistakes and abuses of past ministers and ages."[62] Newcastle gave another view: "We must yeild [*sic*] to the

times," he wrote[63]—a singularly puerile standard for a would-be states-
man to invoke.

Stung by British actions and demands, angered by the South Sea
Company's refusal to forward £68,000, and encouraged on the other
side by reviving Bourbon ties, Spain chose not to make its first payment
on the appointed day late in the spring. Instead, Madrid declared that
it would withhold the money until Haddock had been recalled. With
this step Spain violated the Convention of Pardo; by unilaterally sus-
pending the *Asiento* in the same month it violated the settlement of
Utrecht. The British government now felt it had no alternative. Aided
by Hardwicke, Newcastle had the cabinet in June authorize actions
designed to make war inevitable. Haddock was directed to lie off Cadiz
and "commit all kinds of hostilities at sea." Commodore Brown's
squadron was ordered to seize Spain's bullion fleet. And meanwhile, as
these reprisals were implemented at sea, the British land forces were
to be augmented by eight Irish regiments. There was talk of military expeditions—Newcastle himself hoped for even bolder schemes—but
nothing concrete emerged from the discussions. The duke then told
Keene the truth: Britain had decided "to pursue hostile measures."[64]

The major concern of the ministerial warriors of June was France. In
fact, war had in effect been entered into despite the belief that Louis
XV would come to the aid of Philip V. The Anglo-French alliance of
the 1720's, dying anyway, had not survived the War of the Polish
Succession. The *pacte de famille* had replaced it as the mainstay of
French foreign policy. It is true that Fleury had offered Britain a
renouvellement d'alliance at the opening of 1738, but Britain had been
unexcited at the prospect and France had suspended such desultory
talks as had been held. The recent marriage, followed by rumors of a
Franco-Spanish trade agreement, suggested that the Pyrenees were
indeed crumbling. But France fooled everyone. Instead of war, it tried
for mediation. Britain of course was uninterested; the issues at stake,
apotheosized in public rhetoric, now lay beyond compromise. But
because France's behavior was unpredictable—and because too Britain's own armed forces were not in fighting shape—a formal declaration of war was avoided for several months. Not until early October was
Newcastle prepared to propose the time as opportune. The declaration
followed on the nineteenth.

Newcastle deserves the condemnation he has received for so blithely
courting war in these years.[65] The fault was not that the secretary

wanted hostilities. In fact, no one in authority in either London or
Madrid sought belligerence. Newcastle's readiness to compromise on
the issue of free navigation showed he could elude the snares set by
demagogic sloganeers. He himself, fourteen years later, would say of
these times that "No Search was a cant word."[66] Thus, though it is
proper to regard the conflict as essentially a commercial war, it is improper to think of the duke as acting from economic considerations.
His fault lay rather in his misreading of Spanish character and his weakness before public opinion. The misunderstanding of Spanish character
is easily explicable. The duke had seen Madrid retreat before threats
too often not to think that Spain could be easily intimidated. He had
even been advised by commissioners who had earlier negotiated with
Spain that "small reprisals" only stiffened the kingdom and that a
"capital blow" was the appropriate technique for bringing Madrid to
heel.

The issue of public opinion is more critical and less patient of extenuation. Throughout his political career the duke worked sedulously
to keep public passions banked; but when they nevertheless got stirred
up, the duke was ever ready to obey them. This was an occasion for
such obedience. It is true that by pursuing the path of stubbornness
and resolution Newcastle was doing more than merely responding to
a frenzied public. He was being faithful to convictions enunciated long
before the popular aspect of the dispute emerged. It is similarly true
that Spain itself was far from blameless for the war. But Newcastle, by
virtue of his post and influence, had the best opportunity of any Englishman to choose peace for Britain. He permitted war. There were Britons,
naturally enough, who more unambiguously wanted war, but they were
outside the ministry and without control over events. The duke had
both the office and the prestige wherewith to keep the lid on. Yet he did
not really try to do so. He knew, as a bit of conventional knowledge,
that war ought to be avoided, but he did not know from experience what
pains and difficulties committing a nation to war entailed. Thus he was
too lighthearted about the whole matter. He later learned; the over-
reactions of 1738–39 would give way to the underreactions of 1754–55.
But that was for the future. In 1739, with war declared, Newcastle had
a mission: to guide the kingdom to the military triumph its mercantile
and political communities clearly thought possible.

4

Defense Minister

I

Directing warfare invariably changes the style and pace of a government. So it was with Britain in 1739. As early as June the cabinet operated on a schedule of daily meetings, usually held in Newcastle's office at the cockpit. The duke, feeling uneasy at what he had wrought, was at first reluctant to assume leadership of the war. He tried to avoid countersigning naval orders, fearing putting his name to a document that might some day wind up before the eyes of a hostile parliamentary committee. But he finally could not shirk his responsibility, and for the first two years of fighting—the period in which the West Indies provided the chief theatre—the duke served as *de facto* minister of war. The Admiralty handled details; the ministry, and especially Newcastle, considered and resolved the big issues. The duke's expert advisers were two able septuagenarians, Sir Charles Wager, first lord of the Admiralty, and Sir John Norris, Admiral of the Fleet. But his political advisers were more important. Wilmington and Harrington were generally consulted on military and naval matters, and Hardwicke was asked to advise on almost everything that came to Newcastle's attention. These four men and the still pacific Walpole constituted an inner cabinet. Theirs was the task of planning for victory.[1]

From the vantage point of London the war with Spain had a slow motion quality about it. America lay far off; it took time to convey personnel and equipment to the West Indian theatre, and within that theatre commanders were reluctant to risk the fate of their men through engagements. Thus there were but two signal British battles in the Spanish war: Admiral Vernon's conquest of Porto Bello promptly after war had been declared, and the abortive assault on Cartagena in

1741. The parliamentary opposition seized on this record of inaction, finding in it sufficient justification for delivering some of the most vicious criticisms of the government that a century that admired savagery in its political invective heard. But the fault was not entirely the ministry's. For even though, as shall be seen, it confused ambiguity with delegation of responsibility in some of its strategic directives, it was seriously hampered in hammering out any sort of strategy at all by deficiencies in manpower. Not until May 1740, under strong pressure from Newcastle, did the government adopt Norris's scheme of manning ships with foot soldiers, and even then approval of the proposal had to be virtually wrung from an angry king and a dubious Walpole. Meanwhile, the decision was made—and again under pressure from Newcastle—to recruit volunteers for the army in the colonies themselves, since it seemed quite appropriate to have the traders and smugglers who stood most to benefit from the war carry on a bit of the fighting.[2]

Without enough men Britain's superiority in ships would be vitiated. And that superiority was quite narrow anyway, for even though Britain had 124 ships of the line (not all, however, fit for service) while Spain had only 41 when war began, there was the unknown factor of the French fleet to be considered. If France joined Spain, the combined Bourbon navy would have about 90 large ships. Britain even then would have the edge, but since it would dare not leave Minorca, Gibraltar, or—most important—the Channel undefended, it would have a far smaller navy wherewith to assail New France and New Spain. Its enemies, moreover, were not subject to the same sorts of considerations. Britain had no army to speak of. If the Royal Navy controlled the Channel, the action was defensive. But France and Spain had large armies. If they gained control, an invasion of Britain became possible. And because the Spanish fleet had slipped out of poorly blockaded Ferrol early in the war, this danger was deemed real. The ministry's defense of its record against carping critics was therefore in many ways sound. It would have evoked more sympathy, however, had the government contrived to win a victory somewhere.

That failure did not signify want of effort. Under Newcastle's direction elaborate investigations of past British operations in the West Indies were begun in mid-1739.[3] Some hard choices lay ahead—where to strike, and with what type of force—and the duke wanted the ministry to have the requisite information. In fact, it was not until May 1740 that the final decisions on the nature of Britain's war in

America were reached. The choice of the Indies rather than Europe as the arena for the conflict was easy; only Walpole opposed and he was overridden. Spain was believed more vulnerable in America, where her settlements sat exposed to naval assault and perhaps even to annexation. Moreover, it was in America that Spain's annual treasure fleet could more easily be intercepted and the fragile alimentary tube that supplied Madrid with American sustenance thereby severed. Newcastle had his own additional reason for wanting to emphasize the Spanish Main. It was the field he knew best and, thanks to Hosier's activities in 1726, the only foreign arena in which he had tasted some form of armed success. Spain cooperated fully in reinforcing Britain's decision: the early loss of Porto Bello compelled Madrid to seek vengeance precisely where London wanted to fight.

But the British leaders were divided over what types of forces to use. Vernon speculated that any use of land troops in the Indies would be unduly expensive, costly in lives lost to disease, and largely ineffectual. But the duke was not alone in the ministry—or outside it, for that matter—in believing that something more dramatic than a mere maritime endeavor was called for. So the ministry decided to launch a combined military–naval assault. And, with the exception of Captain Anson's forays against Peru and Panama, it also decided not to disperse its forces in scattered efforts but to concentrate them against one major target in New Spain. The duke chose to dispatch 6,000 British soldiers to Jamaica to unite with a colonial force which, it was hoped, would total 8,000. The ministry considered a variety of possible Spanish targets for this force. Newcastle preferred Havana, the key to the Spanish Caribbean. But Norris and Wager thought Havana too well fortified, and the Admiralty finally recommended Cartagena. Newcastle was unpersuaded, and the ministry, divided and confused, ultimately decided to authorize the joint leaders of the expedition, Admiral Vernon and General Cathcart, to hold a council of war after gathering at Jamaica and only then to designate the target of the assault. The decision is clearly vulnerable to characterization as irresponsible buck-passing, but the charge will not stand scrutiny. Even before the formal declaration of war Hardwicke had persuaded Newcastle that, as civilians without military experience, they would be wise to let career officers in the services work out all but the broad outlines of operations. And with the Indies so far off and the situation there, as Spain prepared for combat, in flux, it seemed an invitation to disaster to bind a commander to inflexible instructions based on information that was probably incomplete and, by the time it was to be acted on, certainly out of date. Broadly speaking, there was no other way to handle the war than the one the duke elected.[4]

All these meetings, and the urgency of the subjects under discussion, frayed Newcastle's spirits and widened the fissure between him and Walpole. The prime minister also vexed the duke by pushing the appointment of Lord Hervey to the office of lord privy seal despite the duke's dislike of the waspish peer. The duke muttered about resignation, but as usual did not act on the threat. Still, Hervey's promotion galled him deeply. Both Lord Hardwicke and Bishop Hare, Newcastle's friend at the see of Chichester, felt obliged in these trying months to caution the duke against separating himself from the prime minister.[5] The advice only annoyed him. Observers could see that the ministry was sharply divided, and Lord Egmont at this time discerned three distinct factions: the Pelhams and Hardwicke, Wilmington and the duke of Dorset, and Walpole and the dukes of Grafton and Devonshire.[6] Biblical images of houses divided leapt readily to eighteenth-century minds.

Even as the cabinet struggled, amid their intestine quarrels, to complete their war planning, events elsewhere generated a far larger conflict that swallowed up the Anglo-Spanish war and replaced Spain with France as the chief threat to Britain. One of these events was the secret French decision to prevent British annexations in the West Indies. Ever since Versailles had surprised London by avoiding war in 1739, the ministers in Britain had been understandably but unduly sanguine about the possibility of limiting the conflict and isolating the theatre. Newcastle, moreover, was encouraged to disregard any rumors of significant French military preparations by the reports he received from the ambassador to the court at Versailles, Lord Waldegrave, filled with assurances of the meaninglessness of Fleury's warnings to London. The duke was too credulous—and without any real excuse, since he himself had earlier recognized the cardinal's dexterity at deception. France was in fact preparing a naval force which would, once dispatched, be authorized to attack Britain's.

When word arrived in September 1740 that d'Antin's fleet was sailing toward the West Indies, Newcastle was thrown into panic and confusion. "Except we can form some new alliance," he exhorted Harrington, "France, (for what I see,) will, sooner or later, overrun Europe, and perhaps America too." If the sailing meant war with France, then Britain's home defenses needed securing. But the West Indies could not be abandoned: "We are no nation," he wrote a friend at this time, "if we cannot be superiour to ye French in ye W. Indies." Newcastle urged massive reinforcements for Vernon,[7] but difficulties in ascertaining the size of d'Antin's fleet and therefore in computing the defense needs of the British isles held up the dispatch of Sir Chaloner Ogle and his fleet of twenty-five ships of the line until late October. Detaining Ogle had meant exposing Vernon, for d'Antin's head start assured the Bourbon forces in the Indies of a temporary advantage that any British delay would only extend. As it turned out, the arrival of the French entailed neither a British naval defeat nor even a state of war—d'Antin and Fleury were wary adversaries—but it did indicate how the intricate pattern of parallel and conflicting interests to which all Europe belonged tended to widen bilateral conflicts into multilateral wars.

The most critical events of 1740, however, were pure happenstance: two continent-shaking deaths. In May Frederick William I, King of Prussia, died and was succeeded by his unpromising son, Frederick II. In October the Holy Roman Emperor Charles VI passed on, leaving his Habsburg hereditary dominions to his daughter, Maria Theresa, and his imperial dignity to whomever the nine electors should select. Almost immediately, on a flimsy pretext, the new Prussian king attacked rich Silesia, one of the holdings of Maria Theresa, and the fierce struggle between the houses of Hohenzollern and Habsburg for dominance in Germany commenced with the so-called War of the Austrian Succession. That Prussia had accepted the Pragmatic Sanction meant nothing to Frederick II; and the Prussian repudiation of the document made it easy for other states, eager to snatch tidbits from the Habsburg table, to cast aside their scruples as well. France made this decision too, against Fleury's advice and less for self-aggrandizement than in the conviction that Bourbons prospered when Habsburgs suffered. Within months the new Austrian ruler found several of her lands under the heavy yoke of foreign armies, her own forces insufficient to deal with the attacks, and her treasury and administration inadequate to mustering the needed additional help. She called on Britain for succor.

London was obliged by the Pragmatic Sanction to defend the integrity of the Habsburg inheritance. It responded first with financial and then with military aid, and even though it accomplished this without incurring war with either France or Prussia, its commitment to Maria

Theresa's cause entailed the eventual subordination of West Indian to European operations. That Britain in 1741 should so readily behave toward Austria in a manner it had eschewed eight years earlier was a clear sign of the altered balance of power within the ministry. Newcastle, not Walpole, was in command, a man whose Austrophile inclinations were strong and undisguised. He had, it is true, recently adopted Horace Walpole's plan for an anti-Bourbon alliance and urged the necessity of securing the new Prussian monarch—"We must buy Prussia at almost any rate we can get"[8]—but those desperate words had been penned before the emperor's death. Now all the considerations that had impelled him to urge war in 1733—the strategic importance of Austria to Britain and the need to keep one's word—operated with even greater force. Additionally, in George II Newcastle had a powerful ally. The king by 1741 had shaken off his dependence on Walpole. On the issue of supporting Austria he agreed with the duke and even nourished hopes of securing more territory for himself as a reward. Against the duke and the king, reinforced as they were by a public opinion that sympathized with the Habsburg queen, neither man nor argument could stand.

The man who might have done so was Walpole, but by October 1740 he was thoroughly dispirited. He might assail various ministerial measures, but publicly he declared that he dared not alter them, and to Newcastle he could even say: "This war is yours. You have the conduct of it, and I wish you Joy of it."[9] Walpole had lost his appetite for command. The argument that might have blocked British aid to Austria was that to help Vienna might invite attack from Versailles. But with d'Antin on the seas and Anglo-French conflict expected anyway, it seemed wiser to secure a major continental ally and thereby assure future cooperation than to find oneself isolated and doubly beset, with only a recently betrayed neighbor as a source of assistance. Britain therefore decided to grant Maria Thersea a subsidy of £300,000 and to supply her with 12,000 troops recruited from the continent.

Rumors that Newcastle was consorting with the opposition in the persons of Carteret and Argyle were becoming prominent by the fall of 1740. They were neither new nor groundless. It was thoroughly understandable why he might treat with the parliamentary enemy: he found them more in sympathy with the sort of vigorous military measures he wanted to pursue than Sir Robert was. With Carteret he had an additional tie as well. Both were sons of Westminster School, and if a report about their drunken tomfoolery after a school feast in 1737 has any truth, it shows that while politics may have divided them, memories of shared boyhood experiences could perhaps sometimes eclipse politics.[10] But talking with opponents, even in secret, is not equivalent to betraying allies. There is no evidence that the duke ever tried to have Walpole ousted. He quarreled with the prime minister, raged at him, and occasionally shrank from him, but he did not, so far as is known, seek to destroy him politically.

Nor, upon consideration, is this surprising. It is true that the opposition tended to focus its fire on Sir Robert as the one man to be rejected. But Newcastle was too wise to leap to the inference that it sought only that one change and was prepared to cooperate with Walpole's ministerial colleagues to get it. Newcastle knew he had no assurance that an assault on the prime minister, if successful, would not bring the southern secretary down too. After all, the opposition was assailing measures as well as a man, and these measures were in general the policies by which the war had thus far been run. Lord Chesterfield, for example, spoke in the House of Lords to the effect that the operations in the Mediterranean were "the worst conducted part of the worst conducted war that was ever carried on by this nation or any other."[11] In fact, since the fiercest opposition of the parliamentary session which began in November 1740 arose in the chamber of peers, the duke could stay neither above nor below the battle. He had to answer charges, repulse efforts to have letters and instructions revealed, and defend his prime minister. Even if he had wanted to reach a rapprochement with the opposition, the war would have been an insuperable handicap.

All his contemporaries agreed that the duke was not a great speaker in the House of Lords. But he did some of the finest parliamentary debating of his career in the session of 1740–41 and proved himself no mean antagonist. He argued effectively against disclosing Haddock's instructions of early 1739 on the grounds that, since they were probably strongly worded, publication would make Britain appear the aggressor. Not an argument to convert an enemy, it was, rather, shrewdly conceived for winning over the uncertain: it suggested, contrary to opposition charges, that the instructions were rigorous, but it laid the onus of exposing British aggression on those who wanted proof. He also defended the ministry against charges of unnecessary delay in dispatching the West Indian expedition—a delay he himself had keenly opposed—on the grounds that France had not yet committed itself at the time, and Britain therefore needed a major part of its fleet in home waters. This line of argument let him quickly add that those in the opposition who had gone on record as believing that France would not intervene had been proven wrong by events. On central points he was unyielding: "I do not still," he is recorded as affirming in January 1741, "repent of the war with Spain."[12] But his greatest moment came on 13 February 1741 when Lord Carteret, cooperating with Samuel Sandys in the Commons, introduced a motion asking for Walpole's permanent dismissal. Lord Hardwicke's eldest son attended the debate in the House of Lords, calling it "the finest I was ever present at there." Carteret, Argyle, Hervey, and Hardwicke spoke. And so did Newcastle, who, according to the lord chancellor's son, "performed remarkably well that day in reply to Lord Carteret."[13]

Newcastle himself was proud of his effort. There is among his papers[14] a page of notes in his own hand that outlines his rebuttal speech. It appears to have been scribbled down while Carteret was actually firing his broadsides. For no other parliamentary address the duke delivered do such complete notes exist. A study of these jottings suggests that if the speech itself followed them, it was thematically complex but intelligently ordered and based on sound argument. In effect, Newcastle adopted three lines of defense: he asserted 1) that the foreign policies of the Walpole years had been well-conceived and wise, 2) that it was ludicrous to attribute to one man alone policies that emerged from ministerial discussions and received parliamentary assent, and 3) that even if policies should sometimes prove bad, it was unconstitutional and ill advised to use quasi-judicial methods to proceed against a minister. He found Carteret's charges, as the core of the notes puts it, "unprecedented, unfounded & dangerous to the constitution." He displayed knowledge not only of Britain's treaties since 1714—that could surely have been expected of a secretary of state—but also of a variety of efforts dating back to Restoration times to punish ministers through parliamentary action. He concluded with a reference to Sir Robert's "character," arguing that neither documentary nor personal evidence permitted one to call Walpole a "sole minister." The address, though partisan, was persuasive. Aided by a split between dissident Whigs and Tories, the ministry defeated both Sandys' and Carteret's motions.

If his complicity in the elaboration of war policy and his fundamental loyalty to Walpole had not been sufficient to keep Newcastle and the opposition apart, another element which intruded itself into politics in May 1741 would have had the same effect. The Septennial Act required another general election. Had it been possible, the ministry would gladly have put it off. The various opposition factions were well positioned for electoral triumphs; the war remained a cheerless venture, and the aging and all-too-familiar Sir Robert Walpole, where he did not evoke outright bitterness, could at best induce a sense of boredom. Newcastle cast himself into the electoral fray with less than his usual enthusiasm, but with an undiminished resolution to wring victories from the constituencies he in some measure controlled. His burgage power in Yorkshire and his fine-honed Sussex machine produced their customary results. In Nottinghamshire, despite some confusion in dealing with an unexpected development at East Retford, the duke also demonstrated his authority. In fact, perhaps because he had recently visited the county for the first time in two decades, he restored some of his earlier influence by gaining a large measure of control over the second seat at Newark.[15] Thus even as Walpole's political authority was being fatally weakened, Newcastle's was being reaffirmed.

In Yorkshire the election ratified a bit of juggling that had occurred in 1735 when, on the death of Jessopp, Andrew Wilkinson had assumed his seat at Aldborough. The arrangement between the duke and the Wilkinsons remained in effect—and Newcastle had strengthened his interest by buying the Boroughbridge burgages of the Stapyltons in 1739—but after 1735 it is appropriate to regard Boroughbridge as the seat of two of Newcastle's nominees, the familiar John Tyrrell and George Gregory, and Aldborough as the seat of the third, John Jewkes. In Sussex all went as expected. Hastings returned James Pelham, to whom the duke had financial as well as family obligations, and Andrew Stone, whom the duke had finally decided to bring into Parliament. Seaford reelected Sir William Gage and William Hay. At Lewes an opposition was mounted by Thomas Sergison, the leader of the nearly successful assault of 1734. But the ministerial Whig slate had been strengthened by the replacement of "Turk" Pelham, dead of drink in 1737, with John Trevor, son of the duke's earliest member from Lewes. Newcastle gave thought to Sergison's suggestion that a deal be struck giving control of one seat to the opposition; the potential financial savings appeared inviting. But the duke finally, and wisely, rejected the scheme. His two candidates, Trevor and yet another Thomas Pelham of Lewes, won with comparative ease. In the county race the duke antici-

pated "a very warm contest,"[16] but the projected opposition, crystal-
lized by the duke's refusal to abandon James Bulter, dissolved before
polling day after its candidate died of smallpox; Butler and Henry
Pelham were again returned. But ten days later Butler himself lay dead
of the pox, and a meeting of eastern county leaders, at which Pelham
represented Newcastle, chose the duke of Dorset's son, Lord Middlesex,
as the government's nominee. Some in the west muttered their discontent that two easterners should represent Sussex, but Middlesex
won without formal opposition.

In Nottinghamshire, though there was a disruption of plans at East
Retford, the important change was at Newark. The Whig-Tory compromise continued to hold at both the county race and at Nottingham.
The duke's candidate for the county was John Mordaunt, a loyal Whig
who had replaced Bennett in 1739. His candidate for the borough was
the reliable John Plumptre. At East Retford, however, the agreement
was destroyed, as William Mellish emerged to pit himself and his free
spending against the incumbents, John White and Sir Robert Clifton.
White won, but he threw his support —and presumably Newcastle's—
behind Clifton and was embarrassed to see Mellish triumph instead.
The newcomer was a Whig, and ultimately a loyal one, but his arrival
had upset the duke's settlement of politics in East Retford. At Newark
the duke's influence was waxing. Richard Sutton had died in 1738 and
Newcastle had replaced him with Lord William Manners, a gambler,
a rake, and Henry Pelham's brother-in-law. Then the duke had come
to terms with Lord Middleton by nominating their common friend
Job Staunton Charlton, who was also Newcastle's estate agent, in
place of James Pelham whom he was accommodating at Hastings.
Against the combined might of Newcastle and Middleton a faltering
opposition petered out before the polling day, and Manners and Charlton, both obliged to the duke, were returned for Newark.

On a nationwide basis the election results were even worse than the
ministry had expected. Newcastle of course held his own, but with so
many powerful figures now ranging themselves with some segment of
the opposition, the ranks of the ministerial Whigs were dangerously
thinned. Cornwall, at the direction of the Prince of Wales, and Scotland, at the urging of the duke of Argyle, had renounced their parliamentary allegiances to the government. As in 1734, Newcastle was
quicker to see the truth—in this case, a desperate truth—than Walpole.
Sir Robert thought the election had provided the ministry with an

edge of forty votes in the Commons; Newcastle computed the figure at only fourteen. Twentieth-century historians have put the number at sixteen to eighteen.[17] Forty itself would have been a slim majority; eighteen was impossible. When majorities shrank to such tiny figures in the eighteenth century, they became thoroughly unstable. Cautious ministerial supporters, fearing that they would stay loyal too long and be caught voting with the government on the division that defeated it, took to absenting themselves. It was precisely this sort of movement that the ministry could expect when it would need to summon the Commons in November.

Sir Robert's son Horace later accused the duke of betraying his father in the election, but even though the duke and the prime minister had often been keenly at odds, the charge would appear to be baseless. Newcastle worked with his customary vigor and success; he intervened directly in Arundel and Chichester to prevent situations that might have damaged the ministerial forces; he resorted to the full range of preelectoral tricks—plying with drink, satiating with food, cajoling with letters, softening with favors—to keep his dominance in Sussex.[18] It is quite true that all this activity was also self-interested and hardly constitutes unambiguous evidence of the duke's support for Walpole. But precisely because their careers were so tightly linked, it would have been very difficult for Newcastle to have tried to use the election against Walpole without in effect using it against himself. By serving his own interests the duke served Sir Robert's. A ministerial Whig was a supporter of both. It is thus this parallelism of interests, coupled with the total absence of any evidence that the duke conspired against his leader, that raises doubts about Horace's charge. Newcastle harbored reservations about Sir Robert's political value and ability; he had no reservations about the wisdom of cooperating with him in the election.

The general election was only the first of several major blows the ministry sustained in 1741. From America came news that set Newcastle spinning: the assault on Cartagena, the target chosen by the Jamaican council of war, had failed with high loss of life. Earlier reports had led the ministry to expect success from the great West Indian endeavor upon which so many political hopes rode. But disease, heat, quarrelsome leadership, bad provisioning, and resourceful Spanish defenses had conspired to shatter Britain's dreams. Some of the blame was the duke's. Better planning would have assured more plentiful supplies, and foresight might have suggested the vulnerability of

Europeans to tropical disease. But not all the blame can be put on Newcastle. The delays in execution were not, in general, his fault, and the fatal animosity between Vernon and Brigadier General Wentworth was unquestionably not. Newcastle called the debacle "a most melancholy affair" and thought immediately of reinforcing Britain's depleted army.[19] But reserves adequate to this goal were not to be found, and Newcastle's only consolation in the tragedy was a political one, a renewal of closer ties with Sir Robert. The prime minister even agreed with the duke that despite the setback Britain would not retreat in America. Misery had made company of sorts.

Hard on the heels of the bad news from America came worse news from Europe. George II, whom neither war nor reproving ministers could keep from his electorate, had begun contemplating protecting his German lands from French or Prussian incursion by declaring Hanover neutral. The ministry was astounded at the news. The military and parliamentary policy that the government had devised and articulated rested on the assumption that Hanover would serve as a *point d'appui* in Germany. This argument had justified both the subsidies squeezed from Parliament for use on the continent and the talks for military cooperation then under way between Britain and the United Provinces. With 40,000 French troops hovering on the Hanoverian frontier, however, George was not disposed to heed remonstrances from Britain. The feared declaration appeared in September, and Newcastle led the ministry in expressing indignation. George's decision to neutralize the electorate, the duke argued, violated his international commitments, pitted George *qua* king against George *qua* elector, and made impossible any reasonable defense of royal actions in the legislature. The duke feared the king's ruin, the ministry's destruction, and—the unspoken dread—a Jacobite counterrevolution in revulsion from the king's disregard of the kingdom's interests. The ill-considered royal decision revealed how markedly British and Hanoverian needs might conflict, and it brought quickly in its train some of the sad consequences the ministry had foreseen. Denmark repudiated its subsidy agreement with London, and the Dutch, hitherto prepared to do their utmost to assist Austria and prevent France from occupying the southern Netherlands, suddenly grew cool. The fear or hope throughout Europe was the same: what the electorate had already done the kingdom might soon do.

Harrington earned Newcastle's wrath in this affair for traveling with the king and accepting his decision; Walpole earned his scorn for his unwillingness to speak forthrightly against the monarch. Hardwicke tried to compose his unsettled spirit with a touching letter: "I consider our views and interests as the same; and our friendship, if you will permit me to use the expression, is the pride of my life; for I am entirely and unalterably yours."[20] But by October both honor and self-interest seemed to demand an extreme response from the duke: his resignation as a protest against ministerial acquiescence in a fatal policy. "If any one was drove out of an administration for measures," he explained to his brother, "and at present I may say for measures only, I am, if I go out."[21] As usual, the threat exceeded the deed. Hardwicke urged him to reconsider, and Pelham seemed more annoyed than sympathetic with his plight. Then too a natural love of politics and a fear of being reproached for deserting a monarch in trouble also served to induce him to stay. For these and similar reasons he did not in the fall of 1741 desert what some now believed to be a sinking ship.

The defeat of British endeavors on the Spanish Main, the subsidy to Austria, and the subsequent declaration of Hanoverian neutrality all underlined an obvious fact: the focus of the war was changing from the New World to the Old and from the seas to the land. Hardwicke had declared in August, "I fear that now America must be fought for in Europe,"[22] and strategic decisions made in London soon reflected that shift as the conflict in the West Indies was permitted to relapse into a quiet commercial struggle, with British men of war restricting their activities to the protection of British merchants, the harassment of the treasure fleet, and the blocking of Spanish trade. Walpole made a useful contribution to Britain's war effort by inducing Maria Theresa to accept a truce with Prussia late in 1741, an action which promised stiffer Austrian resistance to France. But it was Newcastle as senior secretary who was preparing himself to take on the responsibility of the widening continental effort, and in November he drafted a document expressing his strategic views. He saw an immediate need for invigorating the Dutch, without whose help any British war effort seemed to court serious military and commercial risks. He believed that Prussia might be kept accommodated so that Austria could mount a forceful campaign against France. He hoped to secure Russia, to resecure Denmark and some wavering German princes, and to promote an Austro-Sardinian settlement that would attach Turin to the anti-Bourbon camp. Finally, he proposed the formation of a composite army—British, Dutch, and German—to defend the southern Netherlands and help Austria in

Germany.[23] Virtually this entire program was soon adopted by Carteret and made, after that peer's rise to power, national policy. Perhaps, since at Newcastle's initiative the two men had resumed ties the previous summer, the strategic plans deliberately incorporated Carteret's thinking. Lord Hervey had accused Carteret of giving Newcastle his foreign policy ideas even earlier. Whatever their origin, they show at any rate that the duke intended to be no less forward in Europe than he had been in America.

But by late 1741 it had become questionable whether he would in fact hold office long enough to implement his European planning. It was not resignation but dismissal that threatened the duke—a dismissal likely to be forced from the king by a swelling and hungry opposition that, with Parliament reconvened, now had the opportunity to make the ministry pay for Cartagena and Hanover. Sir Robert had judged badly and allowed an enemy to become chairman of the committee that would hear election petitions. Votes in the narrowly divided House of Commons on the disputed elections quickly began to go against the prime minister, though he won more often than he lost. But he could not mobilize support, and a mood of crisis infected Westminster. "God knows how this will end," the duke confided, "for my own part I fear and dread the worst." The duke's sharpest fear was for his office; he was by now convinced that only Sir Robert's resignation could save the rest of the ministry. "By the best accounts I can learn," he told Hardwicke, "all might have been easy, quiet and *safe*, had it not been for the fatal obstinacy of one single man, resolved to ruin, or to rule, the state."[24] But Newcastle was still loyal. The king commanded him and Walpole to behave as if on warm terms, and they obediently dissimulated well enough to dupe observers who ought to have known better. All hinged on Walpole: neither king nor colleagues would insist that the man who had been prime minister for two full decades now retire.

Sir Robert reached the conclusion they wanted only on 28 January, after his seventh defeat in the lobbies. Within a week he quit his office; within another week he was raised to the House of Lords as earl of Orford. Privately he felt betrayed by Newcastle and Hardwicke, expecially by the latter, but because he hoped to keep the Whigs—the "Old Corps"—together, he chose his own resignation over the risk of mass defeat and defection. Upon first hearing intimations of the decision, Newcastle told the duchess that he believed the resignation would let affairs "jogg on tolerably," an expression which, though tepid, meant at least that the duke expected to retain office in the new ministry.[25] The retiring prime minister had been concerned for his own fate. From Hardwicke and Newcastle he secured promises that no parliamentary inquest would seek to defame or confine him. Clearly an era had ended. Yet the age of Walpole had, in several crucial respects, disappeared well before 1742. His political order had begun crumbling in 1733. His ecclesiastical settlement had collapsed in 1736. His command of policy had ended in 1739. In essence, Sir Robert Walpole fell because, though serving as link between Crown and Parliament, he disapproved of a war they both supported. Now Britain would get a prime minister who was committed to the war. Unhappily it would also get—indeed, it already had—disunity of royal and parliamentary views.

II

The collapse of Walpole's administration had not been unexpected. Within and without the ministry the kingdom's politicians had long been preparing for the fateful day. It was George II himself who made the crucial but quite natural decision to retain as many of his friends as possible in the new ministry: Walpole's fall—if the monarch could have his way—would be neither the occasion for a massive turnover in personnel nor the signal for a major alteration in policy. The king authorized Newcastle and Hardwicke to treat with Pulteney and Carteret about the formation of a new ministry. In choosing the duke and the lord chancellor as his agents, the monarch called upon the two members of the old ministry who, by virtue either of wealth and influence or of demonstrated capacity, had the clearest claims to retaining office. In legitimizing Pulteney and Carteret rather than Argyle and the Tories, he turned to those elements of the opposition closest to the ministerial Whigs and most eager for office.

The task given to Newcastle and Hardwicke was not easy. The opposition had just tasted blood; it was unclear whether the repast would sate them or further stimulate their appetites. Gaps in the Newcastle and Hardwicke papers at this climactic moment make impossible a reconstruction of the duke's thoughts, but the course of the negotiations in early February with Pulteney and Carteret suggests that the ministerial team felt its position to be weak. Pulteney was offered Walpole's old post of first lord of the Treasury and Carteret one of the secretarial offices. The former, bedevilled by his frequent renunciation of personal ambition, felt obliged to decline the offer; the latter, who would gladly have stepped into Pulteney's place, found himself barred from the Treasury by royal resistance and accepted instead the proffered seals. The earl of Wilmington thereupon took Walpole's old office and Harrington took Wilmington's. The prompt elevation of Wilmington from the presidency to the Treasury has led several historians to see in all these maneuverings a rather crafty ministerial scheme to keep the bastions of power out of enemy hands. Perhaps this view is correct. Certainly the ministerial negotiators would have sought to exploit any flaws in the opposition, and Pulteney's public professions of selflessness constituted a highly visible weakness. But in light of the series of large concessions to Pulteney and Carteret which followed the disposition of the Treasury—concessions which found the government withdrawing its demand that Walpole be protected from a vindictive Parliament, agreeing to the appointment of Lord Tweedale to a revived secretary-ship for Scotland, and granting to the opposition no less than a majority in the new cabinet, Treasury, and Admiralty—it seems fairer to regard the modest triumph at the Treasury as simply fortuitous and the succeeding debacle as a sounder indication of the old ministry's defi-cient power. Months later, when it became clear that personnel changes were not producing the policy changes desired by the former opposition and that hopes to punish the earl of Orford had been thwarted, it could safely be concluded that the old ministry had survived the loss of its leader remarkably well. But it had done so because it had been lucky. The various anti-Walpole factions had fallen to squabbling among themselves. Unreconciled and mutually suspicious, they had then failed to respond as a unit when George II, in a fit of rage, refused to allow a particularly obnoxious Tory onto the Admiralty Board. By the end of April the triumphant coalition of Sir Robert's foes was shattered. But to infer from this that in February Newcastle and Hardwicke had shrewdly conceded shadow to retain substance would be illegitimate, involving as it does the unfounded ascription of either prescience to Newcastle or dominance to Hardwicke.[26]

Despite the hopes of many, including Pulteney and Wilmington, the new ministry was not broadly inclusive, not, that is, constructed on a "broad bottom." Newcastle and Hardwicke served their own and the king's interests by building it on as narrow a base as was feasible. After Argyle's resignation in March it rested in effect on an alliance among three parliamentary groupings: the numerous but scarcely zealous followers of Sir Robert, whom Newcastle called the "Old Corps;" the small group of adherents loyal to Pulteney or Carteret, dubbed by the duke the "New Whigs;" and the band of about twenty who served the political ambitions of the Prince of Wales. Excluded were the Tories and the more abrasive Whig groups such as Cobham's "cubs." The effective cabinet remained large, numbering seven for over a year, and it was, as most large cabinets tended to be, divided into factions vying for control. One faction was the close political alliance of Newcastle, Hardwicke, and Pelham, who remained as paymaster and sole commoner in the cabinet. Clearly ambitious, these three hoped that Walpole's exit would permit them to accede to his authority. A second faction was the looser Pulteney-Carteret connection. The two men actually had little in common. Pulteney, who took no formal office and soon accepted the earldom of Bath, was unable to parlay his power as an opposition leader into power in administration and found his influence steadily and irrevocably dissipating. Carteret, however, a man of high intelligence and ornamental learning, had never relied so exclusively on fickle public support for his influence and soon discovered in the friendship of the monarch a new basis for political strength. Outside these two factions stood Harrington and Wilmington, the former a crony of the king and the latter a man of moderate views and still more moderate ambitions and talents. Clearly, therefore, the major threat to Pelhamite ascendancy was Newcastle's new colleague in the northern department, the forceful Carteret.

Since the expanding war was the chief problem confronting the new ministry, it was in the formulation of war policy that disputes might most likely arise. But Carteret was a far more avid warrior than Walpole, and his presence at first strengthened rather than reduced ministerial solidarity on the hostilities. The ministry dispatched 16,000 British troops to Flanders to join the multinational Pragmatic Army; and Parliament responded to the new sense of determination by voting a subsidy of £500,000 for use by the Austrians and Sardinians. Still, within this more united ministerial front Newcastle suffered a diminution of power. Major strategic decisions were ostensibly a product of cabinet deliberations, but by virtue of both responsibility and inclination the two secretaries exercised preponderant influence. Although this situation in itself scarcely portended political defeat for Newcastle, it was clearly a setback. Prior to Walpole's resignation the duke had effectively been the kingdom's war minister, the chief director of the naval struggle in the West Indies. But with Carteret's accession to office and with the almost simultaneous recognition that the continental war merited priority of effort and attention, Newcastle's dominance passed. Now he only shared authority, to be sure usually in agreement with his colleague, but often unable to impose his own will in those instances where he dissented from Carteret's views.

Almost immediately upon the creation of the ministry Newcastle faced and submitted to a scheme of Carteret's. The new secretary believed that the allied war effort needed better coordination, especially in the Italian theatre, and he determined to replace a vague anti-Bourbon agreement between Austria and Sardinia with a formal alliance between the two states. To this aim itself Newcastle took no objection. But inasmuch as Austria lay within the northern department and Sardinia within the southern, any British effort to promote such an alliance would require of one secretary that he abdicate some conventional authority. The duke did the abdicating. London became the center of the negotiations and Carteret the director, meeting not only with the Austrian diplomat Wasner but also with the Sardinian representative Osorio. Carteret gained no glory from his efforts, for the discussions long remained unsuccessful, and the Bourbon threat to Italy was checked by June 1742 as a consequence not of Carteret's diplomacy but of the activities of Vice Admiral Mathews's fleet. Still, Newcastle was restive.

In the more important German theatre Carteret's and Newcastle's major aim was to divide Prussia from France, and the conclusion in September 1742 of the Treaty of Breslau, ending the reinitiated Austro-Prussian hostilities, was unquestionably a major advance toward this goal. But this success led in turn to another secretarial struggle, for Prussia and Britain had had divergent intentions in cooperating on the treaty. Frederick II wanted to bring peace to Germany, to get the armies out and make Silesia his own. Britain, however, wanted to isolate the Bourbons so that they could be more advantageously engaged in battle, and with several French armies in or moving toward central Europe, Germany seemed an appropriate area for such engagements. The dispatch of Maillebois' forces from Westphalia to Bavaria in the fall of 1742 lifted the French danger to Hanover and finally permitted the Pragmatic Army to move onto the offensive. Lord Stair, the commander of the army, recommended an invasion of France and received support from Carteret and the king. But Newcastle and Hardwicke favored a less risky advance across the Rhine into Germany. Lent credibility by the memory of Marlborough's rejection of similar advice from Stair, Newcastle's views prevailed, and in 1743 the Pragmatic Army entered the empire. Frederick II was alarmed and embittered at the incursion, but it is not clear that an invasion of France would have left him happier. In truth, so exposed was his position and so fearful was he of isolation that a protracted war, whether fought in France or in Germany, was likely to suck him back in.

The secretaries thus survived their first year in harness without serious policy quarrels, but in the spring of 1743 a fundamental strategy difference finally arose. Newcastle had long viewed Austria as Britain's chief continental ally and had consequently regarded efforts to humble or thwart Vienna as indirect but dangerous assaults on British security. It had been for this reason that he had disapproved of Walpole's refusal to involve Britain in the War of the Polish Succession. Of Carteret's devotion to the house of Habsburg he also nourished some doubts: the northern secretary had seemed remarkably oblivious to Austrian sensibilities in his efforts to secure an Austro-Sardinian alliance, and had then advocated employing the Pragmatic Army where it would be least serviceable to Vienna. Still, these were differences of degree, not direction. But the same could not be said of Carteret's major plan of 1743, slowly revealed to his ministerial colleagues in their role as lords justices only after he had left for the continent with the king. The northern secretary proposed to use concessions to win over to the allied side the new emperor, the Wittelsbach, Charles VII, whose accession to the imperial dignity had proved so galling to the Austrians. Newcastle thoroughly disliked the scheme. Its success, he believed, would bring no benefit to the allied states since Charles VII was desperately weak, and its implementation would certainly infuriate the Austrians.

Aware of his colleagues' attitude but encouraged by the Pragmatic victory at Dettingen, Carteret persevered, and in July concluded the so-called "Treaty of Hanau," wherein the emperor agreed to abandon France and Carteret promised him an income from British sources for an unspecified length of time. Carteret then sought the approval of the lords justices. But his penchant for secrecy and his self-imposed isolation—Newcastle bewailed his "obstinate and offensive silence"—now took their toll.[27] Largely uninstructed by the northern secretary, the ministry could not fathom the rationale for his actions. Newcastle thus had no difficulty in arousing widespread opposition within the regency toward the Hanau settlement. The subsidy, most lords justices agreed, would make the treaty intolerable in Parliament; the new ally, defeated in battle and harried from his patrimony, seemed scarcely worth any purchase price at all; and the secrecy which enshrouded the negotiations could only serve to kindle the distrust of Vienna. The regency withheld its consent, and Carteret abandoned the scheme and the emperor. But the damage could not be undone: he had set in bold relief a major policy difference between himself and Newcastle, and he had done it in a manner which assured maximum ministerial support for the Pelhams.

Provoking as this policy quarrel was for the Pelhams, their growing opposition to Carteret had yet more fundamental roots: the northern secretary threatened to bypass them and replace Walpole as the king's chief counsellor, threatened, in short, to engross all the power. From the inception of the new ministry the Pelhams had sought to strengthen themselves in the necessary twofold way: by restoring a dependable majority in the Commons, and by gaining friendly access to the temperamental but tractable monarch. The first half of the program was succeeding. By mid-1743, aided by a broadening of the bottom of the ministry, Henry Pelham had gained command of the House of Commons, organizing the business of the chamber and winning the trust of independent members. His chief aide was a valuable recruit to the ministerial team, the able William Murray. A native of Scotland, Murray was a brilliant advocate—he had represented the petitioning merchants in 1738—and a close friend of Andrew Stone. It was Stone who recommended him to Newcastle. The duke had already used the young man in private capacities; judging shrewdly, he now elected to charge him with public responsibilities as well. Appointed solicitor general in August 1742 at Carteret's and Newcastle's joint behest and then returned to Parliament by Newcastle at Boroughbridge, Murray retained his Tory friends but lent his distinguished oratorical talents to the ministry. He also became one of the duke's chief advisers. Many years later, in one of his last letters to Stone, Newcastle mused on Murray, by then Lord Mansfield: "Only the most determined resolution and support from me," said the duke, had made Murray's political career possible.[28] Defended by Pelham and Murray, the ministry could regard even the fire of Pitt less fearfully.

But while the Pelhams acted to secure the ministry's authority in the Commons, they saw their own position in the king's counsels imperilled by the northern secretary's ascendancy in the closet. This development had at least two foundations. Carteret spoke German; more important, he was unabashedly in favor of a vigorous foreign policy and not at all chary of advocating measures likely to aid Hanover. Such advocacy cost him whatever favor he had retained with the opposition, but Carteret regarded the exchange of power bases an advantage. As early as July 1742 Newcastle was reported to be apprehensive of Carteret's growing favor in the closet, and by August he was declaring his pre-monitions to Hardwicke. It was "mortifying," wrote the duke, that George ignored the Pelhams: "If this is not alter'd," he continued, in his favorite threat, "I can't go on."[29] Sometimes the severity of the danger abated, for Carteret had no desire to seem all-engrossing; but the rumors of his mounting power in the closet endured and proliferated however moderately he might behave himself. Upon Newcastle's jealousy all these developments played teasingly. Thus, when Carteret left for the continent with George II in the spring of 1743, Newcastle dispatched his close friend the duke of Richmond, master of the horse and fellow Sussex grandee, to accompany the monarch as a Pelhamite agent. And then, when reports of the Hanau conversations added an element of policy disagreement to the power struggle, the Pelhams reached new heights of suspicion. "Lord Carteret," declared Newcastle to Richmond, "has no other view, but his own, absolute, sole, power . . . he is resolved to strike now."[30]

Yet, with the connivance of fortune, it was the Pelhams who struck. Early in July 1743 Lord Wilmington died, and the succession to the Treasury fell open. It had not escaped general notice that Sir Robert Walpole had used his position as first lord of the Treasury and chancellor of the exchequer to mediate between king and Commons. The treasury office was clearly, when held by a commoner, invested with enormous potential and manifestly worth contending for. Orford himself had urged Henry Pelham to try to establish the same authority, and the Pelhams had already secured a promise of the reversion to the Treasury for the younger brother. But at Wilmington's death Lord Bath suddenly emerged from growing inconsequence to request for himself the position that he had earlier spurned. Thus, two separate petitions went to the monarch. In July George II was basking in post-Dettingen glory at Hanover, and the Pelhams, while hopeful that Richmond's entreaties would prevail, keenly feared that Carteret's vaunted influence would effect a royal judgment in Lord Bath's favor. Their fears proved groundless. George II was a man to honor a promise; so, moreover, was Carteret, who felt obliged to recommend that the king fulfil his pledge to the Pelhams. Thus, in late August and after an inexplicable and unnerving delay, the regency learned of Pelham's appointment to the Treasury. Although, in light of Carteret's recommendation, it came under circumstances which served to soften mutual suspicions, it nevertheless gave the Pelhams a fundamental advantage in the incipient struggle with the northern secretary. "It is plain," exulted Newcastle, "we have got the better of him."[31] As usual, Newcastle exaggerated. But not by much, for henceforth until the collapse of the ministry it would be Carteret, not the Pelhams, who would be on the defensive.

III

"We are willing," Newcastle explained to Richmond after Wilmington's death, "Lord Carteret should fully have his share of power; but more he cannot have, with safety to our old friends; or with security to ourselves."[32] But Carteret continued to insist on what the Pelhams thought an inequitable share. In September the long British diplomatic campaign to bring Austria and Sardinia together in defense of Italy ended in a qualified success. With considerable reluctance and after much pressure from Carteret, the Austrians assented to an agreement whereby Sardinian cooperation against the Bourbons would be repaid with Habsburg lands in Italy. Carteret in turn promised British assistance to Austria. Newcastle regarded Carteret's intimidation of Vienna as unwise, but his colleagues persuaded him that the treaty was sufficiently worthwhile to merit British ratification. More contentious and far less easily rationalized was Carteret's supplementary pledge to continue Britain's subsidy to Vienna as long as the court of Austria declared its need of it. Here, rather than being too harsh with Vienna, Carteret was unwontedly being too compliant. And he was behaving in this bold manner without consulting ministers or Parliament. Newcastle liked neither his procedures nor his pretensions. On the former he spoke harshly: "I hope our active Secretary, will at last find out, that dexterity with Princes, to seem to promise all, and intend nothing, will as little do, as with private persons."[33] And by drawing attention to the latter he was able to persuade most of his fellow ministers to oppose the supplementary pledge. At the decisive cabinet meeting, held in November shortly after Carteret's return to Britain, the duke assailed the commitment as dangerously open ended for the Treasury and unnecessarily provocative to the House of Commons. After deliberation the cabinet voted nine-to-four not to ratify the pledge. It was a clear humiliation for Carteret and a triumph for Newcastle. Secretarial enmity thereafter reached new depths, the two men refusing even to dine together.[34]

An issue of still greater political consequence was meanwhile also obtruding itself. In the summer of 1742, when Maillebois' departure had removed the immediate French danger from Hanover, George II decided to cut his expenses by reducing the number of Hanoverians in the allied force. The British government, however, believed that the reduction would seriously impair the strength of the Pragmatic Army and had thus accepted for itself the cost of maintaining the electoral contingent at full strength. Under Henry Pelham's prodding the Commons had agreed to the expense in December of the same year. But the arrangement was vulnerable to the obvious charge that an unfortunate dynastic tie was permitting Hanover to evade its legitimate defense expenditures and to saddle Britain with them instead. George II further aroused the incipient anti-Hanoverianism of his subjects by preferring electoral emblems to British ones at Dettingen. The opposition—especially Pitt and Chesterfield—was not slow to sense that a new issue was arising with which the ministry might be flailed, and hostility to the Hanoverian tie, an attitude which had once seemed Jacobitical, became in 1743 a hallmark of the patriotic loyalty of the opposition.

Anti-Hanoverian impulses could take many different forms, but the most obvious was opposition to the subsidy for the electoral troops. Thus, as it was increasingly attacked by talented opposition essayists, the Pelhams—but not Carteret—slowly moderated their earlier enthusiasm for the payment. Newcastle, ever alert to the public mood, became most alarmed of all: the government, he cautioned in November 1743, must divest itself of all traces of "German politicks; German measures; and (what is perhaps as bad as either) German manners."[35] It was especially necessary to abandon the subsidy: such a step, he argued with conviction, would soothe parliamentary discontent, constitute another major victory over Carteret, and even open the possibility of some sort of reconciliation with opposition leaders. Henry Pelham and Lord Hardwicke, less apt to let personal quarrels muddle their political and military calculations, believed Newcastle excessively agitated and, with Orford's assistance, persuaded the cabinet not to bow to the opposition campaign. The duke thereupon behaved with proper loyalty to the decision and in the parliamentary debate on the subsidy recommended its continuation to his fellow peers. The measure was approved in both chambers early in 1744. But this decision to retain the troops assured the continuation of widespread anti-Hanoverianism. Because it had dynastic implications, anti-Hanoverianism was an unusually poisonous blister to have festering upon the body politic. Newcastle, despite his vote, had gained a reputation within the kingdom as the minister most ready to heal the sore by eliminating the irritant. Carteret had reinforced his emerging image as lackey to a German monarch.

And Carteret's problems multiplied. In February 1744 the Treaty of Worms, which had already damaged his political authority, began clearly to wreak havoc with his foreign policy as well. The Austro-Sardinian alliance had driven the Bourbon powers into closer cooperation, and France by 1744 was ready to shed its role as auxiliary for that of combatant. Rumors and intelligence of a planned French invasion of Great Britain, perhaps with the intention of placing the Pretender on the throne, circulated throughout the kingdom in the early months of the year. Hitherto it had been possible—and even persuasive—to defend British war policy on the grounds that it had prevented the dismemberment of Austria. But suddenly the cost of such assistance threatened to mount catastrophically. Newcastle's information on French plans and movements was extensive but inconsistent,[36] and the duke, deciding not to hazard Britain's security, ordered Norris and his fleet back from the Atlantic and into the Channel. Meanwhile, the enemy squadron stationed at Brest put to sea and moved up the Channel with the intention of rendezvousing at Dunkirk with an ominous collection of French barges and troops. A decisive sea battle seemed imminent in February 1744, and to protect the kingdom against attack should Norris's fleet fail, the ministry summoned regiments to London, stationed marines in garrisons, and called out some county militias. But instead of confrontation, it was dispersion that ensued at sea: a gale swept into the Channel, and neither fleet emerged from the storm in battle worthy condition. France temporarily abandoned its invasion plans but made clear its intentions by belatedly declaring war on Britain in March 1744. George II soon reciprocated. The war continued to broaden.

Initially the invasion scare reduced ministerial squabbling, but as it passed and the realization emerged that Carteret would not even have foreign success to justify his high-handed administration of diplomacy, the ability of the northern secretary to have his contentious plans accepted declined still further. Concurrently, Newcastle's ability rose, and in a succeeding series of policy disputes with Carteret the duke's advice was frequently adopted. In the spring of 1744 Newcastle drafted *Considerations upon the Present State of Affairs* in which he recommended a more coherent war policy. Since he was unimpressed by the Dutch contribution to the allied war effort, he wanted his recommendations forwarded to the republic's envoy not merely as private views but as official ones. Carteret opposed the duke's suggestion, fearing that if Britain demanded more cooperation from the Dutch, they in turn would demand more participation by Hanover—a blatant demonstration of his Hanoverian proclivities. But George II accepted the duke's proposal, and a scheme for discussions among the Dutch, the Austrians, the Sardinians, and the British was urged on the republic. In June it was the Pelhams, and especially Newcastle, who again opposed Carteret's advice in successfully persuading a bitter monarch not to journey to Hanover that summer. Finally, in early August Newcastle led the successful campaign in the closet against the northern secretary's proposal to extend a subsidy to the king of Poland.

But these victories were won at the cost of the anger of the king and his favorite. George II resented any advice, however wise or prudent, which conflicted with his personal inclinations. For both the Hanover trip and the king of Poland he entertained affections. Newcastle's counsel was unpalatable, and if the king dared not ignore the advice, he could at least rebuke the adviser. He accused the Pelhams of seeking to fetter him: "I know what this is," he told Hardwicke during the discussions over Hanover, "it is contention for power and from motives of that kind I am to be confin'd."[37] Meanwhile, Carteret thought the Pelhams timid at war making. He devoted some effort to sniping at Newcastle's Dutch policy by working quietly to destroy whatever forces conducing to greater Dutch activity the duke might have generated with his communication to the republic. But Lord Carteret was not a man to struggle *sub rosa*, and he demanded a showdown with the Pelhams, Hardwicke, and Harrington. It was a challenge that Newcastle from the beginning was particularly eager to accept.

Not until the late summer of 1744, however, did the duke's colleagues finally agree that the showdown was necessary, that either Carteret or they would have to go. Again it was an external force that redirected British politics and made *sauve qui peut* the most appropriate course of Pelhamite action. In August the remaining elements of Carteret's foreign policy disintegrated as Prussia, fearing Austria's ambitions for compensation, reentered the war. In self-defense the Austrians then recalled their British-financed army from France's frontier, and left the French force under Marshal Saxe free to menace Flanders. Worms had completed its devastation: a modicum of Austro-Sardinian co-operation had been bought at the cost of French and Prussian bel-ligerence, an exchange scarcely defensible in any rational court of judgment. Foreseeing parliamentary rage, Newcastle admonished his colleagues to deal decisively with Carteret before the new session began. He was not convinced that the Pelhams would emerge victori-ous, but even if they and not Carteret left the ministry, at least their humiliating treatment by the monarch would be at an end.

This strategic decision to end the coalition with the "new allies" forced two other tactical decisions upon the Pelhams. The first—whom to replace Carteret and his friends with—was easy. Only in the ranks of the opposition could sufficient force be found to compel the king to dispense with Carteret's services and to staff the new administration to the satisfaction of a parliamentary majority. Murray used his friend-ship with Bolingbroke to notify the opposition that the Pelhams were ready to break with Carteret and to urge that it direct its attacks against the northern secretary exclusively. By the decisive month of November the Pelhams had assurances of sufficient, though not univer-sal, opposition support. The second tactical decision—on what grounds to force the king—was more difficult. Newcastle had no doubts that wisdom recommended the candid approach: he would simply have explained to George that he and his friends could not work with so uncooperative a colleague as Carteret. But the others found personal grounds too dangerous and argued instead that the lever wherewith the king was to be forced ought to be a particularly contentious point of policy. The duke yielded to this argument.

Various policy disputes lay to hand. But the most spectacular of them—objections to Carteret's handling of Prussia or to what New-castle called Carteret's "Hanoverian complaisance"[38]—seemed likely to raise ancillary issues that might damage the Pelhams in the eyes of either the nation or the king. So the brothers decided to focus their criticism on Carteret's sufferance of Dutch inaction. It was less electrifying than the others but also less potentially embarrassing. At the request of the Pelhams Lord Hardwicke drafted a memorial in September which, while even more extensive in its indictment of Carteret than Newcastle's *Considerations* of the previous spring, focused major blame upon the failures of Carteret's Dutch policy. The need to act before Parliament met still obtained, and on the first day of November Newcastle initiated the campaign by presenting Hardwicke's memorial to the king, declaring orally that it represented the views of its drafter, the Pelhams, Harrington, Richmond, Devonshire, Dorset, Grafton, and others. The memorial called for British insistence upon a precise formula of Anglo-Dutch cooperation and hinted that if the Dutch remained stubbornly evasive Britain might find it necessary to withdraw from the war unilaterally. George II did not at once fathom the significance of the memorial or of Newcastle's verbal list of supporters, but private talks with his ministers during the following days persuaded him that the dissidents were prepared to resign if Carteret, recently heir to the earldom of Granville, were not relieved of responsibility.

Newcastle briefly hoped that something less than total exclusion—the lord presidency and a garter, perhaps—might suffice as punishment, but the opposition made clear that its support of the Pelhams at this juncture rested upon Granville's ouster from all offices. George II, meanwhile, sought for any expedient whereby to save his favorite, even offering assurances to the Pelhams that Granville would concur in any future proposal they might make. But this too was unacceptable. George was furious: not only was he being fettered, he was being asked to betray wartime allies just as Queen Anne had done. By soliciting Hardwicke to draft the speech from the throne, the unhappy monarch gave some satisfaction to the Pelhams and stalled a bit longer on the fundamental point. But he felt himself helpless, and Newcastle from the beginning had noted that his reactions—"sullenness, ill-humour, fear"—fostered "a disposition to acquiesce."[39] Confronted with the fearful possibility of a mass resignation, George II finally gave way. Granville was informed of the royal judgment, and on 24 November—a victim of bad policies, bad manners, and bad luck—the earl resigned the seals. The Pelhams were a major step nearer their goal.

IV

The rise in Newcastle's political fortunes had, unfortunately, not been paralleled by an increase in personal financial responsibility. As his reputation for squandering his patrimony spread throughout the land, he became the byword for the wealthy peer who, for want of "common sense and conduct," found himself strapped for funds.[40] It is useful to pause in our account at this triumphant moment in his career to examine the manner in which Newcastle handled his great inheritance. The story of his profligate expenditures remains a thoroughly sad one. The general election of 1734, for example, upon which the duke had expended so much energy, had also been the occasion for staggering financial outlays; Sussex alone had cost him at least £3,709. Furthermore, to broaden his already impressive influence in the county the duke throughout the 1730's moved to acquire, through purchase or lease, numerous houses in the crucial borough of Lewes and a variety of lands located in the neighborhood of Bishopstone.[41] For a man under obligation to confine his expenditures to limits imposed by a trust settlement and his official income, these were rash actions. It was a sign of the waning confidence others had in his ability to put his estate in order that as early as 1731, presumably at Henry Pelham's insistence, the duke was compelled to convey certain lands in Sussex to the duke of Rutland, Pelham's father-in-law, as security for Lady Katherine's £10,000 portion.[42] Clearly Newcastle was not felt to be a trustworthy custodian of the family resources.

Revenue figures for the entire Newcastle estate in 1734–35 show that since 1726, the last previous year for which complete statistics are also extant, there had been further reductions in his patrimony.[43] The lucrative Lincolnshire estate had been significantly diminished, and small increases in rental income elsewhere could not compensate for these losses. Since other evidence indicates that rent income would vary from year to year in each county, it would be inappropriate to build too elaborate an argument on figures that have survived by happenstance. But taken together they do suggest that the estate—or at least the revenues therefrom—continued to decline; what had produced £24,028 in 1726 could generate only £22,921 in 1735. Large portions of the income from the Newcastle estate were remitted to Hoare's bank, the administrator of the trust. Otherwise, the duke's two chief agents, Peter Forbes and Peter Walter, received most of the revenue and, insofar as possible, met current household expenses out of it. Theirs was, however, a losing struggle against ducal extravagance. The duke dabbled with thoughts of further self-regulation,[44] but he could not act on these impulses and matters ultimately began to get out of hand.

In 1737 the duke wanted to borrow £1,000 from his brother to cover recent purchases in Sussex. Pelham agreed to provide the necessary sum but at the same time delivered a withering and bitter rebuke to his elder brother. Why, he asked, did Newcastle "deceive" himself? The explanation for ducal difficulties, he continued, was not esoteric but simple: "You have spent more than your income." Pelham then proceeded to remind the duke that the loss of his office and its perquisites was always possible, and he alluded to the devastation such a change would visit upon the patrimony. He urged upon his brother a renewed commitment to austerity leading to a settlement of debts. Only then could Newcastle be what all hoped him to be: "A great, a fine and considerable support to your friends and country."[45] This was a warning. Sadly for the duke, he did not appreciate how truly his brother spoke. Where Pelham had called for economies, Newcastle pressed on with construction expenditures. This heedless rejection of fraternal advice shortly brought precisely the consequences that observers had long foreseen: by 1738, with the rental of the Newcastle estate down to £22,000, the duke was simply out of money, loaded with debts, lacking in any unencumbered lands wherewith to raise new money, and, therefore, financially paralyzed. It was then that creditors finally began imposing their own terms.

Hitherto the duke had abstained from borrowing from Hoare's, but in 1738 he had only the family bank to turn to. The firm agreed to lend Newcastle £22,000 on mortgages, but they insisted on the creation of a new trust, secure against ducal piracy, to assure that the remaining assets of the duke's holding be used to meet debts, not to support aristocratic tastes or political projects. Unlike the trust settlement of 1721, this one included the Sussex estates. The duke would receive £7,000 annually as an allowance, and the bank loan would help repay the massive debts Newcastle owed to Peter Walter, John Cooke, Colonel John Selwyn, and the new steward James Waller, who in 1738 replaced the ailing Peter Forbes. Lord Monson, Charles Monson, and the attorney Hutton Perkins, a Nottinghamshire friend of the duke's, were nominated as trustees, and in accordance with Duke John's will Henry Pelham stood as heir to his childless brother. Acknowledging that the calamity was a result of "my own follies," the duke was clearly submitting to dictated terms. He tried to have a provision included that would permit him to raise his allowance to £10,000 if he fell from office. He also wanted an escape clause inserted in the deed so that if he should still have a son he might bequeath the estate to him rather than to Pelham. Hoare's bank denied him permission for the former; Henry Pelham, in a kind gesture, allowed the latter.[46] Much now depended on the duke, for while the estate was to be administered by men who would in fact succeed in raising its rent revenues somewhat, the success or failure of the scheme rested ultimately on Newcastle's capacity for self-control.

That was surely a weak reed. Newcastle admitted that his "great load of debt" had been "imprudently & wrongly contracted,"[47] but within months of the creation of the trust the duke was arguing that, whatever the consequences for the policy of retrenchment, he could not part with—of all things—his pineapple trees at Claremont. And his entertaining maintained its princely standards. At one memorable Halland feast 96 tables were set, and the necessary provisions included 5 oxen, 39 sheep, 14 calves, 6 hogs, 300 fowl, 40 bushels of wheat, 480 pounds of butter, and appropriately large quantities of port, brandy, claret, Burgundy, Tokay, and beer to wash the meal down with.[48] It was as if the duke lived in a world apart from reality, and yet there may have been more to it than that. It is, for example, quite true that the duke was correct in what appears to have been his operating assumption, namely, that however critical his financial situation might become, friends and relatives, moved by compassion and self-interest, would intervene to protect him from the worst consequences of his own profligacy. He was, in short, immune to the usual social and legal punishments that heedless expenditure courted, and he appears to have known it. His rank, his office, and his prestige were collectively proof against the condemnation of society and impartial law. Others would not let him fall.

The settlement of 1738 was quickly vitiated by the duke's taste for a sumptuous style of life. But the tragic deaths in 1739 of both of Henry Pelham's sons, by altering the family's testamentary picture, compelled the duke's relatives to try yet again to devise a scheme that could bind him to a program of austerity. The barrenness of the duke's marriage and the demise of Pelham's male heirs left Lord Vane and Henry Vane, hitherto rather distant remainder-men in Duke John's will, in prospect of acquiring a significant inheritance. Still, as the Vanes reckoned, the inheritance, encumbered as it was, might be more burdensome than useful, and it did not at all appear to be imminent. They therefore proposed relinquishing their positions as remainder-men if they were paid £60,000 in return for this sacrifice. The duke was willing to break the entail, Henry Pelham offered no detectable opposition, and insofar as the numerous creditors were concerned, any action that made repayment likelier—and breaking the entail offered that hope—seemed obviously beneficial. Thus it was that in the fall of 1741 the fateful decision was finally made to deal with the debts in a new way, by the systematic alienation, through sale or mortgage, of the inherited lands.

Systematization was the key point. Until 1741 shrinkage in the New-castle estate had occurred haphazardly and piecemeal. Now, the entail broken, planning replaced chance. The duke provided his trustees— still the Monsons and Hutton Perkins—with a list of his debts, and they in turn began using the lands in Lincolnshire, Kent, Derbyshire, Dorset, Wiltshire, and Hertfordshire, collectively worth £9,315 per annum, to raise the money to provide the Vanes their £60,000 and to repay ducal debts. Some funds were raised through outright sales; others were acquired through mortgages and loans. Protection was afforded Henry Pelham and his heirs by a new settlement of the remainder of the duke's holdings. One part of the old Newcastle estate—Ifield, Duke John's only Sussex property—went directly to Henry Pelham. For the rest of the Newcastle estate the duke was life tenant. Provisions were included for the duchess's £3,000 annuity to be raised on the estate, and in the event the duke should remarry, he was to be permitted to settle a jointure of £2,000 on his second wife. Furthermore, the duke and Pelham were authorized, if necessary, to charge further debts up to £20,000 on the Nottinghamshire portion of the estate. The duke retained the right to revoke unilaterally the limitations to Pelham's daughters, and thereby to protect any future children of his own. If any disputes were to arise between the brothers, Lord Hardwicke was designated the appropriate adjudicator. The Sussex estate was limited to Henry Pelham for life, and certain lands were set aside to raise portions for his daughters. Various incumbrances on the estate—a part of the duchess's portion and some of the duke's debt—were transferred to the remaining Newcastle estate. At the last minute Pelham angered his brother by demanding and getting £10,000 for agreeing to the alienations. The duke even had to accept a reduction in his annual trust allowance to £6,500.[49] It was a mark of the duke's capacity to keep the different sectors of his life separate that the completion of this sweeping settlement exercised no discernible influence on his political behavior in late 1741. His personal life was not allowed to touch his public life.

But even that separation almost crumbled in 1744, at the very time that the Pelhams were mounting their climactic offensive against Granville. The immediate cause of fraternal altercation was the imminent marriage of Henry Pelham's eldest daughter, Katherine, to her first cousin, the earl of Lincoln, son of Henry Pelham's and Newcastle's sister Lucy. It was a marriage that the whole clan was pleased with, and Newcastle especially so. Katherine was his favorite niece, Lincoln his favorite nephew. After the death of Lincoln's father in 1728 the duke had undertaken the support of the young boy, had acquired the competent John Hume as his tutor, and had looked upon him and his mother as his two dearest blood relations. Lincoln had attended Clare Hall, gained a reputation as a drinker, and toured Europe in preparation for adulthood. His match with Katherine was certain to elicit from the duke whatever generosity straitened ducal circumstances still permitted. But therein lay the rub. The settlement of 1741 had not effected the desired ducal conversion to austerity. Newcastle remained a spendthrift, and his debts now stood at a truly remarkable £174,640.

The brothers did not quarrel over the amount that the duke was to give the new couple. All agreed that so singular and happy an occasion for the enhancement of family unity merited family generosity. From those portions of the Newcastle estate lying in Nottinghamshire, Yorkshire, and Middlesex the duke provided annuities for the newlyweds and assurances of future income for their children. Lord Lincoln was designated Newcastle's heir. The quarrel arose over Pelham's insistence that the duke now abandon his power of unilateral revocation. When this issue had caused discord in 1741, the younger brother had yielded. Now he would not. And the duke was vulnerable, for two recent events had severely compromised his cause. First, Hutton Perkins had carelessly promised that the duke would relinquish his unilateral authority. Then the duke himself had committed the fatal error of signing a preliminary paper vesting the power of revocation in himself and Pelham jointly. When William Murray and Lord Hardwicke advised the duke that the law would unquestionably support Pelham's position, the duke could not restrain his rage and bitterness. He threatened to break off all ties with his brother, and only Hardwicke's vigorous appeal to him to preserve the nation's welfare, couched in terms proving the lord chancellor's continued devotion to his friend, checked this ducal impulse. Still the duke permitted himself a final *cri de coeur*: "No man," he lamented in mid-October 1744, "ever was so hardly, so unkindly, so cruely [*sic*] used, as I am by my brother."[50]

V

In late 1744, as in early 1742, the opposition had proven sufficiently fearsome to drive a minister from office. But the two situations were otherwise dissimilar. At Walpole's fall George II had acted to protect the rest of his ministers; at Granville's he made clear his vindictive eagerness to turn out the Pelhams as soon as possible. Conversely, however, at Walpole's fall the opposition had been enemies of the Pelhams; now they were their allies. As a consequence of the altered foundations of the brothers' power, the Pelhams admitted many of Granville's foes to office, in fact, every leader of the opposition save Pitt. The "New Whigs" made way for the broad group which the Pelhams designated the "New Allies," and the "broad bottom" was at last realized. Chesterfield received the lord lieutenancy of Ireland; the duke of Bedford, who Richmond shrewdly predicted would bring "plague" upon Newcastle, took over the Admiralty, and other "New Allies" moved onto the Treasury and Admiralty Boards and into lesser offices. Walpole's policy of deliberately excluding talent was reversed: the dangerous politician, Hardwicke argued and Pelham certainly agreed, was less able and inclined to make trouble if given responsibility. Chesterfield even joined the small inner circle of those ministers who shaped national policy. Few were displeased with the settlement, and hence the new opposition was small. But since the king was among the unhappy, an extraordinary development ensued: George II became the first Hanoverian monarch to lead the opposition.

Three men, perhaps four, controlled policy. The most powerful ministers were still the Pelham brothers and their *alter ego* Hardwicke. It is Andrew Stone's role at this time that remains unclear. Many of his contemporaries believed Stone to be using his position as Newcastle's private secretary to exercise extraordinary influence over the duke; but precisely because he was an amanuensis, it is futile to try to verify this belief simply by the quantity of Newcastle papers written in Stone's hand. And of other types of documentary evidence of influence— position papers, memoranda, or drafts clearly prepared by Stone for Newcastle—there is very little. It is true that the chief ministers frequently held important meetings at his quarters, but it is necessary to guard against inferring simply from the convenience of Stone's lodgings that he was the power behind the seals. In fact, Newcastle is known at times to have disagreed with his friend, and the best indication that Stone's influence on the duke has been exaggerated is the lack of any significant change in Newcastle's policies or administrative capacities which can be associated with either the rise or the withdrawal of his private secretary. Stone was an influential figure but he was not a prime minister behind the curtain.

Newcastle feared that George II would hold him personally responsible for Granville's ouster and thus deny him that measure of confidence within the closet which gave extradepartmental authority to a minister. Against such royal disfavor the duke sought to guard, first by winning from the lord chancellor a promise of advocacy with the king, and then by suggesting that the brothers and Hardwicke confer on all measures prior to bringing them before the cabinet. On the parliamentary flank less protection was necessary. The reconstructed ministry found the legislature unusually docile: with almost all important critics of Granville's government now in office, and with the excluded Pitt smiling benignly on the administration, formerly contentious matters passed easily. Even a patent subterfuge whereby the unpopular Hanoverian subsidy was to be abandoned but an additional £200,000 given to Austria to hire the same troops failed to arouse the members. All agreed that the war could not be unilaterally suspended, and the new subsidy was construed as a token of the ministry's anti-Hanoverian good faith.

George II despised his new ministers. It was rumored that he planned to overturn the Pelhams before the spring of 1745, and he ostentatiously continued to seek out the advice of Granville. In the closet he was quarrelsome, threatening "to strike a strong stroke" against the Pelhams.[51] On foreign policy he consistently took issue with the brothers. He hampered their efforts to secure a firmer commitment from the Dutch, fearing that a wider Dutch war effort would cost the end of Hanoverian neutrality. After Charles VII's unexpected death he treated the secretaries' efforts to devise a satisfactory imperial policy as an intolerable interference in his own province. Under such conditions, the younger Horace Walpole found it impossible to determine the locus of power in the government: "It is plain," he explained, "that it resides not in the King: and yet he has enough to hinder anybody else from having it." Chesterfield chimed in with a disspiriting report from The

Hague: "Your situation is as well known out of England as in it, and has even worse effects abroad than at home. Some rejoyce at it, some lament it, but, to tell you the plain truth, most laugh at it."[52] And yet a war had to be prosecuted.

The early months of 1745 saw a continuation of Pelhamite war policy. Newcastle had driven Granville from office by adopting the nation's suspicious attitude toward any Hanoverian influence. These suspicions continued to guide his thinking during the first year of the broad bottom. He approved of the removal of the Hanoverian troops from the public accounts; he rejoiced at the creation of a Quadruple Alliance in January 1745, which promised greater Dutch assistance to the British, Austrian, and Sardinian efforts; and he saw in the necessity of choosing a new emperor a chance for Hanover to resurrect its friendship with the house of Habsburg. Adding conviction to the duke's optimism were several successes by Austria against Prussian troops. But in the spring Newcastle's reviving hopes suffered a series of checks. The Dutch proved quite unable to provide the desired number of troops, and private peace talks with France foundered. Then came Fontenoy, a French victory over the large allied army stationed in Flanders, and Hohenfriedburg, a Prussian triumph over the Austrians. Clearly, despite Newcastle's hopes, the old formula still held: the allies simply could not prevail against a Franco-Prussian combination.

By May 1745 Newcastle and Harrington had thus returned to the view that the duke and Carteret had first accepted in 1742, that Prussia had to be bought out of the war. Since Berlin and London were not at war with each other, the secretaries' decision again entailed, as the similar decision of three years earlier had, pressures on Vienna to renounce its claims to Silesia. As northern secretary, Harrington accepted command of this unpleasant but necessary campaign, and he journeyed to the continent with George during the summer to negotiate with the Prussians. The convention of Hanover, agreed upon in August, was Harrington's handiwork. Wrought against the king's will, in it Britain committed itself to work for an Austro-Prussian peace. Austria too expressed its anger at British meddling, but British diplomatic pressure and Prussian military force eventually combined to persuade the court of Vienna to accept Frederick II's terms. The Treaty of Dresden, concluded in December with Harrington's blessings, finally ended hostilities between the two great German powers. More durable than Breslau, Dresden brought peace to central Europe for a decade.

But while British diplomacy was ending war in Germany in 1745,

Britain itself finally became a battleground. Anti-Hanoverianism had been a pernicious doctrine for politicians to be mouthing so glibly. It probably did not drive many people to embrace the Stuart cause, but it certainly cost George II the active support of a significant proportion of his subjects. The Jacobites by 1745 believed that a nation weary of war and royal insults might accept the dynasty it had not rallied to thirty years earlier. Various French leaders, hoping to disrupt the British government, lent considerable support to Stuart plans. In late June 1745 the Young Pretender landed in Scotland, the bastion of Jacobitism, and soon attracted highlanders by the thousands to his standard. The ministry was not tardy in perceiving the danger, but the surprising depth of anti-Hanoverian feeling showed itself in the refusal of many responsible figures to acknowledge that a threat impended or even that the Young Pretender had truly reached the British Isles. The king further complicated the ministry's task by remaining abroad and declaring the rebellion to be a farce. Granville agreed, advising the monarch that there was no need to bring troops home from the continent. The opposition, with its anomalous royal leader, virtually paralyzed the ministry's efforts to alert and defend the kingdom.

Newcastle was the most alarmed of the ministers. In September he wrote that George's crown was in "the utmost danger."[53] He feared less a Stuart triumph, however, than a French invasion. The Jacobites had brought a two-front war to Britain. If the ministry sent its forces northward to engage the Young Pretender's army, it risked leaving the south coast unprotected against a French intrusion. But Jacobite successes in the North, especially the September victory at Prestonpans, suggested that without reinforcements the loyalists would not be able to resist the Stuart troops. The ministry therefore summoned back from Flanders the British contingent there; it requested and received military assistance from the Dutch; it called out various militias; and it placed the king's younger son, the duke of Cumberland, in command of the loyalist forces. In exposed Sussex an ad hoc association created a fund to pay the militia, and each Pelham brother pledged £500 to the cause.[54] From complacency, the popular mood after Prestonpans swung madly toward concern and even despair. Wildly improbable rumors won believers. One report had the Pelhams joining the Pretender. Another had Newcastle fleeing London, and was discredited only when the duke appeared before the curious who had gathered around Newcastle House. A third had the French landing at Hastings or Pevensey.[55] The duke of Richmond, commanding troops in the North, contributed to Newcastle's uneasiness with hysterical appeals for reinforcements, "be they Hessians, Hanoverians, or devils, if they will butt fight for us."[56] Not until late December, when the rebel army had begun its retreat northward from Derby, did the fears subside: London, it finally appeared, would fall to neither Stuart nor Bourbon.

Among the burdens the ministry had had to bear during the tense autumn was George II after his return from Europe. "The closet," Newcastle told Richmond, "grows worse than ever. We are now come to bad language; *Incapacity* to my Brother, Spectator of other people's policy and measures, and yesterday *Pitifull Fellows*." The Pelhams thought often of resignation: "It will," the duke assured Hardwicke, "be the most honourable and happiest day for us that has passed a great while."[57] But the obligations of office in time of internal war made immediate resignation impossible, and so the brothers turned their attention toward winning back some of the support in the Commons which the debacles of the summer had cost them. In November the Cobhamites were approached, and at an amicable meeting Newcastle and Pitt talked foreign policy. The conversation revealed in all its starkness the differences between Newcastle's ambitious hopes and Pitt's restraint. The duke suspected that little benefit would follow from the exchange. He was thus surprised when, in early January, with the Jacobite threat past, the Cobhamites declared a readiness to support the ministry largely on the ministry's terms. The Cobhamites' already modest demands became even more so when George II again blocked his ministers and vetoed Pitt's appointment as secretary at war.

The veto brought the approaching crisis to a head. The ministers could endure no more from the king. The rejection of Pitt showed that, with the Scottish emergency abating, the quarrels in the closet would revive. Indeed, Lord Bath at this time reemerged to urge the king to new heights of stubbornness. Thus, the ministers recalled their oft-considered resolve to expose the king's political weakness through a mass resignation. The plan was worked out in detail on 9 February 1746. On 10 February Harrington and Newcastle resigned their offices. On the next day Pelham, Bedford, and three others did the same. Hardwicke stated that he would retire with the imminent end of the law term, and Chesterfield wrote from Ireland that he would join the parade. In all, about forty-five members of the administration declared their readiness to act with the ministry. It was an extraordinary, unprecedented spectacle. The king's government ground abruptly to a halt—"like the sun stopping in his course at noonday"—and Bath and Granville, to whom the monarch turned for support, were unable to find enough "adventurous" men to fill even the most attractive offices of state. Simultaneously, in fear that the moderate Henry Pelham would no longer command the Treasury, the moneyed interests in the City registered their disapproval of the prospective Bath–Granville government with a massive run on the Bank and the withdrawal of a subscription of £3,000,000. On 12 February the king accepted defeat, and the next day the ministers began returning to office.[58] As no Hanoverian king before or after him, George II had been humbled in a dramatic display of the fundamental weakness of the Crown in eighteenth-century Britain.

The cause of this strange affair had been the king's refusal to give "grace" to the government, to behave as if all ministerial decisions came from him. The ministers had acted when they did because the Jacobite threat had receded and George had not yet secured the independence which parliamentary approval of the basic financial legislation of the year would soon give him. Upon their return to office the ministers demanded and received concessions from the king: the granting of public marks of favor to them, support for their foreign policy, honorable employment for Pitt, and the removal from office of a designated group of men whose loyalty to the Old Corps was suspect. In the light of the treatment he was receiving, George II remained remarkably goodtempered through it all. Only toward Harrington, whose resignation seemed for reasons of old friendship more culpable to the monarch, did he express bitterness. At Newcastle's tearful leave-taking the unpredictable king had even been "very civil, kind enough; and we parted very good friends."[59] The duke had not been surprised that Bath and Granville could not gain the requisite support in the kingdom to build a viable government. Hardwicke put their problem succinctly: "The public voice of the court, city and country united was too strong."[60]

Although clearly a politically inspired action, the mass resignation was nevertheless also principled behavior consistent with Newcastle's political philosophy. "Philosophy" may, it is true, be too dignified a word for the duke's political ideas. As the product of a mind disinclined to engage in abstract or systematic thinking—of a mind, moreover, totally wanting in originality—this philosophy was thoroughly undistinguished. But precisely because it was not novel and was in fact shared by most Whig grandees at mid-century, it has importance for the understanding of the period in which it fructified. It was the new Whiggery, the Whiggery of officeholding, the political philosophy of Shaftesbury as transmuted by Wharton, regulated by Walpole, and distilled by Hardwicke and Newcastle. It incorporated Shaftesbury's aristocratic prejudices, Wharton's love of liberty, Walpole's distrust of democracy, and the Pelhams' emphasis on management. Its most notorious manifestation was the contradictory policy, espoused by almost all Whig politicians of the day, of expressing aversion to forcing the Crown while being at the same time quite ready to employ techniques to that very end. But the inconsistency was more apparent than real. It was simply a natural consequence of the altered position of the Whigs themselves: no longer critics of government, they were now its practitioners and masters.

Newcastle's legacy from earlier Whiggery may be reduced to two principles: that the king should be controlled, and that the landed class—the peerage especially—provided the kingdom's natural leaders. The complementarity of these two principles had been evident in 1688–89, when the landed class had imposed the ultimate sanction on a king who sought to strip them of their local and national authority. But once Whigs had begun accepting places under William III they had found their political program, rooted as it was in resistance to royal authority, becoming highly awkward. Thus they began adapting a doctrine born of opposition to the exigencies of officeholding. By Newcastle's time the difficult transformation had been completed. The duke consequently distinguished, and this is the key to eighteenth-century Whiggery, between the king and the Crown. The former was an individual, prey as all men are to weaknesses of body and spirit. Hence, whoever he was—and Newcastle would serve three different monarchs—he had to be controlled and guided so that neither his ambitions nor his whims could harm the kingdom. "If kings would have their own way," the duke wrote late in his life, ". . . they must be made to feel."[61] The proper body for asserting this control was the ministry, composed chiefly of members of the landed class, "without the preserving of which," Newcastle is recorded as remarking in 1732, "neither our trade nor our constitution could long subsist."[62] But if the king was frail flesh, the Crown as an institution was stable and durable, one of the essential parts of Britain's exquisitely well-balanced constitution. It was

already sufficiently checked by a rival institution, the Parliament.
Hence the Crown should not be further weakened, for a diminution of
its power would upset the constitutional equilibrium. It was, in short,
with respect to the person of the monarch, not the might of the monarchy, that Newcastle stood in the Whig tradition: he would control the
king, not the Crown, and the agency of control would necessarily be the
ministry, not the Parliament.

As a result of these views Newcastle was actually sympathetic to the
prerogative, but only, of course, as exercised by a king who followed
ministerial advice. He expressed this sympathy when he declared in the
House of Lords that "that monarch will be certainly and most permanently popular, who steadily pursues the good of his people, even in
opposition to their own prejudices and clamours." One consequence of
this sympathy for the prerogative was the duke's hostility toward the
claims of the House of Commons. He expressed his refusal to counte-
nance any expansion of the authority of that chamber in 1740: "It might
be for the service of the kingdom that the Lords' jurisdiction be extended; but give no more to the Commons." Years earlier he had
explained that an augmentation of the power of the Commons "would
entirely overturn that balance upon which our constitution depends."[63]
The duke retained as his chaplain during the 1740's the writer Samuel
Squire, noted chiefly for his belief that the Commons was becoming too
powerful and thus raising for Britain the spectre of Polish or Swedish
anarchy. And throughout his own career, whether in snubbing the
ambitions of the Commons in 1754 or in defending the American colonists against George Grenville's extravagant claims of parliamentary
authority in the 1760's, the duke acted on the principle that the power,
the prestige, and the pretensions of the House of Commons should not
be further enhanced.

Another consequence of Newcastle's sympathy for the prerogative
was his readiness to override civil liberties. His willingness to proceed
against an unruly press, visible early in his career, remained characteristic of him even in his final years of opposition. During his years as
secretary of state Newcastle made uncommonly frequent use of general
warrants, the most controversial tool of governmental repression that
still lay, albeit uneasily, within the bounds of legality. Civil order, as
enforced by authority, was the prerequisite of freedom. If authority
weakened, he wrote late in his career, "we must either be governed
by a mad lawless mob, or the peace be preserved only by a military

force; both of which are unknown to our constitution."[64] Thus, while in ordinary times the duke esteemed the British requirement that guilt be ascertained only in regularized judicial proceedings, in times of crisis he was prepared to abandon civil liberties entirely: "It is better," he remarked during the Jacobite uprising of 1715, "a few should suffer for some Days, than that the whole Nation should undergo the dreadful Calamities and Judgments which hang over our Heads."[65]

Over this point, however, a potentially difficult question arose for the new Whiggery. If the ministry controlled the king, who controlled the ministry? In practice Newcastle, for so long a holder of office, was not anxious to have the ministry's power delimited, and he did not address himself specifically to this problem in his writings. But his actions speak where his pen was silent, and his line of thinking can indeed be reconstructed. As a minister he knew full well that his freedom of action was in fact circumscribed by three concentric rings of authority. The innermost ring was the Parliament, especially the House of Commons. To flout its will systematically was to invite a breakdown in orderly government. The second ring was the electorate. Voters' displeasure with a tyrannical ministry or a meek Parliament could find expression at intervals frequent enough to encourage ministerial caution. The outermost ring, generally the most lethargic but also, if aroused, the most invincible, was public opinion. When the attention of the nation focused on a single grievance, as it had done with the Excise Bill of 1733 and would again with the Jewish Naturalization Bill of 1753, nothing could stand before it. The Commons would submit, the electorate would bow, and the ministry would retreat. No other Hanoverian politician was as alert to the currents of public opinion and as ready to go along with them as Newcastle; it was both his strength and his weakness, though probably more the latter. This peculiar sensitivity to the public mood helps to explain in part his remarkable durability.

Was the ministry then a slave to these concentric rings of circumscribing authority? Clearly, as the duke knew, it was not; for if it was the Parliament, the electorate, and public opinion that set the limits of the possible—limits which the wisdom of the landed class was most apt to see—it was the ministry alone that had techniques for manipulating these forces within those limits. Parliament was receptive to guidance through patronage, and the Pelhams became famous as "managers" of the Commons, using the appointive powers lodged in the Crown, the Treasury, the Admiralty, and their political associates to help ensure the friendliness of the House of Commons in all but the greatest crises. Ministerial control over the episcopal bench made the House of Lords compliant. The electorate too could be reached and altered, and by generally favoring a broad interpretation of the county franchise and a narrow interpretation of borough franchises, Newcastle worked systematically in each case for the creation of that type of electorate which would prove most amenable to ministerial direction.[66] Even public opinion could be guided by appropriate journalistic propaganda, but because this was less certain, Newcastle espoused the thoroughly cautious dictum that any measure likely to enflame the mob should simply be avoided. Ministerial freedom was thus vaguely confined, but such ministerial self-restraint was far preferable to provoking the irrational illiterates of the kingdom to some unfortunate action.

An integrated though crude political philosophy can thus be inferred from the duke's words and actions. Governing authority and considerable discretion on policy decisions lay with the Crown, but the reigning monarch was in turn to be clearly and unequivocally controlled by the ministers. Three watchdogs guarded against ministerial misuse of authority: the Parliament, the electorate, and public opinion. Ministers were to be chosen by the Crown, but they were not merely tools of the king. They were, instead, his guides, valuable for the political wisdom which land and leisure allowed them to cultivate and for their ability to make Parliament compliant. George II by early 1746 had worked stubbornly for over a year to subvert the system, "clogging and hampering" and complaining all the while that he was "in slavery."[67] The Pelhams had ceaselessly replied that they were not fettering their master, and in a final explosion of exasperation they resigned and thereby showed the hapless king what true impotence was. To the twentieth-century mind the Pelhamite contention seems disingenuous and the action self-serving. Still, within the framework of Whig thinking it can be maintained that the ministers were seeking merely to make the Crown's freedom operable: if the king was in toils, and obviously he was, the blame rested not with his ministers but with the constitution. The ministry's task was to advise as to what was possible. Often everything possible was distasteful to the monarch. But the ministry did not create the limits of the possible. It was the source of the king's feeling of captivity only in the same sense that a doctor who prescribes a painful operation is the author of the patient's misery.

VI

Never before in Hanoverian Britain had the relations between the king and his ministry been so strained as in February 1746. The Pelhams had demonstrated to the monarch that he could not do without them, but whether he would now graciously accept them or petulantly nurse his injured pride remained a point on which objective viewers could not be sanguine. Yet the pessimists proved wrong: within three months the Crown and the ministry were enjoying amicable relations reminiscent of Carteret's in his heyday. This remarkable reversal in the quality of the association between a stubborn king and an ambitious ministry had two sources. First, there was the king's changed political outlook; in a word, he grew up. He decided to accept political reality and to use rather than harass the two brothers whose influence in Parliament made them indispensable. Had the kingdom been at peace and thus better able to endure an extended quarrel between the Crown and the ministers, it is possible that George II might have resumed the struggle and, even as his grandson would in 1782–84, have ultimately prevailed. Certainly the deeply implanted tendency of most Britons to support their monarch was a weapon that, given the luxury of time, might have let an unhappy king shed an unwanted ministry. But George II did not have time and chose to eschew hopeless troublemaking; the days of a royally led opposition were over.

But still more important as a source of peace at the top was a convergence of foreign policy views between Newcastle and the king. Newcastle's accomodation at this point is famous and even notorious, for having used an expressed hostility to excessive Hanoverianism as a means to rout Granville and frustrate George, the duke suddenly seemed to adopt the very platform he had so long been an assailant of. The change in the duke's views, hinted at in February and evident by May, needs explaining. Quite obviously a major element in the shift was the duke's calculation that the likeliest path to better personal relations with the king was the adoption of views consonant with royal ones. But there was more to the change than mere self-service. By 1746 Prussia had left the war, radically altering, it was believed, the situation in Europe. Contending against a combined France and Prussia had been fatuous, and in disapproving of measures to widen such a war Newcastle had been reasonable. Contending against France alone, however, promised to be less futile, and if few in Britain thought France could be humbled, many in early 1746 believed that more obliging terms at least could be won. Moreover, the withdrawal of Prussia made Newcastle's cardinal principle, the need to retain Austria's friendship, more compatible with George's, the need to protect Hanover. Hitherto, George had feared that major Hanoverian participation in an allied campaign against Prussia would invite Frederick II's mighty legions to devastate the Hanoverian plain. Thus, despite anguished pleas from Vienna, he had persisted in curtailing the electorate's military efforts. Henceforth, however, with the Prussian threat much diminished, Hanover's security was best served by continued attempts to drive France from the southern Netherlands, a policy which neatly complemented Austria's desire to fight on until compensation for Silesia had been won in Italy. By mid-1746 king and secretary found themselves in basic agreement.

This rapprochement added the support of the Crown to all the other foundations of power that the Pelhams had been cultivating. For the first time since the days of Sir Robert Walpole a ministry enjoyed large measures of both royal approbation and parliamentary support. In a sense, the combination was unstable, for the king wanted a widened war effort while the Parliament, or at least many from the "Old Corps" and the "New Allies" alike, wanted a reduced one. But this divergence was not immediately damaging, for the major theatre of the war was now the Low Countries, and however unrelated to British security the campaigns in Germany might have seemed, campaigns against French encroachments in Flanders were demonstrably in the national interest.

The Pelhams had at last reached the heart of power, much of it exercised by Newcastle.[68] His authority extended from diplomatic and military to Scottish and ecclesiastical affairs. He determined the foreign policy of the kingdom, serving in effect as both foreign and defense secretary. All major diplomatic and military decisions were henceforth made either by the duke or with his concurrence. He reassumed the direction of Scottish affairs, suppressing in 1746 the Scottish secretaryship set up in 1742 and taking over its business. His real interest in the northern kingdom remained scant, but for two reasons he dared not ignore the Scots. First, to a man bent on acquiring power, control over Scottish patronage was not a prize to be scorned. Moreover, insofar as Jacobitism posed a threat to British security, either as opposition to Hanoverian rule or as an excuse for a French invasion, Scotland needed surveillance. On the need to reduce the power of the highland clans and hence to limit France's capacity to meddle in British affairs Newcastle was unyielding: "This, I think," he wrote to Cumberland, "is the great Point, which every servant of the King ought to have first in view."[69] For this reason primarily the duke lent an unsympathetic ear to Duncan Forbes's suggestion that the crown declare a general pardon for rebels. On matters of ecclesiastical patronage he was equally strong. In 1747, on the death of the lacklustre Archbishop Potter, Newcastle offered the primary to the ailing Edmund Gibson, whose energetic advocacy of the Hanoverian cause during the recent rebellion had won the duke's gratitude and effaced memories of former quarrels. But age prevented the bishop of London from accepting, and so the duke raised instead Hardwicke's friend Thomas Herring, one of the organizers of the defenses of the North against the Pretender's son. When Gibson finally died a year later, Newcastle single-handedly translated the trusted Thomas Sherlock from Salisbury to London. Since the younger Pelham, through his control of the Treasury, also exercised wide patronage power, only the area of military appointments—the preserve of the king—lay outside Pelhamite control. The brothers were a truly formidable political force.

The preeminent demonstration of their power occurred in the early summer of 1747 when they won an overwhelming victory in a general election they unexpectedly called. Acting to forestall an effort by the Prince of Wales, recently a convert to opposition, to establish a numerically powerful following in the Commons, the brothers decided to hold the election a year prematurely. "The nation is now in good humour," the duke explained to Lord Irwin, "no incident has yet happened to make them otherwise, since the happy extinction of the rebellion; and therefore I verily think we cannot now fail of getting a good Whig parliament."[70] Frederick was caught thoroughly off guard, but even extensive preparations could not have staved off a ministerial triumph of major proportions. So confident was the government of success that it did not even follow the practice of asking officers to send troops home to vote as in 1741. Pelham directed the apparatus of treasury patronage with his wonted shrewdness, and Newcastle personally accounted for the customary fifteen members.[71]

The major complication for the duke in the campaign was the large number of new faces he had to deal with. At Aldborough in 1743 John Jewkes had died, and Newcastle had brought in his Sussex neighbor, the dissenting merchant Nathaniel Newnham. Newnham was reelected in 1747. Death had removed both members for Boroughbridge since 1741, and Newcastle now had the invaluable William Murray and Lord Dalkeith, chosen in the interval at by-elections, sent back to the Commons. At the country level in Sussex Newcastle dropped Lord Middlesex, who had followed the prince into opposition, and replaced him with John Butler. Butler and his running mate, the invincible Henry Pelham, won unopposed. The poll at Hastings was similarly uneventful: James Pelham and Andrew Stone triumphed without opposition. At Lewes and Seaford, however, problems arose. Both members for Lewes had died in 1743. Newcastle had chosen Sir Frances Poole, a cousin by marriage, and Sir John Shelley, his own brother-in-law, as replacements. But Shelley soon discredited himself by homosexual activities and was abandoned by the duke. Without any obvious candidate then and not unwilling to save some money, Newcastle finally struck the compromise that the persistent Thomas Sergison had long urged on him. Thus, Lewes returned Poole and Sergison in 1747, and even though Sergison usually voted with the government, the result should probably be interpreted as a diminution of ducal influence in the borough. At Seaford the duke preserved his authority and demonstrated the weakness of the Gages with an illegal but striking performance. William Hall Gage had replaced his deceased father in 1744, but he too had joined Frederick's forces and thereby earned the duke's enmity. Newcastle put up the veteran William Hay and the rising William Pitt in 1747; Gage and Lord Middlesex opposed them. On polling day, in contravention of statutes prohibiting peers from interfering in elections for the Commons, Newcastle sat at the returning officer's desk, his presence in an era of open voting intimidating many who might otherwise have preferred the opposition slate. Hay and Pitt won.

In Nottinghamshire some confusion prevailed. To be sure, Newark and East Retford posed no problems. The former returned Lord William Manners and Job Staunton Charlton; the latter reelected John White. At the county level the duke actually added to his authority, for, having bought the support of the Levinz family with a post in the customs, he was able to have two Whigs chosen from Nottinghamshire, Lord Robert Sutton and John Thornhagh. But in the borough of Nottingham ducal signals got crossed in a year in which a powerful new political force emerged, and as a consequence a humiliated Newcastle saw his candidate, John Plumptre, withdraw even before the polling day. The mix-up began when on the death of the Tory member early in 1747 the Whig corporation chose to violate the electoral compromise presumably governing Nottingham elections and to run its own candidate, Lord Howe, then serving in Flanders. Howe's Tory opponent, Sir Charles Sedley, won the by-election, but at the general election the corporation invited Howe to stand with Plumptre. Though he had not been involved in these machinations, Newcastle was quickly caught in a cross fire of criticism. To accusations by the Tories that he connived at a covert violation of the compromise he responded with vigorous denials; but these in turn only earned him the wrath of the Whiggish corporation. Perhaps all these liabilities could have been surmounted, but as it grew obvious that the town's new banker and political force, the ambitious Abel Smith, would not support Plumptre, the cause came to appear hopeless. Plumptre's withdrawal saved him money and since it assured Howe's election did not cost the government a vote; but it showed too that even closed boroughs could successfully rebel.

The picture on the national level was cheering for the brothers. The Whigs held more seats than in any parliament since the Hanoverian accession, the Tories fewer. It is true that some of the Whigs were with the opposition, but the ministry still had a working majority of about 125. Such regions as Scotland and Cornwall, whose loss had so hurt Walpole in 1741, now reverted to their custom of returning largely loyalist Whig contingents. "Places where friends to the Government were never chosen before," Newcastle related to Cumberland, "are now the foremost in their demonstrations of duty and loyalty to the king . . . even the city of London."[72] The results showed that the nation was not yet out of patience with the war. They also demonstrated how successful a government could be when it was not forced into elections at inauspicious moments but instead could choose its own time and terms for a contest at the polls. Above all, and this was their most important meaning, they ratified the Pelhamite hegemony.

During the early years of that hegemony the ministry's fundamental task was to secure peace. It was a vexing task, for although it might have been possible to conclude a bilateral peace with France, Newcastle found this doubly objectionable. Not only would it require Britain's negotiating from a decided military disadvantage but it would also entail the certain loss of the Dutch and Austrian alliances in the postwar years. France was currently beseiging and conquering the barrier fortresses in the Low Countries. Marshal Saxe had thus far proved invincible, and the day seemed not far off when French armies would be confronting a totally defenseless Dutch republic. This advance threatened British security as well as Dutch, but the two allies had different plans in mind for checking it. Newcastle wanted to put a larger army in the field, administer some defeats to the French, and then treat under more propitious circumstances. The Dutch, however, had an alternative solution designed to spare the blood of another campaign. They urged Britain to swap its only conquest of the war, the strategic Cape Breton peninsula taken in 1745 by a group of American colonists, for a French withdrawal from the Low Countries. The scheme was simple, but both Pelhams deemed it politically unwise. Six and a half years of war had brought only that one trophy, and the nation would not gladly suffer it to be abandoned. Shaped by such considerations, Newcastle's position on the war emerged in early 1746: a reasonable, honorable, and tolerable peace was possible only if Britain acted militarily to end France's dominance. Britain dared not approach the peace table until it had swept a few battlefields.[73]

In light of its military successes France was surprisingly anxious to reach terms too, and in March 1746, as a consequence of Franco-Dutch talks, the marquis d'Argenson submitted some peace proposals to Britain. The peace faction within the ministry—Pelham, Harrington, and Chesterfield—believed them an acceptable basis for negotiations, but Newcastle demurred: the proposals required the abandonment of Cape Breton and the desertion of the Austrians. After lengthy debate the duke prevailed, the first obvious sign that his views were shifting toward the king's, and on the crucial issue of whether to give Britain's diplomat to The Hague full powers to treat on these proposals it was decided that the powers should be withheld. Meanwhile, in the hope of winning further negotiating advantages, plans were elaborated for a new attack on Canada. Weather and inefficiency delayed the attack force until its departure became impossible, and so only in late summer was it dispatched by Newcastle on an ineffective raid on the French coast. But even its failure served the politically useful purpose of yoking Bedford and Pitt together in cooperation with the elder Pelham.

The Dutch resented Britain's reluctance to negotiate, and some in Britain feared that they would treat with France bilaterally. Hence, when the French invited Britain to send a negotiator to Breda, where they and the Dutch still planned to hold talks, Newcastle accepted. It was a calculated move, for neither Newcastle nor the king really sought a prompt end to hostilities. But British participation served to soothe Dutch rancor, and since France had declared its intention of keeping Spain informed of events at Breda, Britain could usefully seize the opportunity to initiate negotiations under terms which could not fairly exclude Austria at a later time. To make doubly sure, Newcastle passed over Pelham's recommendation for the man to handle the Breda negotiations and chose instead the young earl of Sandwich, whose seat on the Admiralty Board and friendship with Bedford made him sound on Cape Breton and whose youth would conveniently justify the withholding of full powers. Sandwich embarked with temperate instructions from Harrington, his nominal superior, but from Newcastle he had received secret, less conciliatory ones. More remarkably, he was authorized to correspond in private with the duke and to treat commands from Newcastle's office as superseding those from Harrington's. It was a wretched way to treat a colleague who had often helped the Pelhams, but Newcastle had become alarmed at the northern secretary's unseasonable pacifism and believed that in serving his own interests he was serving the kingdom's as well.

Sandwich's chief task at Breda was to delay. Inasmuch as the Dutch could be kept happy only by continued prospects of peace while the British believed that a peace too soon would be a bad one, Sandwich had no choice but to seek to provoke delay. Newcastle meanwhile turned his attention to several expedients whereby France might be weakened and the delay turned to advantage. One was to capitalize on the timely death of Philip V of Spain by seeking to draw his less Francophile successor, Ferdinand VI, away from the Bourbon family compact. Talks to this end involving the experienced Benjamin Keene were held in Lisbon, while at Breda Sandwich also courted the Spanish. But by early 1747 the effort had apparently failed. A second expedient, borrowed from Marlborough's day, was to use Austrian and Sardinian troops, recently victorious in an Italian campaign, in an attack on Provence. For a while Newcastle had magnificent hopes for this enterprise, but it too foundered, on the enduring rocks of Austro-Sardinian suspicions and Genoese rebellion.

Before these disappointments of the new year showed the failure of Newcastle's policy, however, the quarrel between the two secretaries came to a head. Harrington was outspokenly unhappy over his situation throughout the early fall. He received reproaches in the closet from a monarch who despised him for having led the parade of resignations the previous February. He found his advice ignored. And he soon learned the humiliating truth that his colleague was secretly corresponding with Sandwich. Threats of quitting office came readily to Harrington's lips in these weeks, and thus Newcastle was not unprepared when Harrington resigned the seals. He and George II jointly considered the problem of finding a successor, and both seem to have arrived independently at Lord Chesterfield's name. The decision to appoint the lord lieutenant was made without consulting anyone else, even Hardwicke and Pelham; it constitutes one of the most striking proofs of Newcastle's enhanced authority. Pelhamite mercy saved Harrington from outer darkness, and he received the vacant Irish post, a position requiring little contact with the king. To many observers the selection of Chesterfield was perplexing. The earl had not tried to hide his growing conviction that the war was unwinnable and should be ended as quickly as possible. He thus seemed a strange figure to place in harness with the ebullient and still bellicose Newcastle. But he was, of course, qualified, with diplomatic experience at The Hague, and as he later acknowledged, he was indeed briefly of the view that France was demanding unrealistic terms at that time and could not yet be submitted to. He thus began a short and unhappy tenure as Newcastle's colleague.

Sandwich's behavior at Breda delighted Newcastle, but in the absence of military or diplomatic triumphs which could justify the delay, the earl's undoubted success at prolonging negotiations was an empty one. By the early months of 1747 Newcastle felt himself to be contending alone for a greater war effort. To the duke of Cumberland, now the commander of the allied troops in Flanders, Newcastle lamented: "How mortifying it is to me, to hear, every day, the prophecies of those fulfilled, who, I thought, were prejudiced by their passions and views; and to see those measures, which were most sincerely and honestly advised, blamed and traduced, as wild, ignorant, and calculated for selfish ends."[74] The duke now had an additional friend on whom he could rely personally to some extent, his new amanuensis Hugh Valence Jones. But Jones, a nephew of Hardwicke's, was not of the stamp of Stone. Faithful and diligent, and rewarded for his diligence, he was simply a copyist. The duke trusted him but did not seek his advice. Jones thus provided service but no significant moral support. For it Newcastle looked to the king, for while the duke's colleagues advocated steps toward peace, the secretary and the monarch remained stubbornly persuaded that, whatever the difficulties of the past years, their basic strategy—deferring peace until Britain had more trophies to display—was wise. But it promised also be to costly, and even with the Dutch pledges which Sandwich won in January, the burden would fall basically upon Britain.

Just when all seemed darkest for the beleaguered duke, a revolution in the United Provinces replaced the pacific republicans with the more bellicose partisans of the house of Orange. One by one in late April and early May of 1747 each of the seven provinces chose William IV, son-in-law to George II, as stadholder; and the young man, having risen to power in a fashion astonishingly reminiscent of that of 1672, hoped further to emulate William III by revivifying the Dutch nation and driving out the French menace. At this single stroke the nascent peace movement within the British ministry collapsed. Sandwich, who had long been in contact with the chief Orangist advisers, the brothers Bentinck, received Newcastle's commendation: "Your lordship's ministry in The Hague will always be remembered with gratitude and respect."[75] Some observers have inferred from this statement that British funds helped finance the revolution, but despite the obvious convenience for Newcastle of the change in Dutch policy, it seems unlikely that such aid was actually supplied. No evidence of British complicity has ever been discovered, and there is no indication that Newcastle, though noted for his incautious tongue, ever bragged about alleged accomplishments in the Dutch revolution.

Whatever the case, the passage of time slowly showed that the miracle of 1672 could not entirely be duplicated. William IV had neither the capacity nor the energy of his famed ancestor, the republicans retained important offices and hence influence, and, to put it briefly, the Dutch nation was simply exhausted. The change in leadership effected a short-lived improvement in morale, but could not produce troops and money out of thin air. Thus, the succession of French conquests on the barrier continued unabated. Fortunately for the allies, however, France was, for less visible reasons, also uneasy at the prospect of an interminable war. Versailles had broken off the discussions at Breda after the Dutch revolution, but was soon eager to renew them. At Laffeld in July 1747 Saxe's army scored another victory, and the marshal conveniently used his distinguished prisoner, Sir John Ligonier, to dispatch a peace proposal directly to Britain. Saxe hoped that he and Cumberland would be empowered to conclude a treaty on the spot.

Pelham and Chesterfield liked the idea, but Newcastle was suspicious and William IV thoroughly hostile. By proposing that the maritime powers hire some Russian troops, the prince of Orange suggested a method to circumvent current difficulties in putting an army in the field, and so Newcastle again decided to gamble on a favorable turn in allied military fortunes. Saxe's strange proposal was in effect rejected, and Sandwich was returned to the continent to represent Britain in one more conventional and languid set of negotiations.

But by the fall of 1747 the detectable signs all suggested that Newcastle had again been too optimistic. In September the mighty fortress of Bergen-op-Zoom, one of the two military gateways to the United Provinces, fell to the French. The Dutch reacted to the calamity in a manner that Newcastle found puzzling. Rather than whipping the republic on to more valiant efforts, the conquest merely confirmed the Dutch in their odd policy of remaining technically at peace with France. A declaration of war, they argued, might provoke France to further aggressions, and technical peace had at least the virtue of legitimizing the prosperous Franco-Dutch trade. Such reasoning understandably baffled Newcastle, and thus he was further discomfited when this ally who was refusing to forego the profits of commerce sought a broader troop commitment from Britain. "The present conduct of the Stadholder," he confessed, "is to me incomprehensible."[76]

Simultaneously Newcastle's isolation in the ministry was again growing. Pelham was so furious with his brother that frequently they could communicate only through Andrew Stone.[77] Bedford, whose attachment to Cape Breton had hitherto made him an ally of Newcastle's, now realized the impossibility of retaining that conquest and swung over to the pacific side of the ministry. Even Hardwicke, Newcastle's closest friend, was despairing of a strategy which required that serious negotiations wait upon an apparently unattainable military victory. But the unhappiest minister was Chesterfield, reduced by his reawakened pacifism to the role of "commis" for Newcastle. His grievances were like Harrington's: his advice was ignored by a militant monarch, and his department invaded by an aggrandizing colleague. But his docility made him innocuous, and consequently the duke actually hoped that he would not carry through the threat of quitting he so often made. In February 1748, however, pleading poor health, the earl finally resigned the seals. He later justified his action by quoting lines by Addison which could only provoke Newcastle:[78]

> When vice prevails and impious men bear sway,
> The post of honour is a private station.

The duke wanted George to replace Chesterfield with the "angel" Sandwich,[79] but the other ministers feared Sandwich's subservience to the duke and the prince of Orange, and the duke chose not to force the issue. Somewhat reluctantly, Bedford then yielded to the many entreaties that he accept a secretarial post. But because Newcastle wanted direct access to Austrian affairs, he himself took the vacant northern department and left the southern department to Bedford. Sandwich acceded to direction of the admiralty. Each group in the ministry drew some satisfaction from the adjustments: the more pacific approved the new secretary's views, while the warriors took comfort from the thoroughly credible tale that Bedford was simply holding the seat for his friend Sandwich.

To help stave off criticism from fellow ministers Newcastle had assented during the early winter to a scheme that Britain explore the possibility of an alliance with Prussia. After much discussion Henry Legge, a lord of the Treasury, was selected to represent the kingdom on this sensitive mission. Meanwhile, in preparation for the approaching spring campaign, Sandwich concluded another troop convention with the Dutch. But such actions did not really deal with the key issue, the apparent invincibility of French military power. To Sandwich the duke confessed in December that his expectations for improvements in Britain's position, if not exactly "disappointed," were at least "suspended," and he added, with the logic that Pelham and Chesterfield had long been urging upon him, that "if we cannot be in a position to make war we must make peace."[80] Clearly despondent, and increasingly disposed to accept the distasteful views of his more pacific colleagues, Newcastle gamely held out into the new year. The younger Horace Walpole even accused him of "going to greater lengths *in everything* for which he overturned Lord Granville."[81] But then in February the only remaining support for Newcastle's bellicosity, the oratory emanating from The Hague, crumbled into broken Dutch promises and desperate Dutch solicitations. Pleading the anarchy of Dutch finance, Charles Bentinck arrived in London to request a massive loan. The duke of Cumberland, sent to investigate, reported that the military resources of the republic were exhausted. Newcastle's eyes were opened. "We seem to have been all in a dream," he wrote; and even through he apparently expected the customary penalty imposed on those whose policies prove bankrupt—"I shall be sacrificed for my ignorance, obstinacy, and credulity"—a saddened and wiser Newcastle finally turned the kingdom's diplomacy toward peace.[82]

VII

Newcastle's war policy since 1746 had rested on two principles: the need to delay peace talks until Britain's negotiating position had improved and the need to keep the alliance intact. Revelations of Dutch unpreparedness had now compelled the duke to sacrifice the first principle and shortly thereafter forced him to abandon the second as well. The United Provinces were simply defenseless. In western Flanders Bergen-op-Zoom lay in French hands; the other gateway to the republic (and to Hanover), Maastricht, was under seige and its capitulation seemed imminent. Only an armistice could spare the Dutch nation from occupation. Fortunately for Britain France remained willing, despite the achievements of Saxe's army, to come to moderate terms, for it too was hurting from the protracted war. The dominant figures at Versailles believed, moreover, that by concluding a peace under existing conditions France could permanently shatter the anti-Bourbon coalition. Thus, a will to peace energized the policies of the two leading antagonists, and when it became clear that Austria would not accede to British promptings to join in concluding a preliminary treaty, Newcastle sadly authorized Sandwich to sign without the allies. On the last day of April 1748 the earl did so, and the French army stopped its advance. The United Provinces had been saved.

Despite the failure of his key schemes, Newcastle retained unshaken command of British foreign policy, and his chief task in the months after April was to win Viennese consent to a final peace treaty. He chose to regard the abandonment of Austria implicit in the acceptance of the preliminary treaty as only a temporary severing of a valued tie. The previous year he had outlined for Sandwich his commitment to allied cohesion: "The allies should be kept united; and any peace upon that foot is better than a more advantageous one that is attended with disunion, coolness, and dissatisfaction amongst the Powers who ought ever, for their mutual interest to be most firmly tied and united together."[83] Having violated this principle by accepting the preliminaries, the duke determined to avoid any further provocations of Austria. But for two reasons this resolve was difficult to abide by. The first was

Vienna's distrust of Britain, founded on British promotion of the dictated treaties of Breslau, Worms, and Dresden, and recently revived by Legge's mission to Berlin. The second was the preliminary treaty itself, for Austria regarded some of its terms as unacceptable.

The preliminary treaty was essentially a compromise, a product of the peculiar standoff that French military victories and British naval victories had created. Britain agreed to hand back Cape Breton and France promised to withdraw from the Law Countries. But if any nation can be said to have lost the war of 1740–48 it was Austria, and the preliminary treaty reflected this. On Silesia, of course, it had nothing to say, for Prussia had secured its claim to that province three years earlier when it had withdrawn from the war. But for Italy and the Low Countries the treaty did propose settlements, and in each instance the court of Vienna expressed disapproval. The basic principles upon which the Italian settlement was founded were, first, that the Treaty of Worms should be fulfilled, and second, that Don Philip should be provided with territories in the peninsula. To the first principle Vienna was bitterly opposed. By the terms of the treaty of Worms Austria bought Sardinian aid against the Bourbons by promising territory. Sardinia now demanded, and the preliminaries provided, fulfilment of this commitment, even though the anticipated advantages of Austro-Sardinian cooperation had failed to materialize and Vienna had gotten nothing from the purchase. To the second principle Vienna was scarcely less hostile, for the new Bourbon principality would in part be carved out of former Habsburg holdings. In Italy, in short, the Bourbons won decisively, the Sardinians eked out a narrow advantage, and the Austrians paid. Vienna was no happier with the proposed settlement in the Low Countries. The southern Netherlands were, after all, Austrian territory, and yet the treaty proposed reaffirming the same infringements of Austrian sovereignty—Dutch garrisons and fixed tariffs—which the detestable barrier treaties had forced on Austria three decades earlier. Winning Austrian acceptance to this treaty would not be an easy task.

Making it still more difficult was George II's decision to visit Hanover during the summer. At the minimum, the king's journey would slow down peacemaking, since every important negotiating decision would require approval from a monarch on the continent and a ministry in London. But the trip seemed likely to have a substantive impact as well, for as George had shown in 1741, he felt emancipated when in

Hanover and was apt to endorse measures which in the less authoritarian atmosphere of London he would not. Unable to dissuade the king from making the visit, the Pelhams had thus to choose a suitable minister to accompany him. Mindful of how Carteret had used a similar opportunity in 1743 to undercut the influence of the ministers at home, the brothers agreed that Newcastle himself should go. Since it was impossible for the duke to set out as early as the impatient king, the Pelhams then dispatched Andrew Stone to handle their interests until the duke could arrive. It was an unparalleled demonstration of trust in an undersecretary.

In June the duke, overcoming his aversion to the sea, left Britain for the first time in his life to visit the continent. He did not, as he had feared, fall victim to seasickness, and soon his cautious duchess, who had been abroad in 1731, joined him. "Il brillera bien dans les pays etrangers," prophesied Chesterfield wryly, and a stream of reports confirmed the earl's prediction. Foreign gazettes spoke of Newcastle widely and respectfully. His ship attracted crowds of interested spectators. Delighting in the attention that the curious Dutch and Hanoverians showered on him and his wife, he grew expansive and self-confident and often betrayed the insularity of his breeding. If the younger Horace Walpole's report can be trusted, the duke turned an army review in the United Provinces into a farcical approximation of race day at Lewes; and if Lady Bolingbroke can be credited, the duchess marched from town to town trailed by a chaplain, a physician, a surgeon, and an apothecary, a retinue well suited to minister to her varying needs. Joseph Yorke, Hardwicke's son serving with the army on the continent, testified to the duke's ceaseless activity, much of it partying and socializing, and complained of the sheer incomprehensibility of Newcastle's frenetic conversations. The duke was, in short, a character.[84] It is important to recall that if Lord Hervey and Horace Walpole often exaggerated his foibles, the duke sometimes gave his critics superlative examples of them.

All this activity notwithstanding, Newcastle was not inattentive to business. The actual negotiating of the final treaty was done at Aix-la-Chapelle by Sandwich, but the major British decisions were Newcastle's. The lords justices might have exercised more influence over the settlement, but they chose instead to give the secretary wide discretion, almost a free hand. Hardwicke poured out messages of advice and encouragement to the duke, much needed since the fraternal relationship was entering again into a bleak and even vituperative phase. And the duke was not lacking for advice closer at hand; Stone stayed on in Hanover, doubtless as a voice for caution; Cumberland, who honored the duke with praise, was frequently in attendance; and among the king's Hanoverian advisers, above all in Gerlach Adolf von Münchhausen, the duke found men whose views reinforced his own on the centrality of the Austrian tie. Never before, in fact, had a British secretary of state and a Hanoverian minister worked together so cooperatively.[85]

The plan elaborated by Newcastle was simple: any action likely to anger Austria was to be avoided. The duke worked first to quiet Austrian fears about the significance of Legge's mission. Prussia had hoped to use it to draw Britain away from Austria, and such an outcome was precisely what Newcastle feared: "My politics with regard to the King of Prussia," he explained to Cumberland, "are that he should be gained by way of additional strength (if possible) to the old alliance, but not to be substituted in the place of the House of Austria to form a new chimerical system."[86] Thus, largely to demonstrate his affection for Vienna, Newcastle rejected an offer from Prussia to help George II augment his Hanoverian holdings. This action also served to quiet another Viennese fear, that Hanover would seek more territory within the empire. The conclusion of a preliminary treaty had ended the similarity of Hanoverian and Austrian aims that had existed since 1746; with a peace settlement to be constructed, the two states now became rivals for booty. Münchhausen himself did not take George's demands for total control of Osnabrück too seriously, but to the king it was a grave matter. By relieving Vienna Newcastle riled his master; it was the price of Austrophilism in Georgian Hanover in 1748.

In addition to these largely symbolic actions Newcastle took concrete steps to oblige Vienna. Aided by Cumberland he prevailed on Pelham to pay a subsidy of £100,000 to Vienna even though the cessation of fighting meant that the ostensible purpose of the subsidy, the creation of an army, had become irrelevant. Then when the need arose to dispatch another negotiator to Aix to assist Sandwich, Newcastle vetoed the suggestion that Legge, the dupe of Frederick II, be given the post and succeeded instead in winning the appointment for Sir Thomas Robinson, Britain's minister to Vienna, and as acceptable to the suspicious Austrians as any Briton was likely to be. Newcastle's commitment to the Austrian tie even served, in part at least, as a basis for a quarrel with his erstwhile protege Sandwich. The fault was not all the earl's: frustrated by Austrian obstructiveness, Newcastle had in July briefly succumbed to Dutch demands that a final treaty be promptly concluded, without Vienna if necessary. He soon repented of his weakness and instructed Sandwich to keep the Austrian negotiator Kaunitz closely informed. Sandwich, however, thought the Dutch view wiser, and growing confident of his capacity and reputation, did not hesitate to say so. His appeal to the king, however, fell on unsympathetic ears. Newcastle and his master were soon congratulating themselves on denying the secretary's office to the duke's "*élève*" of the previous February and one of Robinson's major tasks in his new role was to assure the perpetuation of a pro-Austrian tendency in the British negotating position.

In the last analysis, however, despite Newcastle's coddling of Vienna it was an ostensible British ultimatum that drove the Austrians to break the negotiating logjam. The duke recognized that if Britain appeared too sympathetic to the Habsburg cause, the Austrians would have no reason to end their delays. What Britain needed was "more management for the Court of Vienna. We can't conclude without them, though I am, if necessary, for making them believe otherwise."[87] Such a necessity appeared undeniable. So, in late August Britain indirectly informed Austria that if Vienna did not agree within three weeks to come to terms, Britain would conclude the treaty alone. Vienna dared not hazard the loss of its overbearing but valuable ally and in September declared its reluctant readiness to accept the commitments of the Treaty of Worms, and with this the pieces of the puzzle began to fall together. If Sardinia was finally to receive what Worms had promised, Britain no longer needed to lend any support to Sardinian pretensions elsewhere in Italy. And if the United Provinces were now to get the final treaty they sought, Britain was likewise relieved of any obligation to support their demands for barrier payments from Vienna. Newcastle, in fact, was thoroughly exasperated with Dutch arrogance: "That poor government," he complained, "that cannot govern one great town of their own, expects to govern us."[88] The Dutch joined with Britain and France in signing the final treaty in mid-October. The Austrians waited a week, the Sardinians a month.

The treaty itself was curiously inconclusive. Spain's gain—more precisely, Elizabeth Farnese's—was the granting of several Italian principalities to the Queen's younger son Don Philip. Of the great issue that had brought London and Madrid to war in 1739, the rights of free ships, the treaty had nothing to say. Perhaps discretion over an issue of declining importance explained this silence, but the omission of a renewal of the Anglo-Spanish trade treaty left the nature of Anglo-Spanish commerce undefined and was unquestionably an error by Newcastle and Sandwich. The duke had not completely forgotten his earlier commitment to the merchants, and almost to the end he held out for a favorable interpretation of the reestablished *Asiento*. But Spain would not accept it, and Newcastle ultimately backed down. In sum, as the duke years later acknowledged, he "found little success" in the war with Spain.[89] But the maritime war had been swallowed up by the continental war, and the treaty recognized this change. The barrier was reestablished, but Austria's obligation to pay for garrisoning the fortresses was left unstated. France disavowed future support for the Stuarts and agreed to dismantle the fortifications at Dunkirk, but Britain submitted to the unusual and humiliating condition that it send hostages to France to assure British compliance with terms concerned with North America. These terms, of course, required the British abandonment of Cape Breton. The treaty was scarcely a triumph, but Britain—except on the seas—had not fought a triumphant war. At any rate, peace was at last restored, and Newcastle knew the satisfaction of accomplishment: "I feel," he told his brother, "the joy of an honest man."[90]

Whatever else may be said of Newcastle's policy as war minister between 1746 and 1748, it seems unquestionably true that it cannot be termed successful. But perhaps the war was unwinnable: certainly both Carteret's and Harrington's efforts to establish British dominance had been similarly ineffective. Moreover, when Newcastle finally came to full power in the middle of the war, he was limited by previous decisions and agreements for which he had not been entirely responsible. A decade later Pitt would show that France truly could be humbled, but even in the Seven Years' War the British-supported army was far from victorious on the continent, and the major difference between the two wars was less the change in allies than the change in theatres. In fact, France in the eighteenth century was apparently impregnable to military assault. Cumberland failed where Prince Ferdinand would later fail and where the great Marlborough himself had scarcely succeeded. And since France was so powerful, the policy which Newcastle adopted in 1741, Carteret pursued in 1742, and Harrington returned to in 1745—the policy of buying Prussia off—was wise. But it was also insufficient. Even without Prussian support, France remained formidable.

The most fundamental of Newcastle's strategic judgments was correct: France could not be opposed through naval warfare alone. If the duke may seem to have made too much of this judgment and to have not merely harassed France on the continent but actually placed priority on the continental war, the fault again was not all his. It was France, not Britain, that chose to make the Low Countries a major theatre of the war, and had Choiseul made the same choice in the next war, Pitt would likely have been forced to assign many more men and supplies to the continent than he did. Newcastle's view never wavered. Britain, he was reported to have argued, dared not retreat behind its insular "wooden walls;" to do so was to purchase short-run tranquility at the price of "all the blessings that make life desirable."[91]

Despite his continental perspective Newcastle was neither negligent of the navy nor incompetent at directing it. Some of its difficulties in the early and middle years of the war were products of the irrational division of responsibility between the secretaries and the Admiralty. And while it is true that credit for the navy's great Atlantic triumphs in the final years of the war must rest primarily with Anson, it is also true that Anson was able to work his will in matters strategic and disciplinary chiefly because he had political influence, an influence rooted in his marital ties to the Yorkes and in the willingness of the Pelhams to support him. Anson, in brief, like William Murray and Philip Yorke before him, was a man whose ability Newcastle recognized and, at least for a time, used.

With striking consistency the duke remained committed to the view that Britain needed Austria's friendship. Pelham once declared that his brother would "take the word of an Austrian minister for true sterling."[92] In the 1720's the duke had struggled against Townshend's hostility toward Vienna; in the 1730's he had criticized Walpole for abandoning Vienna; in 1743 he assailed Carteret for intimidating Vienna; and in 1748 he turned on Sandwich for rebuking Vienna. Because he was committed to Austria, and because he was unalterably English, the duke was chary of Hanoverianism. No minister criticized the king's decision for electoral neutrality more forcefully than he, and when Carteret later converted to the king's view, it was Newcastle who again led the ministerial assault. Once in power himself, he began to change his mind, but less than his critics believed. He even at one point accused his brother, of all people, of being too partial to the electorate,[93] and he courted royal disfavor in 1748 by resisting George's efforts to extort a trophy for Hanover.

From one point of view Newcastle's self-imposed task of maintaining the tie with Vienna was simply impossible. France was Britain's chief enemy, and hence the ministry's major responsibility was the defeating of France. Each measure adopted by the ministry to this end seemed only to corrode the Anglo-Austrian relationship. Britain's first measure was the dissociation of Prussia from France, but since it was Prussia that was Austria's chief foe, Britain clearly indicated by this action that it did not share Austria's hierarchy of enemies. Britain's second measure was the winning of Sardinia's vital assistance against France; but this action, by challenging Habsburg power in northern Italy, also incurred Viennese anger. In short, from Vienna's point of view, Britain was fighting the wrong enemy with the wrong ally. But if in abstract the Anglo-Austrian tie seemed plagued by unendurable disagreements, in practice the prospects for the tie were less bleak. In fact, by the last years of the war there were good grounds for believing a rapprochement possible, and Newcastle perceived them. Neither Britain nor Austria had an alternative ally to whom it could turn: Prussia had behaved of late with such disregard for treaty commitments that Britain dared not entrust its continental fate to the unreliable Hohenzollerns, and Bourbon France remained the symbol of all that the Habsburgs had long resisted. Moreover, Austria recognized that Britain had an abundance of what the Habsburg state preeminently lacked, money to pay for a war. And Britain recognized that Austria still had strong armies, rendered less than effective by Austria's multiple commitments in the recent war but still capable, as in 1744, of inflicting grave punishment on their foes. Finally, there was the barrier, a source of Austro-Dutch suspicion as the war closed, but potentially, in Newcastle's mind, "the cement of union between the Maritime Powers and the House of Austria."[94]

Thus, when Newcastle's massive miscalculation of the ability of the allies to mount an effective offensive finally stood forth in painful clarity in the early months of 1748, the duke had a policy to fall back on. The preliminaries were accepted in Vienna only under duress, but thereafter the duke did all he could, courageously and in isolation, to placate Austrian discontent. The alliance, he vowed, would survive, and it did. Measured against the lives lost in those last two years of war this accomplishment may seem petty, but we must be wary of too quickly judging by our own standards. Sir Richard Lodge, musing over Newcastle's political survival after his stewardship of these last three years, called it "anomalous."[95] Yet the duke had, after all, presided over the peace; he had reassured and resecured Austria; he had persuaded France to abandon its conquests. This is not, one may judge, an imposing list of accomplishments, but the terms of peace were no worse than those Britain would probably have gotten in 1746, and the Anglo-Austrian entente—almost certainly a casualty had there been a settlement in 1746—remained alive. One interesting and highly significant point, moreover, remains to be noted: the Parliament which had shown both Sir Robert Walpole and Lord Carteret—and would later show Lord North—that it would not brook military ineffectiveness would not support efforts to discomfit Newcastle. Indeed, the general election held toward the end of the war returned a House of Commons still more compliant than its predecessor. From this fact at least one conclusion seems legitimate: many in the nation and most in the Parliament thought the duke was doing a moderately good job in very difficult circumstances. The judgment seems sound.

5

Foreign Minister

I

Newcastle's postwar foreign policy rested upon the fundamental conviction that France remained, as it had been for three-quarters of a century, Britain's only important enemy. He judged soundly. Wherever one looked—on the seas of the world, in the forests of America and India, in the courts of Europe—one found France behaving like, and being regarded as, Britain's chief rival. In the years immediately after the peace of Aix-la-Chapelle the rivalry was muted as the French government struggled to quell domestic rancor and rebuild its heavily damaged navy. But most Englishmen saw the French preoccupation with reconstruction as transitory, certain to be succeeded by a return to hostility. Joseph Yorke, observing in Paris in 1750, warned his father and thus Newcastle of "the surprizing force" of France: "The more I examine into it," he wrote, "the more I am struck with the strength and infinite resources of this kingdom."[1] The warning fell on ears well prepared to believe that the maintenance of European peace depended upon the containment of France.

Newcastle's assessment of French strength and intentions entailed a twofold course of action: Britain had to try to detach from Versailles those states which operated within the French diplomatic orbit and to strengthen simultaneously its own ties with London's traditional but currently discontented friends. Both aims necessitated continued British participation in continental affairs, but Newcastle thought the potential rewards well worth the trouble and expense of remaining involved in Europe. If isolated, France, he believed, would not dare to initiate hostilities, and peace would be maintained. Newcastle clearly took Lord Stanhope as his model and seems in these years after the war to have been moved by a profound desire to leave a permanent mark on British foreign policy.² Just as Stanhope had secured a Grand Alliance to intimidate Spain, so Newcastle hoped to create a coalition—a "league," he called it—to restrain France. He almost pulled it off.

The dilemma of the eighteenth-century minister was the classical problem of serving two masters. On the one hand stood the king. To incur his displeasure was to hazard loss of ministerial effectiveness or even dismissal from office. On the other hand stood the Parliament. Its displeasure could be equally disastrous: Newcastle had seen an obstreperous Parliament drive Walpole from office in 1742 and had no desire to be similarly treated. It was fortunate for the politicians of the day that Crown and Parliament were usually in agreement. Domestic issues did not usually divide the two branches, and Parliament tended in any event to look to the monarch and his ministers for leadership. Even when disagreement threatened, a judicious exercise of influence or a cautiously delivered rebuke to the king could often prevent a true split. Thus, for a minister capable of dealing out douceurs and willing to speak out in the closet, the need to choose between the two masters might never arise. The secretaries of state, however, were peculiarly vulnerable, for their major concern was foreign affairs and no other subject of parliamentary debate was so likely to lay bare the gap between what most members wanted for the kingdom and what the Crown wanted from it. These disagreements over foreign policy generally focused on enduring parliamentary suspicions, sometimes justified, that with the elector of Hanover sitting on the throne of Great Britain, London's interests were being sacrificed to Hanover's. When aroused, such suspicions cast discredit on the Hanoverian tie. Secretaries of state, although servants of the Crown, had to tread with great care if they wished to avoid the fate of Lord Granville.

These were the facts of political life which Newcastle weighed as he decided how to implement his two foreign policy aims. The countries to be lured from their French ties were Spain and Prussia. The countries to be more tightly bound to Britain were the United Provinces and Austria. In each instance, whether in undermining France's alliances or in solidifying Britain's, Newcastle might need funds to achieve his goal, and this need would in turn compel him to present his case to a suspicious Parliament. To induce Spain to abandon the Bourbon family compact, for example, Britain could conceivably be forced to accept some of Madrid's demands for payments owed by the South Sea Company. To wean Prussia from France, a more difficult task, as the

Legge mission had shown, Britain would probably have to settle Berlin's claims against recent confiscations of Prussian ships and cargoes. To fortify the Dutch alliance, in which Newcastle saw unjustifiably great significance, Britain might need to offer assistance in restoring the barrier fortresses. Above all, to restore amicability to Anglo-Austrian relations, financial and diplomatic support for the harassed Habsburg state would be required.

Toward those, like Chesterfield and Pelham, who argued for an Anglo-Prussian instead of an Anglo-Austrian alliance, Newcastle remained unsympathetic. He was not unwilling to consider bringing Berlin into his league, for he respected Prussian power and knew how Brandenburg had served in the Grand Alliance against Louis XIV. But he also knew that the issues dividing Prussia and Austria were deep, and that if London, as seemed likely, had to choose between Berlin and Vienna, Berlin's record of diplomatic faithlessness and the Habsburg tradition of resistance to the Bourbons meant that Austria would clearly be the wiser choice. Such rational considerations aside, Newcastle had another reason for wanting to strengthen the frayed Anglo-Austrian tie that he had fought so hard to preserve in the final years of the war. He was a Whig, raised to honor the Protestant succession and revile its enemies. He knew that Britain's most formidable ally in the years of greatest danger to that succession had been Austria. That the Habsburg state was itself Catholic scarcely mattered; what Newcastle remembered was the successful comradeship in arms of the duke of Marlborough and Prince Eugene. The Austrian alliance was, in brief, founded as much on sentiment as on reason. It constituted, in Newcastle's words, the cornerstone of the "antient system." The duke's task was to persuade Parliament and his ministerial colleagues to accept his vision.

But on the morrow of the peace Newcastle and Pelham were at odds. The duke, still abroad, resented his brother's disinclination to give unqualified approval to his diplomatic efforts; Pelham, in London, suspected that the duke was preparing to embark upon some rash foreign venture. For several years the differences in the views of the brothers about the proper type of foreign policy had been visible even though, in the circumstances of a difficult war, not very significant. The return to peace suddenly permitted Britain the luxury of a wide choice of courses to follow in foreign affairs, and the Pelhams' differences acquired an enhanced importance. Henry Pelham's view was a product of his tutelage under Walpole and his adoption of Sir Robert's belief that foreign concerns were properly subordinated to domestic ones: the return of peace in 1748 provided an opportunity to reduce the service on the debt and thereby ease the kingdom's financial burden. In contrast to this doctrine of noninvolvement Newcastle assumed that British security depended on the maintenance of continental ties, an assumption with which neither Townshend nor Carteret, however diverse the interpretations they might have placed on it, would have quarreled. At root the conflict between the brothers was the difference between the Treasury mentality and the secretarial mentality.

II

Newcastle's plans to win France's allies away from Versailles were partly fulfilled in the years after the war. As early as 1745 the duke had considered sending Benjamin Keene to Portugal, where he could observe the Spanish situation. When Ferdinand VI acceded to the Spanish throne in 1746 and finally terminated the influence of Elizabeth Farnese, Newcastle tarried no more. He immediately dispatched Keene to Lisbon, hoping to use the new monarch's suspicions of his mighty Bourbon ally to Britain's advantage. Keene was doubly qualified to serve the duke: he had become a loyal though undistinguished supporter of the Pelhams in the Commons, and he had an uncommon talent for Iberian diplomacy. Circumstances moreover seemed favorable: by 1747 Newcastle was abandoning the narrow ambitions of the South Sea Company, convinced that Madrid would be more tractable if Britain were less stubborn. Keene left Lisbon for Madrid promptly after the war with instructions to secure a commercial treaty and, if possible, a political *entente* with Spain. Thereafter the duke dinned his envoy with the principal points: he viewed the negotiations "not as a commercial, mercantile affair only; but as the first opportunity that has offered of really separating the two branches of the Houses of Bourbon."[3] The commercial treaty was gained in 1750. At the cost of abandoning the worthless *Asiento* and minimizing a variety of claims made by the South Sea Company against the throne of Spain, Keene won for British merchants access to the coveted Spanish home market. The treaty by itself signified a diplomatic triumph for both Keene and Newcastle. But its remarkable consequences showed that Newcastle's hopes for a political understanding had not been vainly founded: nursed along by the Anglophile ministers Caravajal and Wall and by the tact of Keene, Anglo-Spanish friendship prospered. Moreover, as it prospered the threat of combined Bourbon naval activities in wartime against Britain declined: the first of France's former allies had been won.

Efforts to effect a similar rupture between Versailles and Berlin met with considerably less success. For this task Newcastle chose Sir Charles Hanbury Williams, a poetaster and polemicist trying to hitch his political fortunes to the ascendant star of the Pelhams. Hanbury Williams was not Keene's equal in diplomatic ability, and his instructions for seeking Frederick II's friendship were decidedly equivocal. But the greatest obstacle to the creation of an Anglo-Prussian *entente* remained Britain's tie with Austria: only if London renounced this bond would Berlin consider cooperation. With Britain unwilling to abandon Austria, the mission quickly degenerated into a semiofficial spying assignment, livened only by Hanbury Williams's spirited defenses of British creditors and admiralty courts and his candid evaluations of life in Frederician Prussia. Frederick soon asked Britain to recall him, and Prussia remained France's most powerful though not most tractable ally.

In these efforts to break up the French bloc Newcastle worked chiefly through Britain's accredited diplomats; into the parallel task of reconstructing and redefining Britain's ties with the Dutch and the Austrians he entered more personally and energetically. Since, in the early years after the peace, the Dutch were inclined to accept British guidance in shaping their foreign policy, Newcastle's chief concern was Vienna. Many in the imperial capital, especially Count Kaunitz, resented the cavalier attitude recently displayed by various British ministries toward the territorial integrity of the Habsburg domains. But the Anglophile position within Viennese counsels did not lack for able representation, and Count Colloredo led a group whose consistent advice was to retain the British alliance. The views of this group gained credit when, in the spring of 1749, Newcastle persuaded his colleagues—against the advice of Pelham and despite the end of hostilities—to dispatch the final wartime subsidy to Vienna. The impact of this decision was immediate: "It is impossible," Newcastle rejoiced, "for the Court of Vienna to be better than it is just at present."[4]

Placating Austrian discontent was one thing; using the restored alliance as the foundation for an anti-French league was another. The chief obstacle to such a transformation lay not in Vienna but at home, in Pelham's aversion to trying to secure allies through the granting of peacetime subsidies. "In the present circumstances of Europe," the first lord told the Commons early in 1750, "it would be impossible for us to form a continental confederacy, which would not be an incumbrance to us, rather than an advantage."[5] He despaired at the costs involved and had scant faith in the reliability of vague promises elicited from indigent continental princes. Newcastle, on the other hand, had long believed in the value of subsidies. Almost a quarter of a century earlier he had argued that "it ought to be a general consideration, that if those whose alliance we desire are not in a capacity to defend themselves and assist us, they can be of no use unless they are enabled to do it."[6] What Newcastle needed was a scheme that would justify the expenditure of funds to foreign states for some purpose more concrete than the gaining of mere pledges to oppose France if war should break out.

The plan to promote the election of the youthful Austrian Archduke Joseph to the dignity of king of the Romans, a plan elaborated for Newcastle in September 1749 by Hanbury Williams, met this need. The election would assure Joseph's succession to the office of emperor upon the death of his father Francis I; it would thus forestall a succession crisis of the sort that had thrice brought Europe to war in Newcastle's lifetime. It would counteract the divisive tendencies threatening to destroy any chance that the empire could be restored as a counterweight to Bourbon France on the continent. It was, moreover, earnestly desired by Francis and Maria Theresa. To gain the requisite number of votes—two-thirds of the electoral college, an "eminent majority"—Britain and its allies would pay subsidies. But although the overt purpose of the subsidization plan would thus be a successful imperial election, its most useful consequence would be the justification it offered for buying the friendship of several German states. Despite earlier skepticism about a similar proposal, Newcastle now accepted the scheme readily—"a child of my own," he soon called it—and with little difficulty persuaded Hardwicke and George II of its value. "It is the only means I can think of," he wrote, "of establishing any real, solid system for the preservation of the peace and the maintenance of the liberties of Europe."[7]

But Pelham, his eye ever on the accounts, resisted Newcastle's logic through the winter and yielded, unenthusiastically, only in the spring. As long as he withheld his support, the Treasury could not be the source of the subsidies. Fortunately for Newcastle, even as he pleaded with his brother, another source of funds became available to permit him to initiate diplomatic efforts designed to create an eminent majority. The votes of four states could already be relied on: Bohemia and Hanover, the electoral guises of Austria and Britain; and Mainz and Trier, the ecclesiastical holdings of dutiful imperial subjects. Two more needed to be bought. The fortunate proximity of Cologne caught Newcastle's attention: here was an electoral state, formerly a French satellite, lying so close to the United Provinces and Hanover that both the Dutch and George II *in his electoral capacity* were willing to purchase its friendship. Negotiations to that end took place during the winter, and in March Cologne accepted as terms its vote in exchange for an annual Dutch-Hanoverian subsidy of £40,000. Since Britain was not juridically involved at all, Pelham's penuriousness was irrelevant. George's portion came from his private funds. And by gaining a fifth elector, Newcastle stood but one vote away from success.

The next electoral state to turn to was Bavaria. The alternatives were Brandenburg, the Electoral Palatine, and Saxony, but the first two were clearly in the French camp, and Saxony's financial indebtedness to Hanover made ministers in London reluctant to sanction payments which could be represented in the speeches of unfriendly politicians as devious ways to fatten Hanoverian accounts with British funds. Newcastle arranged for negotiations with Bavarian and Dutch representatives to be held in Hanover during the summer of 1750. George II's plans to visit his electoral territories at that time determined this choice of site, for the duke, who intended to accompany his monarch, had resolved to undertake the negotiations personally. Austria finally received formal notification of the election plan in April. Newcastle had withheld such reports through the preceding winter in the belief that publicity would only encourage opposition in hostile capitals, a judgment that proved correct. The ministers in Vienna displayed some pique at this latest example of British paternalism, but chose to comply with the duke's request that a diplomat be sent to Hanover to participate in the Bavarian negotiations. Baron Vorster, the Austrian representative, carried instructions which, in well-chosen words of moderation, directed him to aid the British effort without—a significant exception—sacrificing Austrian resources or honor. A rigorous interpretation of that instruction would have precluded any Austrian financial assistance in securing Bavaria's vote, but on the basis of past experience with Viennese diplomacy and of Austria's clear interest in having Joseph elected, Newcastle hoped that Vorster would interpret his orders loosely rather than rigorously. His hopes were justified.

The negotiations took place during August and surmounted several obstacles on the path to success. Austria, alarmed at careless British talk of the utility of small Habsburg cessions to Munich, was fearful that the British were undertaking a scheme that would ultimately prove a drain on Vienna's treasury. Bavaria's demands were high, not only because its vote would be the decisive one, but also because Newcastle, now offering public rather than private funds, wanted a troop commitment from Munich to make the subsidy more palatable to the Commons. Moreover, the entire plan, involving Austrian payments to Bavaria in return for control of Bavaria's electoral voice, seemed indistinguishably close to bribery, a practice enjoined by the Golden Bull. That these difficulties were successfully dealt with indicates that Newcastle was not without ability as a negotiator. Austrian fears of an unending electoral auction were quieted by the drafting of a general plan wherein Austrian and British responsibilities were defined. Bavarian cupidity was assuaged by the timely British promise of enlarged financial support. And the final agreement, approved in late August, used the technique of treaty proliferation to disguise the embarrassing fact of Viennese participation in an imperial bribery plot. In return for its favorable vote and a commitment to keep 6,000 troops in readiness, Bavaria was promised £40,000 annually for six years. Britain undertook to pay half; the Dutch and the Austrians would pay a quarter each. Pelham approved of the settlement. "The expense to us is a trifle," he wrote, "and I hope the consequence of the treaty will sufficiently make up for that. It does look as if a King of the Romans would be chosen, and that the choice would fall on the Arch Duke Joseph. If so, our bone of contention is removed for two lives; and the House of Bavaria being separated from France may possibly check and disappoint the turbulent and ambitious views of some other German powers." Newcastle exulted: "There is a foundation for supporting such a system upon the continent as may, with little or no expense, preserve the peace with *safety, honour, dignity,* and *advantage* to us and our interests in Europe and America."[8] Only the election itself, a mere formality, remained.

But then, in October, the euphoric mists evaporated. The elector of Cologne declared his dissatisfaction with the terms he had accepted the previous March. He now threatened to renege on his voting pledge if the Dutch and Hanoverians did not renegotiate the treaty. Newcastle was astonished, George II enraged. Both were reluctant to reward perfidy, and the monarch's reluctance endured long after the duke's had abated. The immediate consequence of Cologne's action was the postponement of any plans to convoke the electoral college in the waning months of 1750. Newcastle, who had hoped to crown his summer trip to the continent with an electoral triumph, returned to Britain in the late autumn fearful that his beloved scheme was doomed. Whether the damage was in fact irreparable the coming months alone would tell, but it took no clairvoyant to see that the vital element of momentum had been lost.

III

When Newcastle returned to Britain in late 1750 he was engaged in still another feud with a secretarial colleague. The duke of Bedford, whom Newcastle had cheerlessly accepted in 1748, was proving to be fully as exasperating to the elder Pelham as Richmond had once prophesied. Newcastle had expected to have absolute control of foreign policy in the postwar years, but such control could exist, he knew, only if he had a fellow secretary properly respectful of his twenty-four years of experience in foreign affairs and a team of diplomatic representatives loyal to him and his policy. The second condition had been met: Lord Albemarle at Versailles, Benjamin Keene at Madrid, Lord Holderness at The Hague, and Robert Keith at Vienna fit the duke's prescription. But in light of Bedford's opposition to Newcastle's subsidy diplomacy, his suspicions of the Spanish negotiations, and his refusal to accept Dutch power as a serious factor in European politics, the first condition was clearly unfulfilled, and the constitutional ambiguity of the secretarial office continued thus to vex Newcastle. Like Stanhope, Townshend, and Carteret before him, he set out to impose a single will upon an administrative system singularly uncongenial to such aspirations.

Policy differences aside, Newcastle had other reasons for becoming increasingly irritated with Bedford. The junior secretary seemed to regard his official responsibilities as nothing more than an avocation. He spent as little time in London as possible, he missed important cabinet meetings, and his inattention to business became notorious. His indolence attracted the scorn of Pelham, Hardwicke, and the king himself. All came to share Newcastle's view that Bedford was unfit to hold responsible office. Still, as Newcastle realized, Bedford's distaste for business meant that his capacity to obstruct Newcastle's policy was limited. This in some measure cancelled out his other vices. It was, therefore, a third, political, consideration that was decisive for the duke.

The duke of Bedford threatened the Pelhamite political hegemony. Even alone he would have been no mean figure. He bore the prestigious Russell name, he possessed a vast estate with its attendant political influence, and he moved among the honored of English society. But he did not stand alone. An anti-Newcastle alliance took shape after mid-1748 which had the earl of Sandwich, Newcastle's fallen disciple, as its lynchpin but Bedford as its ultimate leader. The rupture between Sandwich and Newcastle was not significant in itself, but as a consequence of it two men of far greater stature than the young earl also grew hostile to Newcastle. One was Bedford, to whose protection Sandwich had returned when Newcastle's favor failed, and who loyally supported his errant friend. The other was the duke of Cumberland, who had learned to respect Sandwich during the tortuous peace negotiations, and whose efforts at mediating the earl's quarrel with Newcastle in November 1748 only earned him the duke's enmity. With him into the anti-Newcastle alliance Cumberland brought Princess Emily. Thus was effected, in the short course of a year, a sweeping alteration in the pattern of Newcastle's political friendships: the duke had lost his two chief ties to the royal family and was forced to cultivate new ones, Lady Yarmouth, still the king's mistress, and Lord Granville, still the king's friend. Meanwhile, as the allies of Sandwich became allies of each other's, a new Bedford–Cumberland faction emerged. When to Newcastle's irritation at a disrespectful colleague and his contempt for a lazy one there was added the fear of a political rival, all working upon his well-known predisposition toward suspicion and jealousy, a profound and understandable aversion to Bedford began to obsess the duke.

As early as 1749 Newcastle wanted Bedford dismissed, but two difficulties obtruded themselves. George II rather liked the junior secretary's respectful demeanor in the closet, and while not unsympathetic to the complaints of those of Bedford's cabinet colleagues who had to bear the burden of his indolence, the monarch was ready to yield only to the united will of both the Pelhams; and Henry Pelham, true to his conviction that opposition was best controlled when comprehended, showed no willingness to upset the political scene by forcing the king to turn an influential peer out of his secretarial office. The first lord came to believe that awkward as Bedford might be in office, he would be a greater inconvenience if loss of office permitted him to court the king unfettered by the requirements of departmental responsibility. Unable to win his brother's support, Newcastle was long limited to pouring out his fears and irritations upon the sympathetic, yet curiously impartial ear of Lady Yarmouth.

Newcastle's actual campaign to gain Bedford's dismissal opened during the hectic trip to Hanover in 1750. Like Sunderland and Stanhope in 1716, he hoped to use his electoral tour with the king to effect a cabinet change back home. To induce his brother to acquiesce in the change Newcastle resorted to his favorite strategem: he threatened to resign. He would not, to be sure, leave the ministry, but by writing of a shift to the lord presidency or the privy seal he was indicating that he might abandon active political life. It is impossible at the remove of two centuries to disentangle the contrived ploy from the skein of frustration-induced irrationality that marked the duke's thoughts. It is clear that in July, when Newcastle made the threat, he was depressed by slights and rebuffs he believed he was receiving from the king and Lady Yarmouth. George had even begun claiming personal credit for promoting the imperial election plan. But it is also clear that the alternative to his resignation, in Newcastle's mind, was not a correction in royal behavior, but the ouster of Bedford. Hardwicke's wise advice ministered to his friend's reason and instincts alike. After cautioning against rash assaults on the junior secretary, the lord chancellor spelled out for Newcastle what the abandonment of politics would really mean to a man of the duke's deep passion for the game. He suggested that illness or personal problems might explain the king's coolness; and he told Newcastle to rejoice, not carp, at George's appropriation of the election plan: "A prince cannot make a minister a greater compliment than by making his measures his own."[9]

Despite Hardwicke's clear warning that he and Pelham were unwilling to harry Bedford from office, as the summer passed Newcastle perceived signs that his campaign might succeed. The king finally began to recognize Bedford's laziness, and Lady Yarmouth began to speak in behalf of the proposed ouster. Moreover, the death of the duke of Richmond in August, although a keen personal loss for Newcastle, had the happy effect of opening up the office of master of the horse, with which Bedford's fall from grace might, if he wished, be cushioned, and his political enmity thereby diminished. The opportunity for political musical chairs widened still further in September when it became clear that the duke of Dorset, currently lord President, would insist upon receiving the long-promised lord lieutenancy of Ireland. Still, ultimate success for Newcastle depended on Pelham's support, for as the timorous George II told the duke, "You and I can't do it alone."[10] And Pelham remained unconvinced of the wisdom of provoking the anger of a man of influence. For this reason alone, Bedford remained as secretary when Newcastle returned to Britain in November.

Even while this frustrating situation resisted ducal efforts at resolution, Newcastle entered into a closer and rather shrouded relationship with the party of Frederick, Prince of Wales. The nature of this tie and the motives lying behind it remain obscure, but of a few conclusions one may be fairly confident. Like all his ministerial colleagues the duke realized that with the king sixty-seven years old, a change of monarchs within a few years was quite likely; to procure a measure of insurance against the purge that the accession of the prince would trigger Newcastle was eager, as Walpole had been in 1726, to oblige the heir whenever possible. But there may have been more to Newcastle's tryst with Leicester House than that. Frederick approved of the forward style in foreign policy now represented by Newcastle's subsidy diplomacy, and he approved too of politicians who were prepared to feud with Cumberland. Newcastle for his part, at bitter odds with his brother about policy, persons, and property, may have duped himself into seeing in Leicester House a potential alternative base of power. The evidence suggests, in any event, that it was William Pitt and his friends who sought to promote the rapprochement between the prince and the peer.

The chief obstacle to be overcome was the personal animus each bore the other. Newcastle, though scarcely a warrior himself, thought Frederick soft; he also disliked Frederick's readiness, demonstrated over the course of fifteen years, to join the political opposition when it seemed expedient. Frederick remembered Newcastle as a prime mover in the strategy of 1747 whereby the prince's hopes to establish a powerful electoral beachhead had been checked. Even more recently the two men had contended for the post of chancellor of Cambridge University. When Frederick had intimated his desire to stand for that office in 1747, Newcastle had taken alarm. The duke had assumed that whenever the virtually indestructible incumbent, the duke of Somerset, finally died, he himself would be elevated by the electors to the chancellorship from his present office of high steward. The Prince of Wales posed a particularly formidable threat, appealing as leader of the opposition to those voters who disliked the government and as heir to the throne to those who hoped for preferment in the years ahead. Newcastle wanted the office keenly, less it seems for the patronage and influence associated with it (though they were not insignificant) than for its prestige. To weaken Frederick's appeal he secured from George II a declaration that the king did not wish his son chosen, and when Somerset fell ill, the duke's friends, especially the member for the borough of Cambridge, Lord Dupplin, mobilized the voters who would support Newcastle. In the face of such opposition Frederick finally withdrew, and Newcastle was chosen in December of 1748. The following summer, about the time he was made a fellow of the Royal Society, the duke was installed as chancellor during a week of spirited and memorable festivities at Cambridge. By one account the duke was "very owlish and very tipsy at night," and by another he ended at least one evening "with making both himself and his Vice Chancellor exceedingly Fuddled."[11] The duke clearly had a glorious time celebrating his victory over Frederick.

But these were precisely the types of divisions that had to be overcome if Newcastle and Frederick were to be able to cooperate. The duke was willing by 1750 to make the effort: "The Duke and Duchess of Newcastle," recorded Lord Egmont at the end of the year, "have been long paying a secret court to the Prince." And while the paucity of evidence does not permit an analysis of the nature of this effort, it was apparent by the fall that it was succeeding. As the prince's chief adviser, Egmont was not pleased at his master's complacence toward the duke; he was suspicious of Newcastle's motives and tried to dissuade Frederick from becoming too involved with the secretary. He found the prince, however, thinking "very favourably" of Newcastle.[12] Since William Pitt was also courting Leicester House at this time, and would shortly come to terms with it, the possibility of wholesale defections to the prince was more than just a chimera. But it was probably not too much more. Even though it is now apparent that Newcastle was dabbling with the opposition, it remains less than clear what ought to be made of this fact. Buttering both sides of the bread was not an uncommon political practice. The duke may simply have been seeking new ammunition in his struggle against Bedford or seeking to neutralize a pesky opposition. That he planned such a dramatic step as deserting his brother and

Hardwicke seems exceedingly farfetched. It would have cost him psychological and financial pains that he knew he could not endure. Most likely he simply hoped, while keeping his old friends, to gain new ones, while serving the present king, to please the future one. In any event, whatever Newcastle's reasoning, all his plans came to abortive conclusions early in 1751; Frederick unexpectedly died. The new friendship had proved politically fruitless.

But the death itself was not. It was the second of two developments early in that year that persuaded even the cautious Henry Pelham that Bedford ought to be removed. It had been preceded by Bedford's increasingly confident resort to opposition in the cabinet. The southern secretary aligned himself against not only an effort to strengthen the defense of Nova Scotia that had Newcastle's strong backing but also a bill, urged by Pelham himself, to encourage the naturalization of foreign Protestants. What had been an irritant to Newcastle was threatening to become an irritant to the whole cabinet. The prince's demise sealed Bedford's fate. As long as a rival opposition group already existed, Pelham saw little value in driving colleagues from office and thereby giving manpower to his enemies. But with the Leicester House faction stricken, it seemed less dangerous to provoke the creation of another, especially since Newcastle's informants in Leicester House revealed that many of Frederick's former followers would now choose to eschew pointless opposition and join the body of Pelhamite adherents.

In one immediate way, however, Frederick's death actually made the Bedford–Cumberland faction potentially more rather than less dangerous to the Pelhams. The grandchild heir to the throne, Prince George, was still a youth, and the likelihood of a minority reign with disruptive regency politics seemed great. Against this day the Pelhams had now to provide, especially since Cumberland, as uncle of the prospective king, would be widely regarded as the natural regent. Thus, before Bedford could be dealt with, the more pressing threat of a Cumberland regency riveted the triumvirate's attention. The claims of the royal duke could not be altogether denied, but counting on considerable public support for any measure that might circumscribe "the Butcher's" authority, the ministry, after protracted and contentious deliberations, presented a regency bill to Parliament that, in the event of a new reign, would bestow the title of regent on Augusta, dowager princess of Wales, and make Cumberland merely the president of a council chosen to aid the princess. Hardwicke was the major draftsman of the measure, but the floor manager of the bill in the House of Lords was Newcastle. It was a task that demanded a mental dexterity beyond the duke's capacity. He was required to defend the bill against Cumberland's friends, who resented the slight to their leader, against the princess's diminishing following, who disliked the limitations to be placed on her power as regent, and against conservative constitutionalists, who opposed the restraints on royal authority (when exercised by a regent) that underlay the very conception of the measure. Newcastle's advocacy was marked more by ardor and rambunctiousness than by clear understanding, and at one point even his grasp of procedure failed him.[13] But the obedient House of Lords still accepted the amendments voted by the Commons, and at the cost of some royal irritation—Cumberland, after all, was George II's favorite son—the triumvirate averted the danger of an overtly hostile Crown. Bubb Dodington, a political weathervane, read the signs aright and the very next day set out to resume ties with the Pelhams.

Bedford was now without protection. The Pelhams elaborated a strategy which, they believed, would not only spare the king the pain of personally dismissing the magnate, but also assure the departure from the Admiralty of their foe Lord Sandwich, whose retention of office bespoke Bedford's protective loyalty more than Sandwich's administrative capacity. The plan was not complicated. The king would simply dismiss Sandwich, whom he detested; and Bedford, ever loyal to his friends, would resign in protest. The onus of the separation from office would thereby rest on Duke John's diminutive frame rather than King George's stooped one. Nor was the plan a secret. Diplomats as far away as Hanover knew of it at least a day before it was implemented, and Sandwich tried unsuccessfully to forestall its effects for him. But nothing he did availed: on 13 June 1751 Newcastle notified the earl of his dismissal, and the next day, as anticipated, Bedford resigned the seals. Newcastle's relentless campaign to gain command of foreign affairs had at last succeeded. The victory even had its touch of irony: whereas in 1748 Newcastle had used Bedford because he wanted to get Sandwich *into* office, he now used Sandwich as his means of getting Bedford *out* of office.

The duke was determined not to be deterred, as he had been in 1746 and 1748, from his purpose of installing a clerk as his colleague; the victory would be consolidated, not cast away. Newcastle's choice for southern secretary was Lord Holderness, a man, in the duke's mind, of "solid understanding," whose highest recommendation was that he was "most punctual in the execution of orders." Pelham and Hardwicke thought less highly of the earl—or perhaps more of the responsibilities of the office—but made no effort to interfere. More strikingly, Newcastle also won their approval for the appointment of his erstwhile political enemy, Lord Granville, to the lord presidency. His turbulent ambition mellowed by age and spirits, Granville no longer seemed a threat to the duke's power, while his knowledge of Germany and his readiness to endorse continental measures recommended him to a man with Newcastle's foreign policy ideas. "My Lord Granville is no more the terrible man," Newcastle had assured his brother the previous summer, "*Non eadem est aetas, non mens.*"[14] With Lord Anson's appointment to the Admiralty Newcastle was less content, but Pelham and Hardwicke chose to reward a faithful and distinguished naval officer who was, moreover, the lord chancellor's son-in-law. Anson would amply justify their trust. Only one old ally was cast aside: Lord Harrington, having vacated his Irish post to oblige the duke of Dorset, had hoped for another preferment. Desperately unhappy at his eclipse, Harrington pleaded with the Pelhams for their aid. It did not come, and it may be that nothing the brothers might have done could have overcome George's continuing contempt for his former friend. Harrington retired from politics.

For a short time George II was angry at the triumvirate, and especially with Newcastle, for being forced, as he inevitably saw it, to part with Bedford's services. The episode was not a reenactment of 1744, when Granville had been ousted to prevent a disaster in the Commons. Bedford's chief offense, as the monarch knew, was simply Newcastle's dislike of him; ministerial convenience, not ministerial survival, underlay the cabinet alterations of 1751. In his final audience Bedford sought to turn the monarch against Newcastle by distortedly recounting the history of Newcastle's corrosive relationships with his fellow secretaries. The king's irritation with the duke expressed itself in refusals to speak to him at levees and in an oral warning, delivered in the presence of others, to restrict himself to departmental responsibilities. But as Newcastle continued to behave with decorous submissiveness, the monarch's anger, rooted more in the frustrated awareness of his own political impotence than in any transitory affection for Bedford, soon passed. Holderness, moreover, was precisely the sort of secretarial colleague Newcastle had long hoped for; he provided the duke from

his first day in office with the "most perfect satisfaction upon all points."
"It is very agreeable," the duke wrote over six months later, "to have
such a companion, which never happened to me before."[15]

Newcastle's ouster of Bedford should be understood in two perspectives. Clearly the elder Pelham was not a man to tolerate rivals. He was
uncommonly suspicious, anxious, and jealous of the authority of others.
But the psychological perspective is not the whole story. The continuous
quarrel with secretarial colleagues, from Harrington through Chesterfield to Bedford, arose from Newcastle's effort to overcome the un-
functional dual organization of the secretarial office. The kingdom
needed one consistent foreign policy, not two rival ones. But there were
only two ways in which this need might be met: either the king or
prime minister might impose his will on both secretaries, or one secretary might agree to be a subordinate of the other. For a while during the
1720's Newcastle had been Townshend's subordinate. During part of
the 1730's he and Harrington had accepted Walpole's dominance in
foreign affairs. After 1744, however, Newcastle reasonably believed
himself qualified by experience to assert control in his own name. The
only alternative would have been to let Pelham guide foreign policy.
But the duke distrusted his brother's isolationism, which he saw as a
reversion to Walpole's ill-judged policy of the 1730's; and Pelham
himself, whose knowledge of French was only rudimentary, had no taste
for the task. Thus, Newcastle was doing far more than proving his
uncongeniality as he struggled to find a satisfactory colleague; he was
trying to provide Britain with a single-minded foreign policy. Assess-
ments of the policy must be deferred yet awhile, but one need not hesitate in judging Newcastle's efforts to reduce one secretary to the status
of a clerk for the other as reasonable.

IV

The end of secretarial wrangling and the restoration of what Newcastle termed "harmony and union" in the cabinet let the duke resume
his imperial diplomacy.[16] During the winter of British inactivity
Cologne had completed its defection from the ranks of London's
electoral friends by formally allying itself with France. The damage
caused by this defection had therefore to be repaired, and the obstacles
to success had in the meanwhile multiplied as a consequence of a recent
Franco-Prussian agreement to oppose Joseph's election. To fill Cologne's
vacancy Newcastle looked to Saxony. He authorized Sir Charles Han-

bury Williams, now minister to Dresden, to negotiate for the Saxon vote and, with an eye toward Parliament, for Saxon troops as well. Since the Dutch retained their interest in the election plan, they joined the negotiations. In September 1751 Saxony promised its vote to Joseph in return for the payment of £32,000 annually from Britain and for £16,000 from the United Provinces. When the Saxons then tried to construe certain textual ambiguities in an unsatisfactory fashion, New-castle brusquely threatened to suspend the subsidy and Saxon trouble-making promptly ceased. With a minimum of difficulty Newcastle had restored his "eminent majority."

But he was less certain than a year earlier how it should be used. With France speaking darkly of its right, embedded in the Westphalian settlement, to intervene in German affairs, the war-weary court of Vienna was unwilling to provoke Versailles by convoking the electoral college. Confronted with Viennese timidity, Newcastle began to believe that a mere six votes would be insufficient to effect Joseph's election and that France could be placated only if its imperial ally, the Elector Palatine, received some satisfaction for his pretensions against Austria. But before any effort to win over the Elector Palatine could be under-taken, the duke had to deal with an embarrassment at home: opposi-tion in the Parliament to the Saxon subsidy. Encouraged by rumors of Pelham's coolness to the expenditure, the elder Horace Walpole and the duke of Bedford chose the early months of 1752 to assail the treaty and the principles behind it. The treaty itself was in no danger, for the legions of ministerial adherents would not be shaken by a brief outburst in Parliament. But Newcastle counted the many foreign diplomats attending the debates in the House of Lords and knew that they were trying to discern the real mood of the political classes in Britain. He defended his foreign policy in a vigorous address.[17] A continental system, he declared, was essential to British security, subsidies were needed to build such a system, and the most compelling justification for the small expenditures entailed was the avoidance of the immeasurably larger cost of war. His political forces in both houses then dramatized Pelhamite power: the House of Commons in com-mittee approved the subsidy by a vote of 236 to 54, and the Lords did not even bother to divide.

The stage was now set for the duke's last major effort to secure Jo-seph's election. He sent the acidulous earl of Hyndford to Vienna as a complement to the gentlemanly Keith, hoping that a double-barreled approach would prompt the Austrian commitment to stiffen. He authorized Albemarle to sound out French views on the election, hoping to find grounds for a resolution of differences. And he made plans once again, for the third time in five years, to accompany his monarch on the unpleasant trip to northern Germany. Personal diplomacy had eased the road to the Bavarian treaty in 1750; it might be equally efficacious in 1752 for securing a Palatine treaty and then an imperial election. Newcastle, in any event, was optimistic: "I own," he assured his less sanguine brother shortly before arriving in Hanover, "I have no doubt of our election this summer."[18]

The Austrians remained unmoved, however, and much of Newcastle's energy at Hanover was spent in efforts to promote in succession three different schemes designed to bring about the election. At first Newcastle relied on Viennese statements that the consent of Versailles was the sole prerequisite for a peaceful election. He learned from Albemarle that France would let Britain arbitrate any dispute between Austria and the Palatine, and, ignoring the likelihood that the startling French offer might be intended chiefly to sow discord between London and Vienna, the duke accepted with alacrity. The Austrians—"pettyfogging lawyers" Keith was soon to call them—were less impressed.[19] In 1750 they had painfully experienced Newcastle's eagerness to purchase friends with territory not his own, and the prospect of another British-directed negotiation drove them curtly to reject the proposal.

Stung by the "stupid, haughty" court of Vienna, Newcastle turned to a second and older strategem: if France was not to be placated, perhaps it could simply be ignored and the election effected by the existing "eminent majority."[20] To the duke's proposal that the electoral college be immediately convoked and the election forced through with the six well-disposed votes, Austria first responded with honeyed ambiguity. Newcastle thus persisted until late June. But then, at a meeting of Britain's electoral allies, called to prepare them for the convocation, the representatives of Austria and Mainz confounded the duke's plans. The joint resistance was as unexpected as it was unwelcome, and the meeting turned into what the diplomat from Mainz jocularly called "a tumultuous session of Parliament." Newcastle, in the words of the same diplomat, "raised his tone by degrees, and his natural English temper could not withhold itself from expressing his displeasure to me in the strongest terms."[21] But the duke's expostulations failed to weaken Austrian resistance. The meaning of this "skirmish" was therefore clear:

though Vienna was loath to buy French indulgence, it was equally loath to dispense with it.

Newcastle's dilemma was now acute. If Vienna insisted upon an acquiescence it was unwilling to bid for, the duke could either abandon his scheme and thereby acknowledge the fatuity of the Bavarian and Saxon subsidies, or push forward by purchasing French support with British funds. His decision, if he ever really agonized over it, was made easier by his knowledge that Hardwicke and Granville preferred the commitment of more funds to the admission of failure, and at the end of June the duke suggested to the lords justices that Britain promise to pay £50,000 to the Palatine as compensation for its pretensions against Austria if Vienna would pay an equal amount. Pelham, who had earlier expressed doubts about the utility of the Saxon subsidy, was predictably averse to still another expenditure in pursuit of a German will-o'-the-wisp; but after reflecting on the choices, he too preferred the subsidy. He insisted however—and it proved a sage demand—that all funds be withheld from the Electoral Palatine until after the election had been effected. Newcastle accepted this restriction readily. Its wisdom was too manifest for the duke to protest against the fraternal incursion into foreign policy, and in fact he seems almost to have welcomed Pelham's proposal as an opportunity to begin to disengage himself from sole responsibility for a scheme that was souring.

Throughout July even this generous British offer failed to make Vienna more cooperative. The Austrians reiterated their refusal to compensate the Palatine for baseless claims, and Newcastle began to despair. "We are in," he wrote Albemarle, with the hyperbole so characteristic of his disconsolate musings, "the greatest crisis that I ever knew. Half the world is frightened and the other half scarce knows what to do."[22] But when George II abruptly decided to recall Hyndford as a sign of his disgust with Vienna, a panicky change occurred in Austrian behavior. Colloredo persuaded the ministry that it dared not risk a breach with its major ally, and in a stunning *volte-face,* the emperor and empress informed Hyndford at his final audience in early August that they would match Britain's contribution of £50,000. Newcastle was overjoyed: the hopes for success had been rekindled.

These hopes, however, flickered only briefly. For Newcastle the negotiations of the next three months, as he tried to reconcile Palatine avarice with Austrian cupidity, were a cruel experience. Twice he sponsored the drafting of compromise proposals; twice he saw them rejected by the legalistic Austrians. With the duchess seriously ill, Parliament soon to meet, and George himself growing weary of imperial electoral machinations, Newcastle knew he had exhausted all diplomatic expedients and prepared to set out for Britain, his dreams disappointed. What he did not know was that the hopes he had nourished because of Austria's policy reversal of August had been ill-founded from the beginning. Austria had not acted to facilitate an election which it still feared would upset France; it had acted simply to prevent the dissolution of the Anglo-Austrian entente. Austria's aim for over a year had been undeviating: to deter the election but retain Britain's friendship.

Newcastle returned to London a disappointed man. He had hoped to make an enduring mark upon European diplomacy—to emulate Lord Stanhope. But the reward of his promises, manipulations, and expostulations consistently had been recriminations from Pelham and distrust in Vienna. For many months yet he continued to hope for an end to Austrian obstructiveness, and in the spring of 1753 he even sent his favorite diplomatic handyman, Sir Charles Hanbury Williams, to Vienna to try once again to loosen the glacial firmness of Austria's attitude. But Hanbury Williams had as little success as Hyndford before him, and aside from his justly celebrated descriptions of life and leaders in the imperial capital, his venture produced nothing noteworthy.[23] Thereafter, the imperial election plan receded from view. Deep in his heart the duke retained an interest in it, but by mid-1753 he had more important matters to deal with. The office of king of the Romans remained vacant until 1764.

To no other diplomatic enterprise—and perhaps to no other enterprise in his whole life—did Newcastle devote so much time and personal energy. It is therefore important to understand why the plan failed, to assess the duke's responsibility for the failure, and to determine the impact of the failure upon Newcastle's more basic goal of buttressing Anglo-Austrian relations.[24] The cause of the diplomatic miscarriage is plain, for once Austria had decided that an imperial election might jeopardize the continuation of European peace—a decision reached in the winter of 1750–51—it dared not sanction a convocation of the electoral college. Instead, it chose to obstruct the implementation of the election plan, but to do so in a covert manner, awaiting that day when the British, without feeling resentment toward Vienna, would themselves finally weary of it. In this way a dangerous election was to be avoided while the valued entente was to be saved. Thus, all of Newcastle's efforts after that winter were predestined to failure. Until that time the duke had proceeded with a skilful and even a deft touch: he had wisely cloaked the acquisition of Cologne's support in secrecy to delay the organization of an opposition, and he had then induced his diplomatic colleagues meeting at Hanover to come to terms in the Bavarian subsidy treaty. But after the crucial winter, as Austrian policy became more perplexing to Newcastle, the duke's judgment began to falter. He ought not to be condemned for failing to understand Vienna's new position immediately, since the diplomatic signals from the troubled imperial capital were intentionally ambiguous. But he can be faulted on other grounds. It was a mistake to send the sharp-tongued Hyndford to Vienna, a man ill-suited to mollify Austrian discontent. It was a mistake to ignore the warnings of Lord Granville and Gross-vogt Münchhausen about the technical problems entailed in effecting an imperial election. And it was a mistake to invoke the nebulous but potent notion of British honor in justification of prolonging a scheme so inessential to British security. These were errors born of a confrontation with unexpected resistance, and Newcastle revealed through them his most striking weakness as a statesman, a tendency to respond to waxing difficulties with waning flexibility.

Still, it should not be forgotten that it was the quest for collective security against France that first prompted the duke to begin his diplomatic initiative. In seeing the danger of isolationism Newcastle judged rightly. Throughout the interwar period Britain retained continental ties, and when a troublesome frontier war expanded into a general war in 1756 two of these ties helped save Britain. The reference is to Hesse–Cassel and Spain, not Bavaria and Saxony, but had the full war come a year earlier when the electoral treaties were still in force, the imperial election plan might loom much larger in British history. In any event, Newcastle was serving, according to his lights, the defense needs of the kingdom; allies changed, but recourse to continental alliances did not.

V

Although the duke retained his taste for imperial electioneering too long, he had not entirely ignored other approaches to the defensive league he envisioned. In June 1752 Keene announced from Madrid that Spain, Austria, and Sardinia had concluded an agreement about their respective Italian holdings. The treaty in fact involved much less than

Newcastle had hoped for when the negotiations had begun, but he reacted jubilantly anyway, seeing in this limited Austro-Spanish alliance a solidification of his fragile anti-French league. More pregnant with future implications was Newcastle's decision to seek a Russian treaty. George II and the Austrian ministry were both convinced of the utility of St. Petersburg's amity. This great eastern power would serve as the appropriate counterweight to Prussian strength, forcing Frederick II to divert to his East Prussian frontiers troops which would otherwise threaten Austria and Hanover. Moreover, since Prussia was becoming more testy about its dispute with Britain over Berlin's unpaid portion of the Silesian loan and London's unwillingness to reimburse Prussian shipowners, the threat posed by Frederick's armies seemed to be mounting. Henry Pelham's exchequer eye viewed the proposal with the usual suspicion, but he still preferred this prospect of an alliance with a substantial power to his brother's German chimeras. Although the outcome of any Russian negotiations was unclear, the resolution to pursue the treaty was taken in 1753.

Even with the French, against whom his entire diplomatic effort was otherwise directed, Newcastle was willing to treat. In accordance with plans arranged at the peace congress in 1748 commissioners from both countries began to meet in 1749 to seek a peaceful settlement of American quarrels. They were charged with fixing a number of uncertain boundaries and ascertaining the rightful ownership of some disputed West Indian islands, with adjudicating the contentious issue of prizes, and with resolving the difficulties remaining over prisoners. The last two problems posed no serious difficulties, but the first proved intractable. It is true that both Britain and France apparently wanted a peaceful settlement, but there were two obstacles to successful negotiations. First, each country regarded its own case in the disputes as so fundamentally sound that any compromise would involve a needless sacrificing of possessions. France was committed to limiting the British to as little territory as possible, specifically, to bottling them up on the peninsula of Nova Scotia, to establishing the western frontier of Britain's holdings not at the lakes but at the more easterly watershed, and to retaining St. Lucia. Military wisdom argued for these choices, as the French well knew, but the French thought the relevant international treaties confirmed the validity of their position. The British Board of Trade, however, disagreed. At Lord Monson's death in 1748 the duke of Bedford had insisted that the presidency go to an enterprising and efficient man. Newcastle suggested his wife's brother-in-law, the duke of Leeds, but Bedford persuaded the ministry to appoint the dynamic Lord Halifax. Thus, when giving advice on the various American issues, the Board of Trade was in possession of a different set of "facts" than the French, the same understanding of military advantage, and a president shrewd enough to make the most of the situation. The board found the French argument not just disputable but thoroughly specious. Still more obstructive to a peaceful settlement was the behavior of the men on the spot in America, the British traders expanding their commercial empire westward without regard for such abstractions as international frontiers, and the French military commanders fortifying their defensive positions against what they could only interpret, however much Versailles might urge patience, as hostile incursions.

Newcastle was not at first intimately involved in these negotiations. They fell within the province of the southern secretary, and until 1751 Bedford provided the British commissioners William Mildmay and Newcastle's Sussex neighbor, William Shirley, the governor of Massachusetts, with such instructions as they received. But Newcastle was not inattentive to the broader international issues involved. In 1750 he wrote of the need to stand firm on the Nova Scotian territorial claims, even at the cost of "a rupture with France." "If we lose our American possessions," he continued in the same letter, "or the influence and weight of them, in time of peace, France will, with great ease, make war with us whenever they please hereafter."[25] After Bedford's resignation Newcastle assumed direction of the negotiations and in 1752 agreed to their continuation at the ambassadorial level in Paris. But with neither side authorizing its negotiators to compromise, the talks were stalemated. Meanwhile, the duke was evincing a growing desire for effective ties with America, shifting chief authority for the colonies away from secretary Holderness to president Halifax. But events across the Atlantic were steadily outpacing dignified efforts in London and Paris to halt them. French military posts arose to block British expansion at Nova Scotia, and a running though low-key Acadian war had developed by 1750. Soon thereafter Fort Necessity was built to protect British interests in the Ohio valley territory claimed by both the Crown of France and the Ohio Company. Newcastle did not know how to deal with the broad problem of reconciling British and French interests in America. He wanted a continuation of peace—after all, the last war had taught him the grave risks involved in recourse to arms—but he also wanted to maintain Britain's international position intact. He was unhappy with Shirley's expansionist hopes, and yet he would not instruct the commissioners to take their cue from Mildmay's less aggressive inclinations. His state of mind, it can be seen in retrospect, foreshadowed the strange inability to recognize when goals were incompatible that would haunt his days as chief minister. But to those who might have cared to analyze it in 1752 and 1753 it probably seemed quite simply a natural consequence of the relative unimportance Newcastle assigned to the whole issue of Anglo-French talks.

VI

Political life held many enchantments for the duke. One of the greatest was the opportunity it afforded him to distribute offices and bestow favors and thereby to secure compliance. It was for his direction of patronage that he was, in his own day, most notorious with the politically literate of Britain. Such direction involved the political manipulation of men through the offering or withholding of appointments and benefits. All eighteenth-century governments used this tool extensively. Deprived of the prerogative weapons that had served the Tudors and early Stuarts, the Hanoverian monarchs and their ministers were compelled to fall back on this less obtrusive technique of assuring that Parliament would not thwart the will of the executive. The aim— as David Hume among others saw—was to use the Crown's command of a wide variety of places to encourage the aspiring politician to be a compliant politician as well. Advancement was difficult and in some professions well-nigh impossible without royal or ministerial favor, and if such favor was to be bestowed only on those whose politics were satisfactory, a powerful inducement operated on every ambitious man to trim his political views to acceptable Whig specifications.

It was widely believed that political loyalty was the sole prerequisite for attaining appointive office, and Newcastle sometimes professed to adhere to that criterion: "The rule which I have laid down to myself in all recommendations which I have ever made to the crown, has been, first to recommend none whom I did not think most sincerely well-affected to his majesty and his government, and to the principles upon which it is founded."[26] Office, by this theory, was to be reserved for orthodox Whigs; and it would take, the theory further held, a bold man to hew to Tory or radical convictions if he knew they deprived him of almost all chance of success. As a corollary to this rule that only the right-thinking should be appointed it was also widely believed and asserted that only the right-thinking should be retained. Bubb Doding-ton captured the essence of this aspect of mid-century politics in his aphorism: "Service is obligation, obligation implies return."[27] A place-holder who failed in this primal duty was likely to be divested of office.

Instances of patronage manipulation for political ends are legion during Newcastle's years of power. In 1752, to cite a single but repre-sentative instance, William Blackstone, his reputation not yet made, asked his friend William Murray's aid in procuring a professorship of civil law at Oxford. Murray in turn inquired of Newcastle. The duke's power was more extensive at Cambridge than at Oxford, but he was not without influence at the older university and agreed to an interview with Blackstone. The duke was, among other considerations, eager to defuse the Tory bomb he believed Oxford University still to be. He pointedly asked Blackstone if "whenever anything in the political hemisphere is agitated in that University, you will, sir, exert yourself on our behalf." The lawyer replied merely that he would fulfil his lecturing obligations as well as he was able, a reply that the duke rightly thought evasive. The post went to a sounder candidate;[28] political interest was served.

Still, the political system did not always operate with such precision. The duke was not a political automaton, and there could be other considerations on his mind as well when he made selections and rec-ommendations, considerations that would not eliminate political and practical concerns but which might diminish their significance. Some-times the concern was simply friendship. At Newcastle's direction in the 1730's, for example, Lord Essex received the diplomatic assignment to Turin, a post deliberately chosen by the irresponsible Essex because he believed it would involve little work. He served wretchedly there, forgetting to put secrets into code, constantly seeking money, favors, or leaves of absence, debauching himself, and doing neither the Whigs nor the kingdom any good. Friendship with Newcastle alone accounted for this disastrous choice, and only when Essex asked to be relieved of his duties—he found even Turin too taxing—was he removed.[29] At other times the duke's operative consideration was his regard for Sussex. "Sussex people are too fond of *sinecures*," the duke once remarked.[30] But Sussex people kept filling minor posts, less because they were orthodox Whigs—though most doubtless were—than because their gratification lent further strength to the duke's sway in the county. A

South Saxon poetaster described the effect of the duke's indulgence towards his neighbors:[31]

> Favours conferr'd engage the Sussex coast:
> Party still more: their country's welfare most.

> And as you've been a friend, still may you be,
> To George, to Britain, Sussex, & to me.

At still other times Newcastle's prime motive in making appointments was to oblige Pelhams and their relatives. Very early in his career he earned a reputation as a man who sought advantages for his family. "We drank your health," Lord Carteret cheerfully wrote in 1724, "as well as that of all the Pelhams in the world."[32] Many of them would soon be clogging various offices under the Treasury.

Although he revelled in exercising patronage authority, the duke was never all-powerful in the sphere of appointments. Some fields of patronage, most notably the army, were deliberately denied all ministers by George II. Other fields were, in effect, controlled *ex officio*, and Newcastle could not be all officials at once. Still, his might was extensive. As chancellor of Cambridge University he could make and unmake academic careers. As southern secretary he had the right of recommendation to most colonial and many diplomatic posts. After 1754, when he assumed command of the Treasury, he had to relinquish his official power over such appointments. But he continued to exercise wide influence in diplomatic and colonial patronage for several years, not because he was officially entitled to but because his successors were either his tools or, in the case of Pitt, a man unenchanted by patronage manipulations. In taking over the Treasury, moreover, the duke acquired a patronage empire: he exercised the right to superintend the vast number of places under the most capacious department of government. And meanwhile, whether secretary or first lord, independent of any office he held and based simply on his knowledge of ecclesiastical politics, the duke presided over church patronage.

Each field of patronage had its own peculiarities and difficulties and imposed its own requirements. Certain positions, such as university and ecclesiastical posts, demanded a decent level of talent and training of their incumbents; others, such as many revenue positions in the Treasury, required none. Certain types of posts—ecclesiastical ones are good examples—were keenly sought after, and vacancies produced bevies of aspirants to office. Others, especially colonial positions, were so little valued that the duke sometimes had to seek out candidates and prod people to apply. As a consequence of these differences the duke was compelled to handle the various fields in diverse ways. Treasury posts were best for relatives and Sussex friends: they often required no training and little time and in general allowed the appointee to reside away from London if he chose. Colonial posts might have to be filled with people of suspect politics or doubtful deference simply because no one else would accept them. Ecclesiastical posts, however, permitted the most rigorous political sifting because candidates who were eager and technically qualified abounded and the duke did not need to settle for a cleric of dubious political principles. He was, nevertheless, inhibited in ecclesiastical affairs by a different restriction: since he did not want to disaffect his dissenting allies, he had in general to confine his choices to those Anglican divines who were tolerant of nonconforming Protestants.

The duke's record as an administrator of patronage is characteristically spotty. Unquestionably able to discern talent, he nevertheless often found reasons for bypassing it. As a consequence he made some execrable choices. William Cosby, for example, became governor of New York though known to be an obnoxious footlicker. The impecunious Lord Albemarle received the governorship of Virginia so that he might secure revenue to appease his creditors. Sir Henry Poole, a Pelhamite kinsman devoid of talent, later received a treasury post. But Newcastle also made some outstanding selections. He was the chief mover behind the political career of his Sussex neighbor, William Shirley, whose tenure at Massachusetts marked a high point of effective gubernatorial direction for the colony. And he induced Robert Hunter to emerge from retirement to assume the governorship of Jamaica, from which post Hunter successfully led that troubled colony out of financial crisis.

But most of the duke's selections were of a middling sort. He wanted men of ability, but only if they were also docile. This dual standard was most readily invoked in dispensing church patronage. Bishop Warburton called Newcastle's system an "ecclesiastical lottery," and in its suggestion that the system was a vast game the description conveys some truth.[33] But it was not chance that determined who won the coveted ecclesiastical prizes; it was, rather, good churchmanship yoked to deferential politics. Instances of Newcastle acting on political considerations abound. In 1765 the bishop of Chichester was denied the deanery of Windsor because his political behavior had disobliged the duke; in 1743 Dr. Newcomb was required to pledge his support to Lord Fitzwilliam's Whig interest before receiving the deanery of Peterborough; Dr. Newton found himself consistently overlooked because his most outspoken sponsor was Lord Bath. Still, the episcopate that the duke created was somewhat less rigorously Whiggish than Gibson's. Although Newcastle claimed that George II continued to seek only good Whigs for high church offices,[34] the working definition of that term became more flexible after the mid-1740's, and the episcopacy thereafter acquired mild political heterogeneity. This decline of thoroughly partisan church management may in part have reflected the duke's desire to stand well with those who would assume power in the coming reign. But it showed too, despite the duke's own disclaimer, that politics was not his sole standard, and that he regarded scholarship, generosity of spirit, and devotion to the church impressive recommendations for a candidate.

The duke strongly admired certain clerics and favored them whenever decently possible. John Hume, for example, was chosen by the duke to be tutor to young Lord Lincoln and acquitted himself so effectively that his career quickly prospered. He was appointed to a residentiaryship of St. Paul's in 1748, elevated to the see of Bristol in 1756, and in 1758 translated to Oxford and granted the deanery of St. Paul's *in commendam*. He became the duke's closest spiritual adviser in old age. James Johnson also benefited from friendship with the duke. In 1759 Newcastle used his influence to have Johnson translated from Gloucester to Worcester even though some people held the bishop to be a secret Jacobite. Thomas Secker constituted yet another example, a man whom Newcastle chose for Canterbury in 1758 despite the fears of some Whigs that he was hostile to dissenters. But Newcastle knew his man: Secker's hopes to gain advantages for the Anglican church in America were easily blocked, and in other matters the new archbishop proved suitably and humbly cooperative.

In an overview it would appear that Newcastle, during a long career as director of patronage, was neither the fiercely partisan zealot nor the self-aggrandizing empire builder that some have held him to be. It is true that he regularly consulted personal whim and party interest in staffing the bureaucracy; and if he was not blind to ability nor determined to suppress it, neither did he pursue it systematically. But the eighteenth-century context must be recalled. Newcastle inherited a system for filling offices and took delight in running it. It served him and the Whigs well, for although not everyone who received office was a loyalist, the large majority of his appointees supported the government. Eighteenth-century administration was not ruthless, and every minister found in the disposal of places opportunities to exercise compassion or reward talent in addition to assuring votes. Newcastle's notoriety as a patronage manipulator rested not on any efficiency or reforms he brought to the system—he provided neither—but rather on the length of his tenure in command and the unconcealed zest and singular ostentation with which he managed its details. Dr. Newton captured the essence of Newcastle in his role as director of patronage when he called the duke "a good natured man," who "had not the courage to say No to any one, . . . was willing to oblige every one, at the time perhaps seriously intended it, and consequently promised more than he was ever able to perform."[35] Clearly there were more efficient ways to handle the distribution of jobs, but Newcastle's direction met the minimal requirements of his age.

VII

By mid-1753 a general election was approaching. Because the ministry had protected its patronage flank well, it felt itself in no danger from disgruntled politicians. Indeed, among the prominent only Bedford stood in opposition. But its popular flank was inevitably more exposed. A general election gave the entire political nation one of its infrequent chances to make its sentiments known. Should public opinion suddenly become enraged over a transitory issue, duped by demagogic rhetoric, frightened in its understanding, or irrational in its behavior, then the ministry became highly vulnerable, and patronage manipulation irrelevant. More than most successful politicians of the eighteenth century, Newcastle respected, and even dreaded, the force of public opinion in politics. Since tangible expressions of public opinion tended to appear spasmodically rather than continuously, Newcastle reasoned that the proper task of government was not, as modern politicians might conclude, either to guide or capitalize on public opinion, but rather to tranquilize it. It was this attitude, a healthy regard for what he viewed as the disruptive power of inflamed mass irrationality, that explains the duke's extraordinary aversion to change. Change could only upset people, he believed, and ought therefore to be discouraged. Afraid to revive "old Disputes & Distinctions, which are at present, quiet," Newcastle opposed Sherlock's intelligent suggestion that a bishop be sent to America in 1750. He objected to Chesterfield's useful calendar reform in 1751 because he did not want to "stir matters that had long been quiet." He even offered some initial resistance to Hardwicke's thoroughly commendable marriage reforms of 1753.[36] An electorate ablaze, he deeply feared, would be an electorate out of control.

The opposition was also aware of the power of public opinion, and during the winter of 1752–53 it tried to discredit the government by charging it with harboring Jacobite sympathies. The most serious charge, disseminated anonymously by enemies of the Pelhams, especially by the younger Horace Walpole, held that the ministry was not merely listening to the advice of avowed Jacobites, but even entrusting the education of the young prince to adherents of the Pretender. Substantive proof for the accusations was totally lacking, and the contradictory testimony of witnesses hostile to the government made the opposition case singularly unpersuasive. Still, the affair could not be lightly dismissed, for the ultimate targets of the opposition charges were Newcastle's two close friends and advisers, Andrew Stone, formerly the duke's secretary and now the prince's subpreceptor, and William Murray, the solicitor general and member for Newcastle's seat at Aldborough. The two men were exonerated at an unusual cabinet interrogation of their accusers, but the duke of Bedford then introduced the issue of Jacobitism to the House of Lords by questioning the legality of the cabinet session. The ministry took up the challenge. Hardwicke forcefully defended the constitutionality of all the government had done; Newcastle upheld his friends against the imputation of disloyalty. Bedford found few followers and the issue expired. Unquestionably, however, the ministry had been vulnerable, if only because its role as judge could scarcely be represented as disinterested. What is thus interesting in this incident is the failure of the issue to arouse the nation: the days when the cry of "Jacobite!" could summon forth all that was ugliest in the British people were past.

But the ugliness, as Newcastle suspected, was still there, responsive now to other calls. The major political crisis of 1753 was the uproar over the bill to permit foreign-born Jews to become British subjects. It was a measure of reason and tolerance and a reward to the coreligionists of important financial allies of the government. Although the ministry had encountered popular resistance to its efforts to ease the naturalization laws two years earlier, it clearly did not anticipate the frenzied response that the so-called Jew Bill would evoke. Usually attuned to *vox populi*, Newcastle was in this instance as unsuspecting as the rest of his colleagues. The measure passed the House of Lords unobtrusively, but shortly after it reached the Commons popular indignation, compounded of nativism and anti-Semitism, began to emerge throughout the kingdom. The House of Commons approved the bill and the king made it law, but the clamor did not abate.

The parliamentary opposition, ever alert to popular issues with which to assail the ministry, took up the cry. The duke was personally stung when, appearing as chancellor at Cambridge, he was dubbed "King of the Jews" by elements hostile to the Whiggishness of that university.[37] By July the fury of public demonstrations had convinced the duke that the government had erred in supporting the measure: the "mob" was aroused, a most ominous occurrence with an election in the offing. For the duke the situation awakened memories of the Sacheverell and excise madnesses. He saw repeal as the only resort, and finally persuaded his reluctant brother that the government dared not hazard a general election without first placating the antiforeign mood of the kingdom. This meant, above all else, that the Jew Bill had to be repealed. Once this had been decided, strategy dictated that the government should take the initiative rather than letting the opposition gain the double credit of first assailing and then eliminating the measure. And so, when Parliament reopened in November, Newcastle wasted no time in introducing a motion for repeal in the Lords. His speech reflected the embarrassment of the ministry, for in it he tried to defend the wisdom of the original measure and the sagacity of the new one simultaneously. The repeal was quickly effected. Men of reason expressed contempt for the government's pusillanimity, but men of politics, whose judgments cannot be scorned, were almost unanimous in their conviction that repeal was necessary. Had a general election not impended, Newcastle might have had less success in convincing his brother of the need for repeal. But the election could not be avoided, and so the Jew Bill had to be sacrificed.

With the demise of the bill, the ministry seemed advantageously situated for the elections. Public issues posed no threat, and private division within the Pelham family had finally been repaired, though not without some memories of fraternal acrimony. The problem, as always, had been Newcastle's want of financial restraint. It is true that the trust settlements of 1741 and 1744 were not ineffective, for in accordance with their terms large portions of the old Newcastle estate were being steadily alienated, and as a consequence the trust debt which had reached £174,640 in 1744 had been reduced to £97,060. But the duke had continued during these years to live more extravagantly than his trust allowance and income from office justified and had amassed new debts totalling £66,000. As early as 1746 the Monsons and Hutton Perkins had warned that his careless treatment of creditors might lose him the reasonably generous rate of 4 percent at which he was permitted to borrow from friends. But his love for high living burned unabated, and when he traveled abroad in 1750, though still in debt for his trip of two years earlier he nevertheless spent £1,844 for French wines alone.[38] Sam Burt, who managed the duke's London and Claremont properties after the mid-1740's, became a key aide to the duke in these years—Murray called him Newcastle's "maître d'hotel"— but he seems not to have been very vigorous in urging retrenchment. It was thus merely a matter of time before another crisis emerged.

By early 1750 the duke was casting about for financial expedients, hoping that Andrew Stone or William Murray might know someone still willing to advance him cash. But the two friends were unable to supply the needed succor. The duke then hoped to reduce costs by dismissing servants and giving general direction of household affairs over to Burt, but his debt had become too large for such palliatives. By late 1751 he was forced to inform the duchess that his "private affairs" were desperate: everywhere he turned he met demands from "clamorous people" who would no longer brook delay in payment. There was now, he felt, but one recourse: to use the authorization incorporated in the trust settlement to raise a loan of £20,000 on the Nottinghamshire estate.[39] Unhappily for the duke, such action required Pelham's approval, and so once again, despite all that had gone before, the duke was forced to go hat in hand to his brother. He did not relish the task; still less did Pelham relish the request.

Direct fraternal communication broke down completely in the ensuing quarrel. Andrew Stone and Lord Lincoln were pressed into service as intermediaries between the suppliant duke and the disgusted first lord. At first, Pelham was deaf to his brother's pleas: he had already offered more help than duty required, he believed, and he had now to look to the interests of his own family. Privately the duke berated his brother as unmindful of ducal aid in 1726, but Stone, as Newcastle's agent, treated Pelham far more decorously. And slowly Henry Pelham relented, first requiring that Newcastle submit thorough accounts of the disposition of the estate since 1744, and then allowing himself to be moved to mercy by Murray's remonstrations. The first lord still exacted a price: to gain Pelham's cooperation Newcastle was compelled to settle the reversion of parts of the Sussex estate upon Pelham's daughters. Thereupon Pelham approved the new incumbrance on the Nottinghamshire estate, William Murray and a kinswoman to Stone provided the £20,000, and Newcastle was permitted by his newest creditors to retain the Nottinghamshire property as a freehold and collect rents on it.[40] Murray meanwhile examined Newcastle's account books closely, concluding painfully that ducal austerity would be absolutely necessary. "I do assure your Grace," he wrote of these accounts, "they draw tears from my eyes."[41] Newcastle thereupon resolved to live within £6,000 per year, allocating about half of his personal annual income to interest repayment and debt redemption; he reduced his household staff and did not replace Sam Burt, who died unexpectedly in 1752; he leased the Bishopstone farm; and he even explored the possibility of increasing his income through the sale of timber and the raising of rents. Regularly thereafter he submitted his books to the scrutiny of the noted financial writer, James Postlethwayt.

All these measures appear, by 1753, to have eased the duke's situation considerably, and it seems likely that the restoration of fraternal amicability was not unrelated to the improvement of the duke's financial position. Moreover, by 1753 the contentious use of foreign subsidies no longer threatened the sensitive fraternal bond. Clearly fond of each other, the brothers were nevertheless ambitious and thus held power in an uneasy alliance. Their moods and attitudes were contrasting and yet not readily reducible to complementarity. Newcastle was prodigal with his and the kingdom's wealth; Pelham was parsimonious. Newcastle was exuberant in his enthusiasms; Pelham was restrained. Newcastle measured policy proposals against a standard of national glory; Pelham invoked the standard of economy. Both men were uncommonly suspicious, but Pelham was the more censorious and Newcastle the more jealous. It is testimony to the ambivalent nature of their relationship that while they enjoyed each other's company in small and intimate groups, they avoided it at large gatherings: they recognized the tendency of the public arena to change them from friends into enemies.

But politics must be played in the public arena. To reduce fraternal and hence ministerial bickering to a minimum, after 1748 the brothers

and Hardwicke had, in effect, directed Britain as an informal triumvirate. The chief ground rule for decision making within the group was
that matters falling clearly within the official competence of one of the
three men were to be his responsibility.[42] Herein lies one reason why
historians have had so much difficulty in ascertaining where the heart
of power resided in these years. Each brother is known on occasion to
have stated that the other directed affairs; and at different times Hardwicke acknowledged the supremacy of each.[43] Certainly Henry
Pelham was the crucial link between the Crown and the Parliament;
in this sense he was prime minister. But the locus of power lay elsewhere, for if the ministry's viability depended upon the younger Pelham, the direction in which it led Britain depended to a great extent on
Newcastle. The critical test of dominance within the ministry arose in
those situations where issues lay athwart two distinct spheres of ministerial responsibility. On such occasions—the dispute over whether to
subsidize German principalities is the most famous of these years—it
was Newcastle, not Pelham, who customarily prevailed. This dominance was rooted in psychology rather than in institutions. But it was not
enfeebled for want of constitutional soil. It was, quite simply, a consequence of the duke's position as the elder of the two brothers and of his
greater readiness to resort to badgering to settle disputes. Pelham was,
in sum, submissive towards his brother: the political events of the mid-
century years reflect that psychological fact.

During July 1753 Henry Pelham fell ill of a scorbutic disorder and
withdrew for recuperation to Yorkshire. In December the complaint
returned. Newcastle fretted over his brother, and January brought
Pelham relief once again. The political world was thus unprepared for
the outcome of a third attack in February: slowly but inexorably the
disease exhausted the patient, and on the morning of 6 March 1754
Henry Pelham died. Newcastle knew only tears at the most grievous
loss he had thus far borne. But, with a general election still to come,
friends such as Hardwicke and Murray, enemies such as Bedford and
Egmont, and rising politicians like William Pitt and Henry Fox knew
that Pelham's death meant the end of a political system and an era. It
was a truth that Newcastle too would slowly and painfully learn.

6

First Minister

Henry Pelham's death deprived the kingdom of its chief pillar of political stability. He was, under the conditions obtaining in 1754, irreplaceable. Only one man, the duke of Newcastle, could fairly be regarded as Pelham's successor to the leadership of the Whigs and hence of whatever reorganized ministry might now emerge. It is true that at first, because of the pain of loss, the duke disavowed any desire to continue in public life; but soon, prodded by Lord Hardwicke, who assumed command of affairs during ducal mourning, he was adopting a sharper tone, not only talking of remaining in politics but even asserting that no one would be permitted to deny him the dominance that now seemed rightfully his.[1] Once this determination had been reached —and it came within a few days of Pelham's death, under the cover of a public image of persisting grief—the first choice to be made was the post from which the duke would exercise his authority. He hoped at first to remain as secretary of state, a position he found congenial and one for which his experience had prepared him. Various names were bandied about as possible successors to Pelham at the Treasury, and the position was even offered to the duke of Devonshire, a Whig of high reputation and low ambition. But Devonshire declined, and Newcastle and Hardwicke meanwhile concluded that the duke himself would have to assume the duties of first lord. The command of finance and patronage were prizes too valuable to be consigned to others. The duke acknowledged that he would probably find the responsibilities of the post onerous, but if preeminence was to be his, he had to secure it by controlling the key office of state. At a council meeting on 12 March, stage-managed by Hardwicke and unattended by the still secluded Newcastle, it was decided that the duke should succeed Pelham at the Treasury.[2]

With that decision made, a major problem loomed, for three vacancies thus needed filling. Newcastle's decision to take the office of first lord of the Treasury immediately created two departmental vacancies: the post of secretary of state, which the duke would perforce resign, and the post of chancellor of the exchequer, which had to be left with a commoner whenever a peer took direction of the Treasury. Similarly, since Newcastle, unlike the earlier party leaders Walpole and Pelham, was disabled by his title from giving direct leadership to the more fractious and powerful of the two chambers, Pelham's death had presumably created a third vacancy, the post of minister in the House of Commons. The exchequer was quickly disposed of. The duke needed a competent subordinate, able to offer assistance to a neophyte first lord and speak intelligibly in the Commons, and yet unprepared to use his knowledge to try to undermine his nominal superior. Henry Legge was chosen, intelligent but unpolished, and disqualified from aspiring to the highest offices by a voice and accent that invited snickers. The other two vacant posts presented far more vexing problems. The office of secretary of state was, of course, one of the two posts responsible for foreign affairs and many domestic matters; in disloyal hands it could plague a first lord. The minister in the House of Commons was the man chiefly responsible for good relations between the Crown and the lower house. He needed both ability and experience to be effective, and he could not be expected to carry out his functions to good account without some share of treasury patronage authority as well. Clearly someone who met these qualifications and had access to the king too would be a formidable political figure in his own right. Newcastle predictably feared the consequences of delegating so much power to anyone.

The younger Horace Walpole wrote that in the aftermath of Pelham's death three men stood out as possible leaders of the Commons: the fiery William Pitt, paymaster of the forces, the suave Henry Fox, secretary at war, and the reasonable William Murray, the solicitor general.[3] Walpole's comment is both true and false—true in the sense that these were the three ablest commoners, but false insofar as it conveys the impression either that no other men were considered or that the chances of success were at least modest for each of those three. In truth, the public spoke in addition of several other candidates, among whom were Legge before his appointment to the exchequer, Sir George Lee, treasurer of Princess Augusta's household, George Grenville, a lord of the Treasury and a friend of Pitt's, Lord Dupplin, a lord of trade and Pelham's chief aide in handling treasury patronage, and Arthur Onslow, the speaker of the House of Commons. But the one whose name dominated discussion was Henry Fox. Pitt's rhetoric might be terrifying and Murray's logic compelling, but each of Fox's rivals suffered from widely recognized disabilities which made their likelihood of succeeding to Pelham's leadership of the Commons exceedingly remote. Pitt's burden was the king's keen dislike of him. He was in Bath, nursing his crippling gout when the crisis broke, and his absence from the scene of action destroyed whatever dim chances may have remained. Within days of Pelham's death Hardwicke wrote to Pitt to explain gently why preferment would not come his way. Murray's chief burdens were his Scottish birth and the recent charge that he had accepted the Jacobitism of much of his family. Though exonerated by the ministry (and posterity), he suffered the plight of Caesar's wife—the Whigs would not accept direction from one whose devotion had been in question. It would seem as well, though perhaps only as a function of this unpopularity, that Murray was temperamentally disinclined to seek the highest of political offices, preferring instead to keep his career in judicial channels and his eye on the highest of judicial posts. A few days after Pelham's death he declared through his friend Andrew Stone that he had no ambition to succeed to leadership of the Commons.

Thus, Newcastle and Hardwicke had few options. If they wanted a lieutenant in the Commons—and most people presumed the post indispensable—they could look only to Fox. Newcastle undoubtedly would have preferred Murray, an old friend and adviser and a man willing to be a subordinate. Hardwicke would have preferred Pitt, and Newcastle, though less enthusiastic, would have accepted him. Neither, however, was willing to take the dangerous Henry Fox. The man's allies, his odd gaucheries, his inclinations, and even his talents were all computed as liabilities. Fox was a friend of the duke of Cumberland, with whom the Newcastle Whigs were still at odds. Cumberland, "the Butcher," was odious to many in the kingdom. Fox had also been a determined foe of Hardwicke's marriage bill. Of this transgression Hardwicke was unforgiving. Besides this, on the morning of Pelham's death, indeed within two hours of it, Fox had begun canvassing politicians for support. Of this disregard of ordinary decency Newcastle was similarly unforgiving. The duke was, moreover, aware that Fox was a would-be director of patronage in a way that Pitt, who claimed to despise the management of offices, was unlikely to be. If admitted to leadership of the Commons, Fox would bid fair to become an independent political power, cultivating his own widening circle of clients; indeed, friendship with Cumberland might even allow Fox influence over the military patronage that Hanoverian monarchs had so resolutely withheld from their ministers. Finally, Fox was fearsome simply because he was so able. A man of skill and ambition, he would be certain to use whatever advantages might fall or be given to him to broaden his power and thereby threaten Newcastle's command. For this congeries of political and personal reasons Newcastle could not give control of the Commons to Fox. But if Fox was not to be permitted to have it while Murray would not and Pitt could not take it, there was but one inescapable conclusion: the government would have to gamble and try to make do without a minister in the House of Commons.[4]

Denying the post to Fox was not an easy task. The public expected him to receive it, and the king was rather fond of this younger politician who had befriended the favorite royal son. Public disapproval could perhaps be risked, but not royal discontent, and thus there could be no alternative to offering Fox the post. But Newcastle and Hardwicke devised the plan of offering him a restricted leadership, with conditions such as to make likely his rejection of the offer. The men who had engineered Bedford's resignation in 1751 knew that their fellow politicians maintained a certain sense of honor. They planned now to offend Fox's. If successful, their strategy would serve two ends: it would keep Fox from office, and it would do it in such a way as to cast responsibility on him for declining the offer rather than on them. But even if unsuccessful at denying the post to Fox, it would at least severely inhibit his ability to make trouble for the first lord. Lord Hartington, son of the duke of Devonshire, was dispatched to Fox on 12 March to offer him the position of southern secretary with direction of affairs in the Commons. The southern secretaryship had been cleared by plans to shift Holderness to the vacant northern post, presumably to keep Fox in the less important secretarial office should the scheme fail. Fox accepted promptly, even a bit jubilantly. But the following day, after a convivial meeting with Hardwicke, he conversed with Newcastle and learned that the duke proposed to withhold from his new lieutenant both the right of nominations to office and the knowledge of who in the Commons was in receipt of secret service moneys.

It is now clear that Fox exaggerated the importance of the secret

service fund. But he did not misconstrue what was happening. Newcastle maintained that either Fox had misunderstood Hartington or
that Hartington had misunderstood the duke; but Hartington, not
involved in the plot, defended himself and Fox from the duke's accusa-
tory self-exculpations. Bitter and confused at such duplicity, Fox cast
about for expedients, and for a short while it appeared that the duke
might have misread his quarry. But Fox soon repented of his indecision,
decided that he would be neither "fool" nor "knave," and on 14 March
wrote a letter to the duke asking simply that he be allowed to remain
as secretary at war.[5]

Only on 15 March, after Fox had made himself ridiculous by accepting and rejecting office within forty-eight hours, did Newcastle again
appear in public, weeping at the feet of the king. Ostensibly his grief at
the loss of his brother had prevented him from carrying on affairs during
the intervening eight days, but the true story is more complex. That
the duke's sorrow was genuine need not be doubted: he loved his relatives, quarrelsome though they might sometimes be, and he was an
affectionate man in any event. "His excessive grief," Hardwicke wrote
on 11 March, "makes him just now very unfit for business."[6] It would
appear, however, that five or six days after Pelham's death the duke's
demeanor of mourning had acquired a certain element of calculation
to it. He remained shut up, and as late as 15 March a visitor called the
sight of the duke in his despondency "the most tragical Scene he ever
saw."[7] But meanwhile the duke was not only managing private meetings
with Hardwicke, Hartington, and Fox on political mattters, he was even
beginning to collect information about his brother's plans for the
coming general election. Indeed, on the "tragical" fifteenth he plunged
into a series of what were to be almost daily meetings with his key
electoral advisers to prepare for the imminent polls.[8] If unfit for business on the eleventh, he was clearly no longer so within a few days. It
was, one can speculate, useful to maintain the image of the grieving
brother. The charade spared him the importunities of an eager pack
of politicians, and it provided a convenient alibi when it became necessary to explain how he had failed so miserably at conveying the
proper idea of the nature of his offer through Hartington to Fox.

It took Newcastle four days to resolve his remaining problems. Sir
Thomas Robinson was asked to resign the great wardrobe to become
southern secretary, and the duke's old friend agreed. Robinson was
not to be minister in the House of Commons in anything remotely

resembling the way Pelham had been. He was simply to be a conduit or a loudspeaker for the ministry. No one doubted his intelligence, but of characteristics that might make for leadership in the Commons he was almost devoid. He was not even, the duke acknowledged, an adequate public speaker. Newcastle viewed himself as manager of the House of Commons: "The direction of the House of Commons," he told Bubb Dodington on 21 March, "was fallen on him, who had never thought of it."[9] The ministry in short was to be a throwback, an effort to return to the days when a first minister relied chiefly upon the Crown rather than the Commons for political might and endurance. He knew the risks he was running. He had been instrumental in securing Murray's support in 1743 precisely because he knew what debating strength in the Commons meant. But a leaderless Commons now seemed preferable to having Fox exercise much of the authority of Pelham. Perhaps the duke calculated that in peacetime the government was in less danger from truculence and noncooperation in the popular house than it had been in wartime. Certainly he felt that patronage would afford him the opportunity of constructing large and powerful majorities. But William Murray, a man of sound judgment, was visibly upset by the settlement. Unmistakably an element of risk lay at the heart of the scheme.

For this reason the duke made special efforts to placate and resecure the support of the unpredictable William Pitt. This irascible cripple was disadvantaged in any effort to assail the duke's settlement by the fact that he currently sat for Newcastle's interest at Seaford and had been promised a seat at faithful Aldborough at the coming general election. This "peculiar circumstance"—the term is Pitt's[10]—modified such remonstrances as he could make. But he was nevertheless unhappy. Of Robinsons's appointment he was contemptuous: "The Duke might as well have sent his jack boot to lead us." The elevation of such an undistinguished member of Commons was an insult to the house in general and Pitt (and others of talent) in particular. He wrote a noteworthy letter to Newcastle on 24 March to complain of the results of the ministerial shuffling. For a man who had earlier denied any interest in preferment, he was remarkably disgruntled that he had been taken at his word. Both Hardwicke and Newcastle wrote to calm the orator. The lord chancellor gave a short history of the proceedings since Pelham's demise, stressing the need to find solutions that guaranteed continued Whig control of affairs and advancing the hope that with his friends in high places Pitt might look forward to an abatement of the king's dislike for him. Newcastle noted that, though Pitt was discontented, so were many others: he himself, the duke added, had been forced from an office he undertsood and liked "to go to one where I was entirely unacquainted, exposed to envy and reproach, without being sure of anything but the comfort of an honest heart, and a serious design to do my best for the service of the King, my country, and my friends." The duke's fulsome letter evoked Pitt's irony: "If I have not the fruit, I have the leaves of it in abundance; a beautiful foliage of fine words."[11] Pitt was not prepared to join the opposition immediately. But it boded ill for the future of the ministry that a scheme designed to settle the affairs of the Commons satisfactorily should have angered Henry Fox and wounded William Pitt. They could be, they would be, remarkably damaging enemies.

After Robinson's acceptance of the seals, only various odds and ends needed settlement. George Grenville became treasurer of the navy and Sir George Lyttelton became cofferer. Since both were allies of Pitt, their promotions were designed to bring him solace and the ministry peace. Lord Barrington was designated for the Treasury Board but reassigned at royal request to Robinson's old post of master of the great wardrobe because the king wanted a man of economies in the office. The lord chancellor was given a deserved earldom—he retained the title of Hardwicke—and Lady Katherine Pelham, Henry's widow, was granted a generous annual pension of £1,000.[12] Newcastle made financial provisions for himself as well. His secretarial office had brought in almost £6,000 per year, and the salary of the first lord of the Treasury was only £1,600. For a man in the duke's financial straits such a decrease in income could be disastrous, and reflections on that truth may in part have contributed to the duke's reluctance to shift offices. Thus, once established at the Treasury, the duke persuaded the king to permit a payment of £1,050 quarterly to the new first lord.[13] A slight diminution in official revenue was still incurred, but at least personal financial chaos had been averted. The duke could settle down in his new office in the knowledge that his pocketbook was not paying for his decision to keep younger rivals at bay.

The sight of Newcastle at the head of the chief financial office of state and in command of national affairs was alarming to some and astonishing to more. Only in the middle of the eighteenth century was it possible for a man like the duke, so clearly unfit for the leadership responsibilities he now assumed, to reach the pinnacle of political success. To make clear why this is so it is necessary to examine the polit-ical and social setting of the duke's career. He emerged on the scene at a time when the great aristocratic resurgence that had followed the demise of the Puritan commonwealth had reached full tide. Land laws and inheritance laws had been molded by two generations of conserva-tive gentlemen and peers to encourage the accumulation of land by a small number of owners and to discourage the breakup of the landed estates. For a millenium the ownership of land had been associated with, and had often been the key to, membership in the leadership strata of English society. The impact of the new laws was to make these strata, or at least the higher of them, a smaller proportion of the population than they had been for at least several centuries. But the importance of land was more than social. One of the tools of the aristocratic resurgence was the new political use to which land was put. For although the power of the House of Commons within the constitution had been considerably enhanced by the events of the seventeenth century while the cruder techniques by which the aristocracy had once controlled the Commons had passed into desuetude, the accumulation of land in the hands of an ever smaller proportion of the population gave to that proportion extensive power in parliamentary elections. It was precisely these developments in landholding that made the eighteenth century the era par excellence of electoral manipulation. Whether deferential or venal, electorates generally conformed to the wishes of a body of magnates whose power was increasing. Still the question remains as to why eight-eenth-century magnates were so often peers. After all, there would appear to be nothing in the changed nature of the land laws to favor the success of the peerage over the success of the gentry. To some extent, that appearance is simply misleading, for peers were likelier than the gentry to be wealthy to start with, and the laws tended to give in pro-portion to what one already had. But the real reason the peerage ex-ercised the power attendant upon land ownership with greater effect than the gentry was the lingering and potent respect Englishmen continued to have for men of title. Peers were thus the double bene-ficiaries of an ancient regard for nobility and of a new system of land distribution.

Newcastle, of course, believed that in still a third way peers might now be heirs of good fortune. Firmly committed to the notion that the peerage was the fittest ruling group in the country, he yet had to ac-knowledge that for half a century the preeminent political figures in the kingdom had more often than not sat in the Commons. But he apparently viewed this fact as simply a product of the unusual nature of the reigns of Anne and George I. Politics had been explosive in those days, and the Commons had too often been on the verge of chaos. Now all had changed. Order and tranquility had been restored, in part because Jacobitism had faded and in part because, in the duke's view, the Pelham administration had pursued sound policies. When the Commons was volatile, leadership had to be direct, intimate, and continuous. But now in less tempestuous times leadership by remote control from the House of Lords finally seemed likely to succeed. In a sense, Newcastle was right. His fierce adherence to the Old Corps blinded him to the helpful truth that the partisanship of the early decades of the century had deteriorated into factional spirit, but he did perceive that issues of a fundamental nature were receding in importance. Thus, he was not entirely mistaken in judging that the Commons had grown more quiescent and that this was the type of popular house most likely to accept aristocratic leadership. That being so, it was Newcastle who by virtue of his diligence, his wealth, his experience, his Whig background, his belief in the rightfulness of aristocratic control, and his Pelham name stood above all others as the peer most fit to assume command. What the duke failed to perceive was that an effort to implement control of the popular chamber from afar was precisely the sort of action that would revive resentments in the proud Commons. Aristocratic direction of the House of Commons was, in short, impossible because, however sweeping the aristocratic resurgence might be, actions designed to translate it into virtually direct control of the popular chamber would destroy the very tranquility which was the sine qua non of such a translation.

II

When Newcastle became first lord of the Treasury in March 1754, he entered an office of which he had little understanding. Especially foreign to him were the financial operations of his new department. For this reason some observers speculated that a subaltern in the Treasury might well emerge as the real power in the ministry. But the duke was on guard against this threat. He avoided giving any true authority to Legge, even though the new chancellor of the exchequer had been chosen because he seemed a fairly subservient sort, and he relied instead on the men who had been most helpful to his brother. He importuned friends to fill out the Treasury Board, and Lord Dupplin and Robert Nugent accepted. In principle the members of the board collectively bore responsibility for the kingdom's financial health, but in fact the first lord dominated the board's activities. Newcastle was quite prepared to seek the advice of members he trusted, particularly Dupplin, but the real second in command in the Treasury was neither Legge nor any other commissioner: it was James West, one of the two secretaries of the Treasury. West was the perfect aide. Intelligent and shrewd, he was nevertheless not particularly ambitious for advancement. A fellow of the Royal Society, he had extrapolitical interests that consumed both time and energy. He knew the Treasury well; within a few years so would Newcastle. As secretary, West assumed multifarious responsibilities. He conducted interviews, prepared and channeled documents, and imparted a measure of bureaucratic expertise to treasury operations. Though he did not actually make the key financial decisions, he was the man most responsible for keeping the department functioning in its financial role.

But its role was not solely financial, for the first lord of the Treasury had another vital function: he commanded the disposition of treasury patronage. It was precisely this command that allowed the office of first lord to evolve into the office of prime minister. Not every eighteenth-century first lord was really a prime minister—Newcastle, as shall shortly be argued, should probably not be regarded as one—but such prime ministers as the century produced operated, with the exception of the elder Pitt, out of the Treasury. Patronage was the key. Secretaries of state had considerable power, especially in time of war, but it was the first lord of the Treasury who controlled the most effective weapon for creating an obliging Parliament and well-disposed governmental and local officials. Newcastle, however, assumed control of it at an awkward moment. The general election for which Pelham had long been laying plans was just ahead. Newcastle's personal interests in Sussex, Nottinghamshire, and Yorkshire were in order, but the duke knew virtually nothing of the network of promises, commitments, and alliances that his brother had been building in anticipation of the polling. For this reason his primary concern in March was to make himself conversant with this network, and to that end he called upon the almost daily assistance of Pelham's key advisers: John Roberts, a customs officer, and Thomas Hay, Lord Dupplin, a commissioner of the Treasury. Years later Newcastle paid Dupplin a high compliment:

"Je dois principalement a lui le peu de connaissance que j'ai dans les affaires des finances."[14] But the duke's memory was confused; it was West who taught him finances. Dupplin's great contribution was to initiate the duke into the refined art of treasury electioneering.

Within little more than a week of his accession to the Treasury it became clear to the duke that he was already bound by a vast number of decisions and commitments of various sorts that Pelham had made. Some pertained to the small number of constituencies, almost all with tiny electorates, in which the Treasury exercised a powerful and direct interest. For these constituencies decisions about candidates and financial support to be offered them were generally already in effect. Other commitments pertained to a larger number of constituencies with whose patrons the Treasury had struck a deal. Money had occasionally been the price asked by the borough-mongers; more often it had been office or favor or support. But whatever the type of remuneration, for these constituencies too almost all the key decisions had been made. Still other commitments pertained to financial support that was to be extended to a small group of candidates vying for election in various constituencies over which the Treasury exercised no significant influence. Newcastle drew on this category of funds a little to support his own candidates, but even here he was compelled in general to abide by his brother's promises. In all, the Treasury paid out almost £27,000 in contesting the general election of 1754, a modest sum when contrasted with the funds that opponents spent, even in single constituencies. And when the polls were finally closed early in May, in all about seventy members had received their seats as a consequence of at least some help from the Treasury. The general election was a political success. Dupplin gave the ministry 368 members in the new house, and the various oppositions, even when augmented by those of uncertain loyalty, could total only 174. Little of the credit was Newcastle's. Pelham had made the arrangements, and political fires burned so low throughout the kingdom anyway that widespread disaffection was unlikely. Still, Newcastle exulted. "The Parliament," he wrote, "is good beyond my expectations, and I believe there are more Whigs in it, and generally well-disposed Whigs"—here the duke in fact exaggerated—"than in any Parliament since the Revolution."[15]

Part of his joy may have been thoroughly personal. Aided by his new office and the reputation it bore, he had met with unprecedented success in his private electioneering. Fully seventeen members had been returned chiefly through his concurrence, a higher total than he could claim for any previous general election. And throughout his electoral empire he had met little resistance. Only in two boroughs, both in Nottinghamshire, did an opposition go to the polls, and in each the upstart candidate lost. The Yorkshire boroughs voted with their wonted obedience, though with sounder cause than usual. Two of the duke's Yorkshire candidates were men of profound merit: William Pitt, who was chosen for Aldborough, and William Murray, who won at Boroughbridge. Murray was joined by Lewis Watson, who, as second cousin to Lord Rockingham and husband of Henry Pelham's daughter Grace, had seemed eminently well-qualified to succeed the deceased Dalkeith in 1750. The other Aldborough seat, in accordance with long-standing agreement, went to Andrew Wilkinson.

The Sussex constituencies were similarly compliant. The county returned Newcastle's first cousin once removed, Thomas Pelham, in Henry Pelham's stead and reelected John Butler as his colleague. This Thomas Pelham, rising in the duke's favor, was a very recent appointee to the Board of Trade. Lewes reelected both Sir Francis Poole, poor but faithful, and Thomas Sergison, thoroughly converted and hence also faithful. A nascent opposition had been bought off by £1,500 from the Treasury. Hastings obediently returned its two seated members, James Pelham and Andrew Stone; and Seaford, with equal submission, accepted William Hay and William Hall Gage. The latter was fittingly repentent of his recent folly of attaching himself to the late Prince of Wales, and Newcastle, having demonstrated his dominance over Firle in 1747, was relieved to renew an old alliance. The duke even gained command of a new seat in Sussex, or, more precisely, confirmed in 1754 the command he bought in 1749. The seat was at Rye, another of the Cinque Ports. Ever since 1714 Newcastle had recommended to customs posts in the borough, but he had never intruded into electoral matters. When doughty old Sir John Norris finally died in 1749, however, Newcastle was permitted to introduce his nephew by marriage, George Onslow, into the vacant seat after first paying off a debt owed by the borough to Norris's executors. Rye remained grateful in 1754: Onslow won reelection unopposed.

As usual, electoral affairs in Nottinghamshire were somewhat less settled, though only minimally so in 1754. And even though oppositions surfaced in several constituencies, the duke, in a pattern similar to Rye's, consolidated a breakthrough he had achieved earlier and thereby added an additional member to his already unrivalled collection of beholden members of Parliament. For the county the old compromise retained force: the incumbents were reelected, and John Thornhagh, an independent Whig, remained Newcastle's nominee. In the borough of Nottingham, however, a peculiar opposition arose. Faithful to the compromise agreement in the town, Newcastle himself supported both Lord Howe, the Whig who held one of the seats, and Lord Middleton's Tory nominee. But John Plumptre, victimized by the confusion of 1747, also raised the Whig standard and, though running without Newcastle's endorsement, gave the duke a severe scare before narrowly losing in his effort to sneak past one of the incumbents. At Newark too an opposition fought to break through Newcastle's alliance with local powers. It was led by the indefatigable vicar, Dr. Wilson. Three years earlier Wilson had almost engineered the defeat of Job Staunton Charlton, who had been seeking reelection after appointment to office, and the vicar at that time had showed his vindictiveness by dismissing from his school the sons of those who had supported Newcastle's friend and agent. In 1754, supported by the duke of Bedford, Wilson returned to the fray, inducing Edward Delaval to enter the lists by offering him £2,000 if he lost. Charlton and his runningmate received £1,000 of assistance from the Treasury and spent £1,700 in all in their joint campaign. In the end they won, and rather handsomely. But the duke's concern had been justifiable. And poor Delaval, for his part, had to turn to the courts before he could compel Wilson to hand over the promised £2,000. Newcastle's chief northern triumph, however, occurred at East Retford. In 1751 on the retirement of William Mellish, Newcastle had brought in his nephew John Shelley. In the general election following Pelham's death the borough unprotestingly returned both of the duke's nominees, Shelley and John White, and thereby confirmed what the election of 1751 had indicated: that Newcastle could finally dominate both seats at East Retford. He had thus held his own in every constituency he had controlled in 1747, and he had won new clients at Rye and East Retford. In this context the duke's postelectoral joy becomes understandable. He had, he believed, initiated his ministry in the most successful of all possible manners: he had secured a compliant House of Commons.

III

This euphoria was soon shattered by news from America. Although

British and French commissioners had continued their efforts to reach
an agreement on a line of demarcation between the respective American
empires, in the New World itself talk was giving place to military action.
The French established Fort Duquesne on the Ohio River as part of a
plan to secure their defense perimeter, and the Virginians, in retaliation,
sent a detachment under Colonel George Washington to destroy the
fort. Washington's troops won their first engagement but were over-
powered by a larger French force in a second. This defeat occurred in
May 1754, and word of it reached London in early July. Newcastle had
already expressed some uneasiness about the American situation, and
had enunciated as the ministry's operating principle that "the colonies
must not be abandon'd."[16] In June the cabinet had placed on record
its fear that French aggression in America posed a threat to British
trade and conceivably to the viability of Britain's northern colonies.
But the report of Washington's defeat suddenly compelled the ministry
to take seriously what had hitherto been a somewhat abstract concern.
Newcastle was enraged and spoke of national vindication. "All North
America will be lost," he wrote, "if these practices are tolerated, and no
war can be worse to this country, than the suffering such insults as
these."[17] Nevertheless, it was one thing to breathe fire and another to
make adequate military plans. Newcastle was briefly keen for the
former but essentially unqualified for the latter.

The problem reduced itself to a simple gamble: could forces be sent
to America to help in the defense of colonial and British interests without
provoking France into a full-fledged war? The duke was not at all
prepared to suffer France to take liberties with British subjects legitimately trading in areas under the sovereignty or protection of the
British Crown, and he had been persuaded by arguments emanating
from the Board of Trade that what in truth was a questionable British
claim to lands in the Ohio valley was thoroughly sound. But despite his
fierce declarations of July, he was no warrior. Neither his hopes for
financial reforms nor Britain's uncertain international position would
permit recourse to arms. The plans for financial reform are revelatory:
they suggest that Newcastle was stung by the criticism that he was unfit
to direct the Treasury and was determined to prove his merit. The
plans consisted of several parts. One was to effect a reduction in the
interest rate that the Treasury paid the bank for the annual short-term
loan which allowed the government to operate until tax revenues were
collected. "I own," he remarked, "it is hard to pay the Bank 3. p. Cent,

for lending us, (for that is the case,) almost our own money."[18] He
proposed to lower the rate to 2½ percent. A second part of his reform
plan was to bring about a reduction in the rate of interest being paid
on long-term loans from somewhat more than 3 percent (a consequence
of Pelham's conversion scheme of 1750) to the same 2½ percent. Sir
John Barnard, spokesman for the men of moderate wealth in London,
urged the duke to pressure the moneyed interest in order to get his way,
and plans for re-funding were in the works at the Treasury. Beyond
these schemes to lower the rates of interest, the duke also hoped to
pare operating expenses in the large department he now presided over
and to check official complicity at the local level in smuggling activities.[19] These were bold schemes, and the continuation of peace was the
prerequisite for their realization. A vigorous defense of British interests
in America would almost certainly destroy any chances of financial
reform at home.

The international situation was similarly unpropitious for war.
Though Britain had stopped vexing Austria about an imperial election,
London had no assurance that Vienna would come to Britain's aid in a
war with France begun in America. Austria was still very unhappy
about the Barrier. And Britain's other putative ally, the Dutch republic,
was still less useful. Scarcely a military power in any event, the United
Provinces by 1754 were showing a marked disinclination to give aid of
any material sort to a Britain caught up in hostilities. With the Austrians
unreliable and the Dutch impotent, the duke could expect any war
undertaken to be a single-handed effort. Against French might such an
action would, he believed, be folly. Partly as an effort to extricate the
kingdom from semiisolation and partly to please Austria, Britain had
recently approached Russia about an alliance. Newcastle was optimistic that a treaty with the eastern empire could be concluded. But even
if, after long negotiations, it were, it would not affect the situation in
America. The duke also took some satisfaction from the thought that
British diplomacy had shattered Bourbon unity by securing Spanish
friendship. But in the summer of 1754 even this triumph, soon to be
critically important, seemed tarnished. The marquess of Ensenada had
authorized attacks on British loggers in Honduras Bay, and Newcastle
penned a hysterical letter of protest to Ricardo Wall, the Irish-born
Anglophile Spanish minister: "I am frightened out of my wits at these
Ensenada–Orders. . . . *Pour l'amour de Dieu, ou serons nous? Vous et moi,
nous en serons certainment les victimes.*"[20] Britain was prepared to take

counteractions, but Keene again proved his worth by successfully urging Wall to discredit Ensenada, who soon fell from office. Still, as the duke cast his eye over the map of Europe in the summer of 1754 he could find little reason to suspect that a test of arms would prove useful to Britain.

So the dilemma was acute. The least painful way to deal with the French threat would have been to find a scheme to let the Americans defend themselves and British interests without recourse to British troops. If the use of British regulars could be avoided, war on the cheap might be possible. The duke had a surplus of £100,000 in the current budget which could be applied to the recruitment and arming of colonial forces for war. Not that Newcastle wanted war. His most fervent wish was that France, upon seeing that Britain would not backdown, recognize the folly of aggression in America. It was the theory of the deterrent: be strong enough to hurt your enemy and he will stop hurting you. Besides regarding regular troops as too expensive, Newcastle also thought them less suited than colonials for the woodland encounters that seemed likely to characterize any future struggle with France in America. In this view he was supported by Lord Hardwicke and his Surrey neighbor, Lieutenant General Sir John Ligonier.

But it turned out to be no easy task to elaborate a scheme through which to realize colonial self-defense. A major obstacle was colonial division, and only through the creation of a colonial union did it seem that the less threatened colonies could be made to share fairly in the cost of defense. To this end ministerial discussions began in August, but they foundered. Some ministers perceived possible damage to the prerogative if the colonies, at British prodding, effected their own union. Newcastle began to fear the "ill consequences to be apprehended from uniting too closely the northern colonies with each other; an independency upon this country being to be apprehended from such a union."[21] Because no consensus emerged from the discussions, the plans for a colonial union were finally set aside, thus explaining the ministry's inattention in October to the union plan produced by colonials at the Albany Congress. But as early as September, whatever the disposition of plans for colonial union, various forces were operating on the government to make irrefutable the argument for a widened British military presence in America. For on the one hand important colonial governors such as Dinwiddie of Virginia were pleading for such support; and on the other hand it became clear, as authorities on the colonial situation were interrogated, that the Americans were strangely unwilling to risk themselves in military engagements with the French. Newcastle expressed the problem directly: "Though we may have ten times the number of people in our colonies," he commented to Granville, "they don't seem to be able to defend themselves, even with the assistance of our money."[22]

It seemed, therefore, that complements of troops from the home country would be required if the colonies were to be defended. This was a hard decision for the duke, but it was not one he sought to evade. The British made no effort to negotiate the conflict in the Ohio valley after they learned of Washington's defeat, for the government from the first was determined to regain the military initiative before suggesting talks. Newcastle began dismantling his plans for financial reform in September: with the government needing more money, it would be silly to hope that interest rates could be driven still lower. At the same time, probably at Fox's urging, he invited the duke of Cumberland, the captain general, to participate in cabinet discussions devoted to America. His motives in doing so are unclear. Cumberland was an experienced and brave soldier whose advice merited attention. But such advice could have been solicited outside the cabinet. Indeed, Sir Thomas Robinson had been authorized to consult with the royal duke on these matters. By allowing Cumberland into the cabinet Newcastle not only enhanced the reputation of a political enemy, he also brought together at the heart of governmental deliberations two allies, Fox and Cumberland, who had already revealed their hope for vigorous measures and who held offices that might let them effect such measures. Fox, it is true, was not a member of the cabinet, but as secretary at war his importance mounted with each escalation or rumor of escalation. It seems likely, therefore, that in September Newcastle was already preparing the groundwork for later assertions that, if affairs went awry, the fault was not particularly his.

This slow abdication of authority continued as deliberations progressed. Newcastle and Hardwicke suggested that a commanding officer of rank be sent to America, accompanied by some half-pay officers, arms, and money. These officers would then cooperate with authorities in Virginia in devising appropriate defensive measures.[23] Cumberland and Fox advocated stronger action, including the dispatch of additional regiments to America to reinforce the three regular regiments already there, permanently garrisoned at Nova Scotia, and the two colonial regiments, disbanded in 1748, that were now to be raised again. The captain general and the secretary at war won the day, and the cabinet decided in late September to send two Irish regiments to the colonies. When augmented in America, these regiments would comprise almost 1,500 men. Cumberland then selected Major General Edward Braddock as the officer most fit to lead the troops, a judgment which, despite its outcome, was not as outrageous as some have asserted. Newcastle reluctantly assented to these developments, noting to Murray that "we must do it as cheap and inoffensively as we can."[24] The duke could even hope to avoid new appropriations: the Irish troops were kept on the Irish establishment, at an estimated cost to the Treasury of £100,665. One must suspect that the estimate was juggled to correspond with the surplus.

The decisions of September were not, however, immediately acted on. In fact, the duke almost at once repented of his acquiescence and hovered for a week in tormenting irresolution. He had the king's permission to reject the Cumberland–Fox plan, and his own inclinations sent him searching for a less aggressive response. But Murray spoke firmly for strong measures, and Pitt, whom Newcastle queried on 2 October, seemed prepared to argue that all the alternative plans should be merged into a single mighty stroke for British rights in America. Fox delivered Newcastle from his paralysis with a fait accompli. Without notifying the duke, he persuaded George II, whose friendship he retained, to sign the necessary warrants for the officers involved; and he then, still on his own initiative, dispatched them to their posts and requested transports from the Admiralty. Newcastle had ceased directing. A vacuum had been created at the decision-making heart of government, and Fox, prodded by Cumberland, was simply acting because some sort of action seemed necessary while the presumed leader of the government was incapable of it. Newcastle struck one last time: on 8 October he won "a most complete victory in the closet over Mr. Fox. All his orders were suspended."[25] But he relapsed immediately into confusion, and on 9 October the cabinet acquiesced in Fox's actions. Then, to prevent any further tergiversations, Fox promptly placed an advertisement in the *Gazette* announcing the cabinet decision. Hardwicke was appalled at this indiscretion, a clear violation of governmental agreements to keep military activities out of the public eye. The duke, who labeled the action "most ill-judged," wailed: "We are on a precipice."[26] And he had good reason. For even if Fox had felt com-

pelled to force Newcastle's hand in this way, it remained true, as the
duke and the lord chancellor knew, that the advertisement dimmed
hopes that France might retreat from its claims. Publicity had now
raised the question of national honor: where the quiet dispatch of
troops would have left France the option of yielding without appearing
to be intimidated, the noisy send-off left Versailles no honorable alternative to increasing its own stakes in America. The frontier war now
threatened to leap the Atlantic.

It took a month for the ministry to prepare Braddock's final instructions. Newcastle and Hardwicke hoped to limit the objectives of the
troops to the French forts on the Ohio River, but again Fox and
Cumberland, supported by Lord Anson at the Admiralty and by Pitt,
prevailed. Various units were to move against Fort Duquesne, Niagara,
Crown Point, and Fort Beauséjour. The omission of Louisbourg indicated that Britain was still restricting its military activities to those
areas which lay in dispute between the two crowns. But determined and
bitter French resistance could nevertheless be expected. The orders
were assailed by some as too pusillanimous; both Governor Shirley and
Lord Halifax, for example, thought it inexcusable that the troops were
to retreat from their conquests after driving the French out. But Newcastle found them lamentable for their extensiveness, not their caution.
He could not believe that France, however divided its counsels and weak
its will, would be conciliatory when confronted by such a provocative
show of British force.

His judgment, as often, was sound. But since he was better situated
than anyone in the kingdom to have his judgments converted into policy
guidelines, his wailing, though characteristic, became him very ill. The
duke was refusing to exercise the authority that could have been his and
that he had in fact sought. As events began to turn sour, as unexpected
difficulties arose, he retreated into a conception of his office that bore
little resemblance to Sir Robert Walpole's or Henry Pelham's. Lord
Hillsborough, comptroller of the household, noted in October 1754 that
the ministry was sorely divided, with each member running his own
department and no one asserting control. "Nobody impower'd, or
would take the lead" was Dodington's shorthand for Hillsborough's
remark.[27] Newcastle made a virtue of this traditional conception of
government: the ministers were the king's. Their task was to carry out
their departmental duties and accept direction from him, and civilian
ministers were not competent to give more than recommendations on

military matters. It would therefore seem clear that Newcastle ought not to be called a prime minister, at least not in the sense that Walpole or Pelham were. The difference between them lay not in the fact that his predecessors sat in the Commons and he in the Lords. It lay rather in the views that the three men had of their office. All had the support of the Crown. All wielded enormous influence in the Commons, whether directly or indirectly. But whereas Walpole and Pelham had used this strength to seek to superintend affairs—if not all of them, then at least a large number—Newcastle used it to isolate himself whenever things began to go wrong. The duke may have been "first" minister; Pitt at least gave him that distinction. But a prime minister, if the term is to mean anything, he was not. Namier's remark is apposite: Newcastle retained his position as leader "by reducing it to his dimensions."[28] Most of his time as first lord of the Treasury was spent in flight from responsibility. And because that conduct was inappropriate to his office, by it he must be judged fully as responsible as Cumberland and Fox for measures that gravely threatened peace.

IV

The problem of elaborating a strategy for America was not Newcastle's only difficulty in the late summer and fall of 1754. Even though Parliament was not in session and there had as yet been no test of Newcastle's plan to direct the Commons from the Lords, voices began to express doubt that it could succeed. Newcastle was initially confident. He linked Legge, Pitt, and Fox together, each holding office, as the self-appointed leaders of a small, spiteful, jealous opposition. All the advantages, he believed, lay with himself and the Old Corps: "We have as good a body of friends in the House of Commons," he wrote to Hardwicke in early September, "as ever men had; we have the King, we have the nation at present and we have, and shall have, the House of Lords. I hope that we shall not suffer three ambitious men in the House of Commons (of which two are at this time guilty of the highest ingratitude to us) to defeat all our good designs for the public, and to convince the King the we can't serve him without their being our masters."[29] But the confidence began quickly to ebb. Legge pushed the suggestion that the leader of the House of Commons be permitted direct access to the king, and meanwhile Pitt and Fox, through their collusive and successful effort to force Britain into more vigorous defensive measures in America, demonstrated greater strength and support than the duke had at first credited them with. Showing traces of apprehension, Newcastle wrote to the elder Horace Walpole in October to express the hope that he would lend his support to those who sought to defend the king's system against the arrogant claims of those who demanded a minister for the Commons. Still, as late as mid-November, right after the opening of Parliament, he could interpret Legge's insistence that Pitt be treated with confidence and that Fox be given a secretaryship as evidence not of their strength but of their desperation and ineffectiveness.[30]

Of such cocksureness he was soon completely disabused. William Pitt had been growing restive and perturbed for months. As early as May, Pitt had predicted troubles for Newcastle's ill-conceived ministry. He had also begun nursing hopes that he would be summoned into the cabinet. But the duke, having committed himself to a diminution in the authority of the Commons, proved resolute in his pursuit of that goal. Pitt finally ran short of patience. Finding the duke's war preparations appalling, he chose November to unleash a tumult in the Commons. On three celebrated occasions the fire of old flared forth. When Pitt entered a weary house on 25 November to find it laughing about electoral bribery, he poured verbal contempt upon his colleagues' disrespect for the dignity of their chamber and warned, in a quickly famous phrase, that if the Commons did not regain its old prestige, it "should only sit to register the arbitrary edicts of *one* too powerful a *subject.*" That same evening Pitt attacked the unguarded revelations of ministerial prejudgment of electoral petitions that the ingenuous Sir Thomas Robinson delivered; but since Robinson was such an easy target, the paymaster quickly softened his tone and indicated that it was not Sir Thomas whom he blamed but the duke of Newcastle. Two days later it was Murray's turn to feel the heat. In calculatedly ambiguous phrases Pitt spoke of Jacobites still abroad in the land, reminding his auditors of Oxford University and, with glance and gesture, showing he had in mind Oxford's illustrious son, the new attorney general.[31] Murray writhed, and for Newcastle an unexpectedly dangerous situation abruptly emerged: although the ministry could still count on a majority of votes in the Commons, many of those who voted with the government laughed rather with the opposition.

Newcastle now had to recast his plans. Robinson was unable, and Murray generally unwilling, to stand up to Pitt. Either Pitt had to be silenced, presumably by giving him responsible office, or someone had to be found who could match Pitt's debating facility. George II's distaste for Pitt, increased by these latest antics, made the former option unfeasible; indeed, the king wanted to dismiss the rebel from office and had to be dissuaded from doing so by Newcastle's argument that a total severance of ties would only stoke Pitt's rage. Thus Newcastle had to look for a powerful reinforcement. Only Henry Fox fulfilled the requirements, but Fox and Pitt had formed a strange partnership during the fall of 1754. It began with their joint opposition to Newcastle's American program, and it blossomed into a devastating debating duet in the Commons as Pitt trained his fire on Murray while Fox took aim at Robinson. Whether Fox would now break with Pitt and accept the role of defending the government against his former friend's impassioned denunciations was uncertain. But the effort to secure him had to be made. On 29 November George II summoned Fox to suggest that he might become spokesman for the ministry's measures in the Commons. Recalling the deceit of the previous March, Fox was cautious. He expressed some interest, demanded details, and agreed to treat with Lord Waldegrave about terms. But he was, at this time, unwilling to negotiate directly with Newcastle. His conditions, as revealed to Waldegrave, were two: that he be made a cabinet councillor, and that he not be required, in defending the ministry's measures, to assail Pitt. He hoped to be made a secretary of state, but Newcastle demurred at this request, and Fox withdrew it, remaining secretary at war. Fox also agreed to being, in rank at least, behind Robinson in the Commons and declared he did not wish to share in patronage recommendations or the disposition of secret service funds. He finally settled not for a cabinet councillorship, but for the promise of future promotion into the cabinet. Fox's decision to save the ministry at this juncture was a calamitious personal error; it would irreparably blight his political career. He was accepting far less than he had properly rejected nine months earlier, and while he had in March refused to be a flunkey in what appeared to be a strong ministry, he now embraced the same role in a weak one. Henry Fox was an honorable but ambitious man, and his ambition had fatally clouded his judgment.

But it also saved Newcastle's political life. A government that had been tottering now regained a degree of stability. The duke's experiment in remote direction of the Commons had proved a failure, but he had reacted to the danger in time, and had been able to do so, thanks to Fox's misjudgment, at a cheap price. Pitt thereafter muted his rhetoric, and the rest of the session progressed smoothly, as Fox, Murray, and Robinson provided the government with ample might in the chamber. Still, Newcastle showed little gratitude toward his savior. As soon as Fox was admitted to confidence, Newcastle thought he detected a new coolness in the king. Old friends anyway, George II and Fox were, in the duke's view, entirely too chummy. When the duke suggested at the very end of the year that several personnel changes might strengthen the royal household, George II burst into a series of tirades against his first lord. "The Duke of Newcastle," he told a startled Hardwicke, "meddles in things he has nothing to do with." "There is no such thing," he declared to an astonished duke, "as first minister in England, and therefore you should not seem to be so." It is a commentary on Newcastle's inclinations and view of government that the man who sought to evade control of policy simultaneously tried to extend his control of patronage. Hardwicke rebuked the king for publicly disputing with his ministers: such actions could only undermine the "state of ease and quiet" that Newcastle was promoting. Royal behavior thereafter improved—George II had doubtless been venting one of his periodic rages of frustration—but Newcastle found it suspicious that the explosion had coincided so closely with Fox's rise in influence, and the duke held the secretary at war responsible.[32] It was an inauspicious beginning to what was supposed to be a cooperative venture.

America reemerged at the forefront of ministerial concerns early in 1755. As the duke had feared, France responded to the dispatch of Braddock and the Irish regiments with a decision to send reinforcements to its own troops. Newcastle still believed war avoidable, and although he never got around to selecting a successor to Lord Albemarle, who died as ambassador to Versailles in 1754, he was eager to talk the colonial dispute out. Thus there began in January in London the most serious negotiating effort undertaken during the mounting crisis to stave off hostilities. The French ambassador, the duc de Mirepoix, met regularly with Robinson and occasionally with Newcastle to explore suggestions for calming the colonial scene. The ambassador thought well of Newcastle: "Je le crois bien intentioné pour le maintien de la tranquilité et de la bonne intelligence entre les deux Cours."[33] Robinson's instructions directed him to seek a mutual withdrawal from the Ohio valley; Mirepoix nursed similar hopes. Each negotiator wanted peace, and each found his negotiating partner sympathetic. But good will alone could not suffice.

The stumbling block to success was the French insistence that they could not truly negotiate until an armistice had been declared. France feared that without the armistice, military ventures by the reinforced British and colonial armies would give London enormous advantages. Britain felt, conversely, that the imposition of an armistice would allow France to dispatch its reinforcement fleet with impunity, even though its arrival in North America would tip the military situation in France's favor. The duke rejected the advice of those who urged him to have the Royal Navy intercept the French fleet in European waters. His action was an assertion of treasury authority, and it clearly forestalled what would have been an act of war. But his decision immediately raised the new problem of countering the escalation of the conflict that the French reinforcement would represent. Meanwhile, at the negotiating table, Britain was less conciliatory. After initially accepting the Appalachian chain as the British frontier, the ministry, pressured by Halifax of the Board of Trade, altered its position and called for the frontier to be put far to the west of the mountains. Britain also now insisted for the first time that the Nova Scotia boundary be drawn to London's advantage and that certain French forts be razed. Such shifts only increased French suspicions of British intentions and led several powerful French ministers to conclude that Newcastle was playing for time. In this atmosphere of mutual suspicion the negotiations stagnated and in March the French reinforcement fleet took to the seas.

Britain had not let the negotiations prevent it from strengthening its defense forces. In a series of ministerial decisions beginning in January, Britain began bringing its naval crews up to full size by extending impressment and offering bounties to volunteers. The ministry also authorized the expansion of the regiments in America by 2,000 men. The duke of Cumberland was the spirit behind these decisions. Peace with France was desirable, he argued, but in view of the natural enmity existing between the two kingdoms, prudence demanded extensive military preparations. Even Newcastle agreed: he expressed his hope in February that France would accept terms, but he noted that, whatever the outcome of the talks, Britain's fleet would be ready. The question was, of course, ready for what? By March the duke could no longer disguise the bleakness of the picture: negotiations had failed, and French reinforcements were preparing to move toward American waters. And so the cabinet acted. It dispatched a fleet under Admiral Sir Edward Hawke to Torbay and directed him to detach a squadron—it would be commanded by Vice Admiral Edward Boscawen—which was to sail to America to prevent the French from disembarking troops at Louisbourg. The Royal Navy was now under orders to attack the fleet of another nation in non-British waters. That would be an act of war. Mirepoix was not privy to Boscawen's orders, of course, but he understood the situation: "Le gouvernement cède aux caprices du public; le parti est prise, et les dispositions actuelles de la cour tendent ouvertement à un rupture. Le duc de Newcastle, par impuissance, timidité, et légèreté, suit le torrent commes les autres."[34]

The decision to accept war as inevitable did not end the divisions about defense policy that so hobbled the ministry. The old war party, Cumberland and Fox, urged on by George II, now became advocates of extensive military action designed ultimately to bring the conflict home to France on the continent. The old peace party, chiefly Newcastle and Hardwicke, but now independently supported by Legge, hoped instead that the struggle could be confined to America and that the ancient notion of a localized belligerence could be revived.[35] Fox and his supporters, the "land-war-party," were proving faithful to traditional Whig conceptions of the proper way to wage war against France. Newcastle and his friends were now heirs to traditional Tory ideas which emphasized the priority of maritime activities in warfare. But the duke's position was unsound. Much as he might hope that France would accept a prohibition of belligerence in Europe, he knew very well that it was precisely in Europe that Britain, through its tie with Hanover, was most vulnerable. France could scarcely be expected to let Britain triumph in America without seizing Hanover as a bargaining point for peacemaking. Hence any proper strategy needed to presume that France would attack the electorate. And so, because British and French forces were clashing sporadically in America, the rulers of continental Europe began to prepare for war at home: "On viendra a la rupture," Frederick II grimly predicted, "sans avoir eu le dessein et sans savoir comment."[36]

George II recognized the threat that imminent Anglo-French hostilities posed to his German patrimony, and so, despite the exhortations of his ministers that he was needed in Britain, he determined to set off for Hanover in the spring of 1755. While in the electorate, after consulting with electoral ministers, he would prepare a scheme for its defense. But his actions did not absolve the British ministers from the same duty, for it was widely held, even by some who disliked the

Hanoverian tie, that if the electorate were attacked as a consequence of its connection with Britain, London should defend it. Newcastle ultimately assented to this line of reasoning, and the minstry prepared itself to argue that British aid could and should come in time to deter, not just relieve, an attack. The monarch's absence from the kingdom necessitated the creation of a regency council. Shortly before the king's departure Fox was raised to the rank of cabinet councillor to qualify him for appointment to the regency. The promotion occasioned his final break with Pitt. But the decision that surprised many was the selection of the duke of Cumberland to head the council. It was, to be sure, a choice that simply ratified the dominant position Cumberland had come to assume in defense planning. Moreover, with war so close, many now argued that Cumberland was clearly the wisest choice for director of the council. But Princess Augusta, mother of the Prince of Wales, was furious, and the attitude of Leicester House toward the ministry, never favorable, now turned thoroughly hostile.

The council's chief task was the strengthening of Britain's alliances in preparation for the defense of its continental interests and concerns. And although it later rejected the grandiose defense projects suggested from Hanover in June—massive armies in both Germany and the Low Countries—the council knew that such defense would require troops. The Dutch were unlikely suppliers. Sick of war and constitutionally hamstrung, the Dutch government was also engaged in a quarrel with Britain about money that the United Provinces claimed was owed them. But the Austrians seemed a better choice, and Robert Keith was directed to sound them out. Vienna had already expressed a readiness to help protect Hanover and strengthen its own army in the Austrian Netherlands if Britain would also station British troops in the Low Countries and guarantee Maria Theresa's hereditary holdings against Prussia. Newcastle had thought that this proposal offered good prospects for an agreement, but the ministry, with George II concurring just before his departure, had crippled the initial Austrian scheme by declaring that while Britain would pay mercenaries to man the Netherlands, it would not send its own forces. Austria thereupon grew cooler, and after Britain rejected Vienna's de facto ultimatum in June even though the terms were not really extravagant, it became apparent that Vienna's policy was to remain disengaged from any Anglo-French quarrel. Only one British action would then have altered Austria's determination to keep clear, a British commitment to make war on

Prussia. Keith expounded Austrian thinking to the regency, emphasizing Kaunitz's view that Russian aid against Prussia was imperative and relaying Kaunitz's hints that the best solution to the Prussian problem would be a dismantling of the Hohenzollern state. Newcastle rightly thought the last comment "a pretty remarkable statement," and he recognized as well the purpose of the chancellor's reference to the czarist empire. Though Keith was directed to continue pressing Vienna for troop support, the duke sadly remarked that "he might as well whistle— they won't send a man till our treaty with Russia is upon the point of being made and a general plan formed."[37] The road to Hanoverian defense apparently led through Vienna and St. Petersburg.

To the end of securing a treaty with Russia, Newcastle early in 1755 had replaced Guy Dickens with Sir Charles Hanbury Williams as Britain's ambassador to the czarist court. Hanbury Williams used cunning and an appreciation of the venal nature of Russian politics to secure a treaty in August: Russia promised to keep troops poised on the East Prussian frontier and to launch them if Prussia attacked Britain or Hanover; in return Russia would receive an annual subsidy of £100,000 in peacetime and £500,000 if the troops had to be sent into action. It was understood, moreover, that Russia both wanted and expected war. Meanwhile, however, the earlier subsidy treaties with Saxony and Bavaria were now expiring, and Dresden and Munich were displaying considerable reluctance to renew them on any terms that Britain could regard as satisfactory. Ultimately the treaties, to Waldegrave's disgust, were allowed to lapse. Additional continental troop strength from other states was thus needed, and the ministry turned to an obvious source by providing £50,000 for an 8,000-man augmentation of the king's own Hanoverian forces. Then allies were sought. Hesse-Cassel was approached by the ministers at Hanover, including Holderness, who had accompanied the king on his journey. Hesse soon came to terms, promising 8,000 men in return for £60,000. Still later, the Hanoverians secured the support of the Margrave of Ansbach and the bishop of Wurzburg, each agreeing to keep 2,000 men ready. Because public opinion in Britain had turned quite hostile to subsidies—"Sea war, no continent, no subsidy is almost the universal language," wrote Newcastle[38]—the ministry quietly diverted £90,000 from the Civil List and passed it on to Hanover in preference to preparing an application to Parliament for all the funds. Perhaps the treaty with Russia would induce Austria to stand by Hanover; if not, the ministry had at least given the electorate a heterogeneous group of reinforcements. Holder-ness bluntly explained the reason for the ministry's fondness for sub-sidies: "As we pay the piper, it is not unreasonable for us to have the tune we like."[39]

Subsidy treaties were relatively noncontentious within the regency itself. But the broader question of the scope of the coming war was not. It came to a head in the summer of 1755 when the ministry addressed itself to the task of preparing instructions for Admiral Hawke, who waited off Torbay for orders with sixteen ships of the line. Initially Hawke was to have been given hostile orders, that is, instructions to attack any French vessels encountered, whether commercial or ships of war. With such orders he could intercept France's Indies fleets on their return. But Hardwicke, and then Newcastle, blanched at the implica-tions of these plans: any hope of limiting the conflict to America would be swept away by an attack on French shipping in European waters, and Britain would be recklessly choosing war without having secured a strong ally. So Newcastle began to stall. He knew that the public might scorn him as too pacific, but he wanted to avoid the opprobrium of being the aggressor. It was, of course, rather late in the day for such sentiments to emerge, far too late, in fact, considering the instructions Boscawen had sailed under, but the duke showed an unwonted stub-borness in July as the regency agonized over drafts. Cumberland and Fox urged approval for the instructions as originally envisioned; Gran-ville, unpredictable as always, opposed "vexing your neighbours, for a little muck;" Newcastle insisted that some restrictions be placed on Hawke. At first, he proposed that the admiral be instructed to attack only if he thought it worthwhile, but the other lords justices quickly noted that this stipulation would put the entire responsibility on Hawke and probably induce him to avoid any action. The duke then proposed that some weighting formula be devised, authorizing Hawke to attack only if the French fleet exceeded a certain size. Ultimately, under Newcastle's influence, the instructions directed the admiral to engage French war ships but no merchantmen. "The absurdity," Dodington remarked, "is inconceivable."[40] And indeed it was. For whatever may be said in extenuation of the duke's hesitation—that he was a friend of peace, that war had not yet been declared, or that France's attitude was still ambiguous—it remains true that he had already endorsed instructions to Braddock and Boscawen that were certain to lead to war. Indeed, before Hawke's instructions were completed, news of Boscawen's misadventure had arrived. The duke's scruples and fears in mid-summer of 1755 only served to ensure that a war begun unwisely and dishonorably would be undertaken weakly and ineffectively as well.

V

Not until August 1755 did the government learn precisely how awk-ward and precarious its position had become. Reports had reached Lon-don in July of Boscawen's inability to prevent the landing of French troops at Louisbourg. Worse than that failure was the fact that part of his fleet had attacked a portion of the French fleet, capturing two prizes. These were not very valuable, but the action clearly stamped Britain as aggressor. Hardwicke aptly characterized the venture as "*too little* and *too much*" and despaired at Britain's unprecedented plight, without a friend and yet initiating a war with France.[41] Meanwhile, as Versailles now sought Madrid's support, only Keene's mastery of Spanish affairs kept the two Bourbon kingdoms from joining forces. But the unhappiness produced by the account from Boscawen was redoubled in August when London learned that Braddock and many of his men had been slain by French and Indian troops while they were trying to apply European tactics on the American terrain. Jointly the melancholy reports constituted disastrous information: France had succeeded in reinforcing its troops in America while Britain's earlier reinforcements had been significantly diminished; moreover, while failing to gain su-periority in America, Britain had still managed to assume the role of aggressor. Mirepoix left London in anger, and war seemed inevitable. But Newcastle's potion of troubles had not yet reached the brim. Even as the shocks of Boscawen's failure and Braddock's death were being absorbed, intraministerial quarrels led to a stunning act of defiance. Henry Legge, chancellor of the exchequer, refused to sign warrants authorizing the payments of the Hessian subsidy. Though it could not prevent the dispatch of the funds, Legge's action hinted at how wide-spread the doubt about Newcastle's handling of affairs had become. Newcastle would have replaced him immediately but could find no adequate substitute.[42] Three months earlier Dodington had written that "the nation was sinking by degrees, and there was a general indisposition proceeding from the weakness and the worthlessness of the minister."[43] What had seemed true then seemed still truer by August. The minister, the government, and the kingdom were adrift.

As in November 1754, though now with more reason, Newcastle

needed rescuing. Parliament would meet in the fall, primed with questions about the inept conduct of colonial defense and about ministerial divisions over subsidies. A forceful spokesman for the government was needed to counter the anticipated barrage. Newcastle was already harboring doubts about Fox when the disasters of July and August began raining down. Quarrels between the duke on the one hand and Cumberland and Fox on the other had become matters of public comment. And although Fox was a skilled House of Commons man, Hardwicke continued to dislike him for his past while Newcastle continued to distrust him for his tie with the king. Thus the duke was prepared, indeed, had long been prepared, to seek Pitt's help again. As early as April old Horace Walpole had approached Pitt with Newcastle's blessing and gauged his mood to be conciliatory; but the interview turned fruitless when Newcastle disavowed Walpole's intimation that Pitt could expect a secretaryship when next one fell open. By July, with resistance in the Commons to the government's subsidy policy predictable, Newcastle decided that if the seals were the price of securing Pitt, it would have to be paid. The duke even began seeking royal approval, a sure sign that he was serious, and later claimed he had been given "full power" to effect ministerial shifts.[44] But Pitt's attitude was also changing, for as he grew increasingly bitter at Newcastle's repeated snubs and aghast at his incapacity, he renewed ties with an alternative source of prestige and influence, the rising sun of Leicester House. This liaison was desired by Lord Bute, the Scottish instructor to the Prince of Wales and director of Leicester House political activities. If Pitt could be gained, Bute predicted, " 'tis likely a strong party will be formed that will set both Fox and the Cardinal"—an allusion to Newcastle—"at defiance."[45] Thus, although by July Newcastle had come to accept Pitt's April view, he was still behind his quarry. Charles Yorke, one of Hardwicke's sons, met with Pitt at Newcastle's request and found him unfriendly. Tired of promises, Pitt wanted plain speaking. Newcastle, he declared, should specify precisely what needed to be done, who he proposed to have do it, and what offices they would hold to effect these goals. Only then would Pitt give the duke an answer.

Unpromising as these interviews were, the duke initiated a third one in August. This time his representative was Hardwicke. Perhaps because Pitt could recognize the lord chancellor's sincerity, or perhaps because he had been told he could be of more service to the kingdom giving a weak ministry immediate help rather than awaiting the emergence of a strong one, Pitt was not unfriendly. He agreed to meet with the duke, for a face-to-face encounter could not longer be deferred, and not to reject cooperation with him out of hand. Hardwicke advanced no great claims for what he had accomplished, but clearly he felt that the basis for an entente and joint action has been laid. Unhappily, Legge's break with Newcastle intervened between Pitt's interview with Hardwicke and the one with the duke, and the split limited the number of options Pitt had. Granville and then Legge himself frankly predicted to Newcastle that he would not now be able to win Pitt, and their prophecies were shrewdly grounded: Pitt, they believed, would dare not endorse a subsidy policy that Legge, to nationwide acclaim, had repudiated.

At the fourth interview, held on 2 September, both the duke and Pitt were cautious. Newcastle flattered his guest but conceded littled by way of substance. He offered Pitt a cabinet councillorship but not the seals. A discrepancy between the accounts of the two interlocutors then appears: Newcastle later suggested that Pitt insisted on the secretarial office as the price of his support, while Pitt later intimated that the duke had, without prompting, promised Pitt the next secretarial vacancy. Whatever the truth—and neither man was averse to self-serving distortions—it was clear that Pitt was not to become secretary immediately. Pitt focused attention on two issues: the leadership vacuum in the Commons and subsidy diplomacy. On the former question he urged, as Legge had a year earlier, that the leader of the Commons be given direct access to the king and that he be a man "of efficiency, and authority." Pitt went on to assert that Legge would be a splendid person for such a role. On the latter question he expressed a readiness to accept the Hessian subsidy, even though it was buying too few troops for too much money, but he would not swallow the Russian treaty. He denounced Newcastle's subsidy system, to which the duke replied, a bit disingenuously, that two subsidies did not constitute a system. The meeting ended without commitments, save for a vague promise from Pitt to talk again with Hardwicke. But to the lord chancellor Newcastle confided his belief that Pitt would not accept the terms; and Pitt, meanwhile, told Dodington bluntly that "he knew the Duke of Newcastle was a very great liar."[46]

The efforts to enroll Pitt on terms something like Fox's were thus foundering, and the unsettling prospect of a parliamentary assault on the subsidies, led by Legge and Pitt, loomed large. After the early

September interview with Pitt Newcastle consulted with Hardwicke about the possible courses of action for himself: he could resign the Treasury to Fox, he could offer Pitt an immediate secretarial post, or he could make Fox commander of the Commons. The first option seemed to the duke thoroughly honorable and had as well the virtue of assuring that the king's government would be carried on. But Hardwicke feared that the public would suspect an attempted replay of 1746 and thereby completely misunderstand the duke's motives. The second option seemed to both the duke and the lord chancellor unlikely to be practicable unless enormous pressure were brought to bear on George II to part with either Holderness or Robinson, both of whom he admired as accomodating servants. Hardwicke was ready to apply such pressure; he had long thought Pitt's adherence a prize worth some trouble. But Newcastle, stung and a bit disappointed by his talk with Pitt and unwilling to compromise on subsidy diplomacy, preferred the third option, even though, as the lord chancellor reminded him, Fox had the favor at court of both the king and the duke of Cumberland and hence would be much less dependent on those who effected his promotion than Pitt would be. Rather unenthusiastic negotiations with Pitt continued for over a week; the first lord, the lord chancellor, and the paymaster met at least once more. But by mid-September, with the duke unwilling to alter his defense policy just to secure the fiery member for Aldborough, ducal options had been reduced to two: resignation, or the promotion of Fox. Murray and Lord Lincoln urged the first, but Hardwicke and Lord Waldegrave advocated the second. Newcastle, responding more to inner impulse than outer argument, chose to continue in office, if Fox would make it possible.

The secretary at war had known of the duke's lengthy pursuit of Pitt but had adopted the role, thoroughly congenial to him, of a disinterested observer of frantic mankind. Fox's terms, considering his leverage, were surprisingly low. He might have stubbornly withheld his cooperation in the hope that if the minister fell George II would turn to him. But he did not. In return for a promise to defend the treaties in the House of Commons, Fox required no more than the promotions of a few friends. He accepted Newcastle's pledge that he would receive the seals within a few months. To enhance his prestige in the interval, he would be declared leader of the Commons, a post Fox was as anxious to possess as Robinson was to relinquish. But of the questions of patronage and money that had destroyed Fox's chances for that office in March 1754 nothing was said; it was as if the two men concurred that in lieu of a formal agreement they would prefer to contend quietly for control of these aspects of government, each winning what he could. It was, some objective observers thought, another bad bargain struck by Fox. The duke was understandably pleased with the arrangement. As he explained to Lady Katherine Pelham, he had secured a powerful advocate for his treaties. He had, he continued, removed Fox from the office of secretary at war, a shift that might weaken Fox's ties with Cumberland. And he had burdened Fox with the seals, a responsibility that Fox, for all his talents, was not really suited to. The last remark merits reflection. It indicates precisely why the duke was such an unfortunate choice for first minister: at a time when the kingdom was entering a war with the most powerful nation on the continent, the duke was congratulating himself on placing a man he believed unfit for the job in the second most important office of state. He was, in short, chuckling over tricking a political rival when he should have been trembling for the fate of the empire.

Although the choice between Pitt and Fox was Newcastle's chief political decision as the parliamentary session of 1755 drew near, he approached other figures as well. "I have had no view since last session of Parliament," he told a dubious Halifax, "but to bring all men of weight and abilities into the King's service, who would support the King's measures, and act in concert with his servants."[47] Through Philip Adolf von Münchhausen, the Hanoverian resident, he made approaches to Leicester House. Lord Egmont entertained a feeler from the duke, but after some days of consideration he rejected the offer of a remunerative post and remained faithful to Augusta and the Prince of Wales. Sir George Lee made the same decision. Then Lord George Sackville, styling himself free of connections, also declined to commit himself to the ministry. But Bubb Dodington was hungrier. Though privately contemptuous of the duke, Dodington was an eager place-seeker who, while not unprincipled, often found it easy to mold principles to the contours of interests. He was treated with respect because he controlled four seats in the Commons, and in his bargaining with the duke he won impressive concessions before promising his support on most key measures. A similar effort was mounted to court the duke of Bedford, with Fox and Hardwicke applying the persuasion, and although Bedford himself refused to join any ministry directed by Newcastle, he agreed to support the subsidies. He even lent debating help in the House of Lords. All in all, Newcastle was exuding optimism by November. He was cheered, above all, by the generous turnout of parliamentary supporters at the traditional pressesion meeting of the well-disposed. Sixty-three peers had crowded into Newcastle House, and 289 members of the Commons had attended a party at the cockpit. "With margins like these," he wrote cockily to Lord Hartington, "we have nothing to fear."[48]

And, in fact, the long-dreaded ruckus over the subsidies failed to materialize. The Hessian and the Russian treaties passed the Parliament easily, as Whig loyalists such as the duke of Devonshire and old Horace Walpole, though harboring some doubts, moved to support the government. After an initial slip, Fox handled matters expeditiously and well. Pitt, of course, was not silent. He denounced the subsidy treaties but, if the younger Horace Walpole's account is accurate, without the incisiveness of his best rhetorical efforts. His speech included one famous image, likening Newcastle to the "gentle, feeble, languid" Saone and Fox to the "boisterous and impetuous" Rhone: "They meet at last; and long may they continue united, to the comfort of each other, and to the glory, honor, and security of this nation." Several weeks later he launched into another comparison, more acidulous, suggesting that Newcastle was like James I's Buckingham. On still another occasion he denounced "the silly pride of one man" and the "timidity of his colleagues."[49] Meanwhile he shattered Hume Campbell, whom Newcastle had recruited as a defender of the ministry. Fox simply allowed Pitt to rant, for the ministry was having its way on the divisions. And the fact that Pitt chose quiet irony in the debate on the subsidies suggests that he too knew full well that Newcastle had the votes.

As soon as it was clear that Fox was fulfilling his pledge to conduct the business of the House of Commons with dispatch, he was given the seals held by Robinson. Lord Chesterfield noted on the occasion of Fox's rise that "the Duke of Newcastle has turned out every body else, and now he has turned out himself."[50] Though a choice remark, it was also a false one. Rather than turning himself out, he had given himself a new lease on political life. Robinson willingly returned to the wardrobe, from which Newcastle had summoned him a year and a half earlier. In 1761 he was elevated to the peerage as Lord Grantham, and he remained on friendly terms with Newcastle until the duke's death. Other debts were also paid in the closing weeks of 1755. Bubb Dodington was rewarded with the treasurership of the navy, and Lord Gower,

Bedford's brother-in-law, was made lord privy seal. The Board of Trade was reconstructed, with Newcastle, Hardwicke, Bedford, and Fox each being permitted a nomination. Reprisals were finally visited on those who for many months had sniped at the government while themselves being in office: in late November Pitt, Legge, George Grenville, and Charles Townshend were dismissed. Satisfied with affairs in Parliament, Newcastle no longer argued that it was prudent to keep some contact with Pitt. To the vacant exchequer he promoted Sir George Lyttelton, the old colleague of Pitt and Grenville. Then, over the Christmas recess, he made changes in the Treasury Board, bringing in Henry Furness, a friend of Dodington's. Dupplin retired from the board at this time, but he and West retained their roles as Newcastle's chief advisers on treasury affairs. Robert Nugent, another board member, endeared himself to the duke by emerging as his most extravagant defender in the House of Commons. The younger Horace Walpole remarked in November that Newcastle seemed stronger than ever and that Fox shared in much of the power; after these personnel changes were effected he judged the newcomers to be balanced almost equally between the duke's friends and Fox's. Clearly a partnership of sorts had developed, but a partnership that still left the duke with a considerable residue of political might.

Fortune seemed to be smiling on Newcastle's diplomatic efforts too, for late in the fall Frederick II suggested that Prussia and Britain negotiate a treaty to make Germany neutral in the upcoming war. The proposal, which delighted the ministry in London, was not a surprise. Newcastle had appreciated the dilemma that Britain's negotiations with Russia posed for Prussia and had recognized early that Prussia might seek neutrality—just what Newcastle needed for the protection of Hanover—in any future war. "The King of Prussia sees," he explained to an old Prussophile, Horace Walpole, "that by his neutrality, he may be assured, beyond any doubt, of the most ample security for his present great acquisitions, and that by taking part with France, and introducing a war in the Empire, he may draw upon himself, seventy thousand Russians."[51] London responded quickly to the initiative from Berlin. A convention was drafted, declaring each monarch's determination to preserve peace in Germany and containing a British guarantee of Silesia. Neither the Russians nor the French were mentioned by name, and in conformity with Frederick's desire not to anger his ally at Versailles the Low Countries were excluded from the territory protected by the neutrality. Newcastle entertained doubts about Frederick's sincerity, but the Prussian monarch approved the draft with alacrity and on 16 January 1756 the so-called Convention of Westminster was signed. Both sides now expected the outstanding issues between the two countries, chiefly counterclaims for financial payments, to move toward resolution. But most important from London's perspective was another consequence of the Convention: Hanover was finally safe.

But was it? Newcastle thought so, but he ought to have been less positive. War with France was, after all, deemed inevitable. Despite occasionally hopeful signs and the hazily optimistic reports of Sir Joshua Vanneck about French intentions[52]—Vanneck, a financier, was one of Newcastle's advisers on French attitudes—no one in the ministry, not even Newcastle, thought a peaceful settlement of claims truly possible. Newcastle had in fact become a bit of a saber rattler, boasting to friends of the might, capability, durability, and leadership of the Royal Navy.[53] Nor was the boast groundless, for during the fall of 1755, after Boscawen's action had led Britain to the unusual step of authorizing reprisals by the Royal Navy, the British captured some 300 French merchantmen and 6,000 French sailors. This only added the issue of prizes to the already painful list of British offenses committed against the subjects of His Most Christian Majesty, and in December France threatened a declaration of war if Britain failed to do it justice. "All agree a war is unavoidable," Fox wrote in early January, "but Ld Chancellor and the D. of Newcastle are for a little paper war first, for which I shall, I doubt not, receive orders this forenoon."[54]

Fox was right about the paper war, but he was also right about the inevitability of a real war. And the same Prussia that had accepted the Convention of Westminster was France's ally. When war came Prussia would doubtless notify France of its new commitment to Britain, but London could scarcely be confident that Prussia would adhere to this, especially if Austria chose to come to Britain's aid. To be sure, noninvolvement in an Anglo-French conflict was a likelier Austrian course of action, but it could not have escaped notice that Vienna might decide to use the Atlantic war as a diversion to initiate its declared plan of dismantling Prussia. These were grim possibilities, and they ought at least to have made Newcastle pause. But there was also a grim certainty: Russia would interpret Britain's acceptance of the Covention of Westminster as a treacherous action. When the Russian treaty had been concluded the previous August, the Russians had made quite clear that they wanted to use it to attack Prussia and begin earning £500,000 a year. The Convention of Westminster now obliged Britain to resist any warmaking in Germany. Newcastle ought not to be condemned, as he sometimes is, for failing to foresee the coming *renversement des alliances*; far wiser men than he, including Frederick II, made the same error. Nor should he be condemned, as he often is, for trying to form a massive alliance of countries having few common goals and many conflicting desires; Townshend had done as much, Stanhope had set the pattern, and it is in fact common practice for states in distress to seek aid wherever they can find it. Where Newcastle can and should be faulted is in his blindness to the certainty of Russian outrage and to the likelihood of Russian noncooperation as a consequence of the incompatible commitments Britain had now made. One ought not, after all, spoil a friend's party and expect him to be grateful and accomodating.

VI

It was while the Convention of Westminster was being concluded that the ministry finally and belatedly faced the military problems raised by Braddock's death. For five months the names of candidates to succeed him had lain before the cabinet. In January Cumberland ended the indecision by choosing Lord Loudon, a Scots peer who had led loyal highlanders during the Forty-Five. If not a brilliant choice, it was at least an adequate one. But on other American issues the ministry acted less wisely. All reports from America, whether from Shirley (Braddock's interim successor), De Lancy in New York, or Dinwiddie in Virginia, spoke of the need for more troops. Lord Halifax drafted a vigorous plan to meet this need; it called for the dispatch of more regulars to America, the creation of a royal munitions storehouse, and the appointment of a general who would be empowered to convene the colonial governors and exact of them fixed quotas for the troop contributions of each colony. It was probably an impracticable scheme, for it invited a flare-up of intercolonial rivalries. But because both Cumberland and Newcastle found flaws in it, the plan was only partially implemented by the cabinet and thus never fairly tested. Cumberland objected to the use of colonial soldiers, whom he thought incapable of discipline. Newcastle disliked the cost of a royal storehouse. In its final form the cabinet plan provided only for the sending of two additional regiments across the Atlantic and the raising of about 4,000 more Americans. These decisions, when acted upon, increased British troop strength in the continental colonies, including Nova Scotia, to 13,400. It was a sparse force with which to defend the far-flung American empire of Great Britain. And implementation was shamefully tardy, for Loudon's instructions were not approved until 6 May; only then did he embark for the New World.

The decisions of January were made under the shadow of an angry French memorandum that the Abbé de Bernis later admitted was meant to break all ties between the two kingdoms. Britain almost obliged the French on this point, for many in the ministry wanted to declare war. But the fears of driving Spain into France's arms and of disobliging Prussia prevailed, and the formalization of hostilities was again deferred. Nevertheless, with France speaking so stridently, the ministry moved ahead with preparations for the grim and predictable future. Newcastle expected a full-fledged French invasion. "For my part," he wrote to Joseph Yorke, who had warned of ominous French plans to sweep across the Channel, "I own, my opinion is that they are so irritated, think their honour so much wounded and are so much governed by that hot-headed Marshal Belleisle, that I do think they will make an attempt, and most probably more than one, upon parts of our coast."[55] Virtually without defense forces at home, Britain sent for the 8,000 Hessians it had bought in the recent treaty and turned for support to the United Provinces as well. The Dutch were obliged by a treaty dating from 1678 to supply Britain with 6,000 troops in time of war; both in 1715 and in 1745 they had fulfilled this commitment. But by 1756 realists of a neutral inclination dominated Dutch politics. They were bitter that Britain had left the Low Countries unprotected in the Convention of Westminster and fearful that France would invade. The republic notified Britain in March that the troops would not be supplied. At Lord George Sackville's suggestion Britain then hastily summoned some Hanoverian mercenaries. But the British government was determined to deny the Dutch the commercial benefits of neutrality. Hardwicke and Murray set out to formulate what would be called the Rule of 1756, and in September the lord chancellor in effect defined it: neutral carriers would be allowed no trade in time of war that they had not held in time of peace.

But the Dutch were not central to British thinking in 1756. All eyes were on France; most minds expected French raids. Indeed, to understand the ministry's actions in the late winter and spring of 1756 it is essential to recognize how deeply this fear had penetrated the cabi-

net. Anson, Holderness, and Granville shared Newcastle's expectation
of an invasion effort. It is true that in February reports also began
arriving of a French troop concentration at Toulon; and Minorca, over
forty years under British control but still discontented, seemed an
inviting target for any French enterprise in the Mediterranean. But the
cabinet felt that it dared not commit a large detachment to the protection of Fort St. Phillip if such an action meant the overextension of the
defense forces and an intolerable weakening of the home fleet. It was,
after all, upon the navy that Britain's physical defense rested. Perhaps
the 100,000 men encamped opposite the British coast were merely a
trick; but perhaps too it was the Toulon buildup that was the bluff.
The government would stand condemned of criminal folly, if not worse,
if it protected Minorca while it neglected Devon and Hampshire.

In structuring defense priorities, the image that sprang most readily
to the minds of the ministers was that of the human frame: "The
Heart," Newcastle wrote to Fox in May, "must be secured in the first
place." "As our shield," Lyttelton explained a few months later, "was
not broad enough to secure the whole body, it was better to expose our
limbs than our heart."[56] But if the ministry's reluctance to send as large
a force to Minorca as some thought necessary is understandable,
Lyttelton's letter pointed to a difficulty for which it is less easy to excuse
the ministry, and especially Newcastle. The real problem in the spring
of 1756 was that the Royal Navy was not sufficiently large to carry out
all the defense functions that were required of it. Had the war come
suddenly, one might argue that the government ought not to be faulted
for naval insufficiencies; the peacetime fleet would naturally be smaller
than the wartime fleet. But war had not come suddenly. It had been
coming for over a year and a half. Thus the duke's remarkable
statement to Fox—"We are not equal to the work we have undertaken.
We are not singly a match for France"[57]—was really a terrible indictment of the man who made it. It was under his direction that the kingdom had begun the very undertaking now condemned as rash.

Through February and March intraministerial quarrels were tempered by the knowledge of the danger in which the kingdom stood.
The cabinet decided to bring in a militia bill that would raise more
troops for home defenses, and it canvassed various other protective
schemes, including the surveillance of vagabonds and the concealment
of guards in London. A new harrying of Catholics was also discussed.
Appeals for patriotic support quickened national confidence and met

with wide approval. In March the cabinet decided to notify Parliament formally of the French menace. Meanwhile, to meet the possible threat to Minorca, a squadron of ten ships under Admiral John Byng was ordered southward. Fox wished to assign Byng additional ships but Anson and Newcastle successfully blocked this. Byng's instructions, completed on 30 March, were drafted to equip him for a variety of eventualities. He was to sail to Gibraltar, and if the French, as was deemed "probable," had emerged into the Atlantic, he was to follow them to America. If they were still in the Mediterranean, however, Byng was to sail to Minorca. If the island were under French attack, he was to aid it in all ways; if no attack were in process, he was to proceed to the French coast and lie off Toulon.[58] Byng was an unhappy choice for the task. Son of a distinguished naval man, Lord Torrington, he lacked his father's stature. Newcastle had seen these weaknesses in the man for a number of years, but Anson had thought him competent and therefore, with the duke deferring as usual to the views of others, Byng was chosen.

These defense measures directed against Versailles were simultaneous with diplomatic events on the continent that were radically altering the prospective shape of any future war among the European powers. Russia was of course dismayed at Britain's flirtation with Prussia, and Sir Charles Hanbury Williams soon had to report to London that the giant of the East, in its slow and troubled fashion, was reassessing its international position in the light of the Convention of Westminster. Much more startling was the traffic between Versailles and Vienna. In the imperial capital Kaunitz had long been an advocate of Austro-French ties; such an alliance, the chancellor believed, was the only force that could compel Prussia to disgorge Silesia. After Britain failed to respond to Austria's ultimatum of June 1755, Maria Theresa authorized Austrian efforts to come to terms with France. Thus, as London was trying to add strength to its friendship with Vienna by placating St. Petersburg, Vienna was straying from London to Versailles. The obstacles to success in these Austro-French talks crumbled when the world learned of the Convention of Westminster. The pact, with its guarantee of a Prussian Silesia, simply confirmed Austria's reading of Britain. But it stunned France. What Berlin had interpreted as an agreement thoroughly compatible with the French alliance was seen at Versailles as scandalous betrayal. In anger the French leaders suddenly warmed to Austria's patient entreaties, and in May the Treaty of

Versailles was concluded, binding France and Austria together on terms which (especially after a second treaty) were exceedingly generous to Austria. The so-called Diplomatic Revolution had been completed. It was a triumph for Kaunitz, but Newcastle's insensitive diplomacy had been as much a mover of events as the great Austrian chancellor.

Divisions within the cabinet were widening. They did not affect the parliamentary performance of the government, for Fox and Murray cooperated brilliantly to their mutual satisfaction and the approval of the efficiently managed lower house. But behind the scenes disorder and disagreement marked the ministry. By May Fox had made public his bitterness at Newcastle's and Hardwicke's secrecy and assumptions of superiority; and the duke was openly blaming Anson for the comparative paucity of ships. Pitt, well informed on these and still other disputes that lay behind the veil, delivered a harsh judgment on the ministry: "I don't call this an Administration," he said, "it is so unsteady. One is at the head of the Treasury; one, Chancellor; one, head of the navy; one great person, of the army—yet, is that an Administration? They shift and shuffle the charge from one to another: says one, I am not General; the Treasury says, I am not Admiral; the Admiralty says, I am not Minister. From such an unaccording assemblage of separate and distinct powers with no system, a nullity results."[59] The fallacy of Newcastle's conception of the role of the first minister was thereby brutally but accurately exposed. The duke, however, missed Pitt's point. He thought himself the victim of unfair assaults and tried to justify himself on the very grounds which Pitt used to attack him. "I am not able," Newcastle told Hardwicke, "to bear this weight, especially for measures where others have the principal, if not the sole, direction."[60]

Early in May reports reached London that the French had landed on Minorca and were laying seige to Fort St. Philip. Hostilities, once confined to America and then extended to the high seas, were now touching Europe. Britain had not made any diplomatic effort since the fall to reach a negotiated accord with France, and the attack on Minorca ended any possible utility that the perpetuation of technical peace might be presumed to have. On 18 May Britain finally declared war on France. The attack on Minorca also focused attention on Byng's squadron, which suddenly seemed to many to be unequal to the task of saving the island. Reinforcements under Commodore Thomas

Broderick were dispatched, but the chance that they would arrive in time to be useful was scant. Many people quickly became wise after the fact, explaining to eager auditors how all signs had pointed to French duplicity in the troop concentration in the West. To meet these criticisms the cabinet called for reports from the Admiralty which justified the conclusion "that a squadron could not have been sent into the Mediterranean, sooner than the time, when Admiral Byng received orders to sail, with the fleet under his command, without exposing these kingdoms to manifest danger."[61] But obviously the ministry's evaluation of its own actions would carry little weight with the nation. Everything rode with Byng and his ships. And Pitt was expecting and preparing the nation for the worst. His gift for the apt comparison again revealed itself in mid-May when he likened Newcastle "to a child in a go-cart upon the brink of a precipice, and that it was but common humanity to stop it, or to admonish the child's nurse"—here a glance toward Fox—"of its danger."[62] He had already delivered the devastating judgment that Newcastle was deliberately sacrificing Minorca to persuade the nation that peace at any price was vital. Dodington, meanwhile, consulting with Fox, was speculating ominously that one way to save the leader of the government was to find a "scapegoat."[63]

Many weeks were needed for news from the Mediterranean to reach Britain. Thus, although Fort St. Philip, after brave resistance, finally yielded on 20 May, rumors of the loss did not arrive in London until early June, and official confirmation was delayed until July. But the worst had been feared when the government learned at the end of May that Byng had not picked up a battalion awaiting him at Gibraltar. Shaken with disgust at the news, George II greeted it with the angry prediction that "this man will not fight." Newcastle brooded on the same report and in a letter to the duchess began speaking of a remedy that would obsess him in the months to come: "I think Mr. Byng seems to have no intention to attack the fleet. If he don't he will be hang'd, & deserve it."[64] When unofficial word of Byng's failure to fight for Minorca arrived in London, the cabinet acted swiftly; the very next day it instituted a series of changes in command, replacing (among others) Byng with Hawke. A stunned public then turned wrathful when more information about Byng's inactivity drifted into the capital. The admiral, it appeared, might have landed reinforcements at Minorca, but failed to do so. His force, though not notably stronger than the French, was unquestionably not inferior. He avoided combat when everything, his orders, the gravity of the situation, and the eighteenth-century notion of what was appropriate, should have moved him to fight.

Still, try as it might to keep Byng in the limelight, the ministry could not prevent the public rage from extending beyond the admiral to the ministers. Byng had failed, but so had they. A torrent of antiministerial invective began to flow, and it quickly became apparent that the opposition, ever since 1748 grasping for an issue wherewith to galvanize public opinion, had at last found it. An advertisement appeared at the Royal Exchange proclaiming "Three kingdoms to be let; inquire of Andrew Stone, broker, in Lincoln's Inn–Fields." Westminster ballad singers chanted "to the block with Newcastle, and the yard-arm with Byng." An American spending June in London summed up what he saw as the mood of the kingdom: "Whatever is the event of these things, it is certain the Ministry have disgusted the nation extremely in their conduct of this affair. . . . The fault is generally laid on the Duke of Newcastle."[65]

The last fact was what hurt the duke the most. A man who habitually avoided responsibility for mistakes, he now squirmed in misery as much of the blame for Britain's severest international humiliation in over half a century fell upon him. He was determined to transfer it totally to Byng. The admiral was to be, as Dodington had intimated, the scape-goat. "He, & he singly," the duke told his wife, "lost Port Mahon, & a victory over the French." Byng was brought back to Britain under arrest; the ministry was determined to have him court-martialled for violating his orders. And Newcastle's desire to convict him knew few bounds. He wanted the sea officers who would conduct the trial to be instructed not to implicate the ministers. When an anti-Byng deputa-tion from the City visited him, he exclaimed to them "Oh! indeed he shall be tried immediately—he shall be hanged directly."[66] Mean-while, he was doctoring the information being made available to the curious public, eliding from the papers being released such information as might suggest that Byng had been ill-equipped or that disease had weakened his force, but including those data that hinted (sometimes misleadingly) that the admiral was craven.

In the hysteria of the summer Newcastle and Fox reversed their roles of the past two years. Less visibly a target of the enraged populace, Fox retained his capacity for reasonable judgments. He wanted to get an ally for Britain and thought the concession of Gibraltar to Spain a suitable price to win Madrid's support for a campaign to reconquer Minorca. Newcastle was less rational and compromising. Only Ireland, he asserted, was a more important dependency than Minorca. As a means of energizing the kingdom, diverting its wrath, and winning a bargaining counter, he proposed an attack of an unspecified sort on a French possession in the Mediterranean, the West Indies, or America. "Without it," he told Hardwicke, "we must expect everything that is bad." To Fox he wrote even more oddly and desperately: "Let me entreat you to think seriously of some object: we had better fail in the attempt, than attempt nothing. Nothing but some *attempt* will or can retrieve our situation."[67]

Desperation was appropriate to the occasion. With the important exception of Spain, Newcastle's plans for ordering the world outside Britain had simply fallen apart by July 1756: Britain had lost its old ally Austria and its new ally Russia; the "Old System" that he had thought he was strengthening had dissolved; Minorca had fallen to the French; France had captured the initiative in America; and yet, not-withstanding these disasters, Britain stood indicted as the aggressor. It was a sorry record for two years of office. In truth, one can search in vain for a similar performance in modern British history. Not every-thing, of course, was Newcastle's fault. However ill-advised the al-location of the fleet may have been, Byng had in fact arrived in time and with enough strength to save Fort St. Philip. His responsibility for that calamity does not relieve Newcastle of the charges that the duke's treatment of Byng after his return was contemptible and his frenetic efforts to avoid being blamed were spineless. But when Newcastle is criticized for his part in the Byng affair it should be kept in mind that it was Byng who lost Minorca and Newcastle who then gloated over the sacrifice of Byng. The duke's failing was thus one of character, not of war planning, and his behavior in the affair becomes the most shameful chapter of his personal life, but not of his public career. Similarly, neither Braddock's hapless performance nor Boscawen's blunder were Newcastle's fault, except insofar as his hesitations sapped vigor from Britain's entire defense system and left commanders uninspired and confused. The duke, in short, was in part the victim of bad luck. Even in criticizing him for his continental diplomacy in 1755–56 one must be cautious. Newcastle thought that the convention with Prussia consti-tuted not the abandonment of the "Old System" but its preservation. Clearly he was mistaken. But it is easy to draw wrong conclusions about his errors in judgment. It would seem, for example, inconsistent to charge him with failing to perceive the fatal disintegration of the alliance with Austria and then to condemn him for rushing into an alliance with Prussia. If the former tie was in decay, the latter one became thereby desirable, even if Newcastle sought it for the wrong reasons. And it would, in fact, be the alliance with Prussia that would prevent France from turning its full might on Britain in the war to come. All in all, on individual points, much can be said in partial extenuation of the duke. But the overall pattern indelibly remains. Though the duke tried sedulously to shift responsibility, he was still in everyone's mind the leader of a ministry whose hand had blighted almost all it had touched. By mid-summer 1756 Newcastle's avowed foreign system had collapsed. Nor was that all. By that same July it appeared that the duke's domestic system was on the verge of a similar fate.

VII

Newcastle's domestic political system, as adjusted after his initial and ill-advised experiment with studied neglect of the Commons, drew its strength from three sources: the phalanx of members who were prepared to cast their votes with a Whig ministry; the efficient cooperation of Fox and Murray in directing ministerial affairs in the lower house; and the divisions and consequent suspicions among the opposition. Events in the late spring of 1756, however, undermined the latter two sources and threatened, through their combined impact, to sap the first as well. The first problem arose in May when Sir Dudley Ryder, chief justice of the king's bench, died on the eve of his elevation to the peerage. With Ryder's passing William Murray, to whom political avenues were closed by virtue of the accusations of Jacobitism, finally saw the judicial high road open before him. He had already won promises from Newcastle to be named as Ryder's successor, and now, though knowing well what havoc it would bring to the duke's system, he insisted on fulfillment of the obligation. His breathless eagerness need not be wondered at: like many others, he expected Newcastle's ministry soon to founder, and he feared that hesitation in seizing his opportunity might permit the swift-flowing stream of events to inundate the duke and sweep him from office before the vacancy had been filled. Newcastle importuned his friend to remain in the Commons, but Murray was firm. All the duke could win from him, and only after much arguing, was a respite until the fall, during which interval the duke could try to construct a viable political system. Beyond that point Murray would brook no further delays.

The second change of the late spring was the Prince of Wales's coming-of-age on 4 June. It opened up hopeful possibilities as well as problems, but the ministry was uncertain how to deal with either. It seemed conceivable, on the one hand, that the prince, no longer a child, might be won away from his dependence on his mother and thereby made less useful to the opposition. But if, on the other hand, such efforts failed and the prince remained faithful to his mother and her political advisers, he was now, as an adult, able to pose a severe threat to the ministry. The danger arose both from his new freedom and from the actuarial calculations regarding the youth of the heir to the throne and the senescence of the incumbent. The ministry complicated its difficulty by advising the king badly. Hoping to wean the impressionable young man from his mother, they recommended that George II offer him an allowance and invite him to live at court, away from the dowager princess of Wales. The plan backfired spectacularly. The prince shrewdly accepted the allowance and ignored the invitation. He also asked that Lord Bute be named his groom of the stole. Bute's known complicity with Pitt and Legge made him distasteful to Newcastle and Hardwicke and repugnant to the old king. Thus, royal opposition to an appointment that required royal approbation was predictable. Indeed, by the middle of June, Newcastle strongly feared that as a consequence of the prince's actions and requests the tensions within the royal family were about to enter upon one of their periodic public phases. When juxtaposed to the military and international crises of the day, the fissure in the royal family seemed to the duke a "terrible consideration."[68]

There was one course of action open to the duke which, if it led to success, might solve both the dilemma posed by Murray's departure and the problem generated by the prince's majority. This was to secure Pitt's support. If the former paymaster could be won over, Murray's loss would be more than replaced, and the prince's party would be effectively denied the services of the man whose allegiance it most sought. But Pitt now had yet another reason to regret the duke's direction of affairs: the House of Lords, under Hardwicke's prodding, had recently rejected a militia bill that had earlier passed the Commons with Pitt's blessing and would have created a force of over 60,000 private subjects. Pitt knew he was negotiating from strength, and he had no intention of imitating Fox's overhasty grasping for power. The full fruits of office would be his if he merely waited. In a quick June visit to London, therefore, he informed Newcastle that he would refuse all offers of office unless the duke himself resigned. This stipulation was naturally sufficient to dispel from the duke's mind any desire to pursue Pitt further. In consultation with Hardwicke he decided therefore to try to strengthen Fox's courage and thereby induce the secretary, deeply shaken by the plethora of troubles crowding in upon the ministry, to retain his office. But to prevent Fox from concluding that he could name his own terms, the duke also decided to secure a second person—Lord George Sackville was his candidate—to act as Fox's aide and also to remind the secretary that the ministry could get along without him. Inasmuch as Sackville had earlier declined a similar post and was scarcely equivalent to Fox in any event, it seems fair to see in these plans a manifestation of that peculiar optimism that, by the testimony of Fox himself, buoyed up the duke's mood during what ought to have been a fearfully disspiriting early summer. Newcastle sent Andrew Stone to Fox with instructions to gauge the secretary's cast of mind. Fox expressed hope that the king would permit Bute to serve the prince, doubt that Pitt would link up with the ministry, and guarded willingness to defend the government in the Commons as long as ministerial mistakes were not imputed to him alone. It was surely the best that Newcastle could have hoped for.

But it was not enough. By August the international situation was deteriorating still further, for Frederick II, sensing that Prussia's enemies were plotting an assault, was issuing increasingly minatory declarations. And the domestic situation was also worsening, for the nation's wrath over Minorca could not be confined to Byng and was lapping at the ministry and especially at Newcastle. "His old friends," Sir George Lyttleton wrote in August, "and worst enemies, are trying their utmost to make him responsible for this misfortune."[69] In an effort to strengthen his political position the duke authorized attempts to secure new political alliances and reinforce old ones. But they failed. Lord Egmont, after himself initiating informal talks with the ministry, lost interest; and the duke of Argyle, object of a separate feeler, also chose to allow negotiations to lapse. Fox too began more clearly to differentiate himself from his ministerial colleagues, reminding friend and foe that he had favored assigning more ships to Byng. Newcastle left for his annual

Sussex visitation in good spirits, but the cumulative impact of all these developments could not be ignored.

By the end of the month, after his return to London, Newcastle's erstwhile optimism had withered. The alternatives he now foresaw were uniformly bleak: either Pitt's rise to office to the humiliation of the first lord and the lord chancellor, or their joint resignation. He begged Hardwicke's advice and penned a moving lament: "The army is absolutely under other direction, the sea does not love to be controlled, or even advised; and yet I am to answer for any miscarriage in either. . . . My dear Lord, pity me, alone as I am in my present distress."[70] And he did not yet know, when he poured out that *cri de coeur* on 28 August, precisely how overwhelming his problems were. For two weeks earlier, chiefly in consequence of the duke's dilatoriness in appointing Loudon as Braddock's successor, the British fort at Oswego had fallen to the French, adding another military setback to the ministry's already unenviable collection of failures. And forty-eight hours after the duke had finished his epistle, Frederick II sent his troops across the Saxon frontier to initiate hostilities on the continent and further widen a conflict that the duke still hoped, however desperately, to confine. Only in the grimmest moments of the conflicts with the Americans, Napoleon, and Hitler did the kingdom's international situation wear a severer aspect in modern times.

Almost from its inception the ministry's course of action had shown elements of confusion and incoherence. Now under the pressure of military defeats abroad and political disintegration at home these traits came to dominate and characterize ministerial, and especially ducal, behavior. The pressures were patently severe. Byng had at last acquired some defenders, and the extenuating facts that Newcastle had tried to suppress in June finally reached the public. And if few people were prepared to acquit the admiral, many were at least ready to indict the ministry. Newcastle's unpopularity seemed to mount with each passing week, and in September, during a visit to Lady Katherine Pelham at Greenwich, he was forced to seek refuge in the observatory when he ran afoul of the most dangerous mob he had encountered since the days of his youthful and high-spirited defense of Whiggery in 1715. The angry townspeople pelted his carriage with dirt and tauntingly suggested to his coachman that the Tower was the most appropriate destination for his passenger.[71] In the hope of mollifying such discontent, or at least of directing it away from politically dangerous channels,

Newcastle finally assented to Hardwicke's recommendation that the Prince of Wales be given his way, that is, that Bute be appointed groom of the stole and that the rupture between prince and dowager princess not be insisted upon. "I am sure," the duke commented in reviewing his conversion to the lord chancellor's opinion, "we have done right."[72] And certainly from one point of view this judgment was correct. But in practice it availed little: Leicester House showed scant inclination to be grateful to a sinking minister and indeed accused the duke, somewhat unfairly, of packing the prince's household with Pelhamite dependents.

Newcastle's other decisions had even less to commend them. He unwisely pursued the favor of a young lawyer, Charles Pratt, thinking thereby to please Pitt. But he failed to secure his man and only irritated the Yorke clan, who feared that advancement for Pratt might obstruct the path of their own champion, Charles Yorke, another able young legist. Newcastle also embarked upon a reckless attempt to bribe Murray into remaining in the Commons and, meeting failure in that desperate enterprise, then showed a strange coolness toward Robert Henley, designated to be the new attorney general, even though Henley's political power, while not extensive, could clearly be useful. About the military situation the duke was properly unhappy but typically vague. He rightly acknowledged Prussia to be "our only ally," but he had for some time nursed the peculiar idea of grounding the alliance in confessional politics: Frederick, he believed, "will be supported and adored here when he acts for the Protestant cause." One person who was not enchanted by the Prussian king, however, was his British uncle. In fact, George II let his pique so dominate his reason that he was moved to regret the Prussian victory at Lobositz and to contemplate turning to France for assistance against the rising might of the Hohenzollerns. Newcastle may have had the monarch's dislike of Frederick in mind—though there was much else to be gloomy about —when he wailed in September that "if we don't make peace, for God's sake let us make war in a different manner from what we have done."[73]

But the behavior which, if not exactly the oddest, was certainly the most dangerous of all was the duke's treatment of Fox. From Fox alone could prominvisterial rhetoric of a high order be expected, and yet the duke continued to think of the secretary as some sort of underling who should be made to truckle to the first lord of the Treasury. The notion of August that Fox could be intimidated by the putative threat of turning to Lord George Sackville had showed how divorced Newcastle was from political reality. By the fall the duke's new hope was to have Fox resign his office to Pitt and assume a lesser post from which he would, nevertheless, support the government. It was as if Pitt's known veto of the duke were a triviality. Fox for his part was fed up with ducal incapacity and double-dealing. With Newcastle unwilling to pay the price that Fox wanted if he were to remain as spokesman in the Commons, Fox chose what he saw as the only honorable course still before him. On 13 October he in effect resigned the seals. Newcastle was aghast, though more at the timing of the decision than the decision itself, and at first suspected Fox of trying "to put the knife to our throats."[74] This was probably a misreading of Fox's motive. Though he likely would have been willing to return to office under certain conditions, Fox was in fact sick of politics and its burdens. His appetite, though strong, was largely confined to material considerations; of a hunger for control over men he was comparatively innocent. There is no sound reason to suspect him of lying, though, of course, he doubtless witheld the totality of the truth, when he explained to Hardwicke that he had lost his earlier ambitions and sought only a minor post from which he would tender George II his full support. But Newcastle's reaction was also understandable: he now stood naked before a hostile Commons that, within six weeks, would again be assembled.

The duke's initial hope after learning of Fox's intended resignation was the old one of securing Pitt. "I am," he told Hardwicke, "hand and heart for Pitt at present."[75] Newcastle knew that Pitt could name his own terms, though he did not yet know how steep they would be. But the duke was not sanguine, for he remarked sadly: "He will come as a *conqueror*. I always dreaded it." And with an ominous allusion to Aeneas's bloody dispatch of Turnus he tossed in the fateful words that Virgil put in the conqueror's mouth: "*Pallas, te hoc vulnere Pallas immolat.*" Still, the duke did not crumble beneath his fears. He set to work to convince George II of the need to recruit Pitt, the only man in the opposition with the ability and influence to carry on the king's business. To George's apprehension that Pitt would be unwilling to support the king's German, that is, continental and subsidy, policy, Newcastle shrewdly rejoined that office by itself would cure the conquering hero of some of his sillier convictions. The duke even tried to persuade himself that it was more honorable to be defeated by an able and tenacious opponent than by an incapable, calumniating turncoat.

What Newcastle forgot or, despite the tag from the *Aeneid,* did not rightly understand, was that Pitt, as conqueror, would not accept Newcastle as a mere subordinate but would insist that he be absolutely removed from positions of authority. It is true that in his talk with George II on 15 October the duke acknowledged that it was possible that Pitt would make Newcastle's resignation the *sine qua non* of cooperation with the government; and if that were the case, the duke indicated a readiness to hand over the staff. But the rest of the discussion, especially the duke's pointed reminder that he would be unable to serve the king if out of office, suggested that the duke thought Pitt's veto either bluster or negotiable. And meanwhile, anticipating a struggle for power with Pitt, the duke began summoning allies back to London. Newcastle always had a great capacity for self-deception, but Fox perceived the truth: "The Duke of Newcastle's reign is, I verily think, over."[76]

The duke was soon disabused of his final and flimsy hopes. Hardwicke, though weary with years, again agreed to be intermediary for his friend and arranged to meet with Pitt. The conversation, held for three and a half hours on 19 October, brought the truth into broad daylight. The man who virtually everyone now regarded as indispensable explicitly declared that he would not serve with Newcastle. Beyond that requirement he also insisted that the king grant him full rights of access to the closet and extensive powers in the determination of policy, and that the record of Newcastle's ministry be subjected to investigation. It seemed apparent to Hardwicke that Pitt hoped to destroy the duke. He was right. Pitt himself had already privately told George Grenville that he would refuse not only all schemes that involved cooperation with the duke but also "any proposal for covering his retreat."[77] The duke's fall would be uncushioned. Newcastle seemed to accept this fact on 20 October and authorized Hardwicke to inform the king of the necessity of his resignation. But the duke's acceptance was neither manful nor unqualified. Newcastle took the occasion to try to shift responsibility for the ministry's difficulties to anyone else who might have been even vaguely associated with the important decisions of the last two and a half years. Moreover, in the succeeding days he continued his efforts to save himself, first offering the seals to an unwilling Lord Egmont and then proposing that Lord Granville assume the Treasury so that he himself could take the presidency of the council. Only after the failure of the last scheme did he cease trying to stay his execution.

George II, meanwhile, took Newcastle at his word, and with regret, for he was aware of the duke's "integrity and zeal for me." The king hoped at first to persuade Fox to assume control, but it was quickly learned that Pitt's veto covered the southern secretary as well. All alternative avenues were thereby closed to the king, and there remained but the task of making the transition of power as smooth as possible. Newcastle was dejected: "You know, you see," he lamented to Hardwicke, "how cruelly I am treated and indeed persecuted."[78] He even feared that Hardwicke might not choose to resign with him, though, like most of the duke's worries, this one was quite groundless. The lord chancellor was thoroughly melancholy and eager to leave a post he found both onerous and fatiguing. Since Pitt had no knowledge of financial matters and little interest in them, and since he wanted to hold an office that clearly had authority in foreign affairs, he chose to become southern secretary rather than first lord of the Treasury. A figurehead first lord was thus needed, and the faithful duke of Devonshire met that requirement ideally. Meanwhile, the duke remembered friends and relatives as his ministry approached expiration and, while the opportunity still availed, used his influence with George II to win favors for them. John Shelley received a reversion to the pipe office, Tom Pelham got a reversion to the customs office, and James West and Hugh Valence Jones received still other reversions. James Pelham and Sir Francis Poole received pensions earlier than they were due. Sir George Lyttelton was created a peer. Most important, although the duke sought neither place nor pension for himself, he requested and won from the monarch a new title, duke of Newcastle-under-Lyme, with special remainder to Lord Lincoln. Without direct heirs and with Henry Pelham's sons dead, his dukedom of Newcastle-on-Tyne would expire on his own death. The duke planned by this expedient to keep the title "Newcastle" alive and also to reward his favorite nephew. Once all the political and personal arrangements had been concluded, there remained only the final step: on 11 November 1756 the duke of Newcastle resigned the Treasury and returned to private life for the first time— 1746 scarcely constituting an exception—in almost forty years.

VIII

Shortly after the duke's resignation Lord Hardwicke's son, Lord Royston, enumerated what he called the "weak points of conduct" in the duke's management of affairs; and his forbidding list of failures, though confused, is nevertheless illuminating.[79] The various items in the catalogue constitute collectively a convenient starting point for an evaluation of the duke's ministry and for an explanation of its fall. The first error that Royston cited was the duke's false belief that the Commons would be satisfied without a true leader. But one must be cautious about making too much of this point. Royston was right, if all he meant to assert was that Newcastle was initially contemptuous of the Commons. The dispute with Fox and the decision to use Robinson, both products of March 1754, demonstrated his readiness to demote the Commons and to rule it, in the style of a Stuart minister, from afar. But Newcastle soon became aware of the difficulties he was courting. As Hardwicke later attested, it was impossible by mid-century for a peer to control the popular chamber. "All sorts of persons there," the lord chancellor explained, "have concurred in battering down that notion, and the precedents of my Lord Godolphin's and my Lord Sunderland's time have been overruled by the long habits of seeing Sir Robert Walpole and Mr. Pelham there, which go as far back as the memory of most people sitting there . . . reaches."[80] Newcastle's deals with Fox—the pledge of a cabinet councillorship in late 1754 and of the seals in late 1755—showed his recognition of the painful truth that the Commons demanded respectful treatment. And the pattern of events seemed to bear out this understanding, for in the immediate aftermath of both agreements the House of Commons was unusually docile, open to such leadership as Fox provided.

Moreover, if Royston was wrong in failing to notice how the duke's attitude toward the role of leadership in the Commons changed, he was still more in error if he meant to suggest that the duke's fall should be attributed to his inability to maintain control of the Commons. It is important to recall in assessing the contours of Newcastle's years of stewardship that the duke had not suffered any defeats in the Commons. Though it is tempting to see the fall of the Whigs from Walpolean heights to Pelhamite depths as a consequence of a process wherein Henry Pelham sacrificed his mentor's control of the cabinet and Newcastle then squandered his brother's (and Walpole's) control of the Commons, such a reading of the data, at least insofar as it concerns Newcastle, is probably misleading. It is true that because Newcastle resigned before Parliament reassembled, it is impossible to declare with certainty what would have happened had he instead held on to his office and braved the torrent of abuse that doubtless awaited him. But of his ultimate strength in the House of Lords there can be no doubt; the chamber of peers was too beholden to the ministry and too infused with notions of aristocratic duty to let a few renegades lead it into opposition. And there are at least two sound reasons to believe that Newcastle could have kept a majority in the Commons on his side as well.

The first line of argument to support this contention dwells on the tendencies of the Hanoverian constitution: it was highly unusual for a majority of an eighteenth-century Commons to turn against the chief minister. The only relevant comparisons would seem to be offered by the collapse of wartime ministries in 1742 and 1782. But in reality neither is a trustworthy guide to hypothetical events in 1756. In the final year of Walpole's rule Sir Robert's initial margin in the Commons, as set by the general election of 1741, was considerably narrower than Newcastle's in 1756; and thus he was far more exposed than the duke to the impact of any misfortunes. And in the final year of North's rule the military and psychological situations of the country were dramatically unlike those of the duke's day. Militarily in 1782 Britain needed to reduce the number of its adversaries—a step the government was reluctant to take—and psychologically the kingdom was sick of a protracted war that was being fruitlessly waged for constitutionally ambiguous principles. Newcastle's Britain, however, was neither isolated nor war-weary. Prussia was an ally from whom much was expected, and the national mood, such as it can be discerned, was not shaped by a sense of resignation but by a taste for *revanche*. If the putative parallels are thus false, the presumption gains credit that the Commons in 1756 was not prepared to destroy the minister. The second line of argument reinforces this belief. This line focuses on the regard that others (and the duke himself) showed for his influence in the Commons even after he was out of office. For the duke retained—explanation will come later—enormous authority over members in the spring of 1757. Indeed, it was this belief that the duke could make or break Pitt that made his readmission into government so desirable. But if, out of office, he was believed to exercise sufficient power in the lower house to overthrow a minister, it may be assumed that in office, and thus in a position to reward or punish immediately, his might was still greater.

All of the foregoing argumentation suggests that, whatever the emphasis Royston wished to place on the problem of leadership in the Commons, it was not an issue of crucial significance for the viability of the ministry. But Royston had other ducal errors to note, and they merit attention. He lamented Newcastle's unwillingness to intimidate George II into accepting Pitt; he deplored the duke's incautious drift into a war the grounds of which he never understood; he regretted the duke's inability to conceive of broad schemes of government; and he scorned what he felt to be the duke's dismal handling of the affairs of the Treasury. Royston found various ducal omissions particularly damaging: the failure to appoint a successor to Albemarle at a time of mounting Anglo-French tension; the refusal to try to unite the American colonists in anticipation of a French assault; and the blindness to the accretion of power that war would inevitably confer on Cumberland. Still, despite the gravity of these errors, the heart of Royston's critique of Newcastle's ministry would seem to lie in two other points. The first was the assertion that Newcastle made no effort to keep the army under the control of the civilian ministry. The second was the charge that in the disposition of places Newcastle preferred the shadow of power to its substance. Taken together, these points strongly suggest that the duke was a radically weak first minister. And if one begins with these two final points and their implications, the rest of the items on Royston's list fall into a pattern: each was a natural consequence of the duke's refusal to exert the type of power his predecessors as first lord had exercised. What needs to be accounted for, therefore, is the duke's peculiar diffidence in office. The explanation is, of course, partly rooted in the duke's personality; he was temperamentally unable to choose courses of action when guideposts were missing or ambiguous. But it was also rooted in the very nature of the governmental system he inherited, for the duke was in fact not totally without guideposts. The problem was rather that Pelham's recent experience, which served this purpose, had suggested that the best way to preside over a stable ministry was to be hesitant in shaping policy, bland in articulating it, and accommodating to those inclined to oppose it.

The arena that best demonstrated how Newcastle himself might apply these guidelines was not England but Ireland. Too many complications intruded at London to allow the duke a free hand in committing his ministry to particular modes of action and methods of operation. The approach of war, the inscrutability of Pitt, the fact that the choices made had clear implications for his own political survival, these factors prevented the duke from rigorously and consistently hewing to Pelham's pattern. But in Ireland the situation was different. Hostilities could have little bearing on politics in the western kingdom; politicians were self-seeking in more traditional ways and, besides, open to pressure from Britain; and Newcastle's own fate was not at stake. Thus he intervened in Irish politics with shrewdness and effect, showing a clear preference for the management of men over the advocacy of policy. At issue was the choice of means for dealing with Henry Boyle, speaker of the Irish House of Commons and singled out for action because he led those among the Irish who resisted the Crown's assertions of its right to apply surpluses in the Irish treasury as it saw fit.[81] Boyle's chief rivals for influence in Ireland, including the Ponsonby family and George Stone, archbishop of Armagh and Andrew's brother, seemed eager to destroy Boyle; the lord lieutenant, the duke of Dorset, appeared to agree. But Newcastle and Hardwicke, aware of Boyle's great popularity, demurred. They instructed Dorset to try to win him over and, when that failed, Newcastle took two remarkable steps. He himself initiated secret exchanges with Boyle, and he also replaced Dorset with the more tactful Lord Hartington. The new lord lieutenant made some headway with the speaker. He even concluded that peace in Ireland could be effected only through the political retirement, not of Boyle, but of Archbishop Stone. To this advice Newcastle gave his support. Stone then withdrew from political affairs, Boyle reassumed the chancellorship of the Irish exchequer, and a comprehensive government, embracing both Boyle and the Ponsonbys, emerged. Ducal moderation had triumphed, and the price, even allowing for the bitterness of the Stones, was not reckoned too high. Principle had not been defended, but through wise and timely concessions peace and stability had been preserved.

It would appear that this was how Newcastle wished to govern in Britain as well. He hoped from the beginning of his ministry, though apparently without serious consideration of alternative approaches, to perpetuate Henry Pelham's technique of dealing with opposition by comprehending it. It was a way to provide government with stability. Under Pelham the system of comprehension worked fairly well. But it did so only because there was a readiness to sacrifice policy formulation and decisiveness to the needs of keeping a heterogeneous collection of men in harness. For the system, by its very nature, seemed to work only if there were a continuing predisposition to subordinate policy to techniques of personnel manipulation. The tent under which so many politicians found shelter was capacious. But the politicians would stay put only if the chief minister, whether Pelham or Newcastle, advocated nothing that might divide their ranks. Pelham's reforms were thus restricted to treasury affairs; and it was likewise only in treasury affairs that Newcastle hoped to implement reforms. In each case the first lord was pouring such zeal for corrective modification as he had into a proper departmental channel. Only in this way, by confining programs for alterations to the specific department over which he presided, could a chief minister in a comprehensive ministry effect changes and yet not disaffect his colleagues.

From his retirement in the 1760's Newcastle criticized the draft of a eulogy to George II for including the statement that the monarch reposed *"summa confidentia"* in the duke.[82] The term implied, Newcastle believed, that he had been prime minister; and the duke resisted that designation as stoutly in retrospect as he had when in office. He simply did not try in any systematic way to give direction to the apparatus of which he was nominal head. Some problems interested him more than others, the disposal of places, for example, or the conduct of policy toward the German states. In both fields he intervened, to his pain in the former in December 1754 and to the disadvantage of Lord Holderness in the latter in July 1756. But such interventions were spasmodic, unpredictable, and unattached to any broader conception of policy. He would not deliberately alienate his colleagues by promoting distasteful measures.

Unhappily for the duke, however, the system he hoped to preside over was changing. What had worked for Pelham would no longer succeed for him. To say this is not to say that Pelham was indistinguishable from his brother as a handler of politicians, for clearly this was not the case. Henry Pelham was unquestionably an abler manipulator of men than Newcastle, at once more attuned to the private hopes and fears of his dependents and more tactful in discussing and balancing them. Thus the fact that Newcastle took over the reins in 1754 meant that less skilled hands were thereafter directing the government. But this truth has long been obvious and needs no underscoring. What has often been ignored is the slow change occurring within the system itself. For if stability was to be equated with the ministry's ability to absorb politicians, then the limits of stability had been reached by 1754. This would appear to have been so for two reasons. First, with the young prince of Wales slowly emerging from childhood and the old king visibly weakening, Leicester House reappeared on the scene as a significant force. Unlike any other potential focal point of opposition, Leicester House afforded the immunity that the royal blood could give against charges of disloyalty. Its revival certainly made it easier for men who fretted under the protection of the ministerial umbrella to abandon it for a new shelter. Second, the brief era of international peace was closing, and the ministry was confronted with the rending experience of war. To conduct a war successfully a minister must be prepared to make decisions. But decisiveness is precisely what the duke had been taught would destroy his ministry. He was thus trapped in what appeared to him to be a dilemma: to follow Pelham's precepts would be to invite military confusion, but to face hostilities with resolution and determination would be to invite the disruption of the government.

In fact, there was no dilemma at all. A state of hostilities, whether declared or undeclared, alters the rules by which good governance is measured. Whatever was true of politicians and the political nation in time of peace, it was clearly the case that in time of war they wanted action. Newcastle kept behaving as if there were no war and thus, to cap his fatuities, he pursued the path of indecisiveness to try to keep his ministry intact when by that very choice he was making it less cohesive than ever. Because he thought salvation could lie only in irresolution, the major constitutional innovation he sought and achieved was the diminution of the very office he had acceded to. As a consequence of this self-imposed limitation, when military and naval planning became necessary it was left to Fox, Cumberland, and Anson, the men who held the appropriate departmental posts. And Fox, whom both Newcastle and George II felt unfit for handling foreign policy, was thereby given the opportunity that the duke himself had had in 1738–39, the opportunity in fact to play Newcastle to Newcastle's Walpole. But this is simply to point to yet another way in which the duke's hobbled conception of the demands of leadership became a source of his troubles. Newcastle himself, of course, saw a totally different explanation for these troubles. He had been undone, he explained in 1761, by the "cowardly admiral" who had lost Minorca and the "mad unfortunate General" who had cast away Britain's advantages in North America.[83] But precisely because Newcastle disapproved of at least one of these appointments and could have blocked either or both, the real source of the difficulties must be sought not in the mistakes of others but in his own vision of the office he held. His foreign system collapsed because, for reasons which were both psychologically satisfying and logically persuasive, he avoided hard decisions and left planning to others. His domestic system soon followed because such a structure of divided administration offered no inducement to Pitt to join and little to Fox and Murray to stay.

One further interpretive problem remains. If, as was suggested earlier, the collapse of both his foreign and domestic systems did not bring about an end to his power in Parliament itself, if, that is, that power still existed, why did Newcastle resign in November 1756? Undoubtedly a complex of motives lay behind the decision, but the key point would seem to be that the duke simply lost his nerve. Things were going badly and he did not want to face a Parliament that contained not a few caustic critics. In fact, it would appear that during his days of leadership the duke altered his earlier erroneous judgment about opposition in Commons to its equally erroneous contrary, that is, he moved from the conviction that such opposition was impotent to the belief that it was irresistible. The duke had, thus, a streak of cowardice or, if that charge seems a bit harsh, a want of the type of moral courage that stamps the good politician. For he still possessed, after all, the votes he needed to sustain his ministry, even without Fox, Murray, or Pitt; and had he been intrepid enough to endure verbal abuse and see his friends, supporters, and dependents occasionally chuckle at Pitt's *mazarinades,* he could have retained the Treasury. The year would not have been easy. Food prices were already mounting and food riots had begun. Byng's trial and the loss of Hanover lay ahead, neither of which would have been significantly influenced by Pitt's failure to gain office. But Prussian victories also lay ahead, the inflation was soon to abate, and the annual loan of 1757 would almost certainly have been more ably and advantageously handled had Newcastle remained at the Treasury. It thus seems at least arguable that the duke could have completely ridden out the storm. It seems extremely likely that he could have remained in office for a number of months longer.

To make this argument credible, however, it is necessary to say a few words about a type of evidence that would appear to undercut it. This evidence consists of the pessimistic predictions advanced by a variety of advisers and spectators, many of whom saw no alternative for the duke after Fox's resignation except retirement from office. According to the younger Horace Walpole this group included Andrew Stone, Robert Nugent, and Lord Dupplin; and Walpole suggests as well that William Murray may have concurred. Among Newcastle's friends only Lord Hardwicke and Sir George Lyttelton believed that the ministry might yet prevail, even without the services of either Fox or Pitt. Moreover, others beyond the duke's orbit of aides held views similar to Stone's and Dupplin's. Richard Rigby, a dependent of the duke of Bedford, thought it impossible that the ministry could stand without one or the other, and this view was shared by Fox himself.[84] This testimony raises serious questions, for in all efforts to ascertain the limits of the politically possible at any past time the opinions of those who lived through the era deserve major consideration. And while one might try to explain away the pessimistic advice of the duke's counsellors as a devious method adopted by men concerned for their nation and a friendship to induce an incompetent to retire, the statements of Rigby and Fox are not susceptible to such dismissal.

But there is another approach to this difficulty. All those who believed the duke's fate to be sealed were members of the House of Commons. Their membership in that chamber led them to cultivate overblown views of its weight or to fail to distinguish between brilliant but ephemeral rhetorical flourishes and prosaic but enduring influence over votes. It is probably significant that Lord Hardwicke, no simpleton in construing political reality, thought Newcastle could retain office after Fox's resignation, and that Lord Grafton, though urging a reconciliation with Fox, apparently thought such a rapprochement more a convenience than a necessity. And it is surely significant, for it breaks the united front of commoners, that Sir George Lyttelton, not a wise man perhaps but in any case an experienced one, did not regard Fox's resignation and Pitt's veto as entailing the duke's inevitable defeat when Parliament gathered again. He would thus have concurred with the general argument—though not with the particular judgments about persons—contained in the somewhat earlier statement of another member of Parliament, Thomas Potter, that the ministry, even if led in the Commons by such hacks as Dupplin and Lyttelton, could easily muster enough votes to win any division handily.[85] In short, the fact that others could share in (or at least verbally endorse) Newcastle's erring judgment does not convert error itself into truth. For Newcastle in late 1756 was not lacking for a large following in Parliament, and thus he was not wanting in political power. What was missing was rather the will to use it. In a man like Newcastle, that was a deficiency that physical and spiritual recuperation could quickly repair.

7

Minister of Money

I

From the first, Newcastle's retirement was a celebration of power. At Claremont, day after day, he entertained the great of the London political and diplomatic world. Freed at last from the weight of a responsibility he had grown to loathe, the duke became once again the congenial, expansive host of old. Everyone believed that Newcastle's absence from office would be brief, and few dared to slight a man who would soon hold the reins of power again. Newcastle himself so believed. He kept up his lodgings at the cockpit; he received reports on governmental activities from Holderness and Robinson, his allies still in the ministry and court; he followed with close attention the efforts of Legge, again at the exchequer, to secure a loan. When a rumor circulated that Newcastle had retired with a pension of £6,000, he took out a notice in the *Daily Advertiser* to deny the story. He acted, in brief, to keep himself informed and to maintain unsullied his reputation for probity.

The grounds for his ebullient confidence were obvious: as his boasting indicated, he regarded the House of Commons as his. So, moreover, did most of his friends and enemies.[1] But this belief raises some difficulties for historians. Ever since the publication of the work of Sir Lewis Namier it has been clear that the wide power to elect or unseat many dozens of M.P.'s that was once attributed to the duke was vastly exaggerated. Contemporaries had said simply but respectfully that the duke had the authority to choose a House of Commons, and Basil Williams, trying to give precision to that claim, had reckoned that the duke could place sixty to seventy members in the house. But Namier's analysis reduced the number of members who owed their seats to Newcastle's favor to a paltry seven.[2] And even by the more generous standards adopted in this present study, the extent of the duke's power never exceeded seventeen seats. Namier's work, and that of other historians following his lead, put eighteenth-century politics in sharper focus. But if these studies answered certain questions, they raised others. The activities and power of Newcastle in the seven months between his retirement and his resumption of office in June 1757 were easily explicable under the old framework: Newcastle was deferentially attended to because he could control the Commons, destroy the fragile Devonshire-Pitt ministry at will, and prevent any ministry he disliked from being formed. Within Namier's reconstituted framework, however, the struggle for office in these months becomes more perplexing, for if Newcastle could not even dispose of a score of seats in the Commons, it appears strange, especially in the light of his calamitous tenure as chief minister, that he should have been expected to be, and that he was, the pivot upon which the political negotiations of this period revolved.

The dilemma can be resolved only by concluding that Newcastle and his contemporaries did not make the types of distinctions that Namier did. More particularly, not only did they not differentiate between "nomination" and "influence,"[3] they could not even distinguish these types of power from that exercised either *ex officio* or by virtue of rank and standing in society. Thus, they lumped together Newcastle's territorial electoral influence, his personal electoral influence, the Treasury's electoral influence, and the court's electoral influence, and ascribed them all to the man who had most recently exercised them. Newcastle's known passion for electioneering had lent him notoriety as the "Great Elector," and this reputation in turn made the attribution of enormous influence to him, even when he was out of office, all the more plausible. Furthermore, simply because almost everyone believed that his influence in the Commons would assure his return to office, even those not dependent or presumably dependent on him under any of the foregoing categories still found it expedient to participate in the pageantry of power over which the duke presided at Claremont. At its base, this edifice of ducal influence was very narrow, and the whole structure was therefore inherently unstable. If Britain had not been at war, or if the king had liked his new ministers, there might have been enough time for the fragility of Newcastle's power to be revealed. But circumstances decreed that this revelation should be postponed until 1762. In 1757, with the political world still deluded about the nature of political power, Newcastle stood as "arbiter of England."[4]

Everyone of influence sought the duke's participation in the government; no ministry, it was believed, could be stable without his presence.
George II invited the duke to form a new government several times in
the early months of the year. In January he wanted Newcastle allied
to Fox; by February he was willing to take Newcastle, even if unattached to Fox; by May he was prepared to endure Pitt if that was
what was needed to secure the duke. Equally importunate in his
pursuit of the duke's cooperation was Fox. Throughout March and into
April Fox courted the duke, offering him the "management" of
members of Parliament and the "distribution of favours," reserving
only the "management of debates" for himself. Finally, even Pitt, so
recently triumphant over Newcastle, quickly became eager for at least
his unofficial assistance. Pitt's war policy veered sharply toward conformity with Newcastle's, and while the Great Commoner was also
trying to please his restless monarch with this decision, no such alternative interpretation can explain his promise to Hardwicke to make the
inquiry into Newcastle's ministry only pro forma or his unhappiness
with the occasional assaults on Newcastle launched in the Commons by
such Pittites as Charles Townshend and Alderman Beckford. Pitt was
not, to be sure, prepared to give up all his authority to secure the duke;
but he believed that the duke's ambitions for power and his own
were sufficiently dissimilar to allow for a settlement amicable to both.

The duke basked in his role as the sine qua non of government. He
liked to think of himself as indispensable anyway, and the behavior of
all these suppliants, plus the deferential attention of such lesser fry as
Legge and Halifax, certainly reinforced that belief. Several options,
therefore, seemed open to him, but, except as a ploy, he never seriously
considered any except an alliance with Pitt. To resume office without
a powerful ally would be to court the very dangers that he believed had
struck his earlier ministry down; he would not again hazard office
without oratorical support in the Commons. And when considering
where that support could best be secured, from Fox or from Pitt, several
considerations led him to prefer the latter. The recent memory of Fox's
betrayal rankled the duke; Pitt's open opposition seemed more upright
than Fox's deceitful retreat. Moreover, Pitt's known dislike of treasury
affairs and patronage distribution continued to make him far less likely
to want to challenge the duke in those spheres of activity which lay
particularly close to his heart. Finally, and this consideration was
ultimately the most telling, Pitt was allied with Leicester House; by

coming to terms with him the duke, quite conscious of the king's advanced age, could make contact with "the succession" while maintaining ties with "the possession."[5] Early in his triumphal retirement, then, the crucial decision—to seek to join with Pitt—was made.

The first strategic problem to be confronted was one of timing. For several reasons the duke could not immediately link his fortunes with Pitt's. The Byng affair had not yet run its ugly course, and as long as public attention focused on the admiral Newcastle dared not seek a rapprochement with the man who had become Byng's chief public friend. The duke's interest compelled him to insist that Byng be fully punished; any mercy shown or extenuation accepted would shift some of the blame for the loss of Minorca back to the ministers of the previous year. It is true that the king, when considering whether to exercise his right to temper justice with mercy, solicited the duke's advice, and that the duke, rather than supporting execution, suggested that the cabinet be polled. This step, had it been taken, would probably have saved Byng's life.[6] But almost surely it was pusillanimity, or at least caution, and not compassion, that motivated the duke. Byng's guilt under the twelfth article of war was indubitable. All that was problematical for those who sympathized with him was whether a failure to do one's utmost under trying conditions truly merited a penalty as severe as capital punishment. Most of Newcastle's statements indicate that he thought it did, and the king concurred. Early in March Byng was put to death. Aside from the unfolding of this morality play there were two other reasons for ducal delay in seeking affiliation with Pitt. Newcastle was unwilling to resume office until the parliamentary inquiry had cleared his name and until the supplies for the year had been provided. Neither would occur until May. Therefore, because he did not want to antagonize Pitt unnecessarily, because he felt the kingdom needed at least some form of administration, and because he found opposition slightly immoral, Newcastle did not use his parliamentary muscle to destroy the Devonshire–Pitt ministry.

The need to wait upon events before beginning to act caused difficulties for the duke. Not only was he the recipient of a steady stream of suggestions and offers, all of which he had to parry in some manner, but he also found his timetable overturned in early April by the king's decision to dismiss Pitt. The monarch had found the forceful minister and his friends insufferable. When the duke of Cumberland refused to leave to take up his continental command until Pitt was out of office,

George II had the excuse he needed. He dismissed Pitt's brother-in-law Temple, from the Admiralty, hoping Pitt would emulate Bedford's behavior in 1751; but when the Great Commoner stuck to his post, the king fired him too. Devonshire stayed in office, presiding over a caretaker ministry, but he had neither the inclination nor the power to take any initiatives. The king's remarkable action, clear testimony to his distaste for Pitt, appears all the more striking when it is recalled that it left the kingdom without a ministry in the midst of a losing war. George was trying to force Newcastle's or Fox's hand, reasoning that the hesitancy of both could be overcome by creating an emergency situation. Newcastle was unpersuaded, however, and remained unwilling to form a government either alone or with Fox. Only the union with Pitt held the prospect of a durable ministry. He therefore saw that there were two tasks to be simultaneously done: on the one hand, he had to drive Pitt's terms down as low as possible before allying with him; on the other hand, he had to persuade the king to accept Pitt again and the concomitant Leicester House connection.

Much of the duke's deceitfulness during these months can be traced to his belief that whatever conduced to his ultimate union with Pitt was permissible. In March and April, when he was leading Fox to believe that cooperation between them was possible, his representative, Lord Mansfield, was speaking one way to Fox but quite another to Newcastle. In April, when the duke was trying to reduce Pitt's demands and weaken his power base, he entered into ostensibly secret discussions with Henry Legge which he then revealed so that Pitt might see how he was being deserted; and he led Sir George Lee to believe that he would be named to the exchequer so that Leicester House would remain pacified during some tense weeks. Throughout the spring the duke allowed Lord Halifax falsely to believe that he would become a third secretary of state in a new ministry, again serving notice on Pitt that it might be possible to construct a ministry without his participation. Newcastle was waiting for his opportunity.

In May, with the inquiry and the problem of supplies finally disposed of, it became possible for Newcastle to begin an active pursuit of Pitt. He had already begun talks with the princess of Wales and had, in a set of proposed principles, pledged himself to gaining the support of Leicester House for the government. He had also sketched in possible ministerial alignments embracing his own forces and those of Leicester House, though there is no evidence that he broached these proposals to Pitt until the very end of the month at the earliest. Pitt found little in the duke's plans to please him, especially since Temple would not be restored to the Admiralty. He therefore rejected them. Newcastle then began drafting schemes which excluded Pitt and his friends, and a worried Leicester House pressured the Great Commoner to have a personal talk with the duke. That discussion, held on 25 May, only emphasized the disagreements still separating the two men, for Pitt's demands included a Treasury Board with strong Pittite representation (including another brother-in-law, George Grenville, at the exchequer), the attorney generalship for Charles Pratt rather than Charles Yorke, a position in the cabinet council for Temple, and other places for various additional friends of Leicester House. Newcastle responded almost immediately with still more schemes notable chiefly for their omission of all Pittites. To be sure, the nearness of power and its allure began to cloud Newcastle's strategic judgment at this point, for on 1 June he was seriously considering taking the leap into government without either Leicester House or Fox. Hardwicke, however, gently reminded him that such a ministry would be subject to the same stresses that had shattered the duke in October and November, and after a brief period of deliberation, during which it was widely rumored that the duke would take office without allies, Newcastle instead met with Lord Bute to try once again to close the distance between the two sides. And the effort was not unavailing, for Leicester House finally abandoned its insistence on having several representatives in Newcastle's Treasury. Newcastle had won, he believed, his first objective: he had checked Pitt's appetite for power.[7] Now only the king's aversion to Pitt, Temple, and Leicester House stood in his way.

But at this point the political situation unexpectedly changed. George II had watched with growing dismay and even disbelief as the kingdom's foremost commoner and its most powerful peer had prolonged an inherently undesirable wartime interregnum far beyond anyone's expectation. His faith in Newcastle had turned into rage, and he first revenged himself upon the duke by filling vacant ecclesiastical posts that would ordinarily have waited until the resolution of the government crisis. But he had greater plans in mind. "I shall see," he exploded, "which is King of this Country, the Duke of Newcastle or myself."[8] George turned to Lord Waldegrave and to Fox, authorizing them to form an administration. On learning of the king's surprising decision Newcastle was perplexed and angered; he could only protest that he had done everything in his power to oblige the king, but that the concurrence of Leicester House was vital. But he had other ways of protesting as well, and since the king would not listen to what Newcastle regarded as reason, he would be made to bend before force. With deep impatience and a trace of callousness the duke expressed his thinking: "What the king will do, I know not, but I believe he will be forced to yield, what I own I am very long for."[9] Thus, with Newcastle's approval, though perhaps not at his explicit command, Lord Holderness gave up the seals he had retained during six tumultuous years. Other officials promptly declared their readiness to follow him. The meaning of these shenanigans was not lost on the spectators of this drama: Newcastle apparently had the power to topple any government he disliked. Lord Mansfield quickly convinced George II that a Waldegrave–Fox ministry could not succeed, and a chastened king finally submitted to what Waldegrave called "the necessity of the times."[10] The second obstacle had finally been overcome.

The details of the new ministry did not fall immediately into place, but under the guidance of Hardwicke, whom the king deputed to mediate between the two parties, a compromise at least minimally acceptable to everyone was molded. Pitt's chief victories were the choices of Temple for the privy seal and Charles Pratt as attorney general. Newcastle's were the isolation of James Grenville as the only Pittite agent on the Treasury and the restoration of Holderness as northern secretary. The duke was disappointed, though not surprised, that Hardwicke chose not to reenter government in any official capacity, and after much discussion Sir Robert Henley took the post of lord keeper. Hardwicke remained in the cabinet, however, so the duke was not deprived of his invaluable counsel. To soothe royal resentment Fox was given the lucrative office of paymaster. The choice of Anson for the Admiralty was a victory for Newcastle's Whigs, although the duke himself, blaming Anson for the naval catastrophes of 1755–56, remained peculiarly insensitive to the man's talents and personally regarded his membership in the government as a "sad weight upon us."[11] Newcastle took the Treasury, Pitt assumed the southern secretaryship, and the new ministry kissed hands on 29 June. The key compromise which underlay the coalition ministry was an acceptable division of function: Pitt was to direct war policy and Newcastle to guide patronage and parliamentary affairs. Speaking of the new ministry, Lord Temple characterized his brother-in-law as "minister of measures" and the duke as "minister of numbers."[12] It would be equally sound, as well as more alliterative, to regard the duke as "minister of money."[13] But the terminology is less important than the reality: a "complete, strong, and well-cemented" ministry, the most enduring between Pelham's death and North's rise, had finally been formed.[14] Moreover, though no one yet knew it, the world had seen Newcastle's last great demonstration of political power.

II

The coalition in which Newcastle now partook is one of the most celebrated governments in British history. William Pitt brought energy and a transcendent sense of purpose to Britain's military effort, transforming a war clumsily begun and ineptly managed into a triumphant struggle for world supremacy. Newcastle served him superbly, keeping the king happy and the coffers filled, and occasionally even adding some useful element to the war planning itself. Lord Waldegrave, a commentator who studied the duke more disinterestedly than Lord Hervey or Horace Walpole, remarked that Newcastle's peculiar talents suited him for positions below the top one, that he lacked "both spirit and capacity to be first in command."[15] The judgment rings true, and the coalition is the great test of its validity. Spared the burden of directing or at least of being held responsible for all, and given instead tasks graded to his abilities and congenial to his interests, the man who had just led the most calamitous administration of the eighteenth century blossomed into a competent and valuable adjutant. He was not indispensable—only Pitt bears that distinction—but he was performing indispensable tasks. For two and a half years the two men jointly provided the "complete, strong, and well-cemented" administration that Hardwicke had foretold.

Newcastle came quickly to admire and yet to fear Pitt. His attitude toward the secretary of state even contained elements of a childlike dependence. A smile or kind word from Pitt brought joy to his day; a rebuke or, worse still, studied neglect, raised anxiety within his soul. Pitt's forcefulness cowed Newcastle, but while the duke sometimes complained about being overborne, he seems actually to have flourished in the protection thus afforded by Pitt's unshakable readiness to accept responsibility for wartime policy.[16] Moreover, the duke was no fool about recognizing talent. Pitt's dynamism, command of detail, and ability to keep discrete actions subordinated to a grand strategy earned the duke's respect and outweighed the various particular errors committed in pursuit of this global strategy. That strategy itself was one the duke could comfortably accept, at least until its financial cost became too painful. It was not the doctrine of the Pitt who had formerly railed against Hanover. Sobered by office and the need to win the king's favor, Pitt now fitted Hanover into his strategic thinking. Like Newcastle in the previous war, but with flair and a more effective ally, Pitt wanted to attack France in Europe as well as in the colonial world. Military operations in western Germany forced France to disperse its forces to several theatres and also gave vital aid to Prussia. Yet any similarity between Pitt's thinking in the Seven Years' War and Newcastle's in the War of the Austrian Succession is in one basic regard deceptive. Newcastle had seen the continent as the main theatre whereas Pitt viewed it as a secondary one; the duke moreover had hoped to give France moderate defeats in both Europe and America while Pitt planned to harass France in Europe in order to crush it more easily in the colonies. Pitt, in short, had rational priorities and Newcastle did not. It was part of the difference between strategic wisdom and strategic blindness.

The duke's record of turning against his colleagues in government had not gone unnoticed, and there were those who predicted at the beginning of the coalition that he would grow jealous of Pitt also and seek to undermine his power. The prophets were disappointed. The duke could not avoid fits of jealousy and even of anger against his partner, but he did not try to destroy him politically. The rumors which occasionally circulated about efforts by Newcastle to link himself with Bedford against Pitt seem to have been exaggerated. In fact, the duke's loyalty to the secretary was so strong that at least on one occasion he spurned a direct request from the king to lead an anti-Pitt movement. Instead, he served as Pitt's advocate with the Crown, working in the closet with the aid of Lady Yarmouth on a royal master whose whims they knew well to effect conversions to Pittite schemes that would have aroused royal rage had they been heard from the mouth of their creator.[17] The poor old monarch, thus led by the duke, grew slowly to admire his most famous subject and finally to forgive him much of his earlier king baiting. It was one of Newcastle's most important services to the coalition. It indicated too that the duke's reputation as a faithless colleague needed some qualification. Mediocrities and dogmatists, not men of true ability, were the victims of his machinations;

Townshend, Granville, Harrington, and Bedford were his targets, but not Walpole and Pitt.

The duke's chief political function in the new administration was to be "disposing minister," the man charged with handling patronage, appointments to places, and the distribution of honors and favors. It was of course the sort of work the duke loved, and it was largely through his patronage influence that Parliament in this era contained such an uncommonly high number of court officials. He continued to give preference to friends or residents of Sussex: James Yorke, for example, Hardwicke's clerical son, received assurances of his succession to the deanery of Windsor, and "Mr. Philpot of Lewes [was] to be of the king's band of musick, the first vacancy." On many of the more significant appointments he also had his way. Lord Dupplin, soon to be Lord Kinnoull, became chancellor of the duchy of Lancaster and later ambassador to Portugal, Bishop Johnson was translated from Gloucester to Worcester, and Thomas Secker was elevated to the see of Canterbury, all through Newcastle's activities. He also used his authority to have himself made lord lieutenant of Sussex on Lord Abergavenny's resignation in 1760, thereby deliberately putting a capstone on the mutually fruitful ties he had long had with the county of the Pelhams.[18] Beyond the realm of England itself the duke's effective power of appointment was also great, for, as he bragged to Mansfield in 1760, whenever the duke of Bedford, lord lieutenant of Ireland, wanted appointments for his domain or the duke of Argyle wanted them for Scotland, they worked through Newcastle. The duke's authority reached even to the royal family: in 1760 Prince Edward applied to the duke for a peerage, and received one without consulting his brother, the Prince of Wales.[19]

But there were limits to the duke's patronage power and, aside from them, politic considerations that had to be attended to. Pitt was not as uninterested in patronage as he professed to be, and when he made recommendations they were not easily ignored. William Warburton rose to the bishopric of Gloucester and Robert Nugent became vice-treasurer of Ireland at Pitt's behest, not Newcastle's. The secretary of state even drove a Pelham from the excise board to find a place for a protege of Bute's. Military patronage continued to be denied Newcastle, despite arguments that his efforts to prepare for a general election would be significantly facilitated if he could make promises for promotions within the expanded wartime army.[20] The struggle to pry from the king a garter for Temple, who had both Newcastle's and Pitt's support, lasted fully two years. Most telling as an indication of the limits to the duke's authority was his inability to win royal approval for his own candidates for his own Treasury Board; not until the end of 1759 did George agree to the appointment of James Oswald, a man the duke had been touting for over a year. The king was, moreover, often unhappy that so many of Newcastle's recommendations came from the duke's circle of close acquaintances, a practice that the duke could but lamely defend by noting that they were "not the worse for being my friends."[21] Thus, despite contemporaries' beliefs to the contrary, Newcastle was not an omnipotent minister of men. His job was therefore doubly irritating. Not only was he denied the authority he thought he should possess, he was also blamed by outsiders for not doing what it was forbidden him to do.

Because he was generally so acquiescent toward Pitt, Newcastle rose to clear public visibility only on those occasions when he found himself quarreling with the secretary, but these were infrequent. Some of the disagreements turned on domestic issues. In the spring of 1758, for example, the duke successfully resisted Pitt's strenuous efforts to have the law of Habeas Corpus liberalized. Lord Mansfield had declared that writs of Habeas Corpus were not obligatory, but issuable only at a judge's discretion. Pitt thought the judgment unfortunate and had Pratt draft a measure to end judicial discretion on the matter and make such writs mandatory upon request. The Commons approved the bill but in the House of Lords Newcastle and Hardwicke raised a formidable opposition to it. The duke detested what he interpreted as Pitt's playing to the mob, and Hardwicke's judicial temper found Mansfield's decision correct. Pitt tried to "bully" Newcastle into accepting it—"a greater rhapsody of violence and virulence could not be thrown out"—but the duke refused to give way.[22] When the House of Lords ultimately rejected the measure the secretary thought of resigning to register his bitterness, especially since the duke had actively mobilized episcopal opposition; but Newcastle remained confident that a dangerous change in legal practice had been averted, and Pitt came to see that there were more important matters than this to be dealt with.

Differences of opinion between Newcastle and Pitt also arose over the complex issue of the militia. To the duke a militia was objectionable on several counts. In general he believed it "most destructive of our constitution and the liberties of it in many shapes."[23] He was additionally concerned about the contentiousness of a militia and feared that it would be a continual provocation of the sort of public unrest he so sorely distrusted. Pitt on the other hand saw in the militia a home guard that would be very useful if a French invasion should ever threaten. In 1756 the duke had defeated in the Lords a Pittite effort to create a militia, but in 1757, during Pitt's coalition with Devonshire, the Great Commoner had had his way, and a newly structured militia, organized on a county basis, was brought into being. The measure for 1758 was thus the first to be introduced after the political union of the two militia antagonists, and some feared that it might tear the ministry apart. But since the duke had already chosen to resist Pitt on the Habeas Corpus issue, he declined to challenge him on this ground as well. In fact, after successfully attaching amendments to the measure, the duke actually voted in its favor. Still, his suspicions remained, and in 1760 he thwarted an effort to create a Scots militia, a step that might, he believed, have amounted to arming Jacobites. In that same year, even though he had been compelled to acknowledge the marginal usefulness of a home guard with France so menacing, he again could not bring himself to agree to vote for its continuation, though as a mark of respect for Pitt he forebore organizing any opposition. The duke's aversion to a militia endured throughout his remaining years.

The militia raised problems for Newcastle at the local as well as the national level. As lord lieutenant of Nottinghamshire and Middlesex and as the preeminent peer of Sussex, Newcastle bore chief responsibility for providing appropriate leadership in militia administration in all three locales. His known antipathy to the organization did not lead him to disavow his legal obligation. "I care no more for the Militia than you do," he wrote to John White in Nottinghamshire, "but I do care for an Act of Parliament, and should be sorry that the Execution of one which belongs to me as Lord-Lieutenant should be neglected."[24] But the duke could not convert good intentions into the requisite energy, and none of the three counties came close to fulfilling what the law expected of them. In Nottinghamshire his friends could induce only four men, one of them a Tory and another a "mad man," to volunteer for commissions. In Middlesex the turnout was similarly unimpressive. In Sussex only Rose Fuller and George Medley volunteered from among the county leaders, and Newcastle was driven to command Tommy Pelham and John Shelley to accept regiments. In a desperate effort to make good the consequent deficiencies, the duke then tried to raise troops through a subscription, but this also proved inadequate.[25] A verse of the times heaped appropriate contempt on the duke's failure:[26]

> All over the land they'll find such a stand,
> From our English Militia Men ready at hand,
> Though in Sussex and Middlesex folks are but fiddlesticks,
> While an old fiddlestick has the command.

Pitt doubtless concurred.

At various times Newcastle opposed Pitt's war strategy. He was in general distrustful of the raids on the French coast which Pitt authorized, and at least in 1757 that suspicion was sound. Pitt might instead have sent badly needed reinforcements to the duke of Cumberland in Germany. This decision was the Great Commoner's final spasm of anti-Hanoverianism, and an undermanned Cumberland, defeated at Hastenbeck, signed the Convention of Klosterseven, briefly removing Hanover from the war. The king's son was in disgrace and not even his father, alternately abject and enraged, could muster a kind word for him. Cumberland resigned his military appointments, and Pitt, Newcastle, and Hardwicke agreed that Sir John Ligonier should succeed him. When it was learned that the king, despite his years, was contemplating assuming command himself, Newcastle was selected to inform him of ministerial opposition to that folly. George reluctantly assented. But, had Cumberland received the assistance he needed, the whole episode of forcing the able Ligonier on the old king would probably have been unnecessary.

Since years of experience had made the conduct of foreign affairs the duke's chief field of competence and interest, important conflicts between Pitt and the duke in this arena also appeared. They were not in general products of ducal meddling in the war itself; Pitt would tolerate no such presumptuousness, and Newcastle knew his colleague's sensitivity on this point. But not every state in Europe was a belligerent, and with the neutrals something approximating normal relations was the goal of British policy. Into this sphere of relations with nonbelligerents Newcastle was eager to intrude his views. And it was a sphere characterized by peculiar problems. The chief one to arise during the war was the difficulty of remaining on amicable terms with the Dutch and the Danes while simultaneously trying to enforce the rule of 1756 against their expanded trade with France. British privateers roamed the seas, applying the rule with minimal regard for international niceties and scant concern for the indignation felt in Amsterdam and Copenhagen about Britain's unilateral modification of international law. Pitt saw no need to relent in this sea warfare, but Newcastle, who was in frequent consultation with Dutch and Danish representatives, feared that the affected states might be driven to form a northern league by means of which they would seek to defend what they regarded as their rights. Ultimately it was the duke's view that prevailed, and checks were placed on British privateers; still, untoward incidents continued to keep the issue alive until the hostilities themselves ended.

The chief way in which Newcastle kept himself informed on diplomatic events in Europe, despite his separation from secretarial office, was by inviting Joseph Yorke, Britain's minister at The Hague, to send him long and detailed accounts of any information he acquired: "It will not," the duke reminded Yorke, "be the worse either for you or for me."[27] In some ways the prophecy was right. Throughout the war the duke remained remarkably well informed about what was happening in foreign capitals. His most spectacular intelligence success came in the spring of 1759 when he correctly learned that France was preparing for an invasion of Britain; Pitt scoffed at the idea until his own information belatedly confirmed what the duke had long warned of. But the private correspondence which Newcastle invited from Yorke led to an acutely embarrassing incident toward the end of that same year, and before he extricated himself the duke had irritated Pitt and hurt Hardwicke. Joe Yorke transmitted to the duke some letters he had received from "*l'inconnue*"—actually the princess of Anhalt–Zerbst—which spoke of peace terms that might be acceptable to Versailles. Like Yorke, both Newcastle and Hardwicke treated the letters as the humorous trivia they obviously were: George II and the Prussian minister Knyphausen were let in on the joke and were amused both by the epistles and by Yorke's overly gallant replies. But word of the exchange leaked to Pitt, who, in a fury, rebuked the duke and the earl for keeping information about peace feelers away from the responsible secretary of state. When Newcastle meekly protested that he had not intended to establish private peace negotiations, Pitt silenced him with an icy reply: "I believe it, for if you did, you would not be able to walk the streets without a guard."[28]

Having shown himself to be a meddler, the duke now proved himself cowardly as well. Rather than simply accpet Pitt's stinging chastisement, he sought to shift the blame onto Yorke for having sent him "those cursed female letters" in the first place. "I read it to the King for amusement only," he whined to Pitt, "I was sorry when it was sent to me."[29] As if to underline this last contention, the duke then acquiesced in Yorke's dismissal from a negotiation being undertaken with France. Hardwicke could not allow such willful distortions of the truth to stand unchallenged, especially since they threatened Joe's reputation and future. Gently but firmly he reminded the duke that Yorke had simply acted in compliance with the request of the first lord of the Treasury, a request, he shrewdly added, that was not at all inappropriate for "the head of the King's administration" to make.[30] The earl then turned his attention to having Joe's honor restored, a feat accomplished by having him receive royal authorization to proceed "in concert" with Prince Louis of Brunswick in another diplomatic negotiation at The Hague. Newcastle's behavior was shabby throughout the entire affair, but at least he seems to have learned a practical lesson from it: not until Pitt had left the ministry would he again engage in unofficial diplomacy.

Above and beyond any particular points of contention he had with Pitt, Newcastle came to nourish a fundamental disagreement with the Great Commoner's thinking about the entire war. Hard experience had taught him to be wary of the lure of military adventuring. His official duties at the Treasury gave him a new perspective on warfare. Convinced that Britain could neither win nor afford a protracted global struggle, the duke became an advocate of a prompt and moderate peace. Only slowly did he fathom Pitt's purpose; only by degrees did he realize the breadth of the secretary's ambition. When that realization finally penetrated, the duke was almost incredulous: "To think," he wrote in 1759, "of being able to extirpate the French from North America, or, if we could, that our business was done by doing so, or that such a nation as France would sit down tamely under it, is to me the idlest of all imaginings." The duke's unalterable inference from the string of military victories of that *annus mirabilis* was that each removed any previous objections to peace. But Pitt's policy remained unshaken: "The only way to have peace is to prepare for war." A year later, as Pitt prepared to send forth another raid on the French coast, ducal disbelief had turned to despair: "My Claremont road is filled with wagons, heavy artillery, ordnance stores, etc etc. . . . Where they go, God knows. . . . Would to God they were all now at Wesel. I write *treason* and you are guilty of misprision if ever one word of it."[31]

The reference to the Rhenish town of Wesel points up another aspect of Newcastle's strategic estrangement from Pitt. Although the duke wanted hostilities to end, he believed the most important theatre of the war remained Germany, where from 1758 on Prince Ferdinand was leading an allied army with much success against French troops. The duke's commitment to the priority of the German theatre was demonstrated by his efforts, despite the costs they would involve, to have a Baltic squadron aid the allies and to maintain a flow of reinforcements to Ferdinand. This fixation on Germany meant that if the state of belligerence was not amenable to cessation but only to contraction, the activities in Germany should be the last to be sacrificed and the invasion expeditions the first. In sum, the duke's deep conviction that Britain could not bear the financial burden of world war steadily drove him to dissociate himself from Pitt's ambitious schemes. This split developing between secretary and first lord was pregnant with momentous political consequences.

There was one other element to the duke's disquietude as the decade moved to its close. Despite his hopes to the contrary and his efforts to realize those hopes, he could not disguise from himself or others the truth that his political influence was fading. "Mr. Pitt," he had early written to Hardwicke, "shall have his full share of power and credit, but he shall not be my *superior*."[32] Newcastle had promptly sought to reinforce his influence in the cabinet by having Lord Mansfield brought in. But nothing availed against the dynamic secretary. The lord chief justice, although he accepted the duke's offer, disappointed his former patron by expressing himself rarely. Thus, with the doughty Bedford often absent, with an incoherent Granville unheeded, and with Anson and Holderness all too ready to follow Pitt's siren call, only Newcastle and Hardwicke remained to resist the secretary's excesses. But Hardwicke was in declining health, his former vigor flagging, and Newcastle, even when he had the reason, lacked the courage to struggle almost single-handedly against so forceful a figure as Pitt. Thus, the secretary ruled the cabinet and, through it, the kingdom. Holderness' betrayal— for so the duke viewed his colleague's slow transfer of loyalty to Pitt— was an ominous sign. A man of scant ability anyway, Holderness was virtually invisible as Pitt's cosecretary. Whether from ambition or from a fear of antagonizing the Great Commoner, he became, in George II's phrase, "Pitt's footman." He began complaining, and with some justice, that "the Duke of Newcastle had used me shamefully ill," and he simultaneously treated the duke publicly with disrespect.[33] The final rupture between Newcastle and Holderness came late in 1759 when it was Holderness who informed Pitt of Joseph Yorke's correspondence with the duke about *l'inconnue*. For this action neither Newcastle nor Hardwicke ever forgave their former friend.

Hardwicke's poor health and Holderness's defection were but two of the most obvious reasons for the duke's mounting feeling of isolation. Among important men in the government only the king, older even than Newcastle, still treated the duke with confidence and respect; but the monarch was showing traces of heightened emotional instability in his final years, and he had in any event never been more than a broken reed in political infighting. "Pray, my Lord," he tearfully implored the duke as early as 1757, "serve a friend." "I cannot do without you," was his lament in 1759. He often wept in his closet encounters with the duke and seemed still more forlorn than the first lord to whom he poured out his sorrows. Outside of the closet the duke often felt himself useless. By mid-1759 the duke was bewailing his exclusion from affairs, and late in that year he described himself as "an unfortunate old minister, proscribed by a young ———." Unconsulted on policy, unattended in his warnings, bearing at last the physical and psychic toll of advancing age, Newcastle fell victim frequently to a despair that not even his characteristic hyperbole could render amusing: "My present situation," he confided to Hardwicke at the end of 1759, "is such as even my worst enemy, would hardly be so cruel as to wish."[34] It was thus not startling that the duke began to let word leak out that, whenever the old king died, he would use the occasion finally to retire from public life.[35]

Nevertheless, it would be misleading to leave the matter thus. A deep streak of ineradicable optimism, or at least of love of life and society, lay close to the core of the duke's psyche. He lived on hopes and was inexhaustibly resourceful in creating them. Glum moments beset his days in the coalition, but they did not overwhelm them. For each hour of despair there might be found at least one hour of fulfillment. Despite recriminations and suspicions, Newcastle took pleasure in working under Pitt and for his old master George II. Hardwicke told the Great Commoner as late as September 1760 that "I continually hear from my friend the Duke of Newcastle, how harmoniously you go on together; which gives me the greatest pleasure."[36] There was diplomatic exaggeration in Hardwicke's letter, but a fundamental truth as well. On 25 October 1760 the foundation of that truth crumbled: George II died at the age of seventy-six. The duke thereby lost, as he wrote to Joseph Yorke, "the best king, the best master, & the best friend, that ever subject had."[37] He had also lost his political *raison d'être*.

III

The accession of George III was an event of signal political importance. Unlike the change of monarchs in 1727, the shift of 1760 altered the balance of forces within the government, bringing to the throne for the first time in almost half a century a Briton rather than a German. George III was only twenty-two years old; not conditioned by the party strife of the early decades of the century, he failed to share Newcastle's deep belief that Whiggery was the foundation of national stability and tranquility. In fact, convinced that the moral tone of the kingdom had declined under his grandfather, he held the self-proclaimed Whigs who had guided George II to be responsible for this decay. Programatically he sought little more than a restoration of virtue to government, but that in itself, though in a sense a platitudinous goal, had as one clear consequence a sharp reduction in royal trust and interest in Newcastle and his associates. Whigs were not to be purged from government, but neither were they any longer to be automatically preferred. George III intended to promote and advance men of virtue, whatever their political ties. The appearance of the new king entailed the coming to political power of the king's chief friend and confidant, the Scots peer, the earl of Bute. Bute was in many ways naive and can certainly not be credited with possessing a detailed plan by which in the months to come he would drive Pitt and Newcastle from office and thereby assure his own authority. But he was ambitious, and that fact, coupled with the king's unquestioning support of him, boded ill for the coalition partners. As the earl himself stated early in the reign, he would not be "a bare groom of the stole. The king will have it otherwise."[38] And if Bute's power was to be magnified, Pitt's and Newcastle's could only be diminished.

Neither man had been unaware in the final years of the previous reign that the accession of the grandson would bring Bute to authority, and each had sought to remain on friendly terms with the coming favorite. As early as 1757 Newcastle had called the earl "my sheet anchor, with this new connection. I will keep *him* in good humour."[39] But Bute had preferred Pitt to Newcastle in those days, doubtless because his own future ambitions seemed less likely to be confined by Pitt's domination of strategy than by the duke's patronage authority. In a letter to Bute the Great Commoner called his alliance with Newcastle "this bitter, but necessary cup," and he and Bute had talked of the ministry that would follow George II's death. In these discussions, although Pitt had loyally defended Newcastle's right to significant representation, Bute had voiced strong objections.[40] Still, much depended on events. When the old king finally passed on, neither Pitt with his popularity nor Newcastle with his financial ties was regarded as immediately expendable. Both would stay on, but the duumvirate became an uneasy triumvirate, and Bute was clearly *tertium gaudens*.

It was within a week of George II's death that Newcastle decided, despite earlier pronouncements to the contrary, that he would remain at the Treasury in the new reign. The king's reference to Bute as the man who would "tell you my thoughts at large" was ominous, but its force was softened by the further royal assurance that Bute was Newcastle's "good friend."[41] The duke gave brief consideration to fulfilling his promise to withdraw from office, and both Hardwicke and Stone urged on him the propitiousness of the moment. A future in office, they reasoned, could only bring reduction of authority and honor. But on the other side of the question were arrayed the king, the dukes of Devonshire and Cumberland, Lord Bute, Pitt, Lord Mansfield, Archbishop Secker, Lady Yarmouth, and most of the moneyed interest in the city. Against this phalanx there could be no successful resistance, especially for one as habituated to office as the duke. Still, longer perspective leaves little doubt that the decision to stay was personally unfortunate; Newcastle thereby squandered his last opportunity to resign with honor and without recriminations.

The duke was determined, insofar as possible, to retain both place and power. Before assenting to remain at the Treasury he won assurances from George III and Bute that he would be entrusted with management of the general election that both the late king's death and the Septennial Act now necessitated. This promise meant that for a while at any rate Newcastle would continue in general command of patronage. But the assignment met Bute's and George's needs as well as Newcastle's, for neither the monarch nor his favorite knew the intricacies of electioneering, and both were happy to leave the choosing of a new Parliament to an expert who had for a full year been preparing for the task. Putting Newcastle in control did not prevent them from exercising some influence, for the duke was only too eager to please his

new master and new colleague. For a while he was fearful of rumors
circulated by the artful Sardinian diplomat, Count Viry, that Bute
had a list of fully fifty men whom he wanted returned; but the actual
list contained only three names, and Newcastle accomodated two of
them, providing as well for a few unmentioned Bute men. The election
itself was, as it could only have been, a success, for with no opposition
in the land and with all prominent politicians in the ministry, partisan
and factional disputes almost disappeared. Newcastle handled the
election with aplomb. Though there were a few of the inevitable problems, it was in general a remarkably smooth affair.

In those constituencies peculiarly responsive to his personal wishes
the duke duplicated his success of 1754: he again accounted for seventeen members.[42] The Yorkshire boroughs continued loyal. Aldborough
returned Nathaniel Cholmley, who at Lord Rockingham's suggestion
had been chosen to replace Pitt in November 1756; and Boroughbridge
elected Sir Cecil Bisshop, a former foe of the duke who had repented
and accepted the seat in 1755, and Brice Fisher, a friend of Lord Lincoln's and a valued government contractor. Nottinghamshire was
similarly faithful; in fact, all four constituencies experienced unopposed
elections. The county returned its sitting members, of whom John
Hewett—John Thornhagh's new name—was Newcastle's adherent.
The borough of Nottingham chose William Howe, the future com-
mander-in-chief in America, and John Plumptre. Both were Whigs,
but Newcastle disapproved of Howe, who, as younger brother of the
late Lord Howe, had been chosen to succeed him in 1758 by the corporation and against the duke's wishes. The duke's man at Nottingham
was Plumptre, who, though often disappointed in his pursuit of a
seat, finally persuaded Newcastle that he was reliable. At Newark Job
Staunton Charlton was feeling his years and hoped to retire. He was
sufficiently loyal to the duke to acknowledge that if the retirement
seemed likely to open a Pandora's box, he would assent to retaining his
seat. And his fears were not groundless: opposition grouped itself around
Lord Middleton, Dr. Wilson being by now somewhat chastened, and
backed down only toward polling day. But the duke had felt sufficiently confident to let Charlton retire, and the election of Thomas
Thoroton, another of the duke's Nottinghamshire friends, justified the
decision. At East Retford John White and John Shelley were reelected.

In Sussex too the duke met with complete success. The county
returned Thomas Pelham and John Butler for new terms. Lewes gave

the same endorsement to Sir Francis Poole and Thomas Sergison. At Hastings, with both James Pelham and Andrew Stone choosing to retire, the duke faced some difficulties. Though assured by his agent Edward Milward that "the whole corporation, will continue entirely at your Grace's command," the duke was embarrassed that he had no Pelham to nominate for this loyal port,[43] and he actually apologized for this deficiency when asking the borough to accept James Brudenell and William Ashburnham, the latter being at least a distant cousin. Just as Milward had predicted, Hastings responded loyally. At Rye the duke answered the plea of his old friend, the Dutch politician Count William Bentinck, by nominating the count's son, John Bentinck, for the seat he could in some measure control. That the command was less than absolute is suggested by the hint that the duke, as in 1749, assured success by paying off another municipal debt shortly before the polling. Only Seaford gave the duke cause for alarm. He sought the return of the two incumbents, Lincoln's friend James Peachey (who had replaced the late Hay in 1755) and Lord Gage (William Hall Gage with his new Irish title). But an opposition appeared, willing to fight the battle to the end. George Medley led the rival slate, and he shrewdly addressed his appeal to those voters not belonging to the corporation. He ultimately failed in his effort, though only because the membership of the corporation was remarkably steadfast in its support of the duke. But because he displayed a wide influence that was grounded in the appeal of his vaguely democratic principles, Medley was a rising power in Sussex politics and a sign of new forces entering the political arena.

Though the general election was properly viewed as a sign of cooperation between the first lord and the young favorite, this cooperation bore seeds of future trouble for the duke. It would of course have been folly to have willfully angered Bute, but even more important than amicable ties with the favorite was the maintenance of Pitt's confidence. As long as the duke stood well with Pitt, the two men constituted a formidable and independent power base against which not even the combined might of George and Bute could be sure of prevailing. This power base was Newcastle's security; if he should break with Pitt and bind himself to Bute, he would lose his independent leverage and become expendable at Bute's whim. The duchess of Newcastle saw this truth. Early in the new reign she urged her husband to cultivate his friendship with Pitt: "There is no safety for you in any thing else."[44] But the duke, while intellectually aware of this truth, followed instead the behavior pattern that had long characterized his political life: whenever confronted by a threat to his power, the duke was likely to ignore what cool reason prescribed and to react incautiously, short-sightedly, and almost mindlessly. In this instance, seeking desperately to ingratiate himself with the favorite, he became the dupe of those who for their own reasons sought Bute's advance, and he did it in a fashion that could only make Pitt, who was himself fearful of the changing political ambience, deeply suspicious of his colleague at the Treasury.

Bute began the reign as groom of the stole, an office of far less significance than his real power warranted. In January Count Viry suggested to Newcastle, perhaps at Bute's prodding, that the favorite should replace Holderness as secretary of state. Newcastle, who had once already displeased Bute by resisting his efforts to be made an English peer, was eager to restore himself to the earl's good graces and of course throughly in sympathy with any demotion of Holderness. He then learned that his closest friends, Hardwicke, Devonshire, and Kinnoull, found Viry's suggestion commendable, in part because it would make Bute officially answerable for much that he would anyway be the author or promoter of. But Pitt's view was unknown, and as the man most to be affected by a change of secretarial colleague, he clearly would expect to be consulted. In early March, however, without broaching the plan to Pitt, Newcastle recommended to George III that Bute be given the seals. Holderness's dismissal and Bute's elevation followed promptly; Pitt was simply presented with a *fait accompli*. Newcastle meanwhile incautiously concluded this entire maneuver by promising that he would never desert Bute. Viry had induced him to become the chief mover in this political game by raising the spectre of Pitt doing so if the duke lacked the courage. But *divide et impera*, as the duke knew, is generally the first rule of political combat. The experienced Newcastle had fallen victim to it with surprising alacrity.

The three-cornered struggle for place in the ministry was waged in the realm of strategy too. The growing divisions between Pitt and Newcastle had surfaced long before George III's accession. Bute's views were at variance with both men's. He agreed with Newcastle, and dissented from Pitt, in his belief that the war should be brought to a conclusion as quickly as was reasonably possible; but he stood with Pitt, and against Newcastle, in his belief that Germany was the least justifiable theatre of operations. Both Pitt and Bute had more consistent views of the war than Newcastle. Pitt wanted to humble France. Ameri-

ca was the major field, but activities on the continent served usefully to
disconcert the enemy. This aim was as yet unachieved, and so the war
should be pushed ahead until Versailles finally capitulated to terms that
only a worldwide victory could compel. Bute was prepared to declare
that the war was "bloody & expensive," words that enraged Pitt.[45]
And while he was not an exponent of rash concessions nor of the surren-
der of the legitimate booty of war, he was dubious of the value of further
massive undertakings. He shared his royal master's contempt for
Hanover and saw little by way of results to justify the enormous expense
of operations in Germany. Pitt in short wanted to press on until his war
aims were realized; Bute wanted an honorable peace based on the
status quo. Each view, given its value assumptions, was internally
coherent.

Newcastle, however, found himself becoming the advocate of a war
policy which, if not strictly inconsistent, was by most appearances and
explanations vulnerable to that charge. On the one hand he favored a
prompt peace, not dishonorable but not greedy either. The war was now
costing the kingdom £20,000,000 a year, an unprecedented sum, and it
had led to so many conquests that Britain could safely negotiate from
strength and success, restoring enough to France to induce Versailles to
come quickly to terms and yet retaining enough to justify the loss of
men and money that had occurred. But on the other hand, as a consequence of his old-fashioned Whig view of France as a power ever
threatening to burst forth from its frontiers to swallow up much of
Europe, the duke continued to believe that Germany was the preeminent theatre of operations, the one that could least easily be abandoned. It was a view that George II in his day might have applauded,
but one that seemed increasingly indefensible, on either political or
strategic grounds, in the era of a king who prided himself on being a
Briton and in the face of the enormous burden of spending £340,000 a
month to wage war between the Elbe and the Rhine[46] while supporting
Prussia with an additional £670,000 annually. In theory, the two aspects of Newcastle's military thinking can be made to cohere by postu-
lating the ducal assumptions that peace was desirable but that if it was
to be approached through a scaling down of activities, the last area to
be scaled down should be Germany. But in the political climate of 1761
the duke seemed to be blindly inconsistent in simultaneously preaching
the imminence of bankruptcy and the necessity of campaigning in
Germany. The duke of Bedford summed up the opinion of many who

found Newcastle's views incomprehensible with the caustic remark that George II had turned Newcastle "from an Englishman into a German."[47]

Newcastle's commitment to Germany grew as the theatre's apparent value declined. Although Israel Mauduit's celebrated pamphlet had recently blackened the name of the German war and a cautions Pitt had thereupon refused to promote the renewal of the controversial Pussian subsidy in Parliament, Newcastle picked up the unpopular cause and secured the subsidy for another year. In March 1761, faced with resistance from Legge to the payment of £330,000 to Hesse, the duke had him dismissed as chancellor of the exchequer—Hesse was obviously the shibboleth of Legge's treasury careers—and replaced by the less independent Lord Barrington, secretary at war since 1754. "I don't care a farthing for Legge," Newcastle had remarked to Fox.[48] George III and Bute, for their own reasons, were not unhappy at Legge's departure, and the duke was thus serving personal as well as policy advantage in dispensing with his services. But by gaining the assistance of a man of Barrington's experience with German war provisioning, Newcastle was also strengthening his Treasury team for the challenges to continental war making that lay ahead.

The most severe of these challenges, and one that Barrington was especially well equipped to deal with, was the mounting public outrage at the cost of the German war. The Treasury bore responsibility for supplying, victualling, and paying troops in Germany.[49] The government in Hanover had recently triggered another of the increasingly recurrent debates about German war policy by publicly accusing the commissariat of gross corruption. Newcastle knew that the charges touched a raw nerve in the public sensibility; he knew too that some of the assaults on the German war could be diverted if the costs of that theatre could be cut back and the profiteers preying on British supply machinery routed. But fearful of drawing more attention to these difficulties, the duke at first tried to explore reform possibilities quietly. He was shaken from this cautious approach by two embarrassing criticisms of his leadership. In February Pitt accused the duke of making the war expensive so that it would become odious, and he added, in a thoroughly unfair comparison, that during his first ministry in 1757 he had spent only £200,000 on the German war. These charges were followed in March by a broadside from Prince Ferdinand, in which he inveighed against his "monster of a commissariat" and accused its officials of being "as ignorant and as incapable, as they are avid to line their own pockets."[50] No approach to reform that seemed fainthearted could any longer be tolerated, the duke realized, and he quickly set in motion the most searching investigation of the commissariat problem undertaken during the war. But the fruits of the study were bitter: the consequent reforms left untouched the primary source of expense, the war itself.

Lord Bute, once installed as secretary of state, no longer felt any need beyond what decency compelled and caution recommended to treat Newcastle with kindness. The two men became—indeed, from the opening of the reign they had been—rivals for the control of patronage. Newcastle had been deeply alarmed when, within a month of his accession, George III had begun choosing men to fill minor household offices without consulting him. Offense was sometimes meant, for Bute was determined to assert himself against what he saw as Newcastle's engrossing power; but even where no offense was intended, the suspicious duke was apt to infer it anyway. He was, for example, dismayed, probably without grounds, when he was not consulted on the choice of the new queen's household. By July 1761 he was in despair. He could not even get royal assurances of two customs places for Lord Lincoln's sons, and in notes for an intended conversation with the favorite Newcastle described himself as "never consulted—hardly informed."[51] The most humiliating blow of all came in the late summer when Bute revealed his intention of translating Thomas Hayter, bishop of Norfolk, to London, even though it was well known that the duke disliked Hayter. This disclosure could only be resented by a man who had long ruled the *ecclesia anglicana* virtually as a personal fief. Thoughts of resignation filled the duke's mind in August, and at one point he informed Hardwicke that he had already decided to quit and that "*quo modo*" was the only unresolved point.[52] The earl, however, with characteristic incisiveness, scotched these plans. He noted that the duke had no grounds for resignation, either personal or public, which the political nation would regard as sufficient to excuse the abandonment of the Treasury in wartime. So the duke finally swallowed his anger at Hayter's translation, acknowledged that Bute should legitimately be the main minister,[53] and remained as first lord.

Doubtless the duke's distaste for the prospect of retirement made Hardwicke's arguments all the more persuasive. But there was an additional reason why the duke, despite ill-treatment from Bute and George III, should choose to stay in the ministry; for even as a rivalry for influence was driving the duke and the favorite apart, Pitt's adamantine response to French peace feelers was giving, if not identity, at least an aspect of parallelism to the two rivals' war views. In the spring France had transmitted peace terms to Britain which Newcastle thought eminently fair—"if we make use of them, which I much doubt."[54] Most of the cabinet also held them to be reasonable, but at the crucial June meetings, held to prepare instructions for Britain's peace negotiator Hans Stanley, Pitt overrode their inclination to reply moderately to Versailles and made them submit to a firm line. Since France was willing to yield Canada and Minorca, the key issues were Cape Breton and the French fishing rights off Newfoundland. Versailles sought to keep both; Newcastle and most of the cabinet believed that Cape Breton should be retained by Britain; but only Pitt and Temple insisted that France should relinquish the fisheries too. The instructions reflected, with only slight softening, Pitt's views. It was not the first time the duke had seen a French peace move blasted apart by what he regarded as Pitt's megalomania. Bute's behavior at this time was shifty. He sought a middle course between Pitt's intransigence and the majority's conciliatory mood. But in his ultimate willingness to concede to French feelings on the fisheries, he aligned himself with the peace faction and dissociated himself from Pitt's policy. Yet it would be misleading to see the growing parallelism between Bute's and Newcastle's views during the summer of 1761 founded simply on the pacific sentiments of each. In truth, the duke's thinking was far more tortuous.

Newcastle was spending his summer among Germanophiles. Lady Yarmouth, now among the most outspoken advocates of a Hanoverian policy in Britain, was guest of the duke and duchess for several months, and her reiterations of the electorate's desperate plight could only reinforce the duke's sentiments on that point. Also with access to the duke's ear was the duchess herself, "the greatest Prussian of them all," as he once described her.[55] All three brooded over the future which Pitt's firm line seemed to portend for Britain and the German war. They anticipated, and correctly so, that France, stung by the rigidity of British terms, would now determine to redouble its military efforts. And they feared that in her inevitable search for a new ally France would find its Bourbon neighbor Spain far more receptive to alliance proposals than heretofore. The situation in Spain had undergone important changes since Newcastle and Keene had secured its neutrality in the mid-1750's. Keene was now dead, and in 1759 a new monarch, the ambitious and reforming Charles III, had succeeded to the throne. Anglophile ministers like Ricardo Wall were losing influence, and outstanding conflicts between Britain and Spain continued unresolved. Moreover, a neutrality which had seemed reasonable in a struggle between presumed equals appeared far less intelligent when one of the combatants was sweeping the field before it; a Britain that had conquered Canada might also covet Mexico. There was thus in Madrid a growing distrust of Britain and a mounting readiness to revitalize the Bourbon family ties.

The scenario that Newcastle dreaded was an increase in Franco-Spanish cooperation leading to a British war against Spain. Such a war besides bringing considerable harm to British trade, would compel Britain to divert forces against Spanish holdings throughout the world, might involve a commitment to aid Portugal, and would unquestionably raise still further the cost of conducting the world war. From painful experience Newcastle knew that Spain was a resourceful adversary. What the duke feared from all this was that the British government, confronted by the need to wage war with Spain and aware of all that such a decision entailed, would seek to reduce belligerent activities wherever they were expendable, and in no theatre were they regarded as being as expendable as in Germany. Thus, the parallelism in Bute's and Newcastle's war views in the late summer of 1761 belied their dissimilar foundations. Bute's opposition to Pitt's policy is sufficiently explained by noting his conviction that Britain needed peace. But Newcastle's opposition rested on his fear that Pitt's policy would lead to war with Spain, and that such a war would force Britain to end its German activities. Newcastle may have appeared to be a spokesman for peace, but the structure of his pacific views was highly idiosyncratic.

In August Bute finally cast aside all his trepidations about exposing himself to charges of betraying Pitt. He swung into alliance with Newcastle, Bedford, and Devonshire—misleadingly called a peace party by some—and the basis was thereby laid for a showdown with Pitt. A first fruit of the shift in political alliances was a mellowing of Britain's strident voice toward France. Sadly for those who sought peace, however, the showdown came too late. For even as the majority of the cabinet finally found the courage to resist Pitt's demands and to try to forestall a Spanish war, French policy made an irrevocable commitment to the continuation of war and the involvement of Spain. Newcastle glimpsed the truth when he speculated to Joseph Yorke in mid-September that France's new firmness—an "ultimatissimum" had just arrived from Versailles—was a consequence of earlier misunderstandings, and that Choiseul had come to doubt Britain's good faith largely because Britain had so long doubted Choiseul's. Pitt summoned the cabinet on 18 September to hear his evidence, now fairly conclusive, that France and Spain had concluded another *pacte de famille* and to ask it to authorize a declaration of war on Spain. "France is Spain and Spain is France," he dramatically declared. But only Temple supported his brother-in-law. The rest of the cabinet, despite the evidence, hoped that war with Madrid might still be averted, especially since Anson warned that the fleet was not prepared to take on a united Bourbon navy. Newcastle's private resolve to oppose Pitt's policy was stronger than ever, for he had recently received a report on the scarcity of money in the City and the financiers' belief that peace was essential. A British declaration of war was therefore "not sufficiently founded either in *justice or prudence*."[56] The final decisions of the cabinet reflected the majority view: although reinforcements were to be added to the West Indian and Mediterranean fleets, Lord Bristol was to offer logwood concessions at Madrid and to inquire further about Spain's intentions.

The gauntlet had been thrown down before Pitt. As never before, his war leadership had been challenged. His chief opponents—Bute, Newcastle, Devonshire, and Mansfield—assumed that he would retire if he could not have his way. Pitt, however, arguing vigorously for his policy, did not resign immediately. But the auguries were not favorable for him. George III had grown weary of a minister whose vocabulary seemed devoid of terms of peace, and other ministers who had at first held back—Halifax and Henley—stepped forward to announce their opposition to a British declaration of war against Spain. The violence of this assault clearly contained an element of personal animus, as the men who as individuals had long endured the Great Commoner's imperious sway at last banded together to dare to challenge him. Certainly, as Lord Hardwicke acknowledged, Pitt's evidence of Franco-Spanish collusion deserved a more respectful hearing than his colleagues gave it. But Pitt made matters difficult, even for those who might have been impressed by the evidence, by insisting that Britain declare war on Spain. He wanted to strike before the Spanish treasure fleet had crossed the Atlantic with its valuable cargo. Whatever Spain's intentions, however, there was as yet no legitimate provocation for war. Such a declaration by Britain would appear to the world as still another example of the kingdom's high-handed dealing with international law. This reflection weighed heavily on Hardwicke who, despite his respect for Pitt and his suspicion that Spain was in truth bent upon war, finally lent his prestigious support to those who wanted to make a final effort to satisfy Madrid.

The climactic cabinet session occurred on 2 October. Each minister restated views he had already espoused, and Lord Ligonier, respected for his honesty, added the ominous reflection that Spain's military might, boasting almost 60,000 foot and over 10,000 horse, was not to be despised. Newcastle and Bute spoke in manners designed to cast doubt on the reliability of Pitt's evidence. The duke reminded his listeners that it was in France's interest to make it sound as if Spain would break with Britain, and Bute noted that Stanley's reports of widespread expectations of an Anglo-Spanish war described only French, not Spanish, opinion. Pitt responded to his critics with a forceful restatement of his demand for war, declaring that Britain was fighting the Bourbons. But when his colleagues remained unmoved, the most successful war minister in British history made his famous statement of accountability—"I will be *responsible* for nothing, that I do not *direct*"—and in effect resigned.[57] Three days later he handed over the seals. Newcastle had not betrayed him, although Pitt would later make that charge, for the two men had long disagreed on war policy. But the duke had acted from a most peculiar complex of motives, and had shed a friend for an enemy. Thus, if not treacherous, his conduct may at least be called unwise. In fact, to pursue peace with Spain so as to make war in Germany was, it would seem, simply stupid.

Pitt's departure from government, or, more precisely, Newcastle's definitive break with him over policy toward Spain, meant that the duke's continued tenure was now subject to Bute's will. Bereft of the power that a conjunction with Pitt had lent him, Newcastle lacked the resources needed to withstand George III's and Bute's desire to rid themselves of men tainted with service to George II. Even before he had been elevated to the secretaryship Bute had thought that it would be easy to get Newcastle to resign. Now, with Pitt gone, Bute's thoughts again turned to the problem of Newcastle's role. Describing him as a "crazy old man," Bute nevertheless argued that Newcastle's presence could be tolerated for a while longer. The duke was weak, accepted that weakness, and had not denied rumors that he would resign after the peace. It was, Bute therefore concluded, "better to let this old man tide over a year or two more of his political life."[58] One other consideration militating strongly against ousting the duke was doubtless the fact that difficult financial negotiations for the annual loan for 1762 were under way. Unprecedented expenditures were foreseen, entailing sweeping new taxes to fund a massive borrowing operation. Not until January was it clear that this loan would proceed smoothly. Thus, not until January did Bute even dare contemplate the removal of Newcastle.

Long before then, however, Newcastle had realized how Pitt's departure had further reduced his waning influence. The whole government, in fact, seemed weaker, for whereas Pitt was again the hero of London, the ministers were pelted with abuse. "No Newcastle salmon," shouted the crowd when the duke traveled to St. Paul's on the lord mayor's day, and Bute was let off no easier. Many spokesmen foi the City also felt that Pitt's departure had hurt the government.[59] Hard as this situation was, within the ministry the duke's position was still more uncomfortable. George Grenville had become leader in the House of Commons, and Lord Egremont had taken up the seals. These two men consistently united with Bute to place Newcastle in an almost unfailing minority on all issues that divided the four chief ministers. The duke hoped to have Hardwicke made lord privy seal in place of the retiring Temple, but Bute accused Newcastle of seeking only to promote his own friends, an accusation George II had once made, and secured the post for Bedford instead. By December the duke was echoing the lament of the previous summer that "my advice or opinion, are scarce ever ask'd, but *never* taken. I am kept in, without confidence, and indeed without communication."[60] To powerful men in the City Newcastle passed the world that his influence was abating. And not even a massive reception at Newcastle House for eighty peers at the opening of Parliament—a "triumph" the duchess called it—could obscure the truth: the duke was living out his political life on borrowed time.

The key policy problem remained Spain. Despite everything that the cabinet had done, Madrid proved embarrassingly stubborn in its reiterated refusal to give satisfaction to Britain's request for assurances of peaceful intentions. By mid-November Newcastle finally conceded that Spain was truly determined upon war. This truth made the loss of Pitt all the more painful: "I know nobody who can plan or push the execution of any plan agreed upon in the manner Mr. Pitt did."[61] War was finally declared in late December. But in addition to missing Pitt's executive skills, the duke also found that a war with Spain would have precisely the dire consequences for continental warmaking that he had dreaded. Back in September Bute had told Newcastle that if Britain came to hostilities with Spain, the German war would be abandoned. The duke had commented at that time, but to Hardwicke, not to Bute, that "giving up the German war is easier said than done."[62] By the winter the duke was less sanguine about the difficulties preventing an end to German involvement. One by one, various men of importance declared their belief that Britain should begin to get out of Germany. Bute argued in the cabinet in January that a withdrawal from Germany would help pay for the attacks planned on Spanish holdings. Henry Legge sent a financial exposition to the duke that left as its unstated but absolutely clear conclusion the belief that troops would have to be withdrawn from Germany.[63] Bedford let word slip to Newcastle that the king himself was determined to end operations in that theatre, and as if to bring the point to the attention of the public Bedford moved a resolution in the House of Lords criticizing the cost of the German war. It failed to pass, but in this vote the chamber was reflecting simply a desire to avoid embarrassing the government and not the mood of the political nation.

Against this drumbeat of demands for British abandonment of Germany Newcastle and Barrington struggled to keep counterarguments in circulation. His exclusion from the inner circle kept the duke acutely uninformed on key points. He did not know in late December, for example, that Bute had promised 6,000 troops to Portugal, and when Bute hastily assured him that no commitment of funds would be made without consulting the Treasury, Newcastle replied appositely: "My Lord, *Troops are Money.*"[64] Still, even in the face of such insulting treatment, he pressed on. Barrington urged that Portugal be left to Spain's mercies, and Newcastle turned his desperate attention again to the "abuses and corruption" persisting in the commissariat. A new investigation of the continuing cost difficulties revealed that the chief source of malfeasance lay in the forage agreements contracted throughout western Germany. Newcastle thereupon effected personnel changes in the commissariat. The duke also began mustering arguments in favor of staying in Germany. Withdrawal, he felt, would constitute a breach of national faith toward the Prussian ally, and would leave Hanover, indeed, all of Europe, subject to French power and authority. The benefits to be anticipated from withdrawal were in fact insignificant, for if Britain were thereby relieved of an onerous financial burden, France was simultaneously relieved of the costs of keeping 150,000 men in Germany and of paying subsidies to allies. Furthermore, no immediate savings could be realized at all, for the transporting of British troops home would be expensive, and the cessation of support for foreign troops was subject to two months' notice.[65] Though perhaps not fully compelling, these arguments were not foolish. They might have been still more persuasive had they not been advanced by a man who for years had decried the cost of the war. For the duke was still trapped in his primary inconsistency: he could not plausibly extol retrenchment at one moment and German warfare at the next.

There were many aspects to the German war issue, but the one that held the kingdom's attention in early 1762 was the question of whether to renew the Prussian subsidy. Although the duke had been able to coax the subsidy money for 1761 out of a skeptical Parliament, by 1762 the expense seemed less justifiable than ever. Moreover, Prussia's military position had been vastly eased by the change of monarchs in Russia and St. Petersburg's consequent cessation of hostilities with Berlin. Sweden had also abandoned its Prussian war. Britain on the other hand had assumed two new burdens, the defeat of Spain and the defense of Portugal. Simple equity suggested that Britain should now retain the subsidy and Prussia accept the reasonableness of such an action. Newcastle was not unmoved by this line of argument; among his friends Mansfield and Stone made the case for abandoning the expenditure. But Newcastle knew that the decision on the subsidy would be seen in a larger context by most observers. If Britain suspended the payment, it would be interpreted as a sign that Britain had finally decided to end the German war. He was in fact of two minds. "If we could," he wrote Hardwicke, "with honor and safety, save £670,000, it would be a great thing for us, and perhaps prevent great difficulties at the end of the year."[66] But ultimately, persuaded by Hardwicke's argument that Britain ought not to renege on a pledge to Frederick II, the duke came out for continuation of the payment. Bute, Grenville, and Egremont naturally were opposed, however, and in April the duke finally relented before superior force, acquiescing in the abandonment of the subsidy.

Privately, the duke had meanwhile pursued still another way of maintaining Britain's interests on the continent. With Pitt out of office, the lesson of the incident with *l'inconnue* lost much of its force, and the duke, seriously this time, had begun a second round of secret diplomatic initiatives. Even as he was arguing that the Prussian subsidy should be maintained, he was also exploring the alternative possibility of regaining Austria and restoring the "Old System," at the expense of Prussian friendship. The impetus of this exploration lay in reports that Kaunitz and Maria Theresa were unhappy at the Franco-Spanish rapprochement and its implications for Italy. The duke hoped that Austria might now be willing, in these new circumstances, to transfer its support from Versailles to London. He spoke with Bute about these possibilities, and the favorite believed the international situation fluid enough to warrant soundings. Bute then directed Joseph Yorke to try to verify reports of Viennese dissatisfaction and, if appropriate, to suggest that Britain would not oppose Austrian efforts to find compensation for Silesia in Italy. But Newcastle thought Bute's probe insufficient, and independently of the secretary of state the duke authorized Yorke to be more enticing in his promises. Specifically, Yorke was to favor "some regulation" of Silesia itself that would be "satisfactory" to Vienna, an unfortunate promise that reached the imperial capital in the still more extreme form of a pledge to support the restoration of all Silesia to Austria. And he was to endorse an Anglo-Austrian effort to drive the Bourbons from Italy—"That," wrote the duke, "would be a war worth fighting for, worth paying for."[67] Kaunitz smelled a plot, thought the initiative implausible, and let the story leak in its most expansive form to Berlin, where it further damaged Britain's already tarnished reputation. It is true that the duke's misguided diplomatic dabbling probably had little true impact on the alliance; Britain and Prussia were already rapidly drifting apart, not least because Frederick II was secretly hoping and openly working to incite a Russo-Danish war. But in its naivete, its utter disregard of proper diplomatic method, and its strange assumption that Vienna could be a more useful ally than Berlin, the initiative showed the degree to which desperation was clouding the duke's judgment by 1762.

How long Newcastle would have endured the shackling of his influence and the abandonment of his strategy cannot be known. Both developments clearly caused him grief and pain. But in March his insignificance was revealed in a totally new and far more humiliating manner—he was undermined within his own preserve, the Treasury—and the limits of his ability to swallow pride and honor were finally reached. The Treasury had concluded by March that the expanded war effort would necessitate an unprecedented vote of credit of £2,000,000. But neither Bute nor Grenville trusted Newcastle's, Barrington's, and West's reasoning, for they suspected the duke of submitting exaggerated estimates so that public opinion would turn against the Spanish war. They had won over to their side Samuel Martin, West's cosecretary, and he agreed to provide them with inside financial information that might be damaging to Newcastle and his friends. Martin then went further: in late April he drafted a paper arguing that a vote of credit for £1,000,000 would suffice for 1762, although—and here its political import became clear—such a reduction presupposed the ending of the German war. Newcastle was enraged that Bute and Grenville would have meddled, and that George III would have permitted such meddling, in the office of another minister.

The king had authorized the action because he was at last convinced that in no other way could Newcastle be driven out. A man who fought so consistently on behalf of continental warfare could no longer be "tided over." The duke was aware that the incident probably bore this significance, but whereas he thought George intended the financially able Grenville for the Treasury, the king had actually determined to promote the financially unlettered Bute. The duke railed against Grenville, declaring to Hardwicke that "I will never be overruled by Mr. Grenville in a point *singly* relating to the Treasury" and adding later that "Mr. Grenville and I cannot *jointly* have the conduct of the Treasury." The duke also ridiculed Grenville's, and Martin's, alternative budget as an absurd scheme based on the principle of not paying what was owed.[68] He knew he would have to resign, though he could not really decide whether the disavowal of his war policy or the invasion of his department should be the ostensible grounds. In truth, of course, both considerations impelled him to withdraw from office. "Every day convinces me that I grow more insignificant," he grumbled to Devonshire.[69]

On 3 May Newcastle pleaded his financial case to the king. George, however, well coached by Bute and Grenville, remained unsympathetic, announcing that he could never agree to a vote of credit exceeding £1,000,000. The duke replied with what the king interpreted as a virtual promise of resignation, and the monarch, in his report of the conversation to Bute, stigmatized Newcastle as "negligent of the public money."[70] On 5 May, in preparation for a scheduled royal audience the next day, the duke invited his closest advisers to Newcastle House for a final exchange of ideas. Not until that evening had Newcastle seen Martin's draft of April. The paper was an impressive document, and the assembled friends—Hardwicke, Mansfield, Kinnoull, and Stone—all told the duke that it had raised doubts in their minds about the absolute necessity of the £2,000,000. Newcastle himself wavered a bit, though he recovered his commitment to the higher figure the next morning. But the crucial decision taken that night dealt with the duke's future. As many signs had portended, he finally announced his resolve to resign the Treasury. He delayed a day in making his intention public, but on 7 May he surprised George III by first acquiescing in a vote of credit for only £1,000,000 and then stating that he would leave office because he had been deserted by some members of his board. The startled monarch behaved in a "goodnatured and affected" manner, though Bute was less gracious, and at Grenville's request the duke agreed to retain office until the end of the parliamentary session "to avoid everything that could give any disturbance or raise a flame just at the end of the session."[71] Hardwicke promptly promised to follow Newcastle, whether he chose opposition or retirement, but he counseled retirement and reminded his friend that the toll of the years would prevent him from acting for Newcastle as he had in 1757.

For almost three more weeks the duke remained in office, bringing various affairs to a close and concluding accounts. Ever given to rationalization, he elaborated a theory that justified the resignation on the pragmatic grounds that he was dissociating himself from a ministry that would soon court public odium by supporting a lenient peace. He was meanwhile dunned by old allies and acquaintances for the granting of final favors before losing his official authority.[72] At times George III was "barely civil" to the oldest servant of his family, perhaps because he was uncomfortable with the awkward circumstances of the duke's forced retirement, but probably because he had truly come to dislike Newcastle. The degree of royal contempt for the departing first lord may be measured by his vicious statement that the heads of the Treasury deserved "Tower Hill" and in his exasperated declaration that "the more I know of this fellow the more I wish to see him out of employment."[73] On 26 May, with Parliament raised and treasury business wrapped up, the king got his wish: the duke attended the closet to hand over the symbols of office. As often at emotional moments, he wept. Several weeks earlier he had made special provision for Thomas Pelham by having himself made Baron Pelham of Stanmer, with reversion to his favorite cousin. But he turned down the offer of a pension for himself, stating—he had composed his response in advance—that if his fortune had suffered in service to the royal family, "it was my honor, my glory, and my pride."[74] As the evidence makes clear, the exhausting of the ducal fortune was scarcely a consequence of disinterested service to the Crown, but at dramatic moments such as this a touch of exaggeration is not inappropriate. Newcastle knew, the king knew, the political nation knew, that a man who had held office virtually without interruption for a staggering forty-five years was finally retiring. Much can be forgotten or at least forgiven when a veteran ends his career.

In an obvious sense both Pitt and Newcastle resigned because their colleagues were confining their legitimate departmental authority. But from a substantive point of view the resignations were a consequence of the policy isolation into which each man fell. And it is more than merely symbolic that Pitt left office defending Britain's need to push on in America, for it was in the colonies that Spain would be confronted, while Newcastle retired urging Britain to persevere on the continent. When George III became king Bute did not have a master plan for achieving his own supremacy, but he did want both Pitt and Newcastle out of his hair. In Pitt's case this could only be achieved through his ouster from office; with Newcastle, the choice was less stark, for it was possible that the duke would submit to holding office as an underling. In any event, Bute dared do nothing immediately. He could only wait upon events to supply him the opportunities he wanted. It was simply chance that events conspired against Pitt first. But it was, from Bute's point of view, a fortunate happenstance; for the first demotion or dismissal would be the harder of the two. Indeed, it would be possible only if one of the former coalition partners abandoned the other, and it would probably have been less easy to guide the shrewd Pitt into clear opposition to Newcastle than it turned out to be to induce the duke to turn against the Great Commoner. On all major points of political strategy Newcastle seemed befuddled once George III came to the throne. He failed to stand by Pitt, though he knew that only therein lay safety. He continued as well to plead simultaneously that the kingdom could not afford war and that war in Germany could not be abandoned. Such confusions left him naked to his enemies. He retained the Treasury until May 1762 in the new reign not because his power made him feared but because his foolishness made him innocuous.

8

Elder Statesman

Even in the hour of his resignation Newcastle was laying the foundations for future political activity. Rather than promising the king that
he would support the new government's measures, the duke merely
expressed his intention to follow his own conscience, the language, as
George aptly noted, that "every man that opposes uses."[1] Newcastle's
refusal of another proffered pension also intimated, and in a peculiarly
striking way, his independence of the government. So that he might
keep abreast of private governmental activities he authorized several
friends still in office to spy for him. He also took the pulse of the moneyed
interest.[2] Meanwhile, at Claremont, he began to hold vast levees clearly
designed to rival and even surpass Bute's and to demonstrate his own
continuing influence. Of all his episcopal friends only Frederick Cornwallis, bishop of Litchfield, had had the courage (and courtesy) to
attend his last levee in office. But soon the Claremont parties became
celebrated events, popular with ecclessiastics and politicians of all
factions, and as late as the end of August the duke entertained the entire
diplomatic corps at his estate. Invigorated and delighted by a summer
of such fêtes, a summer interrupted only by a triumphal visit to Sussex,
Newcastle was oblivious to Hardwicke's persistent suspicion that social
attendance at Claremont need not portend political support for the
host.[3]

All soon realized that Newcastle wanted to be in power again. The
Treasury was not his goal: his age and the wearisome nature of finances
made the post uncongenial. He had, moreover, been proven financially
wrong by the Bute government, which, by the narrowest of margins,
had demonstrated that a vote of credit for £1,000,000 was indeed sufficient. Instead, as the duke openly avowed, he thought of emulating
Sunderland's influential use of a court or honorific post.[4] Yet, had a

simple return to office been the duke's aim, it could easily have been achieved; within two months of his resignation Bute was trying to lure the duke back into the government and Newcastle declined the opportunity. What the duke was hoping for was much more than the resumption of an isolated office. He wanted nothing less than the restoration of the old Whig system and the ouster of the Scots sycophant. Toward this end neither the king's nor the favorite's support could be expected, and Newcastle was thus choosing to try to storm the closet by way of opposition. That he had spoken often in the past of the wickedness or inadvisability of opposition mattered little; and equally nugatory were Hardwicke's warnings about a "new trade to learn at a late hour."[5] The nature of parliamentary politics—and even old George II had perceived this truth—required of an ambitious but out-of-favor politician that he resort to active opposition.

When the summer of 1762 closed Newcastle had not yet determined how he might best pursue a course of opposition, but he reckoned on having a large army for the coming combat. By his own calculation over forty percent of the House of Lords and thirty-five percent of the members of the House of Commons would stand with him.[6] With potential allies he kept in touch. But he knew what he wanted to hear. When the Yorkes counselled patience and restraint, Newcastle sought guidance elsewhere and slowly fell under the influence of the duke of Cumberland, a foe of lenient peace. The young king's uncle had begun reviving his erstwhile amity with Newcastle when the duke had proved such a forceful defender of continental war in early 1762. He never gained complete command of Newcastle, but political circumstance threw them together, and under Cumberland's prodding Newcastle became an outspoken critic of Bute's conciliatory peace treaty. With Newcastle thus disposed to harass the "poor silly men" of the government,[7] further ministerial efforts to secure his support, led in September and October by Egremont and Halifax, were unsuccessful. Consequently the administration sought reinforcements elsewhere and, in an unexpected action, enlisted the assistance of Henry Fox. More than George III or Bute realized, Fox possessed the one capacity that could demolish the opposition Newcastle led: an accurate view of the nature of political loyalty.

Fox himself was at first conciliatory toward the duke, but when an opportunity presented itself to destroy his pretensions, Fox was not squeamish about seizing it. The opportunity arose out of the growing

estrangement between George III and his lord chamberlain, the fourth
duke of Devonshire. This young peer had loosely allied his Whig
following with Newcastle's, but he had retained office when Newcastle
had resigned, preferring to display his displeasure with ministerial
policy from the sanctuary of the household. George grew angry at
Devonshire's failure to attend meetings of the council, suspected that he
acted at Newcastle's prompting, and on 31 October dismissed Devonshire from his offices. Newcastle's reaction to what he called "these
violences" was explosive: "I believe no Court in Europe (I will scarce
except Russia) ever put such an affront upon one of the first rank, consequence and merit."[8] The duke's deep belief in the prescriptive right
of the aristocracy to advise the monarch was offended by the dismissal;
it seemed an act of war on the Old Corps. But it was not entirely unanticipated either, for Newcastle had already expressed a fear that Fox
and Bute would support themselves "by power *only*" and that Fox "had
courage enough, to execute what was necessary to produce the full
effects of the power."[9]

Devonshire's dismissal pulled down Newcastle's house of cards.
Choosing to make the ouster an issue of national importance, he asked
his supporters still holding offices to resign them, hoping thereby to
cripple the government with what may legitimately be called a strike.
Some acceded to the duke's wish, including Lord Bessborough, Lord
Kinnoull, Lord Rockingham, and John Roberts. But many others,
forced finally to choose between a past tie and a present office, opted
for the latter. The eminently realistic Fox was not surprised that the
duke's following should dissipate when subjected to pressure. He quickly
moved to the offensive, driving from offices high and low many men
whose chief crime was a past connection with the Pelhams. Tommy
Pelham, John Shelley, Andrew Wilkinson, George Onslow, Tom
Townshend, and Lord Gage were among those ousted in this so-called
"purge of the Pelhamite innocents." By December Newcastle's party
was in disarray and his spirit desperate. Abandoned by friends and
appearing "contemptible" in the eyes of the world, Newcastle felt the
final sting of Fox's efficiency on 23 December when he was stripped of
his lord lieutenancies and various honorific offices.

The whole affair was doubly discomforting to the duke. He felt guilt
at being the reason for the "cruelties" laid on his supporters, and he felt
shame in the revelation of the flimsiness of many of the friendships he
had prided himself on.[10] Lord Lincoln's unhappiness with the duke,

surfacing at this time, was largely personal: he felt slighted by New-castle's reluctance to transfer much of the Holles wealth to him, and he feared, with some justification, that the duke's extravagant social life was exhausting the inheritance. Lincoln, however, at least complied with the resignation order, albeit sullenly. But some others, chiefly younger men with their futures at stake, simply refused to heed the duke's command. Charles Yorke, who had earlier warned Newcastle that many rising politicians would disappoint him, agonized and then decided to remain as attorney general. Lord Royston, John Yorke, and Lord Barrington also temporized. Lord Granby protested his "personal regard" for the duke but continued to support the government. Lord Mansfield followed the same course with even less consideration for his former patron's feelings. Still others used the occasion to disavow their allegiance to the duke. The episcopal bench, for example, generally refused to follow his lead in the House of Lords, and Andrew Stone, whose ties with the duke had been weakening for a decade, finally consummated the break. Even James Marriott, his former librarian, turned on the duke in a hostile pamphlet.[11]

The reasons for this personal and political catastrophe are not hard to identify. The government controlled patronage; Newcastle spoke from the weakness of opposition. To be sure, it was an opposition founded in part on principles. The duke was opposing, and seeking to overthrow, what he conceived of, perhaps incorrectly and certainly imperfectly, as a system of government antithetical to the Whig prin-ciples of liberty and aristocratic privilege he had long espoused. In fact, therefore, the decision to use Devonshire's dismissal as the occasion for an attack on Bute's government was in its way logical. The dismissal seemed to represent all that was "unconstitutional" in the favorite's advice to the monarch: his neglect of the great Whig families, his readiness to remove those who disagreed with him, and his tendency to act abruptly and arbitrarily. And the purge that followed dramatically reinforced this interpretation. But the more important reflection is that these principles of Newcastle's opposition, whether right or wrong, were irrelevant to the success of the campaign.

Victory depended on being able to command votes. This the duke could not do. As his key allies in his assault on a system of government that he presumed to be unconstitutional Newcastle had thought he could rely on the support of the many men who had comprised the Old Corps. But he was far too ready to ascribe to them his own foggy vision

of proper government and to regard them as Whigs of his own cast.
He forgot, moreover, that only a few of the Old Corps had received
favors from him in his private capacity. The bulk of them had been
helped *ex officio*—by the Treasury or the Admiralty or even the court—
and had still to look to this institutional benefactor for their security.
This is the key reason for the catastrophe: the duke radically and trag-
ically misunderstood the importance of elemental self-interest in
politics.

The Old Corps was in thorough disarray. Fox and Bute had triumphed dramatically. And yet from the debacle, and largely as a
consequence of it, the cadre of a new party slowly emerged. Just before
Christmas in 1762 several notable victims of the purge proposed the
creation of a regular dining club. Although this suggestion seems not to
have been immediately acted on, a pattern of dinners attended by leaders of the Old Corps slowly emerged, and from these beginnings the
Whigs of the 1760's were born. In personnel the party consisted of the
Old Corps purged of the unfaithful. Initial leadership fell unquestionably to Newcastle: he alone had the prestige and experience to guide a
party. But Newcastle's leadership was essentially honorary; among
party chieftains he was simply *primus inter pares*. Under the wise prodding of Hardwicke and even more of Devonshire, who passed on the
"bon-mot" then making the rounds that the ministers had turned out
everyone the duke had helped bring in except the king himself, Newcastle's spirits quickly recovered.[12] This was, to be sure, no party in the
twentieth-century sense. Unsettled, often divided between "warm"
youth and cautious experience, always relaxed, the party seemed more
akin to a modern social club than a political organization. A certain
air of gentlemanly amateurism continued to mark its parliamentary
activities while defections littered its course. But it was something new
on the political scene, unlike either the court party whose techniques it
would try to emulate or the family factions so prominent at mid-century. It was an alliance of influential men who shared a contempt for
Bute's notion of government and who brought with them their political
dependents. It was a principled union of factions. It was still more:
unlike the factions, it gave a considerable measure of influence to its
younger members. And while it sometimes behaved with as little
apparent regard for principles as the factions it was at pains to distinguish itself from, it nevertheless represented a system of government
which placed primary emphasis upon subjecting the monarch to the

control of men who were not only politically but also socially responsible.

The only way the reconstituted Whigs could hope to oust the favorite from power was by allying themselves with Pitt and his friends, a point Newcastle quickly grasped. The chances for such an alliance brightened considerably in the early months of 1763 when the peace treaty was finally accepted and the issues surrounding it and dividing Pitt from Newcastle lost political force. Pitt's resentment over Newcastle's desertion in 1761 slowly abated, and in early March 1763, at a widely publicized opposition dinner at Devonshire House, Pitt and Newcastle finally came to terms which Newcastle represented as an agreement to "act a firm part, be inseparable from each other."[13] He had characteristically exaggerated Pitt's commitment to cooperation, but for himself he seems to have spoken truly. Because Pitt approved them, for example, Newcastle decided not to make an issue of the army estimates, even though he was alarmed at a proposal to increase the size of the standing army in the colonies. Instead, the Whigs and the Pittites spent the late winter and early spring harassing the government. Newcastle refused to present Cambridge University's address of congratulation on the occasion of the peace to the king. The cider tax was resisted as a hateful excise, and Newcastle's rhetoric was not stilled by the reminder that he had supported Walpole's excise thirty years earlier. A major though unsuccessful effort was mounted to gain control of the East India Company.

The alliance between the Pittites and the Whigs held together through most of 1763. It gained encouragement from the facts that Bute had unexpectedly resigned and that the king had found his successor at the Treasury, the domineering George Grenville, distasteful. George III did not hide his desire to replace Grenville. During the spring and summer the ministry, hoping to protect itself against wholesale replacement by the royal hand, sounded out each wing of the opposition about breaking with its ally and joining the government. Neither was then prepared to disavow the alliance. Such resolution to act together almost succeeded in bringing the opposition into power in late August; George III summoned Pitt for consultations and the Great Commoner hastened to Claremont in the midst of the negotiations to talk for five hours with the duke, to whom he planned to offer a position without official responsibilities. But Pitt overplayed his hand; George thought his demands excessive, and the negotiations aborted.[14]

Soon thereafter the Grenville ministry, capitalizing on the reprieve, gained the reinforcements it needed from among the adherents of the duke of Bedford, and the opposition's greatest opportunity for storming into office was gone. Its unity soon followed. In the early fall the Whigs and the Pittites quarreled over whether Newcastle's friend Charles Yorke or Pitt's friend Charles Pratt should be the opposition's choice for lord chancellor. Then Pitt became angry when none of Newcastle's friends defended him against an attack in the Commons. Most significantly, Pitt and Newcastle disagreed about how to handle the Wilkes case.

The furor over John Wilkes had burst upon the scene in April 1763. Wilkes published an antigovernment paper, the *North Briton*, and in number forty-five of the series he viciously criticized the leniency of the peace treaty. George Grenville consulted his legal advisers. Persuaded that Wilkes had exceeded the bounds of the permissible, he acted to bring charges of seditious libel against the publisher. Under the authorization of a general warrant, i.e., a warrant directed broadly against all engaged in a specified activity rather than narrowly against certain specified men, crown officials entered the printer's office and confiscated many of Wilkes's papers. Wilkes himself was arrested, but later released after Charles Pratt, as chief justice of the Court of Common Pleas, had declared the arrest of a member of Parliament on grounds of seditious libel illegal. Newcastle had been encouraging Wilkes in the months before the appearance of number forty-five, and since Pitt's ally Temple was one of the publisher's staunchest friends, the opposition was fairly united in its initial disapproval of the ministry's action. But fissures soon appeared, for Newcastle was doubly hampered from offering total support to the accused publisher. He was, first of all, embarrassed by the attitude of the Yorke family, who felt the government's action to have been entirely legal and whose judicial judgments, whether emanating from former Lord Chancellor Hardwicke or from Attorney General Charles Yorke, commanded respect. Even more discomfiting was the course of the ensuing legal argument. As it focused on the constitutionality of general warrants, Newcastle found his freedom of action constricted. On at least fourteen occasions while serving as secretary of state the duke himself had issued such warrants: no eighteenth-century secretary had been freer with them.[15] One consequence of this awkward legacy was Newcastle's refusal in late 1763 to support the attack on general warrants, even though the issue seemed at that juncture the one most likely to unite the rest of the opposition. A thoroughgoing defense of Wilkes would have required that Newcastle repudiate the opinions of his friends and the actions of his past. He would do neither. But his refusal in its turn meant that by the end of 1763 close cooperation with Pitt was no longer possible.

Opposition was thus not proving to be an easy road for the duke. Yet he had, in fact, come far since May 1762. Initially he had hoped to return to power with ease, even with a certain feigned reluctance. Painfully he had learned that in politics goals must be actively pursued, and in the aftermath of the purge the Whig party had been reborn as an instrument wherewith the ministry could be harassed. But still the duke had held back from an unqualified opposition: he had refrained from excoriating the government on all points of the Wilkes case, and he had cautioned against raising an opposition to the cider tax—a money bill— in the House of Lords once it had passed the Commons. Newcastle, in short, had not adopted the unrelenting attitude and techniques of his old mentor, Sir Robert Walpole, during that quintessential politician's brief period of opposition. The chief reason Newcastle had not moved faster was his friendship with Hardwicke. The patriarch of the Yorkes quite openly disliked opposition: he thought it disrespectful to the Crown and a stimulus to judging the value of proposals by criteria other than their general usefulness. He also feared that it might destroy the political careers of his talented brood. Because his attitude was known, he was the Whig most frequently approached by representatives of the ministries that were seeking to win over blocs of adherents. But the earl was absolutely loyal to the duke, cooperating in opposition measures he disapproved of and rejecting any ministerial overtures which represented less than a total victory for the opposition. In late 1763, not without misgivings, he even forced Charles Yorke to resign his legal post within the administration. Still, his reiterated advice to Newcastle was to eschew an uncompromising opposition.

The deep and lasting friendship between Newcastle and Hardwicke, a relationship which casts credit on both men, survived the growing divergence in their views in the early 1760's, although not without some problems. Hardwicke was, as usual, the more considerate: his labors for causes he disliked bespoke his affection for his old comrade. Newcastle contrariwise was the more thoughtless: he once even rebuked the earl for the political behavior of his sons.[16] But when in October 1763 Hardwicke was stricken with the first major attack of what would be a fatal cancer, the duke revealed his essentially compassionate nature. Out of respect for his friend he refused to sign a protest from the minority in the House of Lords pertaining to the Wilkes case. Then when the ministry, in an action which suggested either astonishing vindictiveness or consummate bad timing, asked for revisions in Hardwicke's greatest legislative accomplishment, the Marriage Act of 1753, Newcastle passed the word to his followers in the Commons: "I shall never look upon any man, tho' ever so nearly related to me, who does not oppose the repeal of this Bill at this time, to be any friend of mine."[17] In the debate on the proposal he delivered a powerful encomium on the former lord chancellor.[18] To Lord Royston in January the duke wrote of his love for "that great and good man, my Lord Hardwicke." Their friendship, he continued, had been "an intimate and almost daily correspondence, attended with constant marks of confidence and affection, with a reciprocal concern for everything that interested or concerned each other, a continued union of conduct and behaviour and even of opinion and sentiment, more than I have known in any other instance."[19] The earl, meanwhile, passed through several periods of apparent recuperation, receiving the duke when he could. But in February 1764 the final decline began, and on 6 March, ten years to the day after Henry Pelham's death, the earl of Hardwicke died. One need look no further for the major cause of Newcastle's loneliness in his final years.

But if Hardwicke's death saddened Newcastle, it also freed him. In his old age the duke was becoming more responsive to reform politics than he had been in his youth and prime, and this change would seem to have resulted chiefly from the decline of Hardwicke's, and perhaps Mansfield's, influence on him. This influence was frequently remarked on by contemporaries. Yet its limits, or rather, its nature, for its limits were rarely tested, must be understood. During their long friendship Hardwicke and the duke had naturally thought alike on most questions and there had rarely been need for persuasion and conversion. But if the two men had reacted similarly at an affective level, it was Hardwicke's precise and orderly mind that had formulated at the rational level the necessary justifications for positions taken. Here was his great political value to the duke: Hardwicke could provide Newcastle with the appropriate arguments.[20] This congruence of attitudes began disappearing in the 1760's, and although the friendship remained, it increasingly served to confuse rather than reinforce Newcastle's political reflections. Hardwicke's death was, in this sense, timely: he was spared the pain of accomodating a friendship founded on an identity of views when that identity no longer existed. For Newcastle it cleared the air: the Whig conservative could become the Whig activist.

II

The two fundamental principles of Newcastle's Whiggery had long been his beliefs that the English aristocracy was the appropriate source of governors for the kingdom and that the monarch should follow the advice of his chosen ministers. The two beliefs were not incompatible, but until the duke's posttreasury days they had never been significantly yoked. The one great crisis of aristocratic prerogative during the duke's career, the Peerage Bill of 1719, had not raised the issue of ministerial influence; and the great crisis of ministerial authority, the resignations of 1746, had similarly avoided the issue of aristocratic privilege. But in the 1760's, as Newcastle's power waned while an increasingly complex government groped toward a recognition of its need for men with technical skills, the two beliefs finally became fused in the duke's political world view. The duke watched with undisguised disapproval as the Crown he had long served turned to the talents of men like the aggressively systematic Henry Fox and the fearfully efficient George Grenville. He noted with equal distaste that the only peer who truly counted with the new king was not one of the English Whigs but rather a Scots upstart. He was appalled at the government's assaults on the privileges of peers and at the king's avowed desire "to ruin the Newcastle faction."[21] Thus, under the pressure of frustration and unhappiness, the duke came to see that his two foundational beliefs were related and carried unexpected consequences; for if a monarch should be so unwise as to follow the advice of bad ministers, refusing to put honorable peers into positions of authority, the representatives of the Whig truths had no choice but to act in ways designed to overthrow the bad ministers and replace them with aristocratic governors.

The decline of Hardwicke's influence made this fusion of principles easier for Newcastle. The earl had shared some of the duke's contempt for the precept that talent should prevail over birth. Still, Hardwicke was himself an example of how talent could overcome relatively modest origins. He was also a man who had a deep respect for both the Crown and the truth. He saw that the politics of outright opposition, the *terminus ad quem* of mid-century Whiggery in the dawning age of political technicians, could easily weaken the former and sacrifice the latter as well. In short, the memory of his own past and the need to uphold the dignity of the Crown and the British system of government acted as restraints upon Hardwicke, consistently keeping him from pursuing the corollaries of Whig principles to their proper conclusions. He cautioned Newcastle against behavior that would "give a handle to suspicions, insinuations, and malicious reports of caballing and concert."[22] His was a voice against thoroughgoing opposition, against the view that all else should be subordinated to the reacquisition of power. But with Hardwicke's passing the simple logic of the duke's Whig principles met no further obstacle to rationalizing a formed opposition.

In several other ways the duke altered the texture of his Whiggery after Hardwicke's death. For over a decade at least Newcastle had realized the crucial connection between commercial activities and Britain's strength. It was, of course, scarcely surprising that he should, for one of the key points of the Whig creed he had been raised in had been the party's support for the mercantile interest. To his brother in 1750 the duke had urged the necessity of pleasing "every mercantile man in England. And no man in England is more for pleasing them than myself."[23] In that same year he translated words into action by providing significant assistance to those then establishing the African Company.[24] But despite these marks of appreciation of the value of trade, Newcastle had never given full rein to his conviction that trade was vital. He had not in general viewed British foreign policy as a vehicle for promoting British trade nor sought out men of commerce for advice on mercantile policy. By the time of Hardwicke's death, however, the commercial component of Newcastle's Whiggery was finally gaining in prominence. In part the growing interest in merchants reflected simply the conventional tactic of those out of office to seek support outside the parliamentary sphere. In part too it was a response to the angry pleas of men of commerce who, accustomed to the prosperity of wartime, found the postwar depression painful and occasionally calamitous. But in part Newcastle's move toward a more active espousal of mercantile concerns was also a consequence of the fading of Hardwicke's influence. The earl, though well aware of the worth of commerce, had never encouraged the duke to concern himself very seriously with its problems or to shape national policy very closely in accordance with the desires of the commercial interest. He had instead shared, and thereby reinforced, the duke's curiously passive, albeit approving, view of commerce. After 1763 passivity was no longer sufficient.

Hardwicke's death also influenced Newcastle's views of Anglo-American relations. And again, though even more clearly than is the case with commercial interests, it would seem that the earl's passing allowed the duke finally to discover springs of action congruent with long held but hitherto largely dormant principles. The duke's career had often brought him into contact with American concerns, and in dealing with them he had left a record of actions which, considered collectively and as part of the broader pattern of British treatment of America, Burke later dignified as a policy of "salutary neglect." The modern historian who called Newcastle's colonial policy "wise and fruitful" exaggerated;[25] its wisdom was simply the convenience of non-intervention and its fruitfulness was, from the British imperial standpoint, dubious. The Americans learned practical independence under the regime of salutary neglect, and they then asserted true independence when British governments began to replace neglect with intolerable attention. But a germ of truth lay in the adjectival portion of Burke's famous *mot*: as long as Britain avoided excessive meddling in colonial affairs, the colonies and the mother country jointly throve within a transatlantic, English-speaking empire. Newcastle had been a constant critic of men who would meddle. He had long set himself against those Anglican prelates who hoped to introduce an episcopacy in America. While at the Treasury he had resisted all suggestions that he impose new taxes on the colonies, and as early as 1729 an unsigned memorandum emanating from his secretarial office had termed a proposal to extend the stamp tax to America "inexpedient."[26] Newcastle's interest in maintaining American good will had also sometimes had a more positive aspect. Since the early 1750's he had unsuccessfully tried to have the office of President of the Board of Trade raised to a cabinet post, or to have a separate secretary of state for the colonies created. Either change would have symbolized Britain's recognition of the importance of the colonies. As recently as 1763 he had spoken out sharply against plans to create a Canadian government without an elected assembly: "Such an establishment . . . would shake the very foundation of our colonies, who would with justice expect that that would be their fate very soon."[27]

Yet, as long as Hardwicke lived, a powerful constraint operated upon Newcastle's thinking toward America. The earl's legal mind never forgot that sovereignty within the empire rested at Westminster with the Crown in Parliament. Neither he nor his offspring were ever respon-

sive to any American grievance that seemed to challenge Britain's
constitutional supremacy. Newcastle's attitude was different. To be
sure, like all politicians of his era he accepted Parliament's superiority
over the colonies, but to him it was a point best left abstract and un-
asserted. He had never been one to magnify the powers of Parliament
anyway, and he sensed that if Britain insisted on constitutional punctili-
ousness it might provoke a reaction in America far out of proportion to
the importance of the point the government would be trying to make.
He remained an adherent to Sir Robert Walpole's famous principle,
quieta non movere. Hardwicke's passing made the forceful advocacy of this
view fully acceptable.

The slow waning of his old friend's influence thus had two consequences for Newcastle's political behavior: it enormously eased his move
toward the reformist wing of the Whigs on the substantive issues of
America and commerce, and it allowed him to drift away from an older
notion of the unacceptability of opposition to a more moderate stance
which countenanced organized resistance to governmental measures
felt to be harmful to the kingdom. Newcastle's advanced age prevented
him from throwing himself with the energy and abandon of his earlier
years into new schemes of opposition. He was unable to accede to Legge's hope, expressed late in 1763, that he serve as a "secretary" for the
antiministerial forces; he even relinquished his self-appointed and
informal post of "vinegar of the opposition."[28] But he abandoned an
earlier aversion to avowedly political associations and accepted membership in the newly organized Wildman's Club. His attendance at
meetings was rare, for he preferred to leave the festivities of political
clubbery to his "young and zealous friends." But, despite occasional
doubts, he adjudged their political boisterousness "a very good thing."[29]
With similar commitment he participated in a series of opposition activities designed to embarrass Grenville's ministry. When Prince
Ferdinand, the hero of the German theatre in the Seven Years' War,
visited Britain in January 1764 to marry the king's eldest sister, the
opposition compensated for the government's rudely cool reception
with parties and celebrations. Ferdinand sipped tea with Newcastle and
the duchess, showering attention on the man he had once blamed for
his military difficulties. When the opposition introduced a motion into
the Commons to have general warrants declared illegal, Newcastle
endorsed the initiative. It was an issue uniquely suitable for attracting
the support not only of Newcastle's Whigs but of Pitt's followers and

many independents as well. The duke contributed time and energy. He wrote to friends, urging them to attend the crucial sessions. He rejected the advice of those who would have summoned only a small coterie of allies, arguing instead that success depended on numbers and that numbers depended on appealing beyond restricted circles. And even though in the end the government succeeded by the narrowest of margins in averting what would have been a humiliating defeat, Newcastle was heartened by the near success and by the cooperation among opposition factions that underlay it.

But since the ministry had apparently proved itself invincible in Parliament, and since the duke's experience taught that governments in general were unassailable on that battleground, Newcastle looked for other areas in which, though with less effect, the government might actually be bested. Hardwicke's death provided an ideal locus of confrontation: Cambridge University. Here, where Newcastle's influence as chancellor remained considerable, the earl's passing had left the office of high steward vacant. Lord Sandwich, the northern secretary, had already declared his interest in succeeding to the position, and despite George Grenville's plea that he reconsider, Sandwich refused to retreat and was in the popular view the ministry's candidate. Newcastle wanted the new Lord Hardwicke, eldest son of his late friend, to be elected, and a furious campaign, provoked by Sandwich and accepted by Newcastle while the old earl still lay dying, was begun. The duke had not stayed fully abreast of Cambridge politics, but he had allies in the university who could guide his actions. He sent a number of rugged campaigners to the university, including Charles Townshend, Tommy Townshend, Jr., and several of the Yorke brothers. Ultimately, a close and disputed election ensued, and only after the Court of King's Bench in April declared Hardwicke the victor did Newcastle know that his efforts had not been wasted.[30] It was a victory to savor, and scarcely one to be despised. To be sure, the Cambridge campaign had necessitated the absence from Parliament of powerful opposition debaters on important occasions. But the duke's priorities were not confused: he was dispatching troops to the only theatre where a significant victory over the ministry in 1764 was truly possible.

When Parliament finally rose in the spring Newcastle looked back with satisfaction at the accomplishments of the session. But mortality and an incident of political pique suddenly intervened to undo all that had been wrought. In August Henry Legge died and the opposition lost its most fit member to lead the Commons. In October the duke of Devonshire, a major Whig peer although not yet forty-five, also died. These blows caught the Whigs unprepared, and Newcastle was especially grieved at the loss of Devonshire—"my best friend" he had once called him[31]—a fellow duke who, while Hardwicke yet lived and still more in the six months since the earl's death, had given advice both readily and well. Almost simultaneously Pitt declared his complete rupture with Newcastle's Whigs. His reasons for breaking with the duke seem to have been petty and idiosyncratic, but the consequence was far-reaching: the opposition, so recently a force to be feared, was now shattered. In lieu of Devonshire as an adviser Newcastle turned to the duke of Cumberland, whose distaste for ties with Pitt now seemed less harmful since Pitt had already consummated the break. "It is upon His Royal Highness that we must all depend," Newcastle wrote, exhorting the younger Whigs to follow Cumberland's advice and judgment as strictly as he himself, "the oldest of them," intended to do.[32] But no amount of admonition could hide the truth that Newcastle's policy of strengthening Whig influence by associating it with Pitt's popularity and ideas had fallen apart.

The course of Whig woes continued to unfold. Ambitious young men who had supported Newcastle as long as the party seemed to be sailing a course straight to office now began to abandon the foundering ship. Charles Yorke negotiated with Grenville in November over the post of master of the rolls, disengaged himself from the duke, and gained at least the half-victory of receiving from the government a patent of precedency over the solicitor general. Three months later it was Charles Townshend who broke with the Whigs, declaring his intention to support the government and urging the duke not to make a stir over Conway's dismissal. Within six months the Whigs had thus lost the services of the very three men, Legge, Townshend, and Yorke, whom Newcastle had singled out in late 1762 as the party's preeminent leaders in the Commons.[33] That optimism had long since yielded to dejection in the duke's outlook is, in the light of these calamities, scarcely surprising. He now saw Grenville having "*champ libre*," he despaired of the "confusion and absurdity" in the House of Lords, and he determined to attend as infrequently as possible.[34] In March 1765, accompanied by the duchess, Newcastle paid his first visit to Bath. As never before politics had begun to pall.

III

George Grenville was the only prime minister between Henry Pelham and Lord North who, like them, simultaneously headed the Treasury and sat in the House of Commons. From an institutional point of view, therefore, he ought to have been a fairly secure minister, but he lasted scarcely more than two years. His fatal error was a tendency to view the king as a figure to be ignored if possible and bullied if necessary. This alone would doubtless have made relations between the monarch and his first minister less than amicable, but heightening even this tension was the misfortune that Grenville was the successor to the king's beloved Lord Bute. In some measure, at least, George hoped and even expected Grenville to let Bute exercise considerable influence while abstaining from office. But the proud Grenville was unwilling to be anyone's puppet, and as he grew ever more distrustful of his master, the monarch in his turn became increasingly disenchanted with the prime minister. Thus, very early in the new ministry the remarkable situation had arisen in which the Crown was actually seeking an alternative to the group of men it felt itself afflicted with. Only the mid-1740's had witnessed a similar spectacle. This curious intragovernmental quarrel reached its peak in the spring of 1765 when the Grenville ministry bungled its handling of a regency bill and, by inducing the king to approve a draft that excluded his mother from the office of regent, made the monarch appear to be a less than dutiful son. George thereupon determined to be rid of his minister, whatever the consequences, and asked his uncle, the duke of Cumberland, to sound out various opposition leaders on their willingness to form a new government.

All turned on Pitt. Although the ministry George III envisioned was to be a coalition embracing the Whigs, Pitt was the man whom the king most wanted and Newcastle thought indispensable. Cumberland's initial probes, in May, found Pitt very severe, insisting that he would take office only if a series of policies and purges he favored were implemented. Above all, Pitt wanted a royal promise that Bute would exercise no influence whatsoever. The Whigs, and especially Newcastle, were prepared to join Pitt in such an administration, but since George wanted Lord Northumberland at the Treasury, Pitt declined the seals, fearing that Northumberland's marital tie to Bute's family portended the favorite's return to effective power. Without Pitt the Whigs were unwilling to take office, and the king was forced to retain Grenville. Again in June Cumberland surveyed prospects. This time he was authorized to concede all of Pitt's demands if necessary. But even this act of royal desperation failed to win over the Great Commoner, for when Pitt's own choice for the Treasury, Lord Temple, unexpectedly refused to accept the post, Pitt withdrew his own candidacy.

The Whigs were thoroughly confused, and in late June Newcastle still felt it would not avail to form an administration to which Pitt did not belong. But the lure of office was enormous, especially since George III stood by his concessions and expressed his readiness to accept a Whig ministry. At a meeting of party leaders at Claremont on 30 June the Whigs decided by a twelve-to-six vote to form an administration of their own. Newcastle sided with the majority. He now argued that Pitt's formal inclusion in the ministry was no longer essential, for "if, as I am persuaded will be the case, those measures which Mr. Pitt has prepared are followed, Mr. *Pitt* cannot and I dare say will not oppose." The duke gave substance to this argument by drafting a list of Pittite programs which the Whigs should implement: favor toward Prussia, a law against general warrants, restoration of military officers dismissed as punishment for their parliamentary votes, and high office for Charles Pratt.[35] It was the younger Whigs, most particularly those with commercial ties, who were most dubious of the viability of a Whig government unsupported by Pitt, but the office hungry duke dismissed their reasonable objections with the remark that "the Boys of *Wildman's* shall not be the Whig party." Cumberland too was initially skeptical of the possibilities of success, but a visit from Newcastle changed his mind. Within a few days the Whigs, "the Duke of Newcastle's friends" as one observer called them, trooped back into office.[36]

The duke had long made clear that at his age he did not want to head the Treasury again, and so no knowledgeable person was surprised that he accepted the distinguished but not very taxing office of lord privy seal. He himself had once spoken of the position as a reward for elder statesmen.[37] The post bore no official responsibilities and was thus even less demanding than the lord presidency he had been offered in May. Its revenue of £3,000 per annum was also a useful addition to the always precarious ducal budget.[38] During Grenville's ministry, and indeed for much of the eighteenth century, the lord privy seal had not been a member of the inner cabinet, but during Newcastle's incumbency the post was elevated. Additionally, the duke accepted special responsibility for handling ecclesiastical politics, and although he vowed to share this authority with the archbishop of Canterbury, Thomas Secker, in fact he dealt directly with the king on appointive matters and left the hesitant and irritated archbishop in virtual isolation. The duke had episcopal friends whom he wanted to reward, and during his year in office he was able to pay debts to several. John Hume, bishop of Oxford, was translated to lucrative Salisbury, and Litchfield's Frederick Cornwallis, the faithful bishop of 1762, got the deanery of St. Paul's *in commendam*. Others who counted on the duke, however, received less.[39] Even in these later years Newcastle's attitude toward the established church remained tempered by his Whig sensitivity to the fears of dissenters, and he continued to resist Anglican activities that could be interpreted as threats to the power or position of dissent.

The new first lord of the Treasury, somewhat unexpectedly, was the marquess of Rockingham. He had long been particularly favored by Newcastle. He had wealth and political influence. He stood well with Cumberland. He had a reputation for honesty and fair dealing. Above all, his politics were right: he had resigned at Devonshire's dismissal in 1762 and had been ready to resign in 1757; he had served as representative of the Whigs on several recent occasions; and he was perhaps the only aristocrat able to bridge the gap between the youth of Wildman's and the party's older adherents. But Rockingham was not a leader of men. A peculiar lassitude marked his activities, and while friends could attribute it to his less than robust health, his enemies were inclined to think him simply lazy. He hardly ever addressed the House of Lords, largely because he was an inept speaker. Most significantly, he lacked deep political ambition. Like the ministry itself, he appears to have taken office more by default than conquest. Newcastle, in any event, was pleased. Though not present when the crucial decision about the Treasury was made, he thoroughly approved it and remained thereafter a loyal lieutenant of a man who was three and a half decades his junior.

Two aspects of the ministerial changes of July 1765 stand out, their startling scope and the remarkable youth of the new incumbents. Excepting the Bath–Granville fiasco of 1746, such a wholesale evacuation of office had not occurred during the duke's entire officeholding career. General Conway and the duke of Grafton, the latter appointed to represent Pitt's interests in the ministry, became secretaries of state. Lord Hertford, Conway's elder brother, took the lord lieutenancy of

Ireland. Lord Dartmouth succumbed to Newcastle's special importuning—"Your lordship's most excellent character and known disinterestness [*sic*]" were needed[40]—and accepted direction of the Board
of Trade. Only two men who had served with Grenville, Lord Northington the lord chancellor, and Lord Egmont at the Admiralty, remained in high office. In both cases the Whigs submitted to the king's
eagerness to retain known friends, but in the instance of Northington
they were probably privately pleased, since the monarch's desire
spared them the need to choose between the two rivals, Charles Yorke
and Charles Pratt. A reluctant Yorke was persuaded by Newcastle to
become attorney general; Pratt was elevated to the peerage as Lord
Camden, another sop to Pitt. Charles Townshend was made paymaster
of the forces. And while the king's two friends, Egmont and Northington, had both been born before the Hanoverian accession, the Whigs
themselves were clearly of a different generation: Hertford was forty-
seven, Conway forty-five, Rockingham thirty-five, Dartmouth thirty-
four, and Grafton not yet thirty. "Je suis tres content de tres jeunes
gens," the duke wrote to Lady Yarmouth in July,[41] but when one reflects on the psychological estrangement which later developed between
him and his colleagues, it seems likely that much of the problem was in
fact rooted in this age difference.

At the king's first levee after Grenville's resignation Newcastle "was
more caressed than anybody," and the duke was naturally pleased at
this sign of royal favor. He predicted bright days for what he called
"this new, honest, Whig administration."[42] But neither his hopes for
Whig success nor his plans for exercising personal influence within the
ministry were fulfilled. The Whigs were too weak to hold office masterfully. Their accession had been accidental, and while the king clearly
preferred their respectful demeanor to Grenville's abrasive presence,
he nevertheless remained aware that they were Whigs and that stronger, more obedient ministries might be possible. Compounding this
problem was the inability of the Whigs to find forceful leaders for either
house. In the Commons Conway was simply not an effective speaker,
and neither Yorke nor Townshend had the requisite commitment to
Whig thinking. In the Lords Rockingham sat silent, Richmond lacked
stature, and Newcastle lacked incisiveness. Such administrative capacity as the ministry had resided not in the Whigs themselves but in the
ranks of department heads and secretaries whose tenures of office were
slowly becoming independent of changes at the top. For all these rea-

sons the ministry's position was precarious. Denied firm support by both the Crown and the Parliament, it was indeed, as Rockingham called it, a "frail green vessel."[43]

Newcastle entered the ministry with visions of lending his experience and acquired wisdom to "our young ministers," with visions, in fact, of providing a form of inconspicuous leadership to the administration. But these visions quickly faded, for if Rockingham had not been the unmistakable party leader before the formation of the government, his accession to the Treasury conferred that dignity upon him. And from the first he saw that a necessary component of exercising leadership would be to deny the duke the full authority he hoped for. Newcastle recommended treasury appointees, but Rockingham named his own. Newcastle could not even get James West reinstated, apparently a test case for Rockingham's assertion of independence, and had finally to settle for a small pension for his former aide. The duke also sought the wholesale restoration of those who had lost their posts in the winter of 1762–63. He himself was restored as lord lieutenant of Nottinghamshire and steward of Sherwood forest. But except for personal friends, especially from the Sussex gentry, the duke could otherwise not have his way. His view was too narrowly vindictive, while Rockingham, either from a sense of caution or from a conscious desire to return to Henry Pelham's ideas of a comprehensive administration, was unwilling to conduct a purge throughout the ranks. Newcastle even tried to influence Rockingham's choice of a personal secretary. He argued that young Edmund Burke was a Jacobite and a Roman Catholic, and he suggested an alternative candidate. But Rockingham, though not without testing Burke's loyalty, again spurned Newcastle's advice.[44] Within a few months ambitious younger men were rejecting Newcastle's offers of aid, rightly believing that success lay in other connections.

Just as his influence over the choice of personnel was confined, so too was his influence over ministerial activities. Indeed, the duke quickly felt himself isolated from his younger colleagues, his counsel unsought and his sensibilities unrespected. He tried his hand at meddling in the departments of others, but Grafton rebuked him and the duke foreswore further interference. He entertained one and all at Claremont but could not transform feting into wielding influence. The role Newcastle had sought for himself as unofficial leader was actually being played by the duke of Cumberland, and it was to the king's uncle that a dispirited Newcastle was forced to turn in late July to discover precisely what function he was to fulfill in the new administration.[45] His self-pitying laments thereafter form a threnody throughout his correspondence of the late summer and fall. Occasionally there were brighter moments when Grafton and Conway would be "very respectful" and Conway—a revealing concern—would even be "very communicative."[46] But mingling with his colleagues became distasteful for the lord privy seal, and by November, though still summoned to all cabinet meetings, Newcastle attended only if foreign affairs, his field of special interest and competence, were to be discussed.

In the opening months of the ministry the duke of Cumberland was "the head and soul of all,"[47] providing his home for cabinet meetings and presiding over the sessions. The influence of the royal uncle was felt in the administration's political activities. It was Cumberland who negatived a proposal to call a general election. Cumberland's aversion to Pitt meant that the ministry could not undertake additional placatory steps to win over the Great Commoner in the early fall. Newcastle, therefore, though still persuaded that such an alliance was crucial to the survival of the government, recommended that if soundings toward Pitt were felt to be inappropriate, an effort to conciliate some of the followers of Bute was preferable to standing exposed and unmoving. Cumberland was unsympathetic even to this idea, however, and so the foundation of the ministry remained essentially rather narrow. But the health of the king's corpulent uncle had long been deteriorating, and on the final day of October, while hosting Newcastle and Northington, he suddenly collapsed and died. At a stroke the chief obstacle to further pursuit of policies designed to earn Pitt's approbation had disappeared, and Newcastle knew it. He promptly recommended new feelers toward the reclusive Pitt. But such efforts as the ministry then undertook were half-hearted and ambiguous at best. Pitt responded to them with scorn and a firm refusal to associate with Rockingham's friends.

The relationship between Newcastle and Pitt at this time is, in retrospect, tinged with irony. Pitt was inclined to blame Newcastle's influence for every governmental misdemeanor, while the duke was in fact a leading spokesman for the pro-Pitt position within the ministry and, far from being dominating, was virtually impotent. The duke in July 1765 had hoped for power without responsibility; six months later he found himself saddled with responsibility yet in fact devoid of power. Just as Newcastle in opposition had been inclined to exaggerate Bute's influence, so too now did Pitt exaggerate Newcastle's. He railed against the methods of "Claremont"—Pitt's shorthand for Newcastle's political influence—and on at least one occasion actually described the ministry as "his Grace's."[48] A one-sided personal feud was keeping Whigs and Pittites apart. And yet, as reports from America gave mounting and finally irresistible evidence of colonial discontent with the Stamp Act, the need for the Whigs to come to terms with Pitt seemed all the more imperative. Since Pitt was known to believe that he could "never have confidence in a system where the duke of Newcastle has influence," and since the duke was the "*Sole Obstacle*" to a rapprochement,[49] only one action could break the impasse. On 8 January 1766 the duke of Newcastle, who had already altered his foreign policy views to entice Pitt, declared his readiness to resign if his departure would finally let the ministry secure the Great Commoner. And even though the duke deeply hoped that he would not have to make good on the offer, the declaration was the most selfless act of the duke's political career— "very handsome & dignify'd" in the words of the king.[50]

Newcastle was, however, not obliged to make good his offer, for an American crisis swept over British politics and forced the Whigs and the Pittites into an uneasy *de facto* alliance anyway. The crisis had arisen slowly as the American colonies responded with unprecedented resistance to the imposition of the stamp tax legislated in the spring of 1765. At that time, although most of the Whig leadership had been quiescent, Newcastle had foreseen trouble and younger members of the opposition had tried to defeat the measure in the Commons.[51] Only, however, when the colonies exploded with resolutions, protest meetings, and a trade boycott did Britain come to realize the magnitude of colonial wrath. The men in Britain most sensitive to these marks of discontent were the merchants, and since the mercantile community looked upon the Whigs as the parliamentary group most attuned to its concerns, the merchants were not backward in seeking redress from the Rockingham administration. Only repeal, they argued, would open American markets to British goods again. Newcastle was the first important minister to sympathize with this view. Rockingham soon joined him. But others among the Whigs were less convinced that repeal was the appropriate procedure. Charles Yorke asserted that the principle of parliamentary supremacy was at stake, that a British capitulation would in effect suggest that Parliament had no right to legislate for America. He urged a declaration of Parliament's full authority in the colonies. Cast in this perspective, the argument was irresistible to any Whig: Parliament's power and dignity could not be allowed to be impugned. But Newcastle preferred to see the question as one of expedient rather than principle. He accepted the thesis that Parliament in theory could legislate for the colonies, but he was more impressed by the overwhelming need to revive British trade. "The idea of *authority* and *relief* going hand in hand," he warned, "will be found very difficult, and for the one, I should incline rather to be deficient, in that, which is only a declaration in words, than in the other, on which depend the most material interest [*sic*] of this country."[52] From these varying points of view a famous compromise emerged in January 1766: the ministry would support the repeal of the Stamp Act, but only when it was conjoined with a Declaratory Act reasserting Parliament's right to legislate for the colonies.

Though Newcastle was absent from the meetings that reached these decisions, he was prepared to give them energetic support. His assistance was vital: the major arena in the coming confrontation would not be the Commons but the Lords, for it was here that the supporters of repeal were woefully short of voices and even dangerously short of votes. During February Newcastle was extraordinarily active. He spoke regularly in the House of Lords. He attended rehearsal sessions for merchants being prepared to testify before the Commons in committee. He sought to line up episcopal support for the repeal. To the archbishop of Canterbury he explained his conviction "that the very being of this country, as a trading nation depends upon the immediate repeal of the Stamp Act; not as an illegal act, but as the most imprudent, and pernicious one, that ever was made." When George III, initially a proponent of minimal reform of the Stamp Act and never a true convert to repeal, hesitated to rebuke those whose consciences compelled them to oppose the government, Newcastle addressed him bluntly: "Conscience, Sir, is too often influenced by prejudice in favor of persons and things, and . . . courts have ways of letting their opinion be known."[53] George, somewhat cowed, then promised to try to convert some of the peers in opposition.

In addition to his direct contributions to the government's efforts to create a majority in the House of Lords, the duke seems to have been a sort of cheerleader for the Whigs. These were bleak days for the government, for not only was the outcome of repeal in the Lords uncertain, but beyond that concrete issue lay the unresolved question of the fundamental viability of a Whig ministry. George had ominously sought Bute's counsel, and although Newcastle obtained from the king an affirmation of his trust in the existing government, the monarch remained far less than enthusiastic about an administration that advocated a pusillanimous policy in the colonies. It all added up to a forbidding future: the government might lose in the House of Lords—an "alarming" prospect, the duke intimated, that could provoke "insurrections in the great manufacturing towns"[54]—and even if it won it had no assurance that the king would continue to rely on it. When the Lords defeated the government in early February on a minor issue related to stamp tax arrears, Grafton and some other ministers believed that the hour for resignation had come. Newcastle countered their argument with an appeal to honor and duty: a ministry bent on a major reform ought not to let a minor incident disrupt its plans. Resignation under the existing circumstances would be tantamount to desertion. Others clearly felt the same, for Grafton's advice was roundly rejected. But equally clearly, the ministry chose to move forward less from a presentiment of success than from a hope that more honorable conditions for resignation might arise.

The Declaratory Act sped through Parliament easily, but the repeal bill lagged behind. As all had foreseen, it was the House of Lords that threatened to overturn the entire plan. With the showdown in that chamber approaching, Newcastle set himself to his old game of drafting probable voting lists. All early calculations showed a small majority for repeal, but the number of those designated as doubtful was invariably sufficient to make the outcome uncertain. Toward the end, however, Newcastle's confidence grew, and his final prediction was an administration victory of 104 to 74.[55] The central debate itself occurred on 11 March, and the duke addressed the eight-hour session at least three times. It was one of his finest performances. He spoke for all when he defended the right of Parliament to legislate for the colonies—"the Supreme Power must have a Right to bind its Subjects wherever they are by Laws and Statutes"—but he insisted that attention had to be focused on the economic aspect of the crisis. He moved that the petition of London merchants trading with America be read to the house, and after the peers had heard these pleas for aid, he reduced his advocacy of repeal to a single reason: since the end of the war British trade with all the world except America had been ailing, and repeal would assure the continued vitality of this only healthy sector of that trade. Privately the duke also had noneconomic reasons for supporting repeal. He believed the empire essential to Britain's standing as a great power, and he saw the colonies as effective allies in wars against national enemies. But the ministry, anxious to keep the debate out of swampy constitutional bogs, apparently decided to restrict itself largely to the safe ground of economic argumentation. At 11:00 P.M. the bill passed its second and crucial reading, 105 to 71. Only eight bishops voted against the government.[56] Six days later the Lords gave final approval to the measure. It was, though not his alone, Newcastle's last great parliamentary triumph.

In a sense, it was the Whigs' last triumph too. Although they hoped to rebound from success to further success, they found instead the three great props of their ministry collapsing in the spring of 1766. The first prop was the king's trust. It had never been wholehearted, for George had accepted the Whigs and what he called their "strange ideas" only *faute de mieux*, and he had remained alert to possible alternatives. His constitutional scruples had hitherto compelled him to lend support, what Hardwicke and Newcastle had once called "grace," to his ministers. But the drive for repeal made the ministry appear more starkly reprehensible than ever. Royal support waned steadily thereafter. The second prop was Pitt's neutrality. His full support would have been far more effective, but as long as he foreswore active opposition the ministry could subsist. During the repeal crisis Pitt had pursued a course parallel to the government's. Indeed, because the ministry in its eagerness to win Pitt over had molded its final proposal along broadly Pittite lines, many people saw the Great Commoner and not Rockingham as the hero of the campaign. The cooperation of February and March quickly gave way to acrimony, however, for Pitt found the government's commercial policy pernicious. By May the disenchantment of both George III and Pitt with the Rockingham government was complete, a thoroughly ominous situation for the Whigs since the monarch had never disguised his preference for Pitt as his chief minister anyway.

The one remaining prop was ministerial solidarity. Had it endured, the administration might have been able to survive in the face of both royal disaffection and Pittite sniping. But this prop was as fragile as the others. Northington and Egmont were not Whigs at all, but adherents of the king, agents of the very power that only solidarity might have vanquished. Among the Whigs themselves rancors troubled ministerial relations. Newcastle began again to feel isolated, Conway and Hertford were widely reputed to oppose Rockingham on many points, and Grafton grew increasingly uneasy as the chances of winning Pitt over declined. It was, in fact, Grafton who first brought these divisions into the open by resigning the seals at the end of April. Most people saw his action as a condemnation of the ministry's spurning of Pitt. Despite Egmont's efforts to have Rockingham repair the loss by turning to Bute and his friends, the Whigs decided to stick to their own circle. Newcastle wanted young Lord Hardwicke as Grafton's successor, but the head of the house of Yorke pleaded poor health and diminished strength and refused to join. Rockingham's preference was the young duke of Richmond, whose Sussex power was mounting as Newcastle's declined. Newcastle thought Richmond inexperienced and, although he denied it, probably resented his rising influence. Most interestingly, he even considered accepting the seals himself, or, to put it more accurately, he wished others would consider him as a possible candidate. The king, at least, although not Rockingham, obliged, giving Newcastle a chance to savor the pleasure of withdrawing his own name from consideration.[57] Ultimately, for want of an alternative, Richmond took the post. Newcastle accepted the choice with moderately good grace.

But Grafton's defection was not the only sign of Whig disarray. The party's powerful transatlantic commercial support, which had demonstrated its strength as a united force during the repeal crisis, split into its two constituent parts, those trading with North America and those trading with the West Indies, when the Rockingham ministry introduced and carried a measure to establish free ports in Dominica and Jamaica. The act was part of what appears to have been an effort to implement a commercial policy of lower tariffs yoked to stricter tariff enforcement. But West Indian merchants, foreseeing the threat of new rivals, turned against the ministry, and Newcastle himself, perhaps because of ties with men like Rose Fuller, considered the action unwise. It unquestionably hurt the ministry in the Commons.

The Whigs were not blind to their need for firming up their ranks. But they could not agree among themselves whether to seek support from Bute or from Bedford, and so they did neither. Nor could they induce George III to punish with dismissal those governmental officials who had voted against repeal. The ministry also knew of royal approaches to Pitt. Rockingham thought them as unlikely to succeed as previous efforts, but Newcastle suspected that different conditions might eventuate in a different result. Early in July Lord Northington, who had already ceased attending ministerial sessions, used another aspect of the Whigs' lenient policy toward America, its readiness to allow Roman Catholics to hold office in Quebec, as a pretext for resigning the lord chancellorship. It was a heavy blow, for although Northington had always been a king's man, he now informed the monarch that the ministry was impossibly weak. The Whigs hoped to use the vacancy to make good on long standing promises to Charles Yorke, but George moved to consummate his negotiations with Pitt. When the king told Rockingham and Newcastle that Pitt would form a new ministry, they were, in the king's report, "thunderstruck," although neither can really have been surprised at what Newcastle later called this "cruel usage."[58] Newcastle's final audiences with the king were moving. The duke recommended the Whigs to the man who had just defeated them, wrangled a further promise of ecclesiastical preferment from the king, and heard the monarch declare that no man had served the Hanoverian dynasty as well as the retiring lord privy seal.[59] These were consoling and cherished words. On 30 July 1766, proudly spurning the offer of a £4,000 annual pension, Newcastle resigned his last major office under the Crown.

IV

The Whigs were embarking on a course of opposition. But who were these Whigs? What relation did they bear to other eighteenth-century political parties? What relation did Newcastle bear to them? These are difficult, disputed, and important questions. Political parties had been fundamental to the kingdom's political life in the reign of Queen Anne. Practically all M.P.'s were, by their own reckoning, either Whigs or Tories, and each party had in addition powerful support from various groups outside of Parliament. The parties differed in their views about the best foreign policy for the kingdom, the best future for the kingdom, and the best way to rule the kingdom. But the Tories faltered in the race. The Hanoverian accession deprived them of royal support and hence of the manipulative influence that parties in power could exercise. The Jacobite uprising of 1715, supported by Bolingbroke, deprived them of their good name. These liabilities proved ultimately insuperable, and the Tories—as defined by issues from the age of Bolingbroke, Swift, and Oxford—slowly disappeared in the decades after 1715. To be sure, there was the Jacobite uprising of 1745, but it constituted a threat only because Britain was simultaneously at war with France. Moreover, it cost the Tories whatever good will they had retained or reacquired. As an organized movement Toryism was moribund by mid-century. Thereafter, within the political nation, only a few individual M.P.'s characterized chiefly by their independence called themselves Tories.

But even though the Tories as an organization faded into political impotence in the 1720's and into oblivion in the 1740's, a sort of "gut Toryism" remained central to the traditional creed of many Englishmen in all levels of society. Its tenets were emotionally charged: a dislike of foreigners, a bitterness toward merchants and industrialists, a distrust of centralized power, and a support for the principle—though less often for the Whiggish reality—of the established church. Bereft of an organizational base, this Tory sensibility was usually quiescent, but when aroused, it could be fearsome. It was, after all, the chief energizing force behind the antiexcise drive of 1733 and the anti-Semitic activities of 1753. It was this aggressive irrationality of the politically unlettered that all Whig leaders from Walpole through Pelham and Newcastle to Rockingham sought to keep dormant. *Quieta non movere* derived its validity from the recognition of what awakened dogs could do.

The decline of the Tories brought one-party politics to Britain. But one-party politics did not initially mean politics without dissent. Sir Robert Walpole never eliminated opposition from his Parliaments. Indeed, opposition ultimately overwhelmed him, though it did not overwhelm the Whigs. One reason the Whig party survived Walpole's fall was that much of the opposition, unwilling to don the discredited designation of "Tory," assumed the name "Whig." Thus, nomenclatural identity, though it obscured divisions in the House of Commons, did not signify their elimination. But precisely because it obscured such distinctions, it allowed governments to be ousted without a party being overturned. After 1745, however, even opposition began to disappear: Henry Pelham, unlike Walpole, practiced the politics of comprehension and brought representatives of all Whig factions into the government. Only Frederick, Prince of Wales, the embodiment of the "reversionary interest," kept a small group of devotees in opposition. But he died in 1751, and the last three years of Pelham's life mark the nadir of adversarial party politics in eighteenth-century Britain.

This artificial situation could not have long endured. It was a conjunction of two unusual situations that gave Henry Pelham the political peace of his final years, and the impermanent nature of each of the conjoined elements meant that whoever succeeded him in power, even a far abler man than Newcastle, would not long have enjoyed similar tranquility. The death of Frederick had given the government its first real respite since 1714 from the existence of an heir to the throne simultaneously mature in years and hostile in politics. The "reversionary interest" was thus briefly in eclipse. But this situation could not last, for young Prince George was growing up and old George II was slowing down. The grandson would soon replace the son, and an institutional and inviting focal point for an opposition would thus inevitably reemerge. Moreover, in the early 1750's Britain was temporarily devoid of fiery issues. The great disputes of the past were resolved or forgotten; those of the future still lay below the political horizon. For a few sunny years no fundamental wrangle troubled politics. But this situation too was necessarily ephemeral: forces for change were abroad in the land. Change always brought gain to some and loss to others, and thus in a world in flux a bland and undivided political order was impossible.

Consequently, parties reappeared after 1754. War brought pressures on the kingdom far more severe than those engendered by the previous conflict, and while as long as the war endured it also provided justification for muting the very political divisions it was fostering, it at least provided fertile ground for the germination of postwar divisiveness. Many of the great issues of the 1760's—Wilkes, general warrants, America—derived at least in part from the war. Those major issues not attributable to the war —Whig fears of a rising authoritarianism and a declining respect for aristocracy—were rooted in the other great event of the war years: the arrival of a new monarch in 1760. George III had no love and little respect for the men his predecessor had chosen to run the kingdom. From the moment of his accession he wanted virtuous rather than partisan government, and within a few years he also wanted ministers whom he could influence. The Newcastle–Rockingham Whigs seemed unfit by either requirement. Tainted by long contact with what was believed to have been the corrupt politics of place and pension, they were also a group with programmatic ideas. Thus doubly distrusted, they achieved power only briefly in the 1760's, when George decided he would prefer their deferential commands to Grenville's abrasive bossiness, during a period in which a permanent nonparty government was to be slowly organized behind the ministers' backs.

These Whigs, with many others, were descendants of the expansive Whig party of Pelham's years. That vast coalition had fallen apart during Newcastle's unhappy tenure as first minister; Pitt and Fox had gone their own ways, while those whose primary loyalty was to court or office stood by the duke only with deep reservations. Still, the coalition remained strong enough to propel Newcastle back into government in 1757, though largely because the duke's position was ambiguous and the king's desperate. The years after 1762, however, showed how few of the Whigs would stay bound to a leader whose hopes for returning to office seemed dashed. Even many of those who resigned for Newcastle in the first winter of opposition ultimately joined another group. Bute's following waxed, Bedford's established itself, Grenville planted a standard, and all drew from Pelham's earlier Whig army. The term "Whig" became, understandably, more ambiguous than ever, though from the first it was accepted that Newcastle's party was the most deserving of that appellation. Here in fact is Newcastle's first important contribution to the Whigs of the late eighteenth century: their name. As an erstwhile colleague of Walpole's, as Pelham's brother, as a former Whig first minister, the duke symbolized Whig continuity. Where he went, there went the party name. It was Newcastle's presence that assured that the Newcastle-Rockingham faction and not some other was the Whig party.

But if Newcastle gave the Whigs a good claim to their name, he did not bequeath them much in the way of personnel.[60] Many of his younger associates from his years of power—Oswald, Barrington, and Nugent are examples—became adherents of the court. Others such as Lyttelton or James Grenville shifted to rival factions. Still others, most notably Kinnoull, simply retired. Strikingly disloyal were the duke's own relatives: Shelley, Lincoln, Tommy Pelham, and Onslow all retained their places even after the duke hoped they would resign. Only Bessborough moved with the duke from officeholding Whiggery to opposition Whiggery. Moreover, stripped of office and its ability to reward friends, Newcastle found his famous influence in the Commons reduced to a point where, in his final years, only a handful of men—Sir William Baker, John White, John Norris, John Offley, and James West—looked to him for leadership. Long years of power had been inadequate preparation for opposition, nor had they even given men a taste for it. Consequently, when the squeeze came, when one had either to opt for the duke and the wilderness or for the court (or Chatham) and place, the psychological scales were already weighted toward the latter choice. Newcastle gave a name to the Whigs of the 1760's; he did not give them manpower. And it therefore follows—a point often missed by contemporaries—that the Whigs of the post-1762 period were in some ways a new party.

If the duke supplied little by way of personnel to the Whigs, however, he had greater impact in other spheres. In at least two different respects Newcastle left his impress upon these Whigs: he helped commit them to certain policies, and he supplied them with a measure of organizational cohesion. Newcastle's contribution to policy can be seen on two levels. At a specific level it can be said that the duke was one of the principal formulators of the Whig attitude toward America. As late as 1765 it was not clear what that attitude would be, but in the end it was the spokesmen of conciliation, with Newcastle their earliest and most vigorous ministerial representative, who prevailed. To be sure, the Whig policy was ultimately inadequate: it presupposed Britain's right to exercise authority in America and condemned merely the inexpediency of such exercise. Thus the Whigs, useful in 1766, were irrelevant as early as 1768, when the issue at stake had shifted from the proper use of power to the proper locus of power. Furthermore, it seems clear that the Whigs, despite their known disposition to be fair toward America, were in one respect actually harmful to the maintenance of transatlantic goodwill because they represented much that appeared to the Americans to be corrupt and degenerate in politics, an appearance strongly reinforced by Newcastle's association with the party. But in terms of party continuity from one decade to the next, Newcastle's insistence on leniency toward America had important consequences. It was this attitude that gave the Whigs a point around which, in the mounting Atlantic crisis of 1774, they could regroup. It provided them with a perspective which, through its apparent reasonableness, proved a stimulant in that year to a party that had been rendered almost comatose by North. At a more general level, moreover, Newcastle's readiness to minimize the authority of Parliament helped shape the Whig view that the enhancement or even the preservation of parliamentary power was no longer a sufficient justification for actions that were otherwise self-serving or stupid. The Whigs did not, of course, repudiate a party tradition that had long aligned them with those seeking to weaken royal arbitrariness by strengthening parliamentary responsibility. But the new Whigs of the 1760's began to feel—and Newcastle's prejudice eased the adjustment—that Parliament itself could on occasion be arbitrary and oppressive. The same bias that underlay the Whigs' American policy may thus be discerned in their attitude toward the investigation of the East India Company, the Nullum Tempus dispute, and the middlesex election controversy.

Newcastle contributed too to the solidity of the Whigs. In part the contribution was unintentional, a mere by-product of his neurotic need to pour out letters to colleagues, friends, and acquaintances. But in part it was deliberate, for with Rockingham indolent and Burke preoccupied, the task of maintaining a communications network among the leaders of the party fell to the willing duke. A communications network at the top was not sufficient to give the party organizational tautness throughout its ranks, and, whether from weariness of age or, more likely, the absence of helpers like West and Dupplin, Newcastle no longer sought to mobilize forces in the Commons with his eagerness of old. But at least he served the useful function of keeping the leaders in touch, and while it was scarcely a task that no one else could have done, it was certainly a task that no one else was doing.

The Whigs of the 1760's were a party different from the factions that rivaled them, and several considerations point up this difference. They survived as a distinct political entity even though leadership passed from Newcastle to Rockingham, thus demonstrating that their existence, unlike that of the Bedford or Grenville parties, was independent of the political life-span of a single man. They refused offers of office whenever such offers seemed but ill-concealed attempts to dilute and destroy them, thus demonstrating that their talk of principle was more than prating. They had, at least until the early years of the North administration, a comparatively numerous following—over forty peers by Newcastle's counts in late 1766 and early 1767, and at least seventy-seven M.P.'s from a comparison of Newcastle's and Rockingham's lists in 1767—thus demonstrating that they were more than a family faction supplemented by a few hangers-on. They were not of course like twentieth-century parties, but far too much can be made of this thoroughly obvious fact. More germane is the point that they were also unlike parties of the 1720's ,'30's, and '40's. They were an opposition group that did not found itself on a reversionary interest, for Cumberland's support, while unquestionably useful, simply cannot be construed as in some sense a substitute for leadership by an heir to the throne.[61] Likewise they were an opposition group with a semblance of a platform, and

a platform that in an age of reemergent issues could go beyond conventional opposition recriminations against those in power. On the issue
of America, though not without obscurities of their own they stood at
clear variance from the ministries that preceded and followed them. On
the issue of national leadership they adhered to their contention that
even in a changing Britain the possession of ancestral land and wealth
remained the best prima facie test of quality, far more reliable than
appeal to training or native intelligence. On the issue of royal power
they were the least ambiguous of the parties about the need for the king
to accept direction from his ministry. It is not difficult to find the Whigs
behaving contrary to their expressed principles, nor more particularly
to find Newcastle advancing programs incompatible with proclaimed
party aims. But inasmuch as the strategic concession was as wise a political tool then as now—inasmuch too as all men are human and can
err—it would be simpleminded to argue from examples of Whig way-
wardness that Whig rhetoric was meaningless and that the Whigs were
simply another faction. Contemporaries thought otherwise. They
usually saw the Whigs as something unique on the political scene.
Newcastle contributed significantly to both the tone and the substance
of the party. It was his most enduring achievement.[62]

V

"Seventy-three and ambition are ridiculous comrades," wrote Horace
Walpole after the duke's retirement from the privy seal in 1766.[63] As
was often the case, the century's most noted Newcastle watcher mis-
judged his subject. Politicking remained the core of the duke's life in his
final years, not because he was still ambitious—he knew he would not
personally hold office again—but because it met, through its demand on
his energy and its requirements for social intercourse, certain fundamental psychological needs of his basically compulsive psyche. Lord
Kinnoull hoped to guide his old friend into a tranquil retirement, reminding the duke that nature (he alluded to Virgil's *Second Georgic*),
books, happy matrimony, and memories of services performed were the
joys of old age.[64] But the plea was as futile as it was well intended. The
passing years, although knotting his features and constricting his frame,
had dealt kindly with the duke. Only a recurring intestinal indisposition
marred his health. He had the gait and vitality of a far younger man and
appeared, in one observer's view, fully two decades less aged than his
exact contemporary Lord Chesterfield.[65] Repose offered no attraction

to an active man who had never cultivated the arts of leisure and solitude. At the height of the opposition challenge to the government in May 1767 an excited Newcastle confided: "I have not been so well or slept so well of some time as I did last night."[66] The duke found relaxation and such renewal as it brought in busyness alone. Thus he had always been; thus he remained till illness crippled his frame.

The aim of all his activity was the return of the Whigs to power. Initially he thought this might best be done by encouraging as many Whigs as possible to stay at their various posts under the new administration. Having once experienced the uselessness of mass resignations and the difficulties of storming back into office from a position of "formed or formal opposition," Newcastle thought that the future hopes of a Whig return were best served by retaining whatever posts the party could, even at the cost of some dilution: "The remaining of our friends in employment is the surest way to support the party and the cause." This policy was briefly pursued. But Pitt, who quickly chose to accept the earldom of Chatham, was too much his own man—"mad, and drunk" Newcastle called him—to become a hostage to residual Whigs in his nonparty administration, and by November Rockingham had decided that the experiment in guarded opposition at least partially from within the administration was not strengthening Whig chances for a recovery of power. Against Newcastle's advice Rockingham chose to try to force the issue, and at his request seven Whigs resigned. Newcastle commented tartly that the marquess "does not know my Lord Chatham" and, as in 1762, the resignation ploy failed.[67]

As in the earlier years of opposition Newcastle argued that the minority Whigs would need help if they were to succeed in 1767. But instead of Pitt, now ensconced in power and therefore the enemy, Newcastle was generally inclined to see the duke of Bedford as the man whose cooperation was essential. The basis for any such cooperation was uncertain, for Bedford—and, even more, his loose ally, George Grenville—espoused a far less conciliatory American policy than the Whigs. As long as America remained a prominent issue, the viability of any Rockingham–Bedford alliance seemed dubious. Such concerns did not daunt the duke. He was prepared to overlook policy differences, for the time being at least, and was prepared even to accept Grenville at the Treasury if concessions of this sort were needed to create an alliance among those opposed to Chatham.[68] Rockingham was less ready to equivocate on policy differences, however, and although amenable to talks about possible ties with Bedford, he came to feel that Newcastle was threatening Whig solidarity through a deliberate disregard of Whig principles. It was a classic example of an ancient type of political dispute: whether to retain purity and thereby sacrifice a chance of exercising power, or to storm the seats of power at the cost of a retreat from principle. Negotiations aimed at forming an alliance with the Bedford faction were undertaken lightly in March 1767, far more seriously in July, and desperately in October. Newcastle pressed arduously for success on all occasions, prompting Lord Albemarle to exclaim: "What a jealous head and restless mind that old man has."[69] In July Newcastle's London residence became the location for the climactic meeting, and when this still failed to bring Rockingham and Bedford into agreement he made one last effort by inviting the two leaders, each accompanied by a second, to a private session under his own auspices. It is a mark of his recognized eagerness for success that he could be accepted by both chieftains as a mediator. But the meeting failed again, largely because Rockingham remained too wary of a tie with Grenville.

In addition to working to create an alternative to the existing administration Newcastle used the parliamentary session of 1767 to harass "this insufficient administration" on a number of issues. He helped to mobilize the forces that in February stunned the government by reducing the land tax from 4s. to 3s. in the pound. He saw in the government's proposal about the East India Company a clear indication of a despotic intent to undermine the sanctity of property. He sought to arouse resistance to the government's efforts to meddle in the legal affairs of Massachusetts. Despite the weight of his years he spoke often in the House of Lords, sometimes without a single ally. The duchess worried about the burden of his activities, but Newcastle revelled in them. It served to energize him in these undertakings that he still believed his old enemy, Lord Bute, covertly to exercise "absolute power." On occasion he called the ministers the "*Bute* Administration," and he once characterized all the governments since 1762 save Rockingham's as "those Bute fluctuating administrations."[70] Inflating the power of the former favorite was not Newcastle's only misconstruction of politics in the late 1760's. He increasingly fell back on a dichotomized understanding of politics that, born in the bitter Whig–Tory wars of Queen Anne's reign, had little congruence with the multi-factional reality of George III's era. The party of the Crown, like the Tories, was seen as the party of naked force; the various opposition groups, Whigs all, were viewed as the legatees of a patrimony of principle and as defenders of freedom. Apocalyptic visions of a Tory tyranny occasionally tormented the duke,[71] and his last political wars were waged as much against mythical as against real antagonists.

Increasingly also, they were fought alone. The anxiety about isolation from his colleagues that the duke had begun to feel even before the formation of the Rockingham ministry grew more oppressive. It was, moreover, a self-fulfilling anxiety, for as the duke's loneliness grew, so too did his readiness to scold and thereby irritate the very men who he felt were neglecting him. Where recently his advice had been unheeded, it was by 1767 not even sought. "Confidence I do expect," he pathetically lamented to the marquess, "confidence is all I want."[72] But confidence was not to be his, in part no doubt because he could retain a secret no better in his retirement than in his prime, but also because youth would no longer listen to a voice from another era. Lord John Cavendish, before the fall of the Whig ministry in 1766, had commented to a friend that if it was necessary for the duke to be dismissed, he hoped "it might be on a bed of roses, not on a bed of thorns." The remark gained wide currency, and the duke was asking not long after his retirement "Where is that bed of roses Mr. Pitt promised me?"[73] It was not to be; and of the many thorns retirement brought, the most wounding was the loneliness of isolation.

In 1767 age and illness began overtaking the duke, as they had earlier crippled the duchess. Her afflictions had long been notorious and her troupe of physicians a source of jokes. By the mid-1760's she was a disabled old woman, confined to playing cards at her residence at Claremont or at the visiting quarters at Bath. It was common knowledge that she could no longer observe the appropriate social amenities: "A *message* from me," she explained, "is a visit." Walking on her gout-ridden, swollen ankles was painful, possible only with a cane. Her hand was palsied, a condition that embarrassed and depressed her so much that for a time she insisted on dining alone. But despite the unsteadiness of her pen she refused to use an amanuensis when corresponding with her husband, preferring instead to hold her right hand down with her left as she wrote.[74] By contrast the duke's health in what Secker delicately called "the evening of your Grace's life" was not shattered. Walking was his favorite exercise, though he could no longer manage the circuit of the Claremont estate. Fatigue bore him down more quickly now—a visitor to the House of Lords in 1765 said the duke "delivered himself as he was leaning on two young lords, who sat before him"—and his digestive complaints continued.[75] Between duke and duchess were still unshaken bonds of devotion. A slight to the duchess was an insult to the duke. Reassuring, touching letters passed back and forth during their separations. "Dear Claremont," penned the duke evocatively on one occasion, "was never in greater beauty. Every thing green, the trees charmingly come out, the wood delightful, the cuckoos and nightingal [*sic*] have made their appearance, and Mr. Hurdis has seen *two swallows*." And on their forty-ninth wedding anniversary in 1766 he wrote: "I can't forbear writing to my dearest, to congratulate us both, upon this happy day, which by Gods providence, has occasion'd so much happiness to us both, & to wish that it may please to God, to bless us, with many returns of this most happy day."[76]

Old age brought with it painful separation from old friends. Some, like Margaret Shelley in 1758, Lady Lincoln in 1760, and Lord Hardwicke in 1764, passed away. Others, like Hugh Valence Jones, Lord Kinnoull, John White, and John Page, withdrew from close association with the duke. Still others, like Andrew Stone and Lord Mansfield, repudiated him. These last were particularly painful losses. After the collapse of the Rockingham ministry Newcastle laid great stress on regaining the lord chief justice, but Mansfield, though willing to perform small favors for his old patron, refused to abandon his political independence. Of Stone the duke wrote feelingly: "The desertion and defection of Mr. Stone affects me extremely. I have nobody to resort to, not even to tell my own *tale* to; nobody who I can flatter myself will advise me for my own sake; and, what is still worse, none or few of my most *private* and *intimate* friends who like to pass much time with me."[77]

But the most bitter separations of all were those the duke could interpret as betrayals of family ties. "I desire nothing so much," he reminded Lord Monson, "as to shew my affection to those of my near relations, who, by their conduct towards me, shew their friendship for me; I am sorry to say, that is not the case for all of them." "Your Grace knows," he wrote more sweepingly to the duke of Portland, "that I have been abandon'd & deserted by my nearest relations."[78] Lord Lincoln, socially and politically ambitious, found his uncle too long-lived, and despite efforts by Bishop Hume to repair the division, became totally estranged from the duke by 1767. He was angered by Newcastle's refusal in 1765 to step aside and allow him, as new master of Newark, to become lord lieutenant of Nottinghamshire; he resented the duke's unwillingness to compel old friends, the Wilkinson family, to sell him some burgages. Ultimately Lincoln became a flunkey of Chatham's, begrudging his uncle the last years of his life. Equally inconsiderate was the action of "that insignificant *chitt*," Sir John Shelley, another nephew. In late 1766, having already at Newcastle's behest received a back salary from 1762, he accepted the post of treasurer of the household and moved promptly into the Chathamite camp. Newcastle soon dismissed him as a "tool to power" and considered refusing him support when he ran for reelection at East Retford.[79] By 1768 Shelley was thoroughly independent of the duke.

Not everyone who broke with the duke politically also severed the ties of friendship. His nephew Tommy Pelham, obliged by the need of feeding his large family to keep the court happy, found that Newcastle could understand his restricted options. George Onslow, financially straitened, also kept on friendly terms with his uncle, despite his refusal to break with the Chatham administration. But both, unlike Lincoln or Shelley, worked hard to humor the old man and to meet as many of his entreaties as were politically possible. Above all, they gave him attention. Others too—for not everyone turned away—shared their time with him. At the duke's request James West diligently informed him of political activities in London. Visits with Lord Grantham and Princess Amelia brought back memories of happier days. Robert Hay Drummond, archbishop of York, though not always politically dependable, mused on how a stay at Claremont reminded him of "the old way . . . there could not be a better."[80] Some others on the episcopal bench—Hume of Salisbury, Yonge of Norwich, Johnson of Worcester, and Trevor of Durham—still made appointments available to the duke and often graced the halls of Claremont; indeed, the frequency of their calls caused Newcastle to note wryly during a hiatus in 1768 that "all my bishops, & archbishops, are this moment gone." Cambridge University was also faithful. At the commencement in 1766 the duke was shown great consideration and with his speech brought tears to the eyes of some of his auditors. Finally, the people of Sussex were faithful. Newcastle's annual visits in 1766 and 1767 were as satisfying as earlier ones: "I never," he wrote from Halland in the latter year, "met with as much respect, affection, & regard in my whole life, as I have done this time."[81] Still, Newcastle was struck more by the treachery of those who deserted than the fidelity of those who held to the old friendship. His perspective was distorted by the defections, and in one of his bleaker moments he plaintively exclaimed—it captures the tone of his final years—"But, dear Caryl, almost everybody changes but you and I."[82]

Adding to the duke's uneasiness was the sorry condition of his exhausted estate. As recently as 1756 James Postlethwayte had reckoned that it would still bring him about £12,000 a year,[83] but the expenses associated with entertaining and politicking during the duke's second term at the Treasury coupled with continued gross mismanagement and the need to pay off enormous debts forced him to part with further revenue-producing properties in the succeeding years. By 1758 Lady Katherine Pelham feared for the ultimate inheritance of her daughters under Newcastle's inept stewardship and, with John Roberts's assistance, began to collect various family deeds for a thorough legal scrutiny of her family's rights. She was further alarmed when in 1760 the House of Lords in its function as a final appellate court determined that certain properties held by Newcastle and presumably destined for the ladies Pelham were in fact the property of Lord Vane. The pressure of creditors was also mounting, for the scarcity of money in time of war led to a reduced readiness in some quarters to tolerate ducal delays. In 1758 Newcastle gave up all his lands in Lewes to Lord Middleton as security for an earlier loan of £20,000; in 1760 he sold what was left of his Lincolnshire estate; and in the meanwhile he borrowed in a tight money market to pay off his final debt of £13,000 to Hoare's Bank.[84]

That final debt was a major embarrassment. The bank had taken to dunning the first lord of the Treasury and had sent Postlethwayte an extraordinary missive which not very obliquely hinted that it might drag Newcastle, despite his high office, into court: "You will force us into a very disagreeable pursuit of which these times will not allow of any hesitation in . . . We cannot possibly dispense with the severe Disappointment of such a payment."[85] Very privately in late 1759 the duke arranged to borrow from the Clive family, using Newcastle House itself as security. He retained the right to reside there, but he thereby inaugurated financial relations with the Clives that would end only after his death with the sale of Claremont to Lord Clive.[86] Simultaneously plans were formed for completing a settlement with Lord Lincoln whereby the duke's nephew, already eager for the influence land afforded, would lease the manor of Newark from his uncle. When the arrangement was implemented in 1761 it gave Lincoln that financial independence that he was soon to convert into a political independence, but it also seems to have brought the duke relief from importunate creditors and fearful remainder-men.

After his resignation in 1762 the duke's annual rental income was not much more than £6,000, with Clare Market providing about two-thirds of that sum and Sussex the remainder.[87] This was meager indeed when contrasted with the financial condition of his estate four and a half decades earlier. The familiar lament over ineffective management was again heard. And then came a startling change. Newcastle suddenly— and, for the first time, seriously—decided that reorganization was needed to increase estate revenue. He belatedly realized that the duchess, in the event of his death, was not well provided for. Because John Greening's incapacity was part of the cause of the difficulties, the duke agreed to appoint Abraham Baley, agent of Henry Pelham's heirs, as steward over his own Sussex estate and Clare Market. Baley set himself to cleaning out the Augean stables of Newcastle's muddled estate management, demanding back rents from tenants long accustomed to ducal mercy or negligence. Newcastle occasionally overrode Baley when the agent tried to squeeze too much out of suddenly beleaguered tenants, but in general he supported his new steward and as a consequence saw the estate properly run at last.[88]

If loneliness is the companion of old age, religious faith has often been its consolation. But for Newcastle retirement brought, apparently for the first time in his life, doubts about the tenets of the church and, correlatively, about his own worthiness in God's sight. The doctrinal doubts, fortunately, were merely concerns about the efficacy of communion if administered by an unworthy cleric and about the Anglican repudiation of transubstantiation when Christ Himself had stated that the bread was His body. The accompanying anxieties were a more fundamental problem, however, for the duke had long lived piously and charitably and yet he suddenly found himself fearful of his acceptability before God. It was a crisis, not of intellectual adherence to doctrine, but of personal relationship to the Father. John Hume, bishop of Oxford and then Salisbury and the duke's longtime friend, was the man to whom the duke turned for guidance, and Hume dealt skillfully with his troubled charge. He drew on the psychological wisdom of latitudinarianism by reminding the duke that right actions, even if performed with irremediable doubts, were pleasing to God. He argued that to fear one's unworthiness was in itself to demonstrate the baselessness of the fear. At the duke's request Hume sent him prayers, entreating God's aid in his efforts both to fulfil the divine will and to persevere in the faith despite the "manifold changes of the world." Hume also encouraged the duke in several unspecified penitential acts and supplied him with a reading list that included Addison, Tillotson, Sherlock, and Clark. It was a reflection of the duke's difficulties, however, that Archbishop Drummond had to caution him against going "too deep" in his readings, and Hume himself had to remind him that reading was an aid to religion, not a substitute for it.[89] Newcastle sought to hide his spiritual anxieties from everyone but his closest episcopal friends. Even his chaplain, Thomas Hurdis, appears not to have known of them. They seem, happily, to have abated somewhat in his final year of life, when the recovery from a severe illness reconferred on the duke "a lively and unfeigned belief of the truth of the holy gospel; and that our Saviour laid down his life to save sinners, by faith and repentance."[90]

In December 1767 Newcastle witnessed the collapse of all his hopes to bring Rockingham and Bedford together when the Bedford faction, despairing of Whig intransigence, came to terms with the administration instead. Newcastle's last political act, in November, was to warn Bedford, an unheeded admonition, about the direful consequences of Grenville's sniping at the Whigs in the Commons. Plagued by a persistent cold and by coughing and fever, he then traveled to Bath in December to join the duchess and seek aid from the waters. When no relief came he returned to Claremont. Shortly before Christmas his condition worsened, accompanied now by chills, a fluctuating fever, a fast pulse, and a severe pain in the side. Dr. Warren, the duchess's physician, treated him by bleeding. On 28 December the duchess was summoned from Bath; soon thereafter Tommy Pelham and Bishop Hume arrived. By the next day the duke's sickness was the topic of London gossip; Lord George Sackville called him "dangerously ill," and Lord Trevor described his situation as "precarious."[91] In fact, judging from the reported symptoms and the imperfect nature of his recovery, it is not unlikely that the duke suffered a stroke in December 1767. His memory and his ability to walk and write were impaired, but not his spirit. He surprised many by turning the corner early in January, and by the end of the month, though still bedridden, he was considered out of danger.

The nearly fatal illness and its train of disability meant that a political career begun in Queen Anne's day was over. Perhaps even before the full illness Newcastle had premonitions of failing strength, for while he was at Bath in December he told Admiral Keppel that he intended to leave politics and to ask his friends to accept Rockingham's leadership. In January, while he lay incapacitated, he authorized James West and Tommy Pelham to announce his retirement from politics and to add that he was "very desirous that all his friends should concur with my Lord Rockingham in such measures as he shall take, for the support of the Whig cause (which has always been the Duke of Newcastle's great object) and the true interest of the nation."[92] He did not thereafter fully honor his pledge to withdraw from the political wars, for he was soon peppering the party leaders with letters of complaint and advice. But he never again was asked to counsel the Whigs and found disability had cut him off from the one activity that had given a measure of fulfilment to his old age. Newcastle's last year was also his unhappiest.

His partial recovery was slow. Nausea frequently bothered his waking hours, and his pen remained so shaky that he decided to use Hurdis's hand even for letters to the duchess. In grimmer moments he would call himself "a poor old cripple."[93] Also demoralizing was the realization that his memory was slipping. Symptoms of mental confusion seem evident in his failure to recall the proper date of his wedding anniversary, an important annual event for the duke and duchess, and in his eagerness to talk, to the neglect of contemporary politics, of such distant triumphs as Sir Thomas Hanmer's preservation of the Protestant Succession in Queen Anne's reign.[94] Lameness and a tendency to tire quickly made entertaining, for the first time in the duke's life, too difficult; and only for close friends or special occasions, such as a reception for Denmark's Count Bernstorff, did the duke open the doors of Claremont. He lamented how his political friends neglected him, but this familiar complaint was now unjustified, for the very men he most reproached for ignoring him—Rockingham, Portland, and Richmond—were actually reasonably faithful in visiting and writing to their broken old colleague. In truth, the duke's illness served to promote rapprochements among several former friends. The duke prevailed upon Rockingham to resume the ties broken with James West, and he himself came to amicable understandings with Charles Yorke, the duke of Richmond, and Frederick Cornwallis, whose deference to the administration allowed him to succeed Secker at Canterbury in 1768. Yorke even agreed to handle the duke's legal affairs, though he was less diligent in fulfilling this promise than the duke wished.

In the early months of 1768, in preparation for the coming general election, Newcastle worked to protect his fading electoral influence in those constituencies still ready to hearken to him. He had been predicting a general election for over a year and had stated late in 1767 that "it is from the next Parliament that this country must be saved, and the cause of those who wish it best be supported."[95] Still, he was unprepared for it when it came, and found that the power of old was clearly gone. He now regretted the decision to confer the manor of Newark on Lord Lincoln, for Lincoln violated an oral promise to let his uncle continue to exercise the estate's political influence.[96] Thus, in Nottinghamshire and the boroughs of Nottingham and Newark Newcastle was impotent. Only at East Retford did he meet success in the county, and even there painfully. He contended with an opposition that ultimately drove old John White from the race; only one of the duke's candidates, John Offley, won. Affairs were not much more cheering in Sussex. At Lewes he stumbled badly, supporting three separate candidates in succession for one seat and finding his final choice trounced; again only one of his nominees, Thomas Hampden, won. At Seaford and Rye he was somewhat luckier, for neither borough deserted him completely. But even here his options were more limited than in the past, for he had no leverage in these boroughs beyond that created by memories of favors rendered in more influential days. Seaford reaccepted Lord Gage, but Newcastle could not prevent his old antagonist George Medley from winning the other seat. Rye elected Rose Fuller, the Sussex merchant with American ties. Only Boroughbridge and Aldborough remained, as always, peculiarly the duke's own.

At the outside, then, allowing for the difficulties in making firm judgments on these matters, Newcastle helped return seven members. Of these only three—James West and Nathaniel Cholmley at Boroughbridge and Aubrey Beauclerk at Aldborough—were in a clear and direct sense the duke's personal choices. Moreover, since the most obvious reduction in his electoral influence occurred in his (former) territorial boroughs rather than in the treasury boroughs holding faithful to him, it seems clear that had the duke of Grafton at the Treasury chosen to bring pressure upon Seaford and Rye, the number seven would have shrunk to five. People, it was clear, were not prepared to flock to a setting sun. And a briefly vindictive Newcastle, assailing the "base ingratitude" of the voters of Lewes,[97] threatened evictions of those who had voted against his will. Tommy Pelham and the duke of Richmond were able, however, to dissuade Newcastle from carrying out such a cruel and uncharacteristic act of vengeance.

In September 1768 Newcastle made the tiring trip to London so that he could take the oaths for the House of Lords. He had no intention of attending the coming session himself, but by submitting to the oaths he would enable himself to give his proxy to either Portland or Rockingham. Politics had not palled for the duke. In fact, Newcastle's disposition to see the ministers as agents of tyranny, governing by a "doctrine of force," lent an unwonted fervor to his political pronouncements during his year of disability. For the government's decision to require payments from the East India Company the duke had only contempt: "They think they have got an inexhaustible fund; & indeed they seem to have found one; which is, to take People's Property, without their consent." On the issue of Wilkes, who had recently returned from exile in France, the duke—despite the damage done to Newcastle House by a mob celebrating its hero—was forthright: "Wilkes's merit is being a friend to Liberty; and he has suffered for it; and, therefore, it is not an ill symptom that it should appear that this is a merit with the Nation." When the American colonists turned to rioting to protest new duties and when the government then spoke of subduing them with force, Newcastle urged the Whigs to stand fast by the principles of the Stamp Act repeal: "It is the same question."[98]

"It is the same question." These words capture the basic irrelevance of the duke's political vision in his final years. For what he saw as recurrences of old issues on which a Whig position was already defined were in fact manifestations of the reorientation already occurring in the political categories wherewith the British people would comprehend the problems of the last third of the eighteenth century. On the East India Company dispute the duke could see only a challenge to private property; he completely missed the emerging moral problem of Britain's duty toward subject peoples and was blind to the implications for state–company relations that this perspective afforded. In Wilkes he saw simply another man who would defend liberty against a power-hungry House of Commons; he had no inkling that within a year this man would raise doubts about the representative nature of the Commons and consequently about the legitimacy of Parliament itself as then constituted. As for the colonists, the duke continued to believe that tricks of management and accomodation rather than principled policy should govern Anglo-American relations. He failed to comprehend that many colonists had moved beyond debate about the right of Parliament to tax them to debate about the propriety and usefulness of looking to the British Parliament at all for guidance in American matters. In more respects than a simply geriatric one Newcastle's era was drawing to a close.

Early in November the duke returned to London, planning to make Newcastle House his principal winter residence. The duchess soon left for Bath. But then the duke's health suddenly collapsed: complaints of fatigue and a lack of appetite gave way to fainting spells and periods when he neither understood nor could direct the frightened Hurdis. Horace Walpole described the attack as "a stroke of a palsy."[99] Dr. Warren, at first sanguine, soon abandoned hope. Word was sent to the duchess that the end was imminent, and she had her attendant of many years, John Twells, instruct Hurdis that Lord Lincoln was to be forbidden access to her dying husband. Bishop Hume arrived at Newcastle House to give the duke the sacrament, and at 2:00 A.M. on 17 November 1768, at the age of seventy-five, the duke died. The duchess, confined at Bath by immobilizing pain, wept alone. "His behaviour," stated the *Annual Register*, "in his dying moments was perfectly calm, pious, and resigned."[100] Newcastle House, Claremont, Halland, and Bishopstone were promptly decked in mourning. The funeral was held at Laughton in Sussex, and Bishop Yonge presided at the final services, which were almost exclusively an affair for the local people of Laughton and East Hoathly, the duke's most loyal acquaintances. Newcastle's body was laid to rest near his brother's, beneath the chancel of the church at Laughton.[101] It was appropriate that a man so imbued with a love for Sussex should be particularly mourned by his Sussex neighbors and cradled in death by Sussex earth.

The duke's will, which had been drawn up the previous February, contained no surprises:[102] the Sussex estate, in accordance with previous arrangements, went to Tommy Pelham, who now succeeded to the title of Lord Pelham; the rest went to the duchess. The Nottinghamshire estate, having already been transferred to Lord Lincoln, was not mentioned, but Lincoln now inherited the ducal title created in 1756. Both portions of the inheritance were burdened with financial obligations, and the necessary dispersion of the duchess's inheritance as a way of meeting debts had been foreseen. It was Lord Clive, already by the terms of the loan of 1759 a major creditor of the duke's wealth, who bought Claremont for £25,000. He tore down the Vanbrugh home and replaced it, further up the hill, with the edifice of Lancelot Brown's that still stands today. Newcastle House was sold for £8,400, and the furnishings of Halland were sold at auction. Halland mansion itself was later razed by the new Lord Pelham and the ground where it stood converted to farm land. The duke's library was also put on the market. A key portion of the duke's will contained his instructions for handling the enormous collection of personal papers he had amassed in a lifetime of compulsive letter writing. They were to go first to the duchess, who was to remove and destroy any meriting that fate; they were then to be deposited with the owner of the Sussex estate. Ever bitter toward those she believed had betrayed her husband, the duchess refused the second Lord Hardwicke access to the papers. Over a century later, through the kindness of the earl of Chichester, they reached the British Museum. Within a short time of Newcastle's death the duchess moved to Twickenham Park. There she lived for almost six years, and there on 28 July 1776 she died. In her will she provided for Twells, Hurdis, and a daughter of Bishop Hume's. She was buried next to her husband beneath the Laughton church. Devoted in life, they lie together in eternity.

Notes

PREFACE

1. Namier's two major works are *England in the Age of the American Revolution* (2d ed., 1963), and *The Structure of Politics at the Accession of George III* (2d ed., 1963). The essays collected in *Crossroads of Power: Essays on Eighteenth-Century England* (1962) are also important. There are many good treatments of Namier's thought and influence. Among them is one by his closest and ablest disciple, John Brooke, "Namier and Namierism," *Studies in the Philosophy of History: Selected Essays from "History and Theory"*, ed. George H. Nadel (1965).

2. Geoffrey Holmes, *British Politics in the Age of Anne* (1967); Isaac Kramnick, *Bolingbroke and His Circle: The Politics of Nostalgia in the Age of Walpole* (1968); J. H. Plumb, *The Origins of Political Stability in England, 1675–1725* (1967).

3. James, Earl Waldegrave, *Memoirs from 1754 to 1758* (1821); William Coxe, *Memoirs of the Administration of the Right Honourable Henry Pelham* (2 vols., 1829); Evan Charteris, *William Augustus, Duke of Cumberland: His Early Life and Times (1721–1748)* (1913); Bernhard Knollenberg, *Origin of the American Revolution: 1759–1766* (1960); Stebelton Nulle, *Thomas Pelham-Holles, Duke of Newcastle: His Early Political Career, 1693–1724* (1931).

4. John, Lord Hervey, *Some Materials toward Memoirs of the Reign of King George II*, ed. Romney Sedgwick (3 vols., 1931); Horace Walpole, *Memoirs of the Reign of King George II*, ed. Lord Holland (3 vols., 1847); Thomas Babington Macaulay, "Horace Walpole," in *Critical and Historical Essays* (1900); Namier, *England*; Basil Williams, *Carteret and Newcastle: A Contrast in Contemporaries* (2d ed., 1966).

5. Ulrich B. Philips, *Life and Labor in the Old South* (1929), p. vii.

CHAPTER 1

1. See Stebelton H. Nulle, *Newcastle*, pp. 1–8.
2. *Sussex County Magazine*, 2 (1928): 272.
3. Add. MSS 33074, fol. 153.
4. Thus called by his father in 1711 (Add. MSS 33064, fol. 1).
5. Gravestones of Elizabeth Pelham and Lady Grace in Laughton parish church.
6. G. F. R. Barker and A. H. Stenning, eds., *The Record of Old Westministers*, 1 (1928): 471; J. Venn and J. A. Venn, comps., *Alumni Cantabrigiensis* (1922–27), Part I, Vol. 3; John Nichols, *Literary Anecdotes of the Eighteenth Century* (1812–15), 5: 87.
7. Add. MSS 33065, fols. 272–74, 449.
8. Stowe MSS 247, fol. 165.
9. O. R. F. Davies, "The Wealth and Influence of John Holles, Duke of Newcastle, 1694–1711," *Renaissance and Modern Studies* 9 (1965): 22–46.
10. H.M.C. *House of Lords*, 10: 57.

11. A. S. Turberville, *A History of Welbeck Abbey and Its Owners* (1938–39), 1: 225–26, 303–27.

12. Nulle, *Newcastle,* p. 17; *Annual Register, 1768,* 11: 187.

13. Davies, "Wealth and Influence," pp. 44–46; Add. MSS 33065, fols. 272–74.

14. Add. MSS 33073, fol. 3.

15. [John Macky], *A Journey through England* (1714), p. 122.

16. *Sussex Archaeological Collections* 37 (1890): 69–70, 75; Frederick Jones, "Random Notes on Halland Park," *Sussex County Magazine* 4 (1930): 374–75; Viscountess Wolseley, *Some of the Smaller Manor Houses of Sussex* (1925), pp. 111–12; Add. MSS 33064, fols. 257–59.

17. Add. MSS 33077, fol. 154; Add. MSS 33076, fols. 77, 180. See also J. Summerson, *Architecture in Britain, 1530–1830* (1953), pp. 165–72; Edward Wedlake Brayley, *A Topographical History of Surrey,* n.d. 2: 440–50.

18. Rae Blanchard, ed., *The Correspondence of Richard Steele* (1941), p. 526; Abel Boyer, *The Political State of Great Britian, 1719–40,* 10: 323–24.

19. Add. MSS 5832, fol. 114.

20. Nulle, *Newcastle,* p. 75; Thomas Bailey, *Annals of Nottinghamshire* (1853), 3: 20; W. Matthews, ed., *The Diary of Dudley Ryder, 1715–16* (1939), p. 255.

21. H.M.C. *Stuart,* 2: 122–24.

22. Nulle, *Newcastle,* p. 85.

23. Add. MSS 33064, fols. 81–82.

24. Ibid. fols. 114–15.

25. Ibid. fol. 112; David Green, *Sarah Duchess of Marlborough* (1967), p. 209.

26. Laurence Whistler, *Sir John Vanbrugh: Architect and Dramatist, 1664–1726* (1934), p. 208.

CHAPTER 2

1. P.R.O., L.C. 5/157, fol. 47; D. H. Stevens, *Party Politics and English Journalism, 1702–1742* (1916), p. 102; Blanchard, *Steele Correspondence,* p. 499.

2. P.R.O., L.C. 5/157, fol. 180; *The Journals of the House of Lords,* 21: 50, 67, 102, 143.

3. Add. MSS 32686, fol. 269.

4. Ibid. fol. 13; Blanchard, *Steele Correspondence,* pp. 98, 498.

5. On the dispute, see John Loftis, *The Politics of Drama in Augustan England* (1963), pp. 72–75; Calhoun Winton, *Sir Richard Steele, M.P. The Later Career* (1970), pp. 27–28, 142–47, 169–70; Richard Hindry Barker, *Mr Cibber of Drury Lane* (1939), pp. 120–22; Blanchard, *Steele Correspondence,* pp. 143–59; P.R.O., L.C. 5/157, L.C. 7/3; Add. MSS 32685, fols. 27–46.

6. Barker, *Mr Cibber,* p. 122.

7. P.R.O., L.C. 7/3, fol. 57.

8. Ibid. fols. 63–64, 71.

9. Philip C. Yorke, *The Life and Correspondence of Philip Yorke, Earl of Hardwicke, Lord High Chancellor of Great Britain* (1913), 3: 396.

10. On the christening episode, see H.M.C. *Portland,* 5: 541–46; H.M.C. *Polwarth,*

1: 404; Add. MSS 35838, fols. 401, 407; Egerton MSS 921, fols. 84–85; Wolfgang Michael, *England under George I,* trans. A. MacGregor and G.E. MacGregor (1939), 2: 26.

11. H.M.C. *Stuart,* 5: 273–74.

12. Add. MSS 32686, fol. 149.

13. Ibid., fols. 137, 151–53.

14. H.L.R.O., South Sea Papers, Box 157.

15. H.L.R.O., Parchment Collection, B, 58, 61; Stowe MSS 247, fols. 164–66.

16. Add. MSS 9149, fol. 169; Add. MSS 32686, fol. 168.

17. H.M.C. *Portland,* 5: 616.

18. Nulle, *Newcastle,* p. 135.

19. Add. MSS 32686, fol. 358.

20. Stowe MSS 251, fol. 23.

21. Add. MSS 32686, fol. 316.

22. Ibid., fol. 145.

23. Stowe MSS 251, fol. 17.

24. Nulle, *Newcastle,* p. 165. Cf. John M. Beattie, *The English Court in the Reign of George I* (1967), p. 209; Namier, *Structure,* p. 192; Mark Thomson, *The Secretaries of State, 1681–1782* (1932), pp. 147–48.

25. Basil Williams, *Carteret and Newcastle,* p. 61.

26. Add. MSS, 32686, fols. 155–56.

27. For Yorkshire, see Sir Thomas Lawson-Tancred, *Records of a Yorkshire Manor* (1937); Romney Sedgwick, *The History of Parliament: The House of Commons, 1715–1754,* 2 vols. (1970).

28. For Nottinghamshire, see Sedgwick, *Parliament;* John Henry Moses, "Elections and Electioneering in the Constitutencies of Nottinghamshire, 1702–1832," 2 vols. (University of Nottingham Ph.D. thesis, 1965).

29. Stowe MSS 247, fols. 164–66.

30. Moses, *Elections,* 1: 322.

31. For Sussex, see Lewis P. Curtis, *Chichester Towers* (1966); G. H. Nadel, "The Sussex Election of 1741," *Sussex Archaeological Collections* 91 (1953): 84–124; Sedgwick, *Parliament.*

32. Add. MSS 32698, fol. 82.

33. Sedgwick, *Parliament,* 1: 366.

34. Add. MSS 33073, fols. 9–18.

35. Sir Lewis Namier was the first to calculate the proper range of Newcastle's influence.

36. Add. MSS 32686, fols. 151–53.

37. Add. MSS 33073, fol. 16.

38. Kathleen M. Lynch, *Jacob Tonson Kit-Cat Publisher* (1971), p. 159.

39. P.R.O., S.P. 36/39, fols. 170–71.

40. P.R.O., S.P. 36/43, fols. 2–3.

41. Lesley Lewis, *Connoisseurs and Secret Agents in Eighteenth-Century Rome* (1961), p. 75.

42. Add. MSS 33073, fols. 21–22, 94–95; P.R.O., S.P. 36/41, fol. 31.

43. Add. MSS 33064, fols. 127, 129; Add. MSS 32685, fol. 10; H.M.C. *Portland,* 5: 535.

44. Add. MSS 33065, fol. 273. See John Brooke, *The Chatham Administration, 1766–1768* (1956), p. 52.

45. Add. MSS 33065, fol. 273. Although some sources assert that the duke transferred part or all of his lucrative Lincolnshire estate to Pelham, there appears to be no evidence of such a transfer (Nottingham University, Newcastle [Clumber] MSS, NeD 113, NeD 117).

46. *Sussex Archaeological Collections* 37 (1890): 73; John Wilkes, *A Whig in Power: The Political Career of Henry Pelham* (1964), p. 4.

47. Nott. Univ., N(C) MSS, NeC 4273; Add. MSS 33158, fols. 47–50.

48. Nott. Univ., N(C) MSS, NeD 95; Sussex Archaeological Society, Lewes, P 168, P 174, P 175, P 180, P 186, P 187; Add. MSS 33064, fol. 351.

49. Add. MSS 33320, fols. 1–20; Nott. Univ., N(C) MSS, NeA 147.

50. Add. MSS 33039, fols. 309–10; Add. MSS 33065, fol. 425.

51. Plumb, *Origins,* p. 178.

52. Cambridge University, Cholmondeley (Houghton) MSS, Correspondence 1199.

53. P.R.O., S.P. 35/49, passim; P.R.O., S.P. 36/5, fols. 15–16.

54. Add. MSS 32742, fol. 170.

55. P.R.O., S.P. 43/78, n.f. (Delafaye to Tilson, 4 July 1729). See also P.R.O., S.P. 36/12, fol. 55; Peter, Lord King, *Notes of Domestic and Foreign Affairs,* printed in idem, *The Life of John Locke* (1830), 2: 88.

56. H. R. Duff, ed., *Culloden Papers . . . 1625 to 1748* (1815), p. 94.

57. Duff, *Culloden Papers,* p. 107; Duncan Warrand, ed., *More Culloden Papers* (1923–30), 2: 323; P.R.O., S.P. 54/16, fol. 345. See Patrick W. Riley, *The English Ministers and Scotland, 1707–1727* (1964), pp. 270–78.

58. Add. MSS 32738, fols. 178–79.

59. Add. MSS 32742, fols. 290–300; Add. MSS 32743, fols. 183–87; *Cobbett's Parliamentary History of England* (1811)8: 509–10.

60. Add. MSS 32687, fols. 155–59; Add. MSS 32748, fol. 144; Add. MSS 19332, fol. 11.

61. Add. MSS 32750, fols. 216–18.

62. P.R.O., S.P. 94/97, fol. 46; Add. MSS 32746, fols. 71–85, 129–42.

63. *Selection from the Papers of the Earl of Marchmont* (1831), 2: 412–13.

64. J. H. Plumb, *Sir Robert Walpole* (1961), 2: 162.

65. Add. MSS 32687, fol. 215.

66. H.M.C. *Carlisle,* p. 52.

67. For the election of 1727, see Stebelton H. Nulle, "The Duke of Newcastle and the Election of 1727," *The Journal of Modern History* 9 (1937): 1–22; Sedgwick, *Parliament.*

68. Add. MSS 33073, fols. 31–56.

69. William Coxe, *Memoirs of the Life and Administration of Sir Robert Walpole, Earl of Orford* (1798), 2: 518.

70. Coxe, *Robert Walpole,* 2: 641.

71. L. G. Wickham Legg, ed., *British Diplomatic Instructions 1689–1789* (1930), 6: 48–49.

72. Coxe, *Robert Walpole*, 2: 641.

73. Plumb, *Walpole*, 2: 198.

74. Coxe, *Robert Walpole*, 2: 623.

75. Ibid., 2: 676.

76. Ibid., 2: 689–90.

CHAPTER 3

1. Legg, *Instructions*, 6: 86.

2. Ibid., 6: 92–93.

3. Coxe, *Robert Walpole*, 3: 112.

4. Add. MSS 32772, fol. 179.

5. Add. MSS 32769, fol. 143.

6. Legg, *Instructions*, 6: 98.

7. H.M.C. *Egmont Diary*, 1: 82; Add. MSS 33050, fols. 124–34.

8. Earl of Ilchester, ed., *Lord Hervey and His Friends 1726–38* (1950), p. 113.

9. Add. MSS 33073, fol. 66.

10. On the opposition, see Archibald S. Foord, *His Majesty's Opposition, 1714–1830* (1964); Kramnick, *Bolingbroke*; Sedgwick, *Parliament*, 1.

11. Add. MSS 27732, fols. 95, 125–26.

12. Camb. Univ., C(H) Correspondence 1990.

13. Cobbett, *History*, 8: 1238–40; Legg, *Instructions*, 6: 114, 118–20.

14. H.M.C. *Lonsdale*, p. 125.

15. Sir Richard Lodge, "English Neutrality in the War of the Polish Succession," *Transactions of the Royal Historical Society*, 4th ser. 14 (1931): 141–73.

16. Legg, *Instructions*, 6: 126.

17. On the election, see Basil Williams, "The Duke of Newcastle and the Election of 1734," *The English Historical Review* 12 (1897): 448–88; Sedgwick, *Parliament*.

18. Add. MSS 32688, fols. 98, 121, 158, 166, 212; Add. MSS 33058, fols. 343–44; Curtis, *Chichester Towers*, p. 42; *Sussex Notes and Queries*, (1948–49) 12: 86–87.

19. Add. MSS 27733, fol. 63; Add. MSS 33073, fol. 80.

20. Coxe, *Robert Walpole*, 3: 168; Add. MSS 27733, fol. 63.

21. Add. MSS 27733, fol. 102.

22. Coxe, *Robert Walpole*, 3: 168.

23. Legg, *Instructions*, 6: 115, 127, 163.

24. Camb. Univ., C(H) Corr. 2421; Add. MSS 32785, fol. 407.

25. Add. MSS 32787, fol. 368.

26. Lodge, "Neutrality, " p. 165.

27. Hervey, *Memoirs*, 2: 470.

28. Coxe, *Robert Walpole*, 3: 424; Hervey, *Memoirs*, 3: 731, 829–31; G. Menary, *The Life and Letters of Duncan Forbes of Culloden* (1936), p. 109.

29. Add. MSS 35870, fols. 18–36.

30. Add. MSS 35406, fol. 165.

31. T. F. J. Kendrick, "Sir Robert Walpole, the Old Whigs and the Bishops, 1733–1736: A Study in Eighteenth-Century Party Politics," *The Historical Journal* 11(1968): 421–45.

32. H.M.C. *Portland*, 5: 571; H.M.C. *Egmont Diary*, 2: 269; Edmund Calamy, *An Historical Account of My Own Life* (1829), 2: 319.

33. Add. MSS 32686, fol. 316.

34. P.R.O., S.P. 36/41, passim.

35. Coxe, *Robert Walpole*, 3: 209.

36. Yorke, *Hardwicke*, 3: 156.

37. Add. MSS 35406, fol. 64.

38. Hervey, *Memoirs*, 3: 732–33.

39. Add. MSS 32690, fols. 445–46.

40. Add. MSS 33065, fol. 402.

41. Horace Walpole, *Memoirs*, 3: 254.

42. Add. MSS 32686, fol. 251.

43. Yorke, *Hardwicke*, 1: 288.

44. Ibid., p. 231.

45. *The Yale Edition of Horace Walpole's Correspondence*, ed. W.S. Lewis (1937–), 9: 323; P.R.O., T. 29/32, fol. 225.

46. Hervey, *Memoirs*, 1: 209; Norman Sykes, *Church and State in England in the Eighteenth Century* (1934), p. 168.

47. Florence Maris Turner, ed., *The Diary of Thomas Turner of East Hoathly (1754–1765)* (1925), pp. 41–42; W. Shenstone, *Letters*, ed. M. Williams (1939), p. 140; Romney Sedgwick, "The Duke of Newcastle's Cook," *History Today* 5(1955): 308–16.

48. Add. MSS 35406, fol. 50.

49. Add. MSS 32797, fols. 246–54; Harold W. V. Temperley, "The Causes of the War of Jenkins' Ear, 1739," *T.R.H.S.*, 3d ser. 3 (1909): 220.

50. Add. MSS 32796, fols. 94–99.

51. Add. MSS 32797, fols. 34–36.

52. Temperley, "Causes," p. 213 n.

53. Ibid., pp. 219–20.

54. Add. MSS 32797, fols. 356–58.

55. Jean Oliva McLachlan, *Trade and Peace with Old Spain, 1667–1750: A Study of the Influence of Commerce on Anglo-Spanish Diplomacy in the First Half of the Eighteenth Century* (1940), p. 107.

56. Add. MSS 32798, fol. 119.

57. Add. MSS 32799, fol. 39.

58. Ibid., fol. 211.

59. Add. MSS 32800, fol. 77.

60. Add. MSS 32799, fol. 230.

61. Add. MSS 32800, fols. 72–79; L. G. Wickham Legg, "Newcastle and the Counter Orders to Admiral Haddock, March 1739," *E.H.R.* 46 (1931): 272–74.

62. Add. MSS 32800, fol. 294.

63. Add. MSS 35406, fol. 111.

64. Add. MSS 32801, fol. 67.

65. See three excellent studies: McLachlan, *Trade and Peace*; Temperley, "Causes;"

Richard Pares, *War and Trade in the West Indies, 1739–1763* (1936).

66. Add. MSS 32842, fol. 153.

CHAPTER 4

1. Add. MSS 28132, fols. 83, 157; cf. Romney Sedgwick, "The Inner Cabinet, 1739–41," *E.H.R.* 34 (1919): 290–302; Plumb, *Origins*, p. 179.

2. Hervey, *Memoirs*, 3: 939–40; Add. MSS 28132, fol. 82.

3. Add. MSS 32694, passim.

4. Yorke, *Hardwicke*, 1: 225.

5. Add. MSS 32692, fol. 450; Yorke, *Hardwicke*, 1: 239.

6. H.M.C. *Egmont Diary*, 3: 141.

7. Add. MSS 32695, fols. 47, 172; Earl of March, A *Duke and His Friends: The Life and Letters of the Second Duke of Richmond* (1911), 1: 345.

8. Add. MSS 32695, fol. 47.

9. Yorke, *Hardwicke*, 1: 248–51.

10. Hervey, *Memoirs*, 3: 733–34.

11. Cobbett, *History*, 11: 820.

12. Ibid., pp. 769, 1017; 12: 333.

13. Yorke, *Hardwicke*, 1: 202.

14. Add. MSS 33034, fol. 10; cf. Cobbett, *History*, 12: 1096–1223.

15. For the following, see Curtis, *Chichester Towers;* Nadel, "Election," 84–124; Sedgwick, *Parliament;* Clarence Perkins, "Electioneering in Eighteenth Century England," *The Quarterly Journal of the University of North Dakota* 13 (1923): 103–24.

16. Add. MSS 32694, fols. 211–15.

17. Add. MSS 35876, fols. 138–39; cf. John B. Owen, *The Rise of the Pelhams* (1957), p. 7; Sedgwick, *Parliament*, 1: 47.

18. Add. MSS 32696, fol. 31; Add. MSS 32964, passim.

19. Add. MSS 32967, fol. 215; Add. MSS 32993, fol. 154.

20. Yorke, *Hardwicke*, 1: 272.

21. William Coxe, *Memoirs of the Administration of the Right Honourable Henry Pelham* (1829), 1: 22.

22. Add. MSS 32697, fol. 426.

23. Add. MSS 35407, fols. 125–34.

24. Curtis, *Chichester Towers*, p. 95; Add. MSS 32699, fol. 14.

25. Add. MSS 33073, fol. 207.

26. See Add. MSS 18915, fols. 28–30; Owen, *Rise*, pp. 88–112; Coxe, *Robert Walpole*, 1: 701–702; Sedgwick, *Parliament*, 1: 51–53; George Colman, ed., *Posthumous Letters from Various Celebrated Men; addressed to Francis Colman and George Colman the Elder* (1820), pp. 76–83; *Lives of Dr. Edward Pocock, . . . Dr. Zachary Pearce, . . . Dr. Thomas Newton, . . . Rev. Philip Skelton*, ed. Alexander Chalmers (1816), 1: 393–94; 2: 47–58.

27. William Coxe, *Memoirs of Horatio, Lord Walpole* (1808), 2: 58.

28. Add. MSS 32943, fol. 224.

29. Yorke, *Hardwicke*, 1: 303–305.

30. Add. MSS 32701, fols. 13–15.

31. Coxe, *Horatio, Lord Walpole*, 2: 53–54.

32. Add. MSS 32701, fols. 75–76.

33. Add. MSS 35407, fol. 280.

34. Add. MSS 35337, fol. 25.

35. Add. MSS 32700, fol. 314.

36. Add. MSS 5832, fol. 83.

37. Yorke, *Hardwicke*, 1: 347–48.

38. Ibid., p. 346.

39. Ibid., pp. 366–67.

40. H.M.C. *Denbigh*, 5: 201.

41. Add. MSS 33058, fols. 343–44; Add. MSS 33157, passim; Sussex Archaeological Society, A 436–A 438.

42. Sussex Archaeological Society P 205, P 205*.

43. Add. MSS 33320, fols. 174–205.

44. Add. MSS 33173, fols. 365–72, 397–98.

45. Add. MSS 33065, fols. 142–43.

46. Hoare's Bank, Fleet Street, Ledger O; Nott. Univ., N(C) MSS NeD 122, NeD 132; Add. MSS 33157, passim; Add. MSS 33065, fols. 272–74.

47. Add. MSS 35407, fols. 13–16.

48. Add. MSS 33073, fol. 129; John Nichols, *Illustrations of the Literary History of the Eighteenth Century* (1817–58), 4: 501.

49. Nott. Univ., N(C) MSS NeD 117, 122, 124, 132; Sussex Archaeological Society, P 217, P 437; Add. MSS 33065, fols. 401–403; Add. MSS 33066, fols. 258–66; Add. MSS 33322, fols. 36, 37, 53, 57–70.

50. Nott. Univ., N(C) MSS NeD 128, 132; NeC 4406; Add. MSS 32703, fols. 363–66; Add. MSS 32736, fols. 168–69; Add. MSS 33066, fols. 16–19.

51. H.M.C. *Lonsdale*, 7: 125.

52. *Walpole Correspondence*, 18: 552; Sir Richard Lodge, ed., *Private Correspondence of Chesterfield and Newcastle, 1744–1746* (1930), p. 15.

53. Charteris, *Cumberland*, 1: 219.

54. Add. MSS 33058, fol. 458.

55. Yorke, *Hardwicke*, 1: 461, 481–82.

56. Add. MSS 32705, fol. 423.

57. H.M.C. *First Report and Appendix*, p. 115; Yorke, *Hardwicke*, 1: 635–36.

58. Yorke, *Hardwicke*, 1: 499–504; Foord, *Opposition*, pp. 259–60; Owen, *Rise*, pp. 293–97.

59. *Marchmont Papers*, 1: 262–63.

60. Yorke, *Hardwicke*, 1: 508.

61. Ibid., 3: 412.

62. Cobbett, *History*, 8: 1061.

63. Ibid., 12: 1148; 11: 514; 8: 992.

64. Add. MSS 32990, fol. 53.

65. Boyer, *Political State*, 10: 323–24; cf. Add. MSS 33034, fol. 10.

66. Plumb, *Origins*, p. 95; Add. MSS 32919, fol. 287; Betty Kemp, *Sir Francis Dashwood: An Eighteenth-Century Independent* (1967), p. 39; Clayton Roberts, *The Growth of Responsible Government in Stuart England* (1966), p. 20.

67. Yorke, *Hardwicke*, 1: 391; Lodge, *Newcastle-Chesterfield Correspondence*, p. 69.

68. Eg 1718, fol. 16.

69. Warrand, *More Culloden Papers*, 5: 37–38.

70. H.M.C. *Various*, 8: 171.

71. For the following, see Owen, *Rise*, pp. 311–17; Sedgwick, *Parliament*.

72. Add. MSS 32712, fol. 24.

73. Add. MSS 35337, fol. 113.

74. Coxe, *Pelham*, 1: 406.

75. Pieter Geyl, "Holland and England during the War of the Austrian Succession," *History*, n.s., 10(1925–26): 51.

76. Add. MSS 32810, fol. 162.

77. *Marchmont Papers*, 1: 223, 271.

78. Earl of Chesterfield, "An Apology for a Late Resignation," printed in *The Letters and Works of Philip Dormer Stanhope, Earl of Chesterfield*, ed. Lord Mahon (1853), 5: 58–86.

79. *Correspondence of John, Fourth Duke of Bedford*, ed. Lord John Russell (1842–46), 1: 246.

80. Charteris, *Cumberland*, 1: 337–38.

81. *Walpole Correspondence*, 19: 464.

82. Sir Richard Lodge, *Studies in Eighteenth-Century Diplomacy, 1740–1748* (1930), p. 316.

83. Ibid., p. 239.

84. Add. MSS 33064, fol. 387; Add. MSS 33073, fol. 242; *Walpole Correspondence*, 19: 484, 490, 495; H.M.C. *Denbigh*, 5: 164; Yorke, *Hardwicke*, 1: 656–57; Bonamy Dobree, ed., *The Letters of Philip Dormer Stanhope 4th Earl of Chesterfield* (1932), 3: 1162.

85. Walther Mediger, *Moskaus Weg nach Europa: der Aufstieg Russlands zum europäischen Machtstaat im Zeitalter Friedrichs des Grossen* (1952), pp. 437–38.

86. Lodge, *Studies*, p. 360n.

87. Ibid., p. 392.

88. Coxe, *Pelham*, 2: 315.

89. Earl of Albemarle, ed., *Memoirs of the Marquis of Rockingham and His Contemporaries* (1852), 1: 86.

90. Coxe, *Pelham*, 2: 325.

91. Cobbett, *History*, 12: 1158.

92. Coxe, *Pelham*, 1: 339.

93. Yorke, *Hardwicke*, 1: 641.

94. Add. MSS 32828, fol. 66.

95. Sir Richard Lodge, "The Continental Policy of Great Britain, 1740–60," *History*, n.s., 16 (1931–32): 301.

CHAPTER 5

1. Yorke, *Hardwicke*, 2: 173.

2. Ibid., 1: 679.

3. Frederick Manning, "The Duke of Newcastle and the West Indies: A Study in the Colonial and Diplomatic Policies of the Secretary of State for the Southern Department 1713–1754" (Ph.D. diss., Yale University, 1925), pp. 506–07.

4. Add. MSS 32817, fol. 25.

5. Coxe, *Pelham*, 2: 97.

6. J. F. Chance, *The Alliance of Hanover* (1923), p. 632.

7. Add. MSS 32822, fol. 239.

8. Add. MSS 32722, fol. 37; *Marchmont Papers*, 2: 388–89.

9. Yorke, *Hardwicke*, 2: 94–99.

10. Add. MSS 33074, fols. 60–61.

11. D. A. Winstanley, *The University of Cambridge in the 18th Century* (1922), p. 54; G. E. Mingay, *English Landed Society in the Eighteenth Century* (1963), p. 135.

12. Aubrey N. Newman, ed., "Leicester House Politics, 1750–60, from the Papers of John, Second Earl of Egmont," *Camden Miscellany* 23 (n.d.): 193–94.

13. *The Political Journal of George Bubb Dodington*, ed. John Carswell and Lewis Dralle (1965), pp. 116–18; Walpole, *George II*, 1: 114–56.

14. Coxe, *Pelham*, 2: 387, 380.

15. Add. MSS 33074, fols. 78–79; H.M.C. *Stopford-Sackville*, 1: 180.

16. Add. MSS 32829, fol. 113.

17. Haus-, Hof- und Staatsarchiv, Vienna, England, Berichte, fasc. 142; Walpole, *George II*, 1: 247.

18. Add. MSS 32726, fol. 409.

19. Add. MSS 35486, fol. 102.

20. Add. MSS 32727, fols. 204–06, 258–59.

21. Add. MSS 32837, fols. 174–79.

22. Add. MSS 32838, fol. 142.

23. Coxe, *Pelham*, 2: 469–82.

24. See D. B. Horn, "The Origins of the Proposed Election of a King of the Romans," *E.H.R.* 42 (1927): 361–70; Reed Browning, "The Duke of Newcastle and the Imperial Election Plan, 1749–1754," *The Journal of British Studies* 7 (1967): 28–47; idem, "The British Orientation of Austrian Foreign Policy, 1749–1754," *Central European History* 1 (1968): 299–323.

25. Coxe, *Pelham*, 2: 345–46.

26. Add. MSS 32906, fol. 387.

27. *Dodington Journal*, p. 281.

28. John Holliday, *The Life of William Late Earl of Mansfield* (1797), p. 89; see R. J. Robson, *The Oxfordshire Election of 1754: A Study in the Interplay of City, County and University Politics* (1949), p. 78 for dating. On Newcastle and patronage, see D. G. Barnes, "The Duke of Newcastle, Ecclesiastical Minister, 1724–1754," *Pacific Historical Review* 3 (1934): 164–91; M. Bateson, "Clerical Preferment under the Duke of Newcastle," *E.H.R.* 7 (1892): 685–96; Philip Haffenden, "Colonial Appointments and Patronage under the Duke of Newcastle, 1724–1739," *E.H.R.* 78 (1963): 417–35; James A. Henretta, *"Salutary Neglect"; Colonial Administration under the Duke of Newcastle* (1972); Stanley Nider Katz, *Newcastle's New York: Anglo-American Politics 1732–1753* (1968); Norman Sykes, "The Duke of Newcastle as Ecclesiastical Minister," *E.H.R.* 57 (1942): 59–89; Winstanley, *Cambridge*.

29. Add. MSS 27732, fol. 23; Add. MSS 27733, fols. 144–47; Add. MSS 27735, fols. 187–88.

30. W. R. Ward, "Some Eighteenth-Century Civil Servants: The English Revenue Commissioners, 1754–98," *E.H.R.* 70 (1955): 29.

31. Add. MSS 32921, fol. 352.

32. Archibald Ballantyne, *Lord Carteret: A Political Biography, 1690–1763* (1883), p. 115.

33. Quoted in Norman Ravitch, *Sword and Mitre: Government and Episcopate in France and England in the Age of Aristocracy* (1966), p. 115n.

34. Add. MSS 32722, fol. 6.

35. Chalmers, *Lives*, 2: 100.

36. Add. MSS 32721, fol. 158; Mahon, *Chesterfield Letters*, 2: 464; Walpole, *George II*, 1: 344.

37. Robson, *Oxfordshire Election*, p. 90.

38. Add. MSS 32736, fols. 168–69; Add. MSS 33066, fols. 29, 203, 341–47; Add. MSS 33074, fols. 49–50, 124–25; Nott. Univ., N(C) MSS NeD 132, fol. 20.

39. Add. MSS 33074, fols. 112–13.

40. Nott. Univ., N(C) MSS NeC 4409; Sussex Archaeological Society, P 438.

41. Add. MSS 33066, fols. 341–47.

42. *Marchmont Papers*, 1: 253.

43. Richard Pares, *King George III and the Politicians* (1953), p. 177; Coxe, *Pelham*, 1: 485–86.

CHAPTER 6

1. H.M.C. *8th Report*, App. 221; *Anecdotes of the Life of the Right Honourable William Pitt, Earl of Chatham*, ed. John Almon (1793), 1: 258.

2. Yorke, *Hardwicke*, 2: 191–92.

3. Walpole, *George II*, 1: 379.

4. Yorke, *Hardwicke*, 2: 206; Walpole, *George II*, 1: 379–80; Earl Waldegrave, *Memoirs*, p. 24.

5. Earl of Ilchester, *Henry Fox, First Lord Holland: His Family and Relations* (1920), 1: 194.

6. Yorke, *Hardwicke*, 2: 208.

7. George W. Pilcher, ed., *The Reverend Samuel Davies Abroad: The Diary of a Journey to England and Scotland, 1753–1755* (1967), p. 83.

8. Add. MSS 32734, fol. 237; Add. MSS 32995, fols. 63–67.

9. *Dodington Journal*, pp. 259–61.

10. *Memoirs and Correspondence of George, Lord Lyttelton from 1734–1773*, ed. Robert Phillimore (1845), 2: 451.

11. *Correspondence of William Pitt, Earl of Chatham*, eds. W. S. Taylor and J. H. Pringle (1838–40), 2: 467.

12. P.R.O., T 1/380, fol. 154.

13. Add. MSS 33075, fol. 4; Add. MSS 33038, fol. 300; Add. MSS 33039, fols. 309–10.

14. Sedgwick, *Parliament*, 2: 119. For an analysis of Newcastle's role at the Treasury, see Reed Browning, "The Duke of Newcastle and the Financing of the Seven Years' War," *The Journal of Economic History* 31 (1971): 344–77.

15. Sir Lewis Namier and John Brooke, *The History of Parliament: The House of Commons, 1754–1790* (1964), 1: 62. For this election, see Namier, *Structure*, passim.

16. Add. MSS 32735, fol. 597.

17. Add. MSS 32850, fol. 218.

18. Add. MSS 32737, fol. 5.

19. Add. MSS 32995, fols. 299–302; P.R.O., T 27/27, fols. 118–39; P.R.O., T 29/32, fol. 205; P.R.O., T 11/25, fol. 167.

20. Quoted in L.H. Gipson, "British Diplomacy in the Light of Anglo-Spanish New World Issues 1750–57," *The American Historical Review* 51 (1945–46): 639.

21. Add. MSS 32995, fol. 309.

22. Add. MSS 32736, fol. 432.

23. Add. MSS 32995, fol. 319.

24. Add. MSS 32736, fol. 591.

25. Add. MSS 33075, fol. 17.

26. Julian S. Corbett, *England in the Seven Years' War; A Study in Combined Strategy* (1907), 1: 10.

27. *Dodington Journal*, p. 292.

28. Sir Lewis Namier, *England*, p. 73.

29. Yorke, *Hardwicke*, 2: 216.

30. Coxe, *Horatio Walpole*, 2: 370; Yorke, *Hardwicke*, 2: 219–20.

31. Walpole, *George II*, 1: 408–12; Waldegrave, *Memoirs*, p. 147.

32. Yorke, *Hardwicke*, 2: 223–27.

33. Paul Vaucher, ed., *Recueil des instructions données aux ambassadeurs et ministres de France depuis les traités de Westphalie jusqu'à la revolution francaise: Angleterre* (1965) 25.2.3: 358–59.

34. Richard Waddington, *Louis XV et le renversement des alliances* (1896), p. 93.

35. H.M.C. *9th Report*, App. 241; Add. MSS 32857, fol. 1; Yorke, *Hardwicke*, 2: 283.

36. *Pitt Correspondence*, 1: 132–33.

37. Add. MSS 32855, fols. 256, 353.

38. Add. MSS 32857, fol. 363.

39. D. B. Horn, *Sir Charles Hanbury Williams and European Diplomacy (1747–1758)* (1930), p. 227.

40. *Dodington Journal*, pp. 311–13, 319–20.

41. Yorke, *Hardwicke*, 2: 284.

42. Add. MSS 32857, fols. 37–39.

43. *Dodington Journal*, pp. 298–302.

44. Add. MSS 33075, fols. 41–42.

45. G. F. S. Elliot, *The Border Elliots* (1899), p. 342.

46. Yorke, *Hardwicke*, 2: 237–44; *Dodington Journal*, pp. 324–26; Waldegrave, *Memoirs*, pp. 44–45.

47. H.M.C. *Various*, 6: 31.

48. Add. MSS 32860, fol. 480; Add. MSS 33075, fols. 61–64.

49. Walpole, *George II*, 2: 58, 68, 113.

50. Ibid., p. 45.

51. Add. MSS 32860, fol. 151.

52. Add. MSS 32856, fols. 214–15; Add. MSS 32860, fols. 111, 326.

53. *Dodington Journal*, pp. 333–34.

54. Ilchester, *Fox*, 1: 303.

55. Yorke, *Hardwicke*, 2: 286–87.

56. Earl of Ilchester, ed., *Letters to Henry Fox, Lord Holland* (1915), p. 79; *Lyttelton Memoirs*, 2: 522–23.

57. Ilchester, *Fox Letters*, p. 80.

58. H. W. Richmond, ed., *Papers relating to Loss of Minorca* (1911), pp. viii–x.

59. Walpole, *George II*, 2: 189.

60. Yorke, *Hardwicke*, 2: 289.

61. Add. MSS 32996, fol. 427.

62. Yorke, *Hardwicke*, 2: 290.

63. *Dodington Journal*, p. 342.

64. Add. MSS 33075, fol. 75.

65. Walpole, *George II*, 2: 288–89; *The Grenville Papers*, ed. W. J. Smith (1852–53), 1: 173; H. Trevor Colbourn, "A Pennsylvania Farmer at the Court of King George: John Dickinson's London Letters, 1754–1756," *Pennsylvania Magazine of History and Biography* 76 (1962): 444.

66. Add. MSS 33075, fol. 88; Yorke, *Hardwicke*, 2: 306; Walpole, *George II*, 2: 230–31.

67. Add. MSS 32997, fols. 18–19; Yorke, *Hardwicke*, 2: 307; Ilchester, *Fox Letters*, pp. 86–87.

68. Yorke, *Hardwicke*, 2: 296.

69. *Lyttelton Memoirs*, 2: 522.

70. Yorke, *Hardwicke*, 2: 310.

71. *Grenville Papers*, 1: 172.

72. Yorke, *Hardwicke*, 2: 315.

73. Add. MSS 32867, fols. 317, 358.

74. Yorke, *Hardwicke*, 2: 318.

75. Ibid., p. 319.

76. *Bedford Correspondence*, 2: 203.

77. *Grenville Papers*, 1: 178.

78. Yorke, *Hardwicke*, 2: 323, 334.

79. Add. MSS 35595, fols. 4–5.

80. Add. MSS 32875, fol. 316.

81. See especially: J. L. McCracken, "The Conflict Between the Irish Administration and Parliament, 1753–56," *Irish Historical Studies* 3 (1942): 159–79.

82. Winstanley, *Cambridge*, p. 228.

83. Yorke, *Hardwicke*, 3: 334.

84. P.R.O. 30/29, i/14 fols. 498–500; Walpole, *George II*, 2: 260–61.

85. *Pitt Correspondence*, 1: 161.

CHAPTER 7

1. Add. MSS 32997, fols. 66–67, 101–2; Add. MSS 33075, fols. 126–27.

2. Williams, "Election," 454; Namier, *Structure*, p. 146.

3. Namier, *Structure*, pp. 142–43.

4. *Walpole Correspondence*, 21: 76.

5. Yorke, *Hardwicke*, 2: 392.

6. Add. MSS 32870, fols. 125, 127.

7. Add. MSS 32997, fols. 133–37, 148, 177–78, 193, 207, 214–15; [Richard Glover], *Memoirs by a Celebrated Literary and Political Character* (1814), p. 138; Dobree, *Chesterfield Letters*, 5: 2226.

8. Add. MSS 32870, fols. 378–79.

9. Add. MSS 33075, fols. 148.

10. Waldegrave, *Memoirs*, p. 131.

11. Add. MSS 33075, fol. 158.

12. *Grenville Papers*, 1: 405.

13. See Reed Browning, "Seven Years' War," pp. 344–77.

14. *Pitt Correspondence*, 1 : 235.

15. Waldegrave, *Memoirs*, p. 14.

16. Add. MSS 33076, fol. 47; Add. MSS 32899, fols. 141–42.

17. Add. MSS 32997, fols. 341–50.

18. Add. MSS 32906, fol. 460; Add. MSS 32997, fol. 337; Add. MSS 32896, fol. 246; Add. MSS 32879, fol. 8; Add. MSS 32902, fols. 398–99; Add. MSS 33063, fol. 20.

19. Add. MSS 32908, fol. 379; Romney Sedgwick, ed., *Letters from George III to Lord Bute, 1756–1766* (1939), p. 41.

20. Add. MSS 32889, fol. 155.

21. Add. MSS 32909, fol. 439.

22. Yorke, *Hardwicke*, 3: 44–45.

23. Add. MSS 35420, fol. 88.

24. Add. MSS 32882, fol. 289.

25. Add. MSS 32891, fol. 433; Add. MSS 32893, fol. 406; Add. MSS 32895, fols. 506–10.

26. J. R. Western, *The English Militia in the Eighteenth Century* (1965), pp. 159–60.

27. Yorke, *Hardwicke*, 3: 216.

28. Add. MSS 32897, fol. 512.

29. Ibid., fol. 287; Yorke, *Hardwicke*, 3: 68–69.

30. Yorke, *Hardwicke*, 3: 71.

31. Add. MSS 32890, fol. 130; Add. MSS 32894, fols. 121, 130; R. Whitworth, *Field-Marshal Lord Ligonier* (1958), p. 335.

32. Yorke, *Hardwicke*, 3: 31.

33. Add. MSS 32897, fol. 288; Add. MSS 32892, fol. 26; *Grenville Papers*, 1: 291.

34. Add. MSS 32895, fol. 204; Add. MSS 32892, fols. 58–61; Add. MSS 32898, fols. 104, 138; Yorke, *Hardwicke*, 3: 170.

35. Add. MSS 32889, fols. 136–37.

36. *Pitt Correspondence*, 2: 71.

37. Add. MSS 32913, fol. 399.

38. Add. MSS 32919, fol. 285.

39. Add. MSS 33075, fol. 152.

40. Romney Sedgwick, "Letters from William Pitt to Lord Bute," in *Essays Presented to Sir Lewis Namier*, ed. Richard Pares and A. J. P. Taylor (1956), p. 124; Add. MSS 32886, fols. 384–86.

41. Add. MSS 35420, fols. 105–6.

42. For the following, see Namier and Brooke, *Parliament*.

43. Add. MSS 32916, fol. 133.

44. Add. MSS 33076, fol. 129.

45. D. A. Winstanley, *Personal and Party Government: A Chapter in the Political History of the Early Years of the Reign of George III, 1760–1766* (1910), p. 41.

46. Add. MSS 32922, fols. 145–48.

47. Sedgwick, *Letters from George III*, p. 109.

48. Henry Fox, "Memoir on the Events Attending the Death of George II. and the Accession of George III.," in *The Life and Letters of Lady Sarah Lennox 1745–1826*, ed. Lady Ilchester and Lord Stavordale (1901), 1: 39.

49. Reed Browning, "The Duke of Newcastle and the Financial Management of the Seven Years' War in Germany," *Journal for the Society of Army Historical Research* 49 (1971): 20–35.

50. Sir Reginald Savory, *His Britannic Majesty's Army in Germany during the Seven Years War* (1966), p. 303.

51. Add. MSS 32925, fol. 85; Add. MSS 33076, fol. 163.

52. Add. MSS 32927, fols. 69–70.

53. Add. MSS 32926, fols. 352–54.

54. Add. MSS 32921, fol. 272.

55. *Memoirs and Papers of Sir Andrew Mitchell, K.B.*, ed. Andrew Bisset (1850), 1: 296.

56. Add. MSS 32928, fols. 60–64, 211, 248.

57. Add. MSS 32929, fols. 18–23.

58. *Grenville Papers*, 1: 395–96.

59. Add. MSS 32929, fols. 13–14; *Pitt Correspondence*, 2:167.

60. Add. MSS 32932, fol. 363.

61. Yorke, *Hardwicke*, 3: 338–39.

62. Add. MSS 32928, fols. 362–65.

63. Add. MSS 32934, fols. 351–52, 411.

64. Add. MSS 32932, fols. 419–20.

65. Add. MSS 32934, fols. 410–16.

66. Add. MSS 32935, fols. 74–75.

67. Add. MSS 32933, fols. 112–15.

68. Add. MSS 32937, fols. 13–16, 183, 450; Add. MSS 33040, fols. 342–45.

69. Add. MSS 32937, fol. 93.

70. Sedgwick, *Letters from George III*, pp. 96–97.

71. Add. MSS 32938, fols. 85, 111.

72. P.R.O., T 1/421, fol. 478; Add. MSS 32938, fol. 295.

73. Sedgwick, *Letters from George III*, pp. 94, 97.

74. Add. MSS 33000, fol. 87.

CHAPTER 8

1. Sedgwick, *Letters from George III*, p. 107.

2. Add. MSS 32939, fols. 5–7; Add. MSS 32940, fol. 302; Add. MSS 32941, fols. 245–46.

3. Add. MSS 35332, fols. 244–45.

4. Add. MSS 32943, fols. 90–91.

5. Yorke, *Hardwicke,* 3: 363.

6. Add. MSS 33000, fols. 107–9; Namier, *England,* pp. 386–87.

7. Yorke, *Hardwicke,* 3: 395.

8. Ibid., p. 428.

9. Add. MSS 32943, fols. 332–40.

10. Yorke, *Hardwicke,* 3: 439–43.

11. Add. MSS 33000, fols. 163–64; Add. MSS 33077, fol. 67; H.M.C. *Lothian,* pp. 244–45; Sedgwick, *Letters from George III,* p. 189; [Sir James Marriott], *Political Considerations* (1762).

12. Yorke, *Hardwicke,* 3: 448, 453; *Rockingham Memoirs,* 1: 155.

13. Add. MSS 32948, fol. 291.

14. Add. MSS 32950, fol. 261; John Brooke, *King George III* (1972), p. 105.

15. P.R.O., S.P. 44/82, passim; Thomson, *Secretaries of State,* p. 116.

16. Yorke, *Hardwicke,* 3: 439–43.

17. Add. MSS 32953, fol. 145; Yorke, *Hardwicke,* 3: 564.

18. Add. MSS 35880, fol. 168.

19. Yorke, *Hardwicke,* 3: 560–61.

20. Add. MSS 32935, fol. 331.

21. Sedgwick, *Letters from George III,* p. 187.

22. Add. MSS 32939, fol. 54.

23. Quoted in Manning, "The Duke of Newcastle," p. 296.

24. *Considerations on the Present Peace* (1763).

25. Knollenberg, *American Revolution,* p. 15.

26. Quoted in Manning, "The Duke of Newcastle," p. 236.

27. Add. MSS 32950, fol. 83.

28. Add. MSS 32951, fols. 397–98; Wentworth–Woodhouse Muniments, Sheffield City Libraries, R 146–4.

29. Add. MSS 32960, fol. 332; Add. MSS 32963, fols. 377–78.

30. Winstanley, *Cambridge,* pp. 56 ff.

31. Yorke, *Hardwicke,* 3: 540.

32. Add. MSS 32964, fol. 304.

33. Add. MSS 32945, fols. 280–81.

34. Add. MSS 32966, fols. 82, 110.

35. Add. MSS 32967, fols. 120–27, 142.

36. Add. MSS 32967, fol. 136; Nott. Univ., Portland MSS, Pw F 7480; *The Jenkinson Papers,* ed. Ninetta Jucker (1949), p. 370.

37. Yorke, *Hardwicke,* 2: 328.

38. P.R.O., Ind. 6765. But see Basil Williams, *The Life of William Pitt, Earl of Chatham* (1914), 2: 211 n.; Lord Edmond Fitzmaurice, *Life of William, Earl of Shelburne, Afterwards First Marquess of Lansdowne* (1875–76), 1: 224.

39. Sykes, "Ecclesiastical Minister," pp. 77–83.

40. Add. MSS 32967, fol. 346.

41. Add. MSS 32968, fol. 3.

42. *Grenville Papers,* 3: 217; Duke of Newcastle, *A Narrative of the Changes in the Ministry 1765–1767,* ed. Mary Bateson (1898), p. 31.

43. H.M.C. *Lothian*, p. 258. The story of this ministry is the subject of Paul Langford, *The First Rockingham Administration 1765–1766* (1973).

44. H.M.C. *Charlemont*, pp. 148–49; W–WM, R 1–465.

45. Add. MSS 32968, fol. 90; H.M.C. *Stopford-Sackville*, 3: 21.

46. Add. MSS 33078, fol. 17.

47. *Grenville Papers*, 3: 82.

48. Sir William R. Anson, ed., *Autobiography and Political Correspondence of Augustus Henry Third Duke of Grafton, K.G.* (1898), pp. 58, 62 n.

49. *Pitt Correspondence*, 2:360; Sir John Fortescue, ed., *The Correspondence of King George the Third from 1760 to December 1783* (1927), 1: 210–11.

50. Add. MSS 33001, fols. 46–47; Nott. Univ., Portland MSS, Pw F 7494; Fortescue, *Correspondence*, 1: 212.

51. Add. MSS 32956, fols. 103–4.

52. Add. MSS 32973, fol. 25.

53. Add. MSS 32973, fols. 342–43; Newcastle, *Narrative*, p. 50.

54. Add. MSS 32974, fols. 5–6.

55. Add. MSS 33001, fols. 64–66, 96–104, 113–15, 128–30, 151–53.

56. Add. MSS 35912, fols. 76–97; Add. MSS 33001, fol. 133; Add. MSS 33035, fols. 386–87, 396.

57. Add. MSS 32975, fol. 244; Add. MSS 33001, fol. 229.

58. Sedgwick, *Letters from George III*, p. 253; Add. MSS 33078, fol. 111.

59. Newcastle, *Narrative*, pp. 88–96; Add. MSS 33001, fol. 271.

60. See analysis in Brooke, *Chatham Administration*, pp. 282–89.

61. Reed Browning, "Cumberland, Newcastle, and the Whigs in 1765," *Historical Musings* 1: (1971): 44–48.

62. Herbert Butterfield, "George III and the Constitution," *History* n.s., 43: (1958):14–33; Herbert Butterfield, "Some Reflections on the Early Years of George III's Reign," *J.B.S.* 4 (1965): 78–101; Archibald S. Foord, " 'The Only Unadulterated Whig'," in *Horace Walpole: Writer, Politician, and Connoisseur*, ed. W. H. Smith (1967); W. R. Fryer, "King George III, His Political Character and Conduct, 1760–84; A New Whig Interpretation," *R.M.S.* 6 (1962): 68–101; B. W. Hill, "Executive Monarchy and the Challenge of Parties, 1689-1832: Two Concepts of Government and Two Historiographical Interpretations," *H.J.* 13 (1970): 379–401; Harvey C. Mansfield, Jr., *Statesmanship and Party Government: A Study of Burke and Bolingbroke* (1965), pp. 121–22; Richard Pares, "George III and the Politicians," *T.R.H.S.*, 5th ser., 1 (1951): 143.

63. *Walpole Correspondence*, 22: 444.

64. Add. MSS 33070, fols. 363–68.

65. Add. MSS 33078, fol. 32.

66. Add. MSS 32982, fols. 95–96.

67. Add. MSS 32976, fols. 223, 255; Add. MSS 32978, fols. 35–36; Nott Univ., Portland MSS, Pw F 7511.

68. Add. MSS 32978, fol. 27; W–WM, R 1–726.

69. Brooke, *Chatham Administration*, p. 126.

70. Nott. Univ., Portland MSS, Pw F 7560; Newcastle, *Narrative*, p. 118.

71. Add. MSS 32981, fol. 254; Add. MSS 32986, fols. 58, 391; Add. MSS 32990, fol. 53; Add. MSS 32991A, fols. 125–26; W–WM, R1–1062–64.

72. Newcastle, *Narrative*, p. 116.

73. *Pitt Correspondence*, 2: 407–8; Newcastle, *Narrative*, p. 90.

74. Add. MSS 33077, fol. 40; Add. MSS 33069, fol. 219; Add. MSS 33068, fol. 17; Add. MSS 33078, fols. 76. 177.

75. Newcastle, *Narrative*, p. 137; [Pierre J.] Grosley, *A Tour to London*, trans. Thomas Nugent (1772), 2: 107; Add. MSS 33070, fol. 361.

76. Add. MSS 33077, fol. 153; Add. MSS 33078, fol. 96.

77. Add. MSS 32960, fol. 421.

78. Add. MSS 33069, fol. 111; Nott. Univ., Portland MSS, Pw F 7552.

79. Add. MSS 33071, fol. 40; Add. MSS 32985, fols. 453–54.

80. Add. MSS 33069, fol. 433.

81. Add. MSS 33078, fols. 100, 170, 190.

82. Winstanley, *Cambridge*, p. 140.

83. Nott. Univ., N(C) MSS, NeC 4277a.

84. Add. MSS 32877, fols. 412–13; Add. MSS 32901, fols. 22–23; Nott. Univ., N(C) MSS NeC 4403; Sussex Archaeological Society, P 246; Add. MSS 32913, fol. 259; *The English Reports; The House of Lords*, 1 (1900): 1274–80.

85. Hoare's Bank, Letter Book, "Private Letters from December 1758 to 8 January 1771."

86. Add. MSS 32894, fol. 356; Add. MSS 32895, fol. 40; Add. MSS 32896, fol. 120.

87. Add. MSS 33168, fol. 27; Add. MSS 33323, passim; Add. MSS 33338, fol. 20.

88. Add. MSS 33067, fols. 407, 411, 423, 441; Add. MSS 33069, fol. 113; Add. MSS 33071, fol. 165; Sussex Archaeological Society, A 499–A 504.

89. Add. MSS 33070, fols. 320–21; Add. MSS 33072, fol. 145; Add. MSS 33068, fols. 267, 275–76; Add. MSS 33069, fols. 157–58, 498; Add. MSS 33071, fols. 71–72, 83–84. See Sykes, *Church and State*, pp. 276–83.

90. Add. MSS 33072, fol. 93.

91. H.M.C., *Stopford-Sackville*, 1: 126; *Grenville Papers*, 4: 205.

92. Add. MSS 32988, fols. 23, 25.

93. Add. MSS 32991A, fol. 85.

94. Add. MSS 33072, fol. 266; Add. MSS 33078, fol. 189; *Rockingham Memoirs*, 2: 73.

95. Add. MSS 32986, fols. 391–92.

96. On the election, see Namier and Brooke, *Parliament*.

97. Nott. Univ., Portland MSS, Pw F 7591.

98. W–WM, R146–26; Add. MSS 32989, fol. 299; Add. MSS 32991A, fols. 11–12, 94–96.

99. *Walpole Correspondence*, 10: 269.

100. *The Annual Register* 11 (1768): 186–87.

101. L. B. Smith, "The Pelham Vault," *The Sussex County Magazine* 4 (1930): 371–72.

102. Somerset House, Secker, 428, proved 21 November 1768 and 27 January 1769.

Bibliographical Essay

Manuscript sources

The major sources for this work are the documents listed in this section. Of these the Newcastle Papers in the British Museum are incomparably the most important and valuable. Almost entirely unpublished though widely quoted, they include copies of many of the thousands of letters Newcastle sent and the originals or copies of even more letters that he received. The collection also contains numerous memoranda, minutes, voting lists, estate records, intercepted communications, financial notes, and a wide variety of other types of documents. The Hardwicke Papers are also rich, but researchers have long had easy access to parts of them since many of the politically important letters were printed or paraphrased in Philip C. Yorke, *The Life and Correspondence of Philip Yorke, Earl of Hardwicke, Lord High Chancellor of Great Britain* (3 vols., 1913). (When I make citations from the Hardwicke Papers I refer to the Yorke volumes when possible.) The sources consulted in the Public Record Office treat aspects of the duke's activities as lord chamberlain, as secretary of state, and especially as first lord of the Treasury. The material at Hoare's Bank, the Newcastle (Clumber) MSS, and the collections at the Sussex Archaeological Society all bear upon his dreary personal financial situation. The Wentworth–Woodhouse Muniments, the Portland MSS, and the Cholmondeley (Houghton) MSS are ancillary sources for the politicking of men with whom the duke associated. The material in the Haus-, Hof- und Staatsarchiv deals with the imperial election scheme of 1749–54.

1. British Museum

(i) *Additional Manuscripts*
   Add. MSS 5832 Various.
   Add. MSS 9152, 9200 Coxe Papers.
   Add. MSS 18915 Pulteney Papers.
   Add. MSS 19332 Instructions to Hosier.
   Add. MSS 27732–35 Essex Papers.
   Add. MSS 28132–33 Norris Journals.
   Add. MSS 32685–33083 Newcastle Correspondence.
   Add. MSS 33157–67, 33320–26, 33337–38, 33344 Pelham Papers.
   Add. MSS 34728 West Papers.

Add. MSS 35406–35408, 35337, 35420, 35465–78, 35486–92, 35595, 35838, 35870, 35880, 35912, 36132 Hardwicke Papers.

(ii) *Stowe Manuscripts*

Stowe MSS 227 Robethon correspondence.

Stowe MSS 247 Letters to James Craggs (the younger).

Stowe MSS 251 Townshend correspondence.

(iii) *Egerton Manuscripts*

Eg MSS 921 Papers of Sir Robert Walpole.

Eg MSS 1718 Bentinck Papers.

2. Public Record Office

(i) *Lord chamberlain's department*

LC 2/20(2)

LC 3/7 Establishment of chamber and bedchamber.

LC 5/127 Lord chamberlain's warrants.

LC 5/157–58 Entry books of lord chamberlain's warrants.

LC 7/3 Theatrical warrants and correspondence.

(ii) *Treasury papers*

T 1/358–421 Treasury Board papers.

T 11/24–26 Treasury, out letters, customs.

T 22/5

T 27/27–28 Treasury, out letters, general.

T 29/32–34 Treasury minutes.

T 64/96 Hunter–Münchhausen correspondence.

T 64/133

(iii) *State papers*

S.P. 42/78 Naval.

S.P. 43/78 Regencies.

S.P. 44/82 Entry book.

S.P. 54/16 Scotland.

S.P. 94/97 Spain.

(iv) *Miscellaneous papers*

Ind. 6765

PRO 30/29 1/14

3. Somerset House

Will of John, Duke of Newcastle, probated 16 July 1715 (P.C.C., 202, Fagg, 1715).

Will of Thomas, Baron Pelham, probated March 1712 (P.C.C., 58, Barnes, 1712).

Will of Thomas, Duke of Newcastle, probated 21 November 1768 (P.C.C., 428, Secker, 1768).

4. House of Lords Record Office

Parchment Collections, 57–63.
South Sea Papers, Boxes 157, 158.

5. Hoare's Bank, 37 Fleet Street

Books of loans ("Money lent on bond and other security"), 1696–1718, 1718–43, 1743–73.
Current accounts, F.
Ledgers O–Q.
Letter book, December 1758 to January 1771.

6. Cambridge University Library

Cholmondeley (Houghton) MSS, Correspondence 1160–3297.

7. Nottingham University Library

(i) *Newcastle (Clumber) MSS*
NeA 147
NeC 4263–4295, 4386–4414.
NeD 95–151, 510–12.

(ii) *Portland MSS*
PW F 7435–7605. Portland correspondence.

8. Sheffield City Libraries (all MSS cited in Wentworth–Woodhouse Muniments)

R1/1–1120 Rockingham correspondence.
R9 Negotiations of July 1767.
R13 Cumberland's narrative of negotiations of 1765.
R14 Lists of those recommended for restoration in 1765.
R146 Letters in Lady Rockingham's possession.
M1 and M2 Correspondence of first Lord Rockingham.
F35 and F43 Papers of second Lord Fitzwilliam.

9. Sussex Archaeological Society (Lewes)

A436–499
Pl68–261 and P437–38
SM94–97

10. Haus-, Hof- und Staatsarchiv (Vienna, Austria)

England, Berichte, fasc. 137, 139, 142–44.

England, Weisungen, fasc. 138, 140, 141, 145.
St K Hannover, fasc. 6, 7 Vorster's reports and instructions
R K Braunschweig–Hannover, Berichte, fasc. 4a, 4c.
Wahl- und Krönungsakten, Josef II, fasc. 68 Negotiations of 1750.
Wahl- und Krönungsakten, Josef II, fasc. 87b, 87c Negotiations of 1752.

Published Primary Sources

The chief published sources for an examination of Newcastle's career are
the memoirs, diaries, and collections of correspondence and records penned
by the duke and his associates and contemporaries. Some are well edited,
some are not; some are outrageously expurgated, some are not. In any
event, all those cited below are useful. Somewhat arbitrarily I am dividing
these sources into two categories: 1. those of extensive relevance to a study of
the duke's career; and 2. those either of less wide-ranging pertinence or of
concern only for a particular incident in the politics of the era.

1.

The single richest published source of documents bearing upon the duke
is Philip C. Yorke, *The Life and Correspondence of Philip Yorke, Earl of Hardwicke, Lord High Chancellor of Great Britain* (3 vols., 1913). This monumental
work is both a biography of Newcastle's closest friend and a sampling of
papers from the magnificent Hardwicke collection in the British Museum.
Many of the papers are letters from or to the duke, and many others deal
with affairs with which the duke was intimately concerned. Scarcely a phase
of his public career from the 1730's on is unnoticed. Almost as valuable is
William Coxe, *Memoirs of the Administration of the Right Honourable Henry
Pelham* (2 vols., 1829), a work of a similar nature assembled by the remarkable archdeacon who remains one of the most fair-minded historians to
explore the period.

Four contemporaries composed memoirs which, by virtue either of the
impressions they recount or the information they contain, are particularly
important. John, Lord Hervey, the witty author of *Some Materials toward
Memoirs of the Reign of King George II*, ed. Romney Sedgwick (3 vols., 1931),
despised the duke, and this attitude pervades his writings. But his powers of
observation were great and his judgment considerable: appraised cautiously,
his memoirs have enormous value. Horace Walpole was another who held
the duke in contempt. But all biases can be allowed for, and Walpole's two
works, *Memoirs of the Reign of King George II*, ed. Lord Holland (3 vols., 1847),
and *Memoirs of the Reign of King George the Third* (2 vols., 1845), are rich with
accounts of Newcastle in action. In his correspondence (especially the exchanges with Horace Mann) Walpole was far more spontaneous. Superbly
edited, *The Yale Edition of Horace Walpole's Correspondence*, ed. W. S. Lewis

(1937–) is the version to be consulted. James, Earl Waldegrave, *Memoirs from 1754 to 1758* (1821), recounts what one man, at times a participant, saw occurring during the most tumultuous and nerve-wracking years of Newcastle's public life. George Bubb Dodington penned a *Political Journal*, ed. John Carswell and Lewis Dralle (1965), that contains many portraits of the duke. Though not without principles, Dodington was an adept timeserver. Sensitized to even faint political signals, he picked up a great many rumors. Much of this information, some of it spurious, then found its way into the journal. It is a rich but sometimes suspect source.

Finally, there are two important published collections of portions of Newcastle's correspondence. Richard Lodge has edited the *Private Correspondence of Chesterfield and Newcastle, 1744–1746* (1930), letters which speak chiefly but far from exclusively to diplomatic concerns. They suggest, among other things, that Newcastle was neither a fool nor a precisian. Mary Bateson collected a number of the duke's letters to his Nottinghamshire friend John White under the title *A Narrative of the Changes in the Ministry 1765–1767* (1898). In these twilight years the duke was no longer privy to all that was happening, but that consideration discredits neither his portrayal of a ministry in confusion nor the expressions of his own disquietude at being unable to shape policy as he wished.

2.

Thomas Curson Hansard, ed., *The Parliamentary Debates* (vols. 7–16, 1811–13), records a number of the duke's parliamentary addresses, but since the reporters of this era were wont to paraphrase or even virtually invent speeches, this work must be treated cautiously. It includes, however, Archbishop Secker's parliamentary journal, a more reliable source. *The Journals of the House of Lords* from 1714 to 1768 contain information pertinent to the duke's career as lord chamberlain and then as first lord of the Treasury. Abel Boyer, *The Political State of Great Britain* (60 vols., 1719–40), publishes occasional documents of importance, especially for the earliest years of the duke's public life.

The number of sources bearing particularly upon the first two decades of the duke's public career are comparatively meagre. Several important letters dealing with the duke's dispute with Sir Richard Steele appear in *The Correspondence of Richard Steele*, ed. Rae Blanchard (1941). An exchange of letters about Irish church affairs between Newcastle and Archbishop Stone is printed in *The English Historical Review* 20 (1905). In addition to his biography of Pelham, Archdeacon Coxe has prepared lives of the two Walpole brothers: *Memoirs of Horatio, Lord Walpole* (2 vols., 1808), and *Memoirs of the Life and Administration of Sir Robert Walpole, Earl of Oxford* (3 vols., 1798). Both contain extracts from a variety of pertinent documents. A glimpse into the meetings of Sir Robert Walpole's ministry is afforded by Peter, Lord King, *Notes of Domestic and Foreign Affairs*, printed in the second volume of his *The Life of John Locke* (1830). Newcastle appears in these notes as a hard working, circumspect lackey. The publication by the Historical Manuscripts Commission of *Manuscripts of the Earl of Egmont*; *Diary* (3 vols., 1920–23) casts some light, albeit faint, on the duke's doings in the 1730's.

For the 1740's there is a larger quantity of useful sources. *A Selection from the Papers of the Earl of Marchmont* (3 vols., 1831) contains many references to the duke, as does [Richard Glover], *Memoirs by a Celebrated Literary and Political Character* (1814). Both works are from the pens of men who were, in general, numbered among Newcastle's political enemies. The duke's panicky response to the Forty-Five receives brief notice in *Culloden Papers . . . 1625 to 1748*, ed. H. R. Duff (1815), and wider attention in *More Culloden Papers*, ed. Duncan Warrand (5 vols., 1923–30). Lord Lyttelton's views, not as revealing as one might hope, are expressed in *Memoirs and Correspondence of George, Lord Lyttelton from 1734–1773*, ed. Robert Phillimore (2 vols., 1845). The same judgment holds for the correspondence of Newcastle's friend, the duke of Richmond, published in *A Duke and His Friends: the Life and Letters of the Second Duke of Richmond*, ed. earl of March (2 vols., 1911). (The Newcastle Papers in the British Museum reveal Richmond as a racy correspondent whose unblushing epistolary manner, in our own era of easier standards, need no longer be confined to the archives.)

After the middle of the century several other sources become important or more important. *The Correspondence of William Pitt*, ed. W. S. Taylor and J. H. Pringle (4 vols., 1838–40) is consistently pertinent on the Pitt–Newcasle duel of the 1750's. Pitt was a man of many disguises, and his letters reveal his masks, not his soul. Still other sides of the man are revealed in Romney Sedgwick, "Letters from William Pitt to Lord Bute: 1756–1758," in *Essays Presented to Sir Lewis Namier*, ed. Richard Pares and A. J. P. Taylor (1956), as Pitt and Bute jockeyed for future power at Newcastle's expense. The *Correspondence of John, Fourth Duke of Bedford*, ed. Lord John Russell (3 vols., 1842–46) is almost as valuable as Pitt's, though Bedford was neither as powerful nor as acute as the Great Commoner. *Letters to Henry Fox, Lord Holland*, ed. earl of Ilchester (1915), show Newcastle as seen by a man who grew to regard the duke as a major obstacle to his own advancement. Aubrey Newman, ed., "Leicester House Politics, 1750–60, from the Papers of John, Second Earl of Egmont," *Camden Miscellany* 23 n.d., shows what the opposition that gathered around the heir to the throne thought of Newcastle and how they hoped to deal with him.

With the accession of George III another group of documents becomes important. *The Correspondence of King George the Third from 1760 to December 1783*, ed. Sir John Fortescue (6 vols., 1927), contains references to the duke, though the reader should be ready frequently to consult Sir Lewis Namier, *Additions and Corrections to Sir John Fortescue's Edition of the Correspondence of King George III* (vol. 1) (1937). *Letters from George III to Lord Bute, 1756–1766* (1939), more authoritatively edited by Romney Sedgwick (1939), show the royal mind, with all its moral narrowness and childish self-deception, hoping for the destruction of Newcastle and his Whig friends. *Memoirs of the Marquis of Rockingham and His Contemporaries,* ed. earl of Albemarle (2 vols., 1852), help account for some of the Whig difficulties in the years after 1762. *The Grenville Papers,* ed. W. J. Smith (4 vols., 1852–53) reveal the perfect bureaucrat perplexed by human nature. *The Life of William, Earl of Shelburne, Afterwards First Marquess of Lansdowne,* ed. Lord Edmond Fitzmaurice (3 vols., 1875–76), though it deals largely with the post-Newcastle period, is doubly useful, both for Shelburne's views and the editor's discernment. Henry Fox wrote a tantalizingly brief relation, "Memoir on the Events Attending the Death of George II. and the Accession of George III.," printed in *The Life and Letters of Lady Sarah Lennox 1745–1826,* ed. Lady Ilchester and Lord Stavordale (vol. 1, 1901), that answers (but also raises) a variety of questions about what happened when the youthful George III assumed the crown. The materials assembled in the *Report on the MSS of Mrs. Stopford-Sackville of Drayton House, Northamptonshire* (vol. 1, 1884), published by the Historical Manuscripts Commission, contain much that touches on the duke in the last decade of his life.

Several other publications of the Historical Manuscripts Commission contain occasionally useful material. Listed alphabetically, they are: *Bath* (1-2, 1904–1908), *Buckinghamshire* (1895), *Carlisle* (1897), *Dartmouth* (3, 1896), *Denbigh* (1911), *Lonsdale* (1893), *Polwarth* (1, 5, 1911–61), *Stuart* (2, 1904).

Not easily categorized but nevertheless interesting and (if cautiously used) valuable are two other works. *The Diary of Thomas Turner of East Hoathly (1754–1765),* ed. Florence Maris Turner (1925), is the journal of a Sussex gentleman, and while Newcastle only occasionally intrudes personally, his spirit—or, more precisely, the awareness of his existence and rank and power—colors much of the work. Tobias Smollett's *Humphrey Clinker* presents a fictionalized Newcastle who is a biting caricature of the real duke. Bearing in mind that exaggeration lies at the core of caricature, the curious reader can find much in Smollett's depiction to enhance an understanding of the duke.

Secondary Sources

The number of secondary sources to which a historical researcher turns is necessarily vast. And since the influence of the ideas and impressions gleaned from such works is sometimes slow to be felt and imperceptible in its growth, I have found it impossible to prepare a list of works which I can with great assurance advance as complete. The works cited below doubtless reveal much about my outlook and biases, but I believe they constitute a more than adequate introduction to the politics of eighteenth-century England and an indispensable entree to the career of the man I have written about.

1. Background studies

The works I include in this category are those most useful for securing a clearer conception of the social and intellectual world Newcastle inhabited, an enriched understanding of the nature of eighteenth-century politics, and a wider knowledge of matters which, though in some ways peripheral, nevertheless have implications for any depiction of the duke.

Two articles that largely shaped my views of the nature and peculiarities of landholding in the eighteenth century are H. J. Habakkuk, "English Landownership, 1680–1740," *Economic History Review* 10 (1939–40): 1–17; and F. M. L. Thompson, "The Social Distribution of Landed Property in England since the Sixteenth Century," *Economic History Review*, 2d ser. 19 (1966): 505–17. Mark A. Thomson, *The Secretaries of State, 1681–1782* (1932), stands as the only useful examination of the office Newcastle held for so long. Lucy Sutherland, "The City of London in Eighteenth Century Politics," in *Essays Presented to Sir Lewis Namier*, ed. R. Pares and A. J. P. Taylor (1956), makes the political role of the metropolis clear, perhaps to a misleading degree. Patrick W. Riley, *The English Ministers and Scotland, 1707–1727* (1964), delineates the political role of the northern kingdom and examines Newcastle's part in bringing the Scots to heel. Particularly useful for identifying the evolution (or conscious creation) of political conventions are Romney Sedgwick, "The Inner Cabinet, 1739–41," *The English Historical Review* 34 (1919): 290–302, and Richard Pares, *King George III and the Politicians* (1953).

On the complex problem of finding appropriate descriptive matrices for the political world of the century, a number of works have been useful. Geoffrey Holmes, *British Politics in the Age of Anne* (1967), rebounds too precipitously from Robert Walcott's excesses but stands as the best introduction to the political stage Newcastle walked onto when he reached his majority. J. H. Plumb, *The Origins of Political Stability in England, 1675–1725* (1967), identifies the manner in which Sir Robert Walpole, Newcastle's mentor, achieved a virtual monopoly of political power. John M. Beattie, *The English Court in the Reign of George I* (1967) provides the most detailed picture and analysis now available of the structure of the early Hanoverian court. Isaac Kramnick, *Bolingbroke and His Circle: the Politics of Nostalgia in the Age of Walpole* (1968) sketches the ideological fissures separating Walpole, Newcastle, Pelham, and Hardwicke from their principled enemies (not all of their opponents merit that adjective). This theme is resumed for the later years by

Thomas W. Perry, *Public Opinion, Propaganda, and Politics in Eighteenth-Century England: A Study of the Jew Bill of 1753* (1962); and Betty Kemp, *Sir Francis Dashwood: An Eighteenth-Century Independent* (1967). And in a less controlled but often illuminating manner John Carswell, *The Old Cause: Three Biographical Studies in Whiggism* (1954), touches on many of the same court-country issues.

The historiographical quarrel over the nature of factions after 1754 remains open. I have presented my views in the text and profited from the study of several important analyses. John Brooke writes with conviction and knowledge of "Namier and Namierism," in *Studies in the Philosophy of History: Selected Essays from "History and Theory"*, ed. George H. Nadel (1965). Ian Christie, *Myth and Reality in Late Eighteenth-Century British Politics* (1970), defends the Namierian analysis of the politics of the 1760's, and several of Namier's own essays, printed in *Crossroads of Power: Essays on Eighteenth-Century England* (1962), remain exciting and powerful reading. But I am more impressed by the tenor of the views advanced in such works as G. H. Guttridge, *English Whiggism and the American Revolution* (1942); Herbert Butterfield, "Some Reflections on the Early Years of George III's Reign," *The Journal of British Studies* 4 (1965): 78–101; and W. R. Fryer, "King George III, His Political Character and Conduct, 1760–84; a New Whig Interpretation," *Renaissance and Modern Studies* 6 (1962): 68–101. Herbert Butterfield's earlier monograph, *George III and the Historians* (rev. ed., 1959), exaggerates in places but also serves as a useful correction to hyperbolic nominalism. Interested readers will also profit from B. W. Hill, "Executive Monarchy and the Challenge of Parties, 1689–1832: Two Concepts of Government and Two Historiographical Interpretations," *The Historical Journal* 13 (1970): 379–401, and Harvey C. Mansfield, Jr., "Sir Lewis Namier Considered," *The Journal of British Studies* 2 (1962): 28–55.

Finally, the reader should examine Donald Grove Barnes, "Henry Pelham and the Duke of Newcastle," *The Journal of British Studies* 1 (1962): 62–77. Though I often dissent from Barnes's conclusions, I find his analysis sobering.

2. *Political Histories*

When taken together the following works provide a virtually continuous, and often overlapping, narrative of British politics during the Newcastle years. I have included a few articles because, though touching only on isolated events, they have what I deem to be particularly important things to say about the course or nature of politics. The best single volume for the period is Dorothy Marshall, *Eighteenth-Century England* (1962). More detail, though not necessarily sounder judgment, is available in the two relevant volumes of *The Oxford History of England*: Basil Williams, *The Whig Supremacy 1714–1760* (rev. ed., 1962); and J. Steven Watson, *The Reign of George III*

1760–1815 (1960). Another valuable survey, albeit an exercise in tunnel history, is Archibald S. Foord, *His Majesty's Opposition, 1714–1830* (1964). Basil Williams, *Carteret and Newcastle: A Contrast in Contemporaries* (2d ed., 1966), unhappily brief, is the only treatment of the entirety of the duke's life, but the comparison is marred by the author's clear affection for Carteret and clearer distaste for Newcastle.

The politics of the opening years of Newcastle's adult life are coherently related in Wolfgang Michael, *England under George I*, vol. I: *The Beginnings of the Hanoverian Dynasty*, trans. L. B. Namier (1936), and vol. 2: *The Quadruple Alliance*, trans. A. MacGregor and G. E. MacGregor (1939). J. H. Plumb's biography of Sir Robert Walpole is still incomplete, but its two highly readable and authoritative volumes, *Sir Robert Walpole: The Making of a States-man* (1956), and *Sir Robert Walpole: The King's Minister* (1961), carry the political story down to 1734. Plumb's work may be supplemented by Ste-belton Nulle's pioneering study, *Thomas Pelham-Holles, Duke of Newcastle: His Early Political Career, 1693–1724* (1931), pre-Namierian in outlook but manifestly relevant; and by William T. Laprade, *Public Opinion and Politics in Eighteenth-Century England* (1936), which relies heavily on newspapers and evinces much insight. Two articles by E. R. Turner, "The Peerage Bill of 1719," *The English Historical Review* 28 (1913): 243–59; and "The Excise Scheme of 1733," *The English Historical Review* 42 (1927): 34–57, deal with political crises of considerable importance to Newcastle. The story of the late 1730's may be followed in Foord.

For the opening of the fifth decade of the century John Owen's cautious and well-researched study, *The Rise of the Pelhams* (1957), picks up the thread, though with insufficient attention to the role of foreign affairs. It may be supplemented and extended beyond 1747 by John Wilkes, *A Whig in Power: The Political Career of Henry Pelham* (1964), a work of uneven quality covering a neglected administration. Several biographies become important for this and the succeeding decades. Basil Williams's magnificent *The Life of William Pitt, Earl of Chatham* (2 vols., 1914) is a scholarly encomium written by a man not burdened with any sense of guilt about the exercise of power. Thad Riker, *Henry Fox, First Lord Holland: A Study of the Career of an Eighteenth-Century Politician* (2 vols., 1911); and earl of Ilchester, *Henry Fox, First Lord Holland: His Family and Relations* (2 vols., 1920) are both examinations of the most complex of the midcentury politicians. Lucy Sutherland, "The City of London and the Devonshire–Pitt Administration, 1756–7," *Proceedings of the British Academy* 46 (1960): 147–93, makes sense of one of the century's briefest ministries, and Williams's *Pitt* is the obvious source for an account of the great wartime coalition.

With the accession of George III genius takes the historiographical stage: Sir Lewis Namier's *England in the Age of the American Revolution* (2d ed., 1963) is really a study of the politics of the opening years of the reign, enormously rich as all of Namier's writings are. Also rewarding are D. A. Winstanley's two volumes, *Personal and Party Government: A Chapter in the Political History of the Early Years of the Reign of George III, 1760–1766* (1910), and *Lord Chatham and the Whig Opposition* (1912). Products of an earlier era of scholarship, they retain all of their vigor and much of their utility. Paul Langford, *The First Rockingham Administration 1765–1766* (1973), provides a useful analysis of the duke's final year in office, and John Brooke, *The Chatham Administration, 1766–1768* (1956), covers the close of Newcastle's life. I have dissented at important points from both studies. Brooke's biography, *King George III* (1972), perceptively analyzes some of the political events of the reign. Two articles merit attention: D. H. Watson, "The Rise of the Opposition at Wildman's Club," *The Bulletin of the Institute for Historical Research* 44 (1971): 55–77, for an analysis of a crucial component of the opposition Newcastle was helping to shape after 1762; and Reed Browning, "Cumberland, New-castle, and the Whigs in 1765," *Historical Musings* 1 (1971): 44–48, for what the author believes to be a corrective to a recent misunderstanding about the organization of that Whig opposition.

3. *Diplomacy and War*

This is a much-explored field, but in recent years it has fallen into un-justified neglect. Consequently most of the important works are not of recent origin. Particularly valuable as sources of diplomatic correspondence are *British Diplomatic Instructions 1689–1789*, vol. 6: *France, 1727–1744*, ed. L. G. Wickham Legg (1930), and vol. 7: *France, Part IV, 1745–1789*, ed. L. G. Wickham Legg (1934). Paul Vaucher has edited French instructions in *Recueil des instructions données aux ambassadeurs et ministres de France depuis les traités de Westphalie jusqu'à la revolution française: Angleterre* (25–2. vol. 3, 1965), which contain illuminating comments on English politics and diplomacy as seen from Versailles. D. B. Horn, *Great Britain and Europe in the Eighteenth Century* (1967), is the authoritative survey for the entire period.

Basil Williams explored the foreign policy of part of the Walpole years in a series of six articles published in *The English Historical Review* 15–6 (1900–1901). J. F. Chance, *The Alliance of Hanover* (1923), details the complexity of the diplomacy of the mid-1720's. The chief line of the story can then be picked up in Arthur McCandless Wilson, *French Foreign Policy during the Administration of Cardinal Fleury, 1726–1743; A Study in Diplomacy and Commercial Development* (1936); and Paul Vaucher, *Robert Walpole et la politique de Fleury, 1731–1742* (1924). Sir Richard Lodge, "English Neutrality in the War of the Polish Succession," *Transactions of the Royal Historical Society*, 4th ser. 14 (1931): 141–73, though nominally a review essay, casts clarifying light on the obscure 1730's and on Newcastle's role in its war. Three works are indispensable for understanding the outbreak of hostilities between Britain and Spain in 1739 and for assessing Newcastle's responsibility for that outbreak. Jean Oliva McLachlan, *Trade and Peace with Old Spain, 1667–1750*: *A Study of the Influence of Commerce on Anglo-Spanish Diplomacy in the First Half of the Eighteenth Century* (1940), provides the richest historical background; Richard Pares, *War and Trade in the West Indies, 1739–1763* (1939), is the most dazzling in its *aperçus*; Harold W. V. Temperley, "The Causes of the War of Jenkins' Ear, 1739," *Transactions of the Royal Historical Society*, 3d ser. 3 (1909): 197–236, is the harshest on the duke. All three are model studies.

British diplomacy in the War of the Austrian Succession is the subject of Sir Richard Lodge, *Studies in Eighteenth-Century Diplomacy, 1740–1748* (1930), a superb example of scrupulous diplomatic history. Lodge also published many articles on the same period in *The English Historical Review* and the *Transactions of the Royal Historical Society* between 1928 and 1933. Newcastle emerges in Lodge's pages as a dunce. The course of the naval war may be followed in Sir H. W. Richmond, *The Navy in the War of 1739–48* (3 vols., 1920), a work that is also highly critical of the duke. Kinder judgments are found in Evan Charteris, *William Augustus Duke of Cumberland: His Early Life and Times (1721–1748)* (1913), and Walther Mediger, *Moskaus Weg nach Europa: der Aufstieg Russlands zum europäischen Machtstaat im Zeitalter Friedrichs des Grossen (1952)*, the latter work being especially valuable by virtue of its central European perspectives. Arthur H. Buffinton, "The Canada Expedition of 1746: Its Relation to British Politics," *The American Historical Review* 45 (1940): 552–80, and Jack Sosin, "Louisburg and the Peace of Aix-la-Chapelle, 1748," *William and Mary Quarterly*, 3d ser. 14 (1957): 516–35, examine two particular wartime incidents in which the duke figured prominently. And for a broader view of strategic thinking the reader should consult Richard Pares's justly renowned "American versus Continental Warfare, 1739–63," *The English Historical Review* 51 (1936): 127–51, and G. S. Graham, "The Naval Defense of British North America, 1739–63," *Transactions of the Royal Historical Society*, 4th ser. 30 (1948).

Newcastle's interwar diplomacy is examined in two articles by Reed Browning, "The Duke of Newcastle and the Imperial Election Plan, 1749–1754," *The Journal of British Studies* 7 (1967): 28–47, and "The British Orientation of Austrian Foreign Policy, 1749–1754," *Central European History* 1 (1968): 299–323; and in two articles by D. B. Horn, "The Origins of the Proposed Election of a King of the Romans," *The English Historical Review* 42 (1927): 361–70, and "The Cabinet Controversy on Subsidy Treaties in Time of Peace," *The English Historical Review* 45 (1930): 463–66. The reasons for the resumption of Anglo-French hostilities are explored, within varying sets of interpretive assumptions, by a number of authors. Richard Waddington, *Louis XV et le renversement des alliances* (1896), is the classical study, generally fair-minded if a bit harsh on Ludovician diplomacy. Patrice L. R. Higonnet is too wont to see symmetry in his study "The Origins of the Seven Years' War," *The Journal of Modern History* 40 (1968): 57–90, but his argument, when less single-mindedly advocated, merits attention. Thad Riker, "The Politics Behind Braddock's Expedition," *The American Historical Review* 13 (1908): 742–52, lays bare the confusion in the British ministry at this time, a view authoritatively confirmed in Stanley Pargellis, *Lord Loudon in North America* (1933). D. B. Horn's recent piece, "The Duke of Newcastle and the Origins of the Diplomatic Revolution," in *The Diversity of History: Essays in Honour of Sir Herbert Butterfield*, ed. J. H. Elliott and H. G. Koenigsberger (1970), is clearly relevant, if a bit contrived, and demonstrates that the late dean of British diplomatic historians retained to the end of his life the interest manifested in his earliest and still valuable monograph, *Sir Charles Hanbury Williams and European Diplomacy (1747–1758)* (1930). On the Seven Years' War and Newcastle's role in it the reader should turn to Julian S. Corbett, *England in the Seven Years' War; A Study in Combined Strategy* (2 vols., 1907), a work that praises the duke, and Brian Tunstall, *Admiral Byng and the Loss of Minorca* (1928), a work that assails him. On Byng himself John Creswell's revisionist interpretation of naval tactics, *British Admirals of the Eighteenth Century; Tactics in Battle* (1972), is illuminating. Creswell pours scorn on the admiral's ineptitude.

3. *Government Finance*

Government finance in the eighteenth century has not been a subject of extensive research. Still, there exists a body of literature which, when taken together, provides much information about Newcastle's activities as head of the chief department of government. For an introduction to the operations of the eighteenth-century Treasury the student should first consult Alice Clare Carter, *The English Public Debt in the Eighteenth Century* (1968). Four other works are available for richer detail on the Treasury: Henry Roseveare, *The Treasury: The Evolution of a British Institution* (1969); J. E. D. Binney, *British Public Finance and Administration 1774–92* (1958); E. Hughes, *Studies in Administration and Finance, 1558–1825* (1934); and the magisterial P. G. M. Dickson, *The Financial Revolution in England* (1967). William Kennedy, *English Taxation, 1640–1799: An Essay on Policy and Opinion* (1913), examines the chief method of gaining revenue in the century but must be treated with caution. W. R. Ward, *The English Land Tax in the Eighteenth Century* (1953), lucidly explains the operation of the most important of the various taxes. What could not be raised by taxation was acquired by borrowing. E. L. Hargreaves, *The National Debt* (1930) considers the consequences of hiring money. L. S. Pressnell, "The Rate of Interest in the Eighteenth Century," in *Studies in the Industrial Revolution*, ed. L. S. Pressnell (1960), explores the forces determining the price of the money to be hired. C. L'Estrange Ewen, *Lotteries and Sweepstakes: An Historical, Legal, and Ethical Survey* (1923); Jacob Cohen, "The Element of Lottery in British Government Bonds, 1694–1919," *Economica*, n. s, 20 (1953): 237–46; and R. D. Richards, "The Lottery in the History of English Government Finance," *Economic History* 3 (1934–37): 57–76, examine the inducements that treasury officials used to pry these funds from potential creditors.

Newcastle's own tenure at the Treasury is the subject of two articles by Reed Browning, "The Duke of Newcastle and the Financing of the Seven Years' War," *The Journal of Economic History* 31 (1971): 344–77, and "The Duke of Newcastle and the Financial Management of the Seven Years' War in Germany," *Journal of the Society for Army Historical Research* 49 (1971): 20–35. Two pieces by Lucy Sutherland, "Samson Gideon and the Reduction of the Interest, 1749–50," *Economic History Review* 16 (1946): 15–30, and "Samson Gideon: Eighteenth-Century Jewish Financier," *Transactions of the Jewish Historical Society of Englan* 17 (1951–52): 79–90, treat the manner of Treasury mangement under Newcastle's immediate predecessor, and most of the methods there explained were retained during Newcastle's days.

4. *Colonial Administration*

American-born historians have contributed extensively to all facets of the study of English history, but understandably they have shown uncommon interest in trying to account for the great rift that shattered the English-speaking world in the last third of the eighteenth century. For an examination of the multiplicity of topics with which recent historians of the American Revolution have dealt the reader can refer to Jack P. Greene, ed., *The Reinterpretation of the American Revolution, 1763–1789* (1968). The rest of the publications I include here touch specifically on Newcastle's colonial views and actions.

Bernhard Knollenberg, *Origin of the American Revolution: 1759–1766* (1960), is the strongest advocate for the essential wisdom of the duke's orientation in colonial matters: his argument must be treated cautiously, however, for Knollenberg sees adherence to principle as an explanation where the evidence to me suggests pragmatism instead. Philip Haffenden, "Colonial Appointments and Patronage under the Duke of Newcastle, 1724–1739," *The English Historical Review* 58 (1963): 417–35; Stanley Nider Katz, *Newcastle's New York: Anglo-American Politics, 1732–1753* (1968); and James Henretta, *"Salutary Neglect": Colonial Administration under the Duke of Newcastle* (1972), all propose to determine whether the duke handled colonial patronage skillfully and responsibly. Alison Gilbert Olson, "Anglo-American Politics, 1675–1775: Needs and Opportunities for Further Study," in *Anglo-American Political Relations, 1675–1775*, ed. Alison Gilbert Olson and Richard Maxwell

Brown (1970), speaks briefly to the same issue. Haffenden surveys only the years prior to the War of Jenkins' Ear: within that span he gives the duke fairly high marks. Katz examines the duke's dealings with New York and reaches a harsher judgment. Henretta's conclusion is also critical, but the work is marred with errors and obscurities and is therefore of suspect validity. Carl Bridenbaugh, *Mitre and Sceptre: Transatlantic Faiths, Ideas, Personalities, and Politics, 1689–1775* (1962), and Arthur Lyon Cross, *The Anglican Episcopate and the American Colonies* (1902), examine the duke's behavior in mediating between Anglican proponents of an established church in the colonies and dissenting opponents of such a scheme. On the centrally important Stamp Act controversy the reader should consult Edmund S. Morgan and Helen M. Morgan, *The Stamp Act Crisis: Prologue to Revolution* (1953), and Allen S. Johnson, "British Politics and the Repeal of the Stamp Act," *The South Atlantic Quarterly* 52 (1963): 169–88. Finally, to gain some measure of the perceptual prisons confining the vision of all British politicians in their dealings with the colonies the reader should turn to Jack P. Greene, "The Plunge of Lemmings: A Consideration of Recent Writings on British Politics and the American Revolution," *The South Atlantic Quarterly* 57 (1968): 141–75, and Edwin G. Burrows and Michael Wallace, "The American Revolution: the Ideology and Psychology of National Liberation," *Perspectives in American History* 6 (1972): 167–306.

5. *Ecclesiastical Administration*

Church affairs were the realm of national politics in which Newcastle exercised influence for the longest time. The reader should begin his survey with Norman Sykes, *Church and State in England in the Eighteenth Century* (1934), a work that treats the Hanoverian church with uncommon sympathy and which first disclosed the true force of Newcastle's Christian convictions. A reading of the relevant portions of Sykes's *From Sheldon to Secker, Aspects of English Church History, 1660–1768* (1959), will add to the story a chronological perspective (and suggest how time tempers judgment). Edmund Pyle, *Memoirs of a Royal Chaplain, 1729–1763*, ed. Albert Hartshorne (1905), reveals the mind of a not atypical careerist Hanoverian clergyman and contains striking depictions of Newcastle in his role as ecclesiastical politician. Two important articles bearing on our understanding of the political role of the clergy in Newcastle's time are T. F. J. Kendrick, "Sir Robert Walpole, the Old Whigs, and the Bishops, 1733–1736: A study in Eighteenth-Century Politics," *The Historical Journal* 11 (1968), 421–45, and R. W. Greaves, "The Working of the Alliance: A Comment on Warburton," in *Essays in Modern English Church History*, ed. G. V. Bennett and J. D. Walsh (1966). Three authors have specifically examined Newcastle's conduct as ecclesiastical minister. Mary Bateson, "Clerical Preferment under the Duke of Newcastle,"

The English Historical Review 7 (1892), and D. G. Barnes, "The Duke of Newcastle, Ecclesiastical Minister, 1724–1754," *Pacific Historical Review* 3 (1934): 164–91, contain some amusing tales, but the views they express must be treated with caution when at variance with the judgments incorporated in Norman Sykes's more authoritative "The Duke of Newcastle as Ecclesiastical Minister," *The English Historical Review* 57 (1942): 59–89. Lewis P. Curtis, *Chichester Towers* (1966), a minor masterpiece of historical narrative, gives an entertaining account of Newcastle's efforts to balance ecclesiastical and parliamentary politics in Sussex in 1740–42. For an examination of the duke's attitude toward the thorny issue of whether to create an Anglican establishment in the American colonies the reader should begin with Bridenbaugh and Cross (see the section on colonial administration above).

6. *Electioneering*

Electoral manipulations were Newcastle's favorite political activity. He devoted large amounts of time and money to what was in many ways his hobby. In the study of his career as the "Great Elector" the reader should bear in mind that the years 1754–1761 constitute a separate phase: both before and after those years Newcastle's eye focused chiefly on Yorkshire, Nottinghamshire, and above all Sussex, whereas during his Treasury days Newcastle had the entire kingdom to fret over.

The reader should begin his survey with Sir Lewis Namier, *The Structure of Politics at the Accession of George III* (2d ed., 1963), still a work of authority and, by its example, inspiration. The relevant volumes of *The History of Parliament* have been published: Romney Sedgwick, *The House of Commons, 1715–1754* (2 vols., 1970), and Sir Lewis Namier and John Brooke, *The House of Commons, 1754–1790* (3 vols., 1964). Both are invaluable sources of information about constituencies, and both, the Namier–Brooke portion especially, contain important introductory essays. For information on particular elections the reader can supplement the data provided in *The History of Parliament* with several important studies. For 1713 see Sir Thomas Lawson-Tancred, *Records of a Yorkshire Manor* (1937). For 1715 and 1722 see Nulle (see the section on political histories above as well). For 1727: Stebelton H. Nulle, "Duke of Newcastle and the Election of 1727," *The Journal of Modern History* 9 (1937): 1–22. For 1734 see Basil Williams, "The Duke of Newcastle and the Election of 1734," *The English Historical Review* 12 (1897): 448–88 (recall that this pioneering effort magnifies the extent of the duke's influence out of all proportion). For 1741: G. H. Nadel, "The Sussex Election of 1741," *Sussex Archaeological Collections* 91 (1953): 84–124; Clarence Perkins, "Electioneering in Eighteenth Century England," *The Quarterly Journal of the University of North Dakota* 13 (1923): 103–24; and Curtis (see also the section on ecclesiastical administration above). For 1747: Owen (see political histories above). For 1754 and 1761 see Namier, *Structure*.

Newcastle's role in the politics of Cambridge University is entertainingly set forth in D. A. Winstanley, *The University of Cambridge in the 18th Century* (1922).

7. *The Private Man*

Not much has been published about Newcastle's private life and domestic interests. Nulle and Williams (see the political histories above) shed some light on his family background, and Nulle also contains some information about the opening phases of the duke's unhappy financial career. O. R. F. Davies, "The Wealth and Influence of John Holles, Duke of Newcastle, 1694–1711," *Renaissance and Modern Studies* 9 (1965): 22–46, analyzes the wealth of the powerful uncle whose favor started Newcastle on his political way. A. S. Turberville, *A History of Welbeck Abbey and Its Owners* (2 vols., 1938–39), reconstructs the story of the litigation over the duke's inheritance from his uncle. Sketchy information about the duke's various homes may be gleaned from Thomas Bailey, *Annals of Nottinghamshire* (4 vols., 1853); Edward Wedlake Brayley, *A Topographical History of Surrey* (5 vols., n. d.); Cornelius Brown, *History of Nottinghamshire* (1891); Walter H. Godfrey and L. F. Salzman, *Sussex Views* (1951); Frederick Jones, "Random Notes on Halland Park," *The Sussex County Magazine* 4 (1930): 373–80; A. H. Marks, *Historical Notes on Lincoln's Inn Fields* (1922); *Victoria History of the County of Sussex* (1907–); T. E. C. Walker, "The Clives at Claremont," *Surrey Archaeological Collections* 65 (1968): 91–96; T. E. C. Walker, "The Water Supply to Claremont," *Surrey Archaeological Collections* 59 (1962): 91–92; Laurence Whistler, *Sir John Vanbrugh; Architect and Dramatist, 1664–1726* (1934); Viscountess Wolseley, *Some of the Smaller Manor Houses of Sussex* (1925). The duke's devotion to Gallican cuisine is entertainingly described in Romney Sedgwick, "The Duke of Newcastle's Cook," *History Today* 5 (1955): 308–16. The tombs of the Pelhams are described in L. B. Smith, "The Pelham Vault," *The Sussex County Magazine* 4 (1930): 370–72, a useful piece since the vault is no longer accessible.

Additional Bibliographical Note

Professor Ray Kelch's *Newcastle A Duke Without Money: Thomas Pelham-Holles, 1693–1768* (1974), appeared while the present work was in press. It is essentially an examination of Newcastle's personal finances. Kelch and I agree in attributing the duke's difficulties less to electoral expenditures *per se* than to a grand style of living which entailed conspicuous and excessive consumption. But in important ways Kelch's and my figures do not agree with each other. Reexamination of the sources persuades me that mine are essentially correct, especially with regard to the income the duke received from his two inheritances (see Kelch, p. 37; but see Davies, "Wealth and Influence," pp. 44–46; Add. MSS 33065, fols. 272–74, 449; and, for suggestive reinforcement, H.M.C., *Egmont Diary*, 3: 244) and the income he was compelled to live on in his final years (see Kelch, p. 191; but see Add. MSS 33168, fol. 27, and Add. MSS 33323, passim; and, for suggestive reinforcement, *Pitt Correspondence*, 2: 206n).

Index